'BONEY' FULLER

'BONEY' FULLER

Soldier, Strategist, and Writer
1878–1966

Anthony John Trythall

RUTGERS UNIVERSITY PRESS

NEW BRUNSWICK, NEW JERSEY

First published in the USA by
Rutgers University Press, 1977
Library of Congress Catalog Card
Number 77-76775
ISBN 0-8135-0844-4

Filmset in Photon Imprint 11 on 12½ pt and
printed in Great Britain by
Richard Clay (The Chaucer Press), Ltd,
Bungay, Suffolk

For Celia

Contents

Illustrations

* *By kind permission of Rutgers University, New Brunswick, New Jersey, U.S.A.*

Acknowledgements

I should like to begin by recording my deepest gratitude to Lady
Liddell Hart. Her help, encouragement, kindness and advice when
I was researching this book were quite invaluable. She was gen-
erous with her time and hospitality when I visited States House
to read the Fuller Papers there and smoothed the way for me
when I visited America to read the papers Fuller left to the late
William Sloane of Rutgers University Press. I also thank her for
allowing me to quote from her husband's books and letters.

My thanks are also due to Kenneth Parker, who helped in the
early stages of writing and to Brian Bond of King's College,
London, for much wise help and advice. It was he who first
introduced me to Fuller's books when I was a student on the
King's War Studies MA course, and who became my supervisor
when I began to research Fuller later for an MPhil thesis, which
never got written.

I am very much indebted to my own Corps, which selected me
for the King's War Studies course, and to Major General Ken
Hall, once my Director in MOD, who encouraged me to burst
into print.

Thanks are also due to the following:

The Controller of HM Stationery Office by whose permission
transcripts of Crown Copyright records in the Public Record
Office appear.

The Trustees of the Liddell Hart Centre for Military Archives
at King's College, London for permission to use the Fuller and
Liddell Hart papers.

The Commandant of the Staff College, Camberley, for permission to quote from the Junior Division files of 1923 and *Owl
Pie*.

Rutgers University Press, and particularly Helen Stewart, for their hospitality, kindness and help, and for permission to quote from letters in their files.

Rutgers University Library, and particularly Donald Sinclair and his staff, for the kindness and hospitality they showed me and for permission to use the Fuller papers and to reproduce numbers of photographs.

Mrs Estelle Fuller, Fuller's sister-in-law, and Mrs Alison Starr, wife of Fuller's life-long friend Meredith Starr, for sparing time to talk to me, for helping me in numerous ways and for allowing me to quote from their conversations.

Gordon Grey for lending me Fuller's letters to Meredith Starr.

Sir Oswald and Lady Mosley for giving me lunch, talking about Fuller and allowing me to quote from their conversation.

Jay Luvaas for inviting me to spend a delightful weekend in his house at Meadville to talk about Fuller and for giving me copies of his notes on Fuller.

James Leutze, who entertained me in Chapel Hill, N Carolina, and talked about Fuller.

Michael Foot for permission to quote from letters he wrote when Editor of the *Evening Standard*.

The Fuller Estate which, through David Higham Associates, gave me permission to quote extensively from Fuller's papers and books.

I am grateful to the following for permission to quote from the numerous sources cited:

The Editor, The Army Quarterly
Associated Newspaper Group Ltd (extracts from *News Chronicle* and *Daily Mail*)
Constable Publishers (J. F. C. Fuller: *The Dragon's Teeth*)
Curtis Brown Ltd, London, on behalf of the Estate of Major-General Fuller (J. F. C. Fuller: *The Last of the Gentlemen's Wars*); (Stephen Foot: *Three Lives*)
Faber & Faber Ltd (G. LeQ. Martel: *Our Armoured Forces*)
David Higham Associates (B. H. Liddell Hart: *Memoirs*)
Hodder & Stoughton (E. D. Swinton: *Eyewitness* and A. G. Stern: *Tanks 1914–18*)
Hutchinson Publishing Group Ltd (James Leutze (ed.): *The London Observer: The Journal of General Raymond E. Lee 1940–41*; and J. F. C. Fuller: *The Reformation of War,*

Sir John Moore's System of Training, British Light Infantry in the Eighteenth Century, The Foundation of the Science of War and *Machine Warfare*)
Michael Joseph Ltd (Heinz Guderian: *Panzer Leader*)
London Express News and Feature Services (extracts from *Evening Standard*)
John Murray (J. F. C. Fuller: *Tanks in the Great War*)
Royal United Services Institute (*RUSI Journal, Cavalry Journal*)
Royal Tank Regt Publications (*The Tank*)
Times Newspapers Ltd (extracts from *The Times*)
University of Chicago Press (Jay Luvaas: *The Education of an Army*)

I have dedicated this book to my wife without whose understanding, patience and forbearance Fuller would still lack a biography. Moreover, she typed the manuscript twice and was in that and in so many other ways unstinting in the gift of her time.

1. Fritz Fuller— 1878–1907

John Frederick Charles Fuller was born at five o'clock in the morning on September 1st, 1878, in Chichester. His father, the son of a Chichester solicitor, was an Anglican clergyman, at that time Rector of Itchenor. His mother, born Thelma de la Chevallerie, was French, but had been educated and brought up in Germany where her father lived at Naunhof near Leipzig. In later life Fuller stated that he was already a heretic by the age of five and attributed this to his descent from Roundheads on his father's side and Huguenots on his mother's. With a predilection for the occult which characterized a great deal of his thinking throughout his life, he also found significance in the facts that his paternal grandfather was born in 1789, his father in 1832 and his mother in 1848, 'all revolutionary years'.[1] Heretical or not, Fuller's background was impeccably middle class and undeniably European as well as English. As a boy he was known as Fritz and signed his letters home with that extremely Germanic contraction of his second name until his middle thirties.[2]

His very early years were almost certainly secure and happy ones, except perhaps when he became the victim of his own fecund and sometimes fevered imagination. His parents were comfortably off; his father's strict religious principles did not then come between them as they were to in later years, while his mother was obviously a woman of very considerable charm, intelligence and education, and Fuller was devoted to her. When his younger brothers, Lionel and Walter, were born the young Fritz showed himself a kindly and considerate brother as he did also to his sister, Maxie. She was an imbecile and, although kept at home until her middle twenties, was eventually placed in a convent in France where she lived until she was sixty. This was, however, a solitary cloud. For most intelligent, middle-class boys it was a good time to be born; for the middle classes the last decades of the nineteenth century were times of confidence and growth, of stability tempered with reform, of belief in progress and absence of doubt, at least for most, and of strength and Empire. In 1878 Hiroshima was still sixty-seven years in the future, the outbreak of the First World War thirty-six and of the Boer War twenty-one years away. There were no tanks, aeroplanes or radio communications; there were no communist or fascist governments and guerilla warfare was associated with the Peninsular War. It was at this time that Robert Louis Stevenson could make a British child say:

> Little Indian, Sioux or Crow,
> Little frosty Eskimo,
> Little Turk or Japanee,
> Oh! don't you wish that you were me?

Into this secure environment arrived the infant Fritz. His formal education, which was in total remarkably short for one who was to lead so very intellectual a life, began at a dame's school in Chichester,[3] the sort of school which has today grown into the pre-preparatory establishment usually occupying a large and run-down house in a quiet surburban or provincial road. In his *Memoirs* Fuller protests that he did little work at any of his schools; however one must take leave to doubt this assertion. Perhaps he neglected some of the arid tests he was set, but on the other hand his early letters and later erudition and intellectual ability are evidence that he must at least have been a lively pupil. However, when he was eight, the family moved to Lausanne and he accompanied them. He went to a number of schools in Switzerland and remembers paying 'twopence at some fête or other to see a cannibal bite the heads off rabbits', and also running 'several miles to the village of Lutry to watch a murderer have his head off with a broadsword'.[4] Unfortunately on the latter occasion he arrived too late to witness the gruesome spectacle.

In 1889, at the age of eleven, he was sent back on his own to England to become a boarder at Fulmer House, a preparatory school in West Worthing. He took with him a small address book,[5] and he must have used it a great deal because he enjoyed writing letters—or perhaps found solace in doing so, since he was

short and slight (and remained so all his life) and cannot often
have come off best in the minor hostilities of a boys' boarding
school. His mother treasured these letters; she kept many of
them and they can now be seen in the Centre for Military
Archives in King's College, London.[6] They show Fuller to have
been a dutiful son, capable of writing very competent English
and interested in such things as stamps, fossils and outings. The
most remarkable thing about them, however, is that many are
illustrated with macabre pen and ink drawings of devils and
castles executed with great care and not a little talent. There is a
feeling of Gothicism about them which is striking and indicates
that Fuller's later passionate interest in the mysterious and the
occult had an early dawn. Indeed he tells us in his *Memoirs* that
he first read Dante's *Divina Commedia* at the age of five in an
edition illustrated by Gustave Doré and that he spent 'hours
turning over its pages to gaze upon its dreadful pictures: men and
women frozen in the mud, blazing in hell fire, turned into gnarled
trees and into crawling spiders'.[7] Such food is strong meat for the
infant mind.

While Fuller was at Fulmer House his parents moved from
Switzerland to Sydenham where they settled on retirement permanently into The Lodge, at 7, Sydenham Hill. Fuller himself
moved on to Malvern in 1893, as he admitted, 'at the somewhat
advanced age of fourteen'. He disliked the school intensely. His
grandfather in Leipzig wanted him to join the Army, and so he
was put into the Army Class, where he found that he was left very
much to his own devices, which suited him well enough since he
was able to spend his time reading novels.[8] The drawings in his
letters home at this period were still beautifully executed but
more stereotyped and redolent of the heavy humour of the later
Victorian *Punch*,[9] except when he reverts to the macabre theme.
In one letter, probably written in 1894, there is a rather frighten-
ing drawing of 'Death' complete with a snake growing out of the
skull's eye socket. This same letter contains a request for the *Pall
Mall Magazine*, 'as I want to see something about Porchester
Castle in it and Portsmouth'.[10] One takes away the impression of
a slight, intelligent, somewhat solitary boy, and one who would
take unkindly to the group solidarity and conventional ethos of
the Victorian public school.

Perhaps partly for this reason, but also because he was

obviously incapable of passing the Sandhurst examination without some rather more specific education, he was taken away from
Malvern in 1895, after only two years, and sent to a crammer's in
London. He enjoyed 'Jimmy's'—as the crammer's was called,
after its principal, Captain James—and the fact that he preferred
the crammer's to the public school is further evidence of his early
departure from the norm of male, middle-class values prevalent in
the 1890s.[11] He described Captain James as 'small, almost diminutive, as clever as a monkey'[12] which reads oddly like a piece of
self-description. James did not appear to be much concerned with
cramming, and his tutors, although often able, kept no sort of
discipline. Aspirants for the RMC were, however, enabled to pass
the examination because James was either 'a clairvoyant or he
bought the examination papers from the printers a little in
advance'.[13] Probable questions and their answers were distributed
to the victims some few days before the examination, which took
place in the cellars of Burlington House. Fuller would have us
believe that it was this excellent examination-defeating system
which got him through, but since his performance was exceptional in geography, history and freehand drawing, and otherwise
indifferent except for a miserable eighteen out of five hundred
marks in latin, it is possible to doubt him.[14] Like very many
others with gifted and original minds, he refused to apply
himself to those areas of learning which did not interest him,
but his performance when he was doing what he wanted was
high.

Although he qualified academically for Sandhurst, he failed
to measure up to the required correlation of age, height,
weight and chest girth for a commission, and was only offered
a place on condition that he would not be commissioned
unless his weight and critical measurements improved by the
end of the course. At this time, when he was almost nineteen,
he was five foot four and weighed only eight stone five.[15] The
new gentleman cadet arrived at Sandhurst in September 1897
and his father was obliged to pay £150 a year for this
privilege.[16] He soon put on weight, and presumably height, which
was a good thing for him since in his first few weeks the height
and weight standards were altered. This caused a French master
to compose a poem for translation by the cadets which read in
part:

No longer like one man the army throbs
With insult
Generalled by such mites as Bobs
. . .
For now the mild cadet is shown the door
If under five foot five and nine stone four.[17]

His small physical stature was not Fuller's only problem at
Sandhurst. Shortage of money began to be a preoccupation since
he was now having to compete in a more or less adult environment with brother cadets, and later brother officers, whose parents were rich rather than comfortably off like his own. 'How
delightful it must have been,' he wrote to his mother in October,
'for the ancient caveman who never had to bother his head about
money.'[18] The narrowness of his room irked him at first, but he
got used to it after a term and asked his mother to look out some
carpets for him.[19] It is at this time also that he began to articulate
his views about hypocrites and fools, categories to which he often
consigned a large majority of mankind. In another Sandhurst
letter to his mother he wrote: 'these canting hypocrites have the
cheek to write one down as an atheist, heretic, infidel because one
refuses to believe some such incident as that Jonah was swallowed by a whale. I verily believe that if it were written in the
Bible that the whale was swallowed by Jonah they would just as
readily believe it.'[20] In the same letter he puts into words the sort
of intellectual idealism one expects more from the gentleman
commoner at Oxford than the gentleman cadet at Sandhurst: 'the
great aim of life is not merely happiness or suffering but a far
greater wider and nobler aim namely Development'.

Development was not, it appears, the aim of the Sandhurst
course. Sport was important and what Fuller later called the
'cricket-complex',[21] but the heart of the military curriculum was a
combination of drill and some rather old-fashioned tactics. For
much of the time the cadets were occupied with copying pictures
of redans, gabions and wooden fuses into 'green-covered note-
books'. They then painted these 'every imaginable colour'. Fuller
rather liked this work but had no idea why he was called upon to
do it. Military law is best described in his own words.

Once a week for two hours at a stretch we sat in a classroom
and read the *Manual*, and when we had exhausted those

sections dealing with murder, rape, and indecency, we either destroyed Her Majesty's property with our penknives or twiddled our thumbs. Fortunately our instructor was as deaf as a post, for this enabled us to keep up a running conversation, broken on occasion by a wild Irishman, named Meldon, banging on his desk to make our teacher look up. Then Meldon would solemnly say: 'Please, sir, may I come and kick your bottom?' And our unsuspecting master, not having heard a word, would invariably reply: 'Come to me afterwards, boy; come to me afterwards.'[22]

The course lasted a year, and as a preparation for what was so soon to come it had distinct limitations. Fuller described the atmosphere as 'Crimean, the Governor and Commandant, Lieut.- General Sir C. J. East, dated from that war, having joined the Army in 1854.'[23] He had actually served in the Crimean War and the Indian Mutiny more than forty years before Fuller met him.

On August 3rd, 1898, Fuller was granted a commission and gazetted to the 1st Battalion of the Oxfordshire Light Infantry— the 43rd.[24] He was then ordered to report to his regiment in Ireland on or before September 3rd.[25] As the regiment was about to move from the Curragh to Mullingar in Westmeath, Fuller, complete with much new uniform and a bank book from Cox and Co.,[26] joined it in the latter locality. By this time—with the exception of his three years in Lausanne and his intellectual intimacy with his European mother—he had received an entirely conventional, Victorian, middle-class upbringing. Of this he was the product, but many of his characteristics were developed as a reaction against it. He must have soon appeared to be a rather odd fish to his fellow subalterns of the 43rd. Of course there has always been, contrary to much popular belief, a tradition of tolerance, within limits, amongst young officers in many regiments and corps in the British Army, but this tradition is stronger in the cavalry than it is in the infantry. However, light infantry are perhaps an exception to that rule. Be that as it may, Second-Lieutenant Fuller appears to have survived and later, in the First World War, it was partly his 'difference' which endeared him to his brother officers in the Tank Corps.

He spent the winter of 1898–9 in Mullingar and there certainly found himself out of sympathy with the predilections of his brother officers. Conversation 'was limited to foxes, duck and trout' and this left Fuller silent. Moreover he found that his pay—of £7 15s. 8d. a month after tax—was inadequate and did not allow him to keep a horse.[27] He received a small allowance from his father, and this was obviously essential, but even so his financial circumstances reinforced his personal inclination and kept him out of the society of the chase. He drilled in the morning, practised with a sword four times a week, and in the afternoons sometimes went shooting alone because this gave him an excuse to get out.[28] There were also route marches, and he spent a lot of time and effort in producing a route sketch of the area north of Mullingar.[29] For the most part his spare time was spent in reading, not novels now, but such works as Carlyle's *Heroes and Hero Worship*, Huxley's *Science and Christian Tradition*, Lang's *Modern Science and Modern Thought* and *Problems of the Future*, the *Meditations* of Marcus Aurelius and a book called *Early Greek Philosophers*.[30] His letters home dwelt on his dislike of society and preference for reading, and in these sentiments a note of priggishness is detectable as it is in a sort of declaration of faith he made to his mother at the time. 'I am as good as most people,' he wrote, 'and not without boasting perhaps a little better. I intend to leave the world a little better than I found it'.[31] He wrote about his interest in painting, particularly Rembrandt, Burne-Jones and Rossetti, but the burden of most of his letters to his father was financial: the extreme difficulty of living on his pay and a small allowance. He was also concerned with acquiring the correct items of uniform from various shops in London, particularly 'the proper sort of plain leather shooting boots rather than wellingtons'.[32]

In the spring of 1899 the 1st Battalion returned to the Curragh 'to carry out field training and musketry on orthodox Brown Bess lines'. In his *Memoirs*, published, it must be remembered, thirty-seven years after the event, Fuller is scathing about the training he was then given. 'Even then,' he wrote, 'though I took no interest whatever in things military, it all appeared to me very ridiculous; yet what did it matter?—we had to fill in time somehow, and what had been good enough for Wellington was good enough for us. There our sojourn passed pleasantly enough; for though daily we assaulted Gibbet's Rath in orthodox fashion, that is to say, in the most suicidal possible manner, there was plenty of time over for fishing and bicycling around.'[33] His interest in the macabre reasserted itself on one such bicycling expedition during which he discovered, to his delight, some petrified bodies in a church vault.[34] However, the regiment eventually returned to Mullingar and then, on September 5th, left Ireland to travel to Holyhead, and thence by train to Crown Hill Barracks near Plymouth.[35] The Boer War was only a few weeks away and he was about to have his first serious encounter with danger, anguish and despair. No premonition of such an event troubled the somewhat contrived and adolescent sentiment of the letter he wrote home after his arrival at Plymouth:

> The French nation ought to be abolished the more I read about them the more absolutely disgusted I get with their venomous qualities. They literally stink with oily backstair skunkiness.... They have a few good points but I am sorry to say many bad ones as well being gross cowardly and essentially effeminate and always were so in the time of Caesar when in a state of barbaric savagery they even used soap, curious as it may seem. What fine nation could ever spring from a soapy savage? None. What is needed is a good, lousy, stinking, rancid Saxon or Goth, not a hair-combing toe-nail-clipping Gaul.[36]

The Gauls had to wait their turn, as it transpired; it was the Boer nation which was about to be abolished.

The 1st Oxfordshires remained in Plymouth for only a short while but the officers were much concerned that they might miss the war in South Africa which, like its successor, would obviously be over by Christmas.[37] On November 23rd the Regiment moved to Oudenarde Barracks, Aldershot, and on December 4th began to mobilize.[38] This principally consisted of the embodiment of reservists, the issue of khaki drill uniforms and the de-pipeclaying of equipment. The red and blue uniforms of the nineteenth century were discarded, helmets were distributed, carbines were substituted for swords, at least for dismounted officers, belts and straps were sand-papered free of pipeclay and great-coats and mess tins were provided with khaki covers. Fuller recognized this later for the military revolution it was, but he also recognized with hindsight that no mental revolution accompanied it, that the

1st Oxfordshires had not been trained for war: 'we knew nothing about war, about South Africa, about our eventual enemy, about anything at all which mattered, and upon which our lives might depend'.³⁹

Just before Christmas he was able to take a little leave at Sydenham, which he nearly overstayed, and had to persuade a hansom driver to gallop from the Elephant and Castle to Waterloo in order to catch his train.⁴⁰ On December 22nd the regiment marched to Farnborough station, went by train to Southampton and by four in the afternoon were all on board R.M.S. *Gaika*, an old liner of about five to six thousand tons, then laden with some 1,650 passengers, of whom 660 were Oxfordshires. At 4.30 p.m. the *Gaika* weighed anchor for the Cape, and to the cheers of spectators the three-week voyage began. It is becoming increasingly difficult today to recapture the emotional content of such an event; both patriotism and distance have grown less important. At the end of the nineteenth century, the chest-swelling, heart-filling notes of the military band and the gay, and yet pathetic, flutter of handkerchief or long-skirted dress from a slowly fading quayside, coupled with a sense of duty and a belief both in the efficacy, almost anywhere in the world, of British military force, and in the justice of the imperial cause—these experiences and values must have been a heady mixture. That Fuller was affected by them intellectually rather than emotionally tells us something important about his developing character. His chief occupations on the voyage appear to have been reading, and playing poker with a view to augmenting his income. The men drank bottled beer and played ''ouse', an early precursor of Bingo, which Fuller much disliked. After a short call at Tenerife and a trip ashore at St Helena, where he was shown a house said to be occupied by an old lady who had as a child been fondled by Napoleon, he arrived off Table Mountain at midnight on the 13th. Next day the Oxfordshires disembarked at Cape Town.

The military situation which awaited them was gloomy. The Boers had invaded British territory, then confined to Cape Colony and Natal; Ladysmith, Mafeking and Kimberley were besieged, the Orange river bridges were in the hands of the enemy and there had been British reversals at Magersfontein, Colenso and Stormberg. All this, however, was rather above the heads of newly commissioned infantry subalterns, who were more concerned with getting men off ships and into trains, a difficult operation on February 14th, 1900, it appears, because the principles of 'last on, first off' loading had not been observed at Southampton. At about 6 p.m. the train carrying the Oxfordshires, less their baggage, steamed out of Cape Town and puffed its hot and dusty way north across the Karroo desert. Sixty-eight hours later, at 2 p.m. on the 17th, the train arrived at their destination, Naauwpoort, 'a dust heap in a dust flat sprinkled with stones and occasional kopjes',[41] in fact a railway junction some fifty miles south-west of the Orange river border between Cape Colony and Orange Free State. It was here that Fuller experienced his first taste of operations—'outpost' duty— and also heard his first shots fired in anger, or at least in fear. These were fired by one of his sergeants at three soldiers of the Cape Mounted Rifles, on the principle that since all Boers were mounted, all mounted men must be Boers. Fuller prevented anyone being hit by knocking the sergeant's rifle out of his hands, but it is interesting that his very first experience of war should have been susceptible to the very formal logical analysis of the false syllogism.

On January 24th the Oxfordshires moved some fifty miles south-east to a place called Thebus with the task of covering the repair of the railway line to Stormberg, where the Army was held up. Here Fuller made the mistake of occupying a temporarily dry river bed and only saved his men from being enveloped in a 3ft.-high wall of boiling mud, when it rained upstream, by having a sentry wake them up by firing a fusillade over their heads! The Oxfordshires' stay in Thebus was short, and on the 30th they began a train journey much farther north which ended early in the morning of February 1st at Modder River. Here Fuller heard his first gun of the war, a five-inch shooting in the direction of Magersfontein, then occupied by the Boers who were preventing British access to Kimberley. A troop build-up was in progress but Fuller's principal contribution to operational preparation was an arduous visit back down the railway line to De Aar to seek out a lost consignment of mess stores and buy up all the whisky he could find. He took the opportunity of posting a letter home at De Aar and this letter provides considerable insight into his state of mind at the time of this journey—a journey which could so very easily have been almost his last.

I really begin [he wrote on February 6th] to wonder what we are fighting for, for this country is quite impossible—for the whole lot is not worth a twopenny d . . . . . and unless the Transvaal turns out to be a Paradise flowing with milk and honey I shall really think that the leaders of the English nation are deserving cases for Broadmoor. . . . I have not been in the army very long but quite long enough to see that nine officers out of every ten, I might say ninety-nine out of every hundred, know no more of military affairs than the man in the moon and do not intend or want to know more. . . . It is no more a profession than shooting pheasant or hunting foxes. . . . That we ultimately will win in this war is highly probable, but unless the tactics of our generals change it will be simply through sheer force of numbers. . . . War as everything else nowadays is reduced to a science. . . . I think William the Conqueror could teach us a thing or two.[42]

This is strong, thoughtful and critical language for a young infantry subaltern of twenty-one in the middle of an uncomfortable war.

At 10 p.m. on February 10th they entrained again and travelled in coal trucks twenty miles south to Enslin. Here they bivouacked beside the track and Fuller began to feel extremely ill. He had a high fever and sharp pains in his abdomen. In the morning the medical officer had him transferred to the bell tent which served as a hospital where he was given peppermint and castor oil, both of which made him violently sick. Next day the Oxfordshires marched off to take part in the Paardeberg campaign but Fuller was left behind on a stretcher. First the tent and next the stretcher were removed by the medical officer, who then himself departed. Fuller and some other casualties had been abandoned. Fortunately he had the presence of mind to order a soldier to stop a passing train and he was carried to an empty carriage. The train took eighteen hours to cover the thirty-five miles to De Aar. Here he was taken to the Orange River Hospital where his illness was diagnosed as 'a twisted gut'. Nothing was done and he got steadily worse. He managed to write a letter to his mother on the 16th in which he told her that he had been laid up with an attack of inflammation of the bowels 'and I have never suffered such agonies in all my life before. I am getting all right again now. . . . The inflammation is nearly all down except in my right side which is still painful.'[43] Whether this was written in self-deception or to prevent his mother worrying there is no means of knowing. On the 19th he was discovered by one of the Oxfordshire subalterns who had reported sick with an ulcerated heel; this officer got him transported in a hospital train back to a main base hospital at Wynberg near Cape Town, where his illness was rapidly and correctly diagnosed as appendicitis. He was also told that in a few more hours he would have been dead. This information was not, however, imparted to him until he had been successfully operated upon. He took a long time to recover, and had drain tubes in his wound for some time. On the 28th he wrote home, obviously still in considerable pain and fever, and told his mother about the operation. This letter contains one of Fuller's most unguarded and heartfelt sentiments. 'Oh,' he wrote, 'this war is an awful thing. When will it come to an end?'[44] So ended Fuller's own first personal experience of war. On April 25th he was invalided home on the *Kildonan Castle* and docked at Southampton on May 14th, just under five months after he had left it.

He remained in England on sick leave for five months and never imagined that he would take any further part in the conflict. However the war began to move into a phase of anti-guerilla operations, and there was some of it still going on when Fuller recovered. On October 17th, 1900, he set sail again for Cape Town, once more in the *Kildonan Castle*, and arrived there on November 4th after a voyage in which he found playing whist with military officers distasteful because 'that biped is a great deal too uninteresting for me'.[45] Eventually, on November 27th, he rejoined his Regiment at Heilbron, a little south of the Vaal river border between the Orange Free State and the Transvaal. A few days later he was sent some miles away to Leeuwport to act as second-in-command of a detachment guarding a railway line. Life was very similar here to that which British soldiers then experienced on the North-West Frontier of India and were to become familiar with in a score of internal security or counter-insurgency operations after 1945. One could be shot at, and very occasionally someone was killed, or some more major disaster occurred, but the greatest danger often lay in misunderstandings and jumpiness amongst one's own sentries and pickets. The 1st Oxfordshires lost only thirty-two officers and men killed by enemy action in the whole war. For Fuller life was often dull, and while at Leeuwport, for instance, he learnt the whole of the *Rubáiyát* of Omar Khayyám! He also seriously considered making his career in the Indian Army and was recommended for a transfer. He wrote to his father about this and told him that he believed 'one can live on one's pay or nearly so, the only thing is one has to live in India most of one's life'.[46] On March 16th he wrenched his knee while riding and had to return to Heilbron for treatment.

For the next three and a half months he was based with the Regiment in Heilbron and engaged in what he later described as 'peace under canvas'.[47] Only three Boers were killed by the troops in Heilbron during that time. Fuller himself was required to make a sketch of the camp and its defences and was then sent to carry dispatches to Pretoria. During this trip, by horse and train, he won forty pounds from a drunken hotel landlord in Elandsfontein and had trouble with officious Railway Staff Officers because he did not have a ticket. On one occasion he was helped out by a Yeomanry officer called Baker, whom he knew, and who had previously served in a Prussian cavalry regiment, but had been specially authorized by the Kaiser to join the British Army for the war. Fuller wrote to his father about this officer and delivered himself of some uncharacteristically anti-German sentiments which included the view that, in any fighting between the British and Germans, by the time the latter had finished saluting each other the British would have won the battle.[48] This letter contains some other interesting views and shows Fuller to have been much more seriously concerned about military affairs at the time than his subsequent books admit. He believed that the British Army had gained immense experience in South Africa while other European armies still conducted manoeuvres on the principles of Napoleon and Moltke, which in modern conditions would 'spell annihilation'. 'If this present war has shown anything it is that mobility is of crucial importance.' Here obviously lay the germ of much of Fuller's later thinking. However, later in the same letter he aired some typical military prejudice:

I have never yet found reason to change my opinion that the army . . . needs primitive men who enjoy the heirlooms of

> prehistoric times such as hunting, shooting etc. A certain
> amount of intellect is of course necessary to keep step with
> the scientific principles of modern warfare but animal cun-
> ning and courage hold the first rank still. . . . People who talk
> of trying to induce a better class of man to join the army are
> fools and their talk is abjectly foolish, it is the savage we
> want not the simpering counter-jumper and shop keeper's
> sons, the former is much more easily disciplined than the
> latter who has an awakening reason which is detrimental to
> all discipline and courage.

A few days later he put the corollary to his mother, that it was
necessary to have gentlemen as officers because under stress
butchers would revert to butchery.[49] This, however, did not deter
him from telling his father at almost the same time that had he
been a Russian he would have become a Nihilist and that Russia
might become great after its Revolution.[50]

On June 27th the Oxfordshires left Heilbron and marched south
to Kroonstadt on the Walsch river where they arrived on July 1st.
The next five months were spent by Fuller in what he called
'blockhousing'. This was an operation aimed at pacifying the
countryside and killing or capturing the remaining militant
Boers, somewhat similar in concept, although not in execution, to
the 'clear and hold' operations of the Malayan Emergency of the
1950s. The whole theatre of war was divided up with wire fences
along which, at intervals of about a mile, depending on the
terrain, blockhouses, or small forts, were built. This isolated the
enclosed area and it could then be swept clear of the enemy. Boer
civilians were moved into concentration camps. The subaltern's
job was to supervise the construction of the lines and to command a number of blockhouses, and this Fuller did in various
parts of the Orange Free State—Jordaan Siding near Kroonstadt,
Koodoosrand on the Modder river, the Vlakfontein line and
around the Lace Diamond Mines between Kroonstadt and the
Rhenoster river. He appears to have become a specialist in the art
of foraging, particularly from military sources, and perfected
systems for obtaining coal from passing freight trains with the
aid of a rope held taut across the top of a truck, and fodder
from bullock wagon supply columns by means of various
distracting devices! The coal was required for cooking while the

fodder was needed for Fuller's unauthorized pony, Nigger. Life
was sometimes exciting, as when one of the 'Black Watch', the
native force employed to guard the wires, inadvertently shot
another. The victim, John No. 4, had been hit in the forehead and
Fuller gave him whisky out of a teapot and stuffed his brains back
into his head with the handle of a fork. He wrote to his mother
some days later about the incident: 'Any ordinary civilized
individual would have fallen down dead at once, but I suppose
these semi-savages use their brain so little that it doesn't much
matter if they lose a part of it.'[51] For most of the time, however,
life was uneventful. He read at least one book a week during his
time in South Africa and these included such works as
Kropotkin's *Memoirs of a Revolutionist*, Tennermann's *History of
Philosophy* and Haycraft's *Darwinism and Race Progress*. As he
told his mother: 'I have not wasted my time though presumably
employed in hunting my fellow men I have spent most of my
time in reading books.'[52] He also began to write poetry of a
distinctly macabre variety.[53] His hopes of obtaining a transfer to
the Indian Army were growing dimmer and never materialized.
On November 24th something exciting did happen. The Colonel
sent for him and offered him a job as Intelligence Officer outside
the Regiment. He jumped at the offer and reported at District
Headquarters at Kroonstadt on the 29th to a Captain Cox who
was blessed with the grandiloquent title of Deputy Assistant
Adjutant General (Intelligence).

Now began one of the most adventurous and not the least
formative of episodes in Fuller's life. Freed from the constraints
of regimental soldiering when the Colonel, the Second-in-
Command and the Company Commander were all God-like
figures to be obeyed, or dangerously and secretly ignored, he was
given seventy unreliable Kaffir scouts to command and the job
of watching, to the west and north-west of Kroonstadt, 4,000
square miles of only partially pacified Orange Free State in order
to 'find the enemy, report his whereabouts and keep him under
observation'.[54] The scouts were divided into two groups, each
under a white agent, and for most of the time these were Holland,
a trustworthy Canadian, and Bethune, a Scots South African
who had served a prison sentence for illicit diamond buying.
Holland was thirty and Bethune forty-two years old; Fuller was
twenty-three.

He was given, or perhaps merely allowed himself, very great freedom of action. The District Provost Marshal, head of the local military police, provided him with a pass which authorized him to go 'anywhere, anyhow and at any time',[55] and he took full advantage of this. His activities for the next seven months bore at least some resemblance to those of a 'lawman' in the American West. He rode the veldt with his horsemen, exchanged shots with chance-met Boers, raided and searched homesteads, captured and interrogated prisoners, and guided parties of more regular troops in raids and minor assaults. It was hot, exciting, dangerous and stimulating work; in one way it was like a gloriously uninhibited Boy Scout 'wide game'—and Scouting had its origins here, of course—while in another it was the deadly serious precursor of later counter-insurgency operations. Fuller told the story of his exploits in *The Last of the Gentlemen's Wars* which was in turn based on a diary he wrote at the time. It must suffice here to mention a few incidents. First there was the apparently bed-ridden Boer, Old Smit, who refused to give away any information even when dragged across the veldt to his home on a hide, and subsequently encouraged to imbibe a whole bottle of whisky, but who was so frightened by Bethune firing his rifle at a dog that 'he leaped from his bed and bolted out of the door and covered a hundred yards in record time'.[56] On another occasion Fuller 'galloped' a number of farms at Damhoek, captured three Boers and only narrowly missed capturing six more because one of the prisoners, an old man and former acquaintance of Bethune's called Prinsloo, pulled the trigger of his rifle on being caught under a bed and so warned his companions that a raid was in progress. At a farm called Schotland West he became involved in a running battle with Kritzinger's and Harman's commandos and saw a Maxim gun used by the South Africa Constabulary with devastating moral effect. With one Kaffir, Fuller himself rode through the enemy lines to deliver dispatches from Kitchener to the headquarters of a Colonel von Donop at Wolmaranstad. His presence along a blockhouse line in the dark was announced by the playing of a cornet in the absence of a telephone line. In the course of these and many other adventures Fuller and his scouts captured large numbers of sheep, cattle and poultry, and also shot buck and guinea fowl, and caught fish in the rivers—the messes he was attached to being often fed well in consequence. His last action of note took place on May 7th when he was almost caught and shot while engaged in posting up peace proclamations in farms near Bothaville.

The reason why he would have been shot had he been captured needs some explanation. Fuller was in the position of a federal agent in the American West using armed Indians to fight the local settlers. He himself agreed that the Boers fought chivalrously and normally the worst that befell prisoners was to be stripped and turned loose on the veldt. However those who armed and led Kaffirs had broken the rules of South African life by undermining white supremacy, and the Boers showed no quarter to either the leaders or the led; similarly, according to Fuller, the Kaffirs showed no quarter to the Boers. One of Fuller's scouts, Simon, was captured, tied to a horse's tail and dragged for some four hundred yards while the Boers shot at him at a distance from a flank. Fuller discovered his body later, 'blown out like that of a dead mule and surrounded by a horrible stench ... hit in many places, certainly through the knee, heart, breast, head and elbow'.[57] Just before discovering Simon's body, Fuller saw a notice pencilled on a whitewashed farm wall which read:

> *Pray to God you are not caught for we will shoot every one of you as we did Simon and the English officer too who leads you.*

In *The Last of the Gentlemen's Wars* he commented: 'Though the English was not faultless, for I was still alive, its meaning left the reader (particularly myself) in no doubt. Under this dramatic obituary I wrote one word. . . . .'[58] The point was that in some respects the Boer War became too serious, undermined too much the fabric and structure of South African society, to be of uniform gentlemanliness. Even so, and in spite of the particular dangers he endured, Fuller still found time to read and to write long discursive letters home which illustrate both his logic and his growing tendency to take the extreme view. In one letter, for instance, he inveighed against anti-vaccination campaigns in London: 'It is one thing to give a responsible and knowledgeable human being freedom of conscience but as nine tenths of the human kind are nothing but a thinly veneered set of brutes ... it is an absurdity.'[59] In another letter he tells his father: 'The more

Boers we can wipe out now the better for the future.'[60] This latter sort of sentiment, which he excludes from *The Last of the Gentlemen's Wars*, published thirty-five years later, was probably close to what the Boer-chasing subaltern felt in 1902.

In May the war was petering out, and it ended officially on the 31st. On being told the news next day, Fuller replied, 'Well, I *am* sorry,'[61] and this sums up concisely the enjoyment and exhilaration he had experienced as an Intelligence Officer. He made a trip to Pretoria in early June to try to get a job with the South African Constabulary because he feared a return to regimental routine with its curse of 'intellectual standardization'.[62] However he got nowhere, and on the last day of the month he rejoined the Oxfordshires. Life did again become routine except that he managed to make £200 by joining Agent Holland, who was still in Kroonstadt, in a cattle-buying venture. They bought sixty-five animals at as little as seven and sixpence each, had them fattened up by a friendly farmer, and sold the thirty which survived for an average of £15 a head in Johannesburg.

Returning to the Regiment, however temporarily profitable, confirmed his fears about the future. The Commanding Officer publicly called him 'a damned fool of a subaltern'.[63] 'The army,' Fuller wrote to his father, 'is only a passtime its no profession if I left it tomorrow I should have nothing to fall back on such as one would have if one were a lawyer, doctor or bricklayer being a passtime it naturally is only fit for one thing "amusing myself" and amusing oneself is always a costly job, and if in the army one can't amuse oneself well it is no good attempting to do so badly.'[64] He went on typically, and without telling his father about his financially successful cattle operations, that because of his poor pay and the fact that his father could only allow him £100 a year, he must find some other 'billet'.

August passed slowly but on September 7th the Regiment left Kroonstadt by train and, after a very slow journey, boarded the SS *Winifredian* in Cape Town harbour on the 12th. Next day they sailed, and after an uneventful voyage during which Fuller won another forty pounds at poker, this time from a 'noble lord' in the Brigade of Guards, they reached Southampton on October 4th and later that day arrived at Chatham, where the Regiment was to be stationed for the next year. As Fuller, still a Lieutenant and only twenty-four years old, settled down at Chatham he must have looked back on the war in South Africa with growing nostalgia, for it was in that country that he grew up. His experiences of pain and death, of responsibility and independence, were strongly formative and led him to become an even sterner and more perceptive critic of the prevailing military doctrine and organization than he had been either at Sandhurst or in Ireland. Few shibboleths were safe from his challenge and the sight of the Royals encumbered with one Cape cart of baggage per officer appears to have particularly enraged him. So that he was not surprised when he heard that one Royals officer and his orderly had chased a Boer for five miles brandishing their swords, a chase which was abruptly ended when 'the Boer pulled up, jumped off his horse and as they galloped up shot both at point-blank range'.[65] He was also critical of the concentration camp system, or so he claimed in *The Last of the Gentlemen's Wars*, because the burning of farms and the evacuation of women and children not only caused lasting bitterness but also drove the male Boers into the hills where they were more difficult to catch.[66] He certainly continued his self-education during the war and read widely, but his activities were obviously not entirely intellectual. Nevertheless out of action came theory, as later it was to do from the observation of action in the First World War. He was fortunate that in planning and executing simple attacks on farms, and in pursuing small parties of enemy, he had been able to see clearly the essential shape and direction of tactical operations, the frontal, flank and rear attack, the processes of envelopment and penetration. This clear and simple vision was to be very helpful to him in later life, both in planning operations and in thinking and writing about war.

Chatham held no appeal for Fuller. He thought it a sordid town and 'full of sordid women against whose low animal natures discipline was no more than a paper shield'.[67] Most of his brother officers spent their evenings in London. We do not know how Fuller spent his evenings but we do know that he was not displeased when the 43rd were posted to India in the autumn of 1903. The Regiment first went to Ambala and then, in early 1904, to the Simla Hills. From there Fuller was sent to Rawalpindi for a course and subsequently rejoined the Regiment at Lucknow. Apparently life was quiet for the 43rd and he found plenty of time to become fascinated with Indian culture, a fascination which developed his earlier predilection for the mystic into a full-blooded passion for the occult which he regarded not primarily as magical or supernatural but as concerned with the hidden or anterior meaning of things. The strangeness of India attracted him and he read widely about it; through his 'munshi', or native language tutor, he met numbers of Indians—holy men, yogis and radicals. He studied the *Vedas* and the *Upanishads* in translation and became deeply interested in Yoga—all extremely unusual activities for an ordinary Edwardian subaltern except that a few of those officers stationed in Edwardian India developed similar interests.[68] It was in the middle of 1905 that he first made contact with Aleister Crowley, probably the most well-known, and notorious, British mystic of the first half of the twentieth century. Crowley was staying in Darjeeling leading an expedition to Kangchenjunga, and Fuller corresponded with him there about obtaining copies of Crowley's books.[69] At this time Fuller, now a Captain, was beginning to write for publication himself, and in 1905 he published two articles in the *Agnostic Journal*, a somewhat rash venture for someone still dependent on an allowance from his clerical father. In a letter to his mother written in October he told her that he would mark anything in his letters which ought to be kept from his father.[70] He also took a great interest in the Russo-Japanese War and admired the Japanese, although it was obvious that their victories stirred the growing nationalist sentiments of the Indians.[71] His political views at the time were a mixture of traditional British military distaste for politics overlain with some highly rationalized anti-socialism. A letter to his youngest brother, Walter, written from Lucknow in February 1906, is evocative of Fuller's state of mind:

> To me the name politician is in most cases a synonym for 'canaille'.... I do not think the increase in Labour members is the beginning of the end, though everything must have an end, or rather a transformation, even Empire and Kingdom.... That the masses are socialistic is not a very grave danger; for socialism is but the scum on the democratic cauldron. Socialism is anti-progressive, tending to level the higher to the lower, true democracy is diametrically the reverse it raises: the former is but a passing

phase bubbling to the surface, a cleansing, a semi-education, the latter a step in the evolutionary ladder.[72]

This letter was written while Fuller was recovering from a serious attack of enteric fever during which he was delirious for over three weeks. He was in hospital in Lucknow for about six months and became wasted and debilitated. When he was discharged in April 1906 he was ordered home via the Suez Canal for a year's sick leave. During this leave he met Crowley in person[73] and began to draw closer to him and to become increasingly immersed in the study of the occult. Many of Crowley's letters to Fuller survive but much of their content is not readily intelligible to the uninitiated. One extract from a letter written in November 1906 will serve to show the strangeness both of Crowley and of the relationship between the two:

> You must be careful—you left a devil behind you last Sunday that came within an ace of killing me! It had a sharp pointed beak (curved) no eyes, a hunched back, no arms or wings, no legs, but a single tapering tail, balanced on a rounded piece of its own excrement.[74]

Perhaps Fuller was still drawing the pen sketches which illustrated his letters from school. It was in 1906[75] also that he married Margarethe Auguste Karnatz, the daughter of Christian Heinrich Karnatz from Hamburg, who had emigrated to Australia where he was a salesman.[76] Margarethe was known throughout her life by many names—Gretel, Gretchen, Daisy, Margot and Margaret—but she became known generally as Sonia, and Fuller calls her by that name throughout his *Memoirs*. The Karnatz family came originally from Poland where they used the name Carnatsky, Sonia having been brought up by an aunt in Hamburg after her father had gone to Australia. She spoke with a German accent all her life and she was, according to Fuller's sister-in-law, 'the most insulting person I knew'. Fuller's mother only put up with her because if she had not allowed everything to pass her by she would never have seen her son.[77] However, in 1906 all this was in the future. In December he married Sonia and decided, as a consequence, not to return to India.[78]

2. The Soil is Prepared— 1907–16

In peacetime the British Army is not a particularly difficult organization for the young officer to manipulate to some modest degree for his own ends, once he has achieved three 'pips'. Sometimes, however, the consequences of attempts at such manipulation can be disastrous or even exactly the opposite of what was intended. Also, outside the well-ordered and predictable routines of regimental soldiering, there used to be, and sometimes still are, opportunities of a surprisingly varied nature for both the enterprising, and the idle, for the future field marshal and the future golf club secretary. Fuller took one of those opportunities when early in 1907 he applied for the adjutancy of the 2nd South Middlesex Volunteers. First he had to pass a medical board, so he and Sonia went to Osborne for a convalescent holiday, and here Crowley addressed more of his odd letters.[1] The next step was to appear before the board which was helped in making its decision by the the fact that in Fuller's case fitness for general service would mean service at home since he had by this time been promised the adjutancy provided he passed the board. In April he took up the appointment and was once again virtually his own master, since in Volunteer units the adjutant was the only regular officer and, as such, generally had things very much his own way.

The new adjutant of the 2nd South Middlesex was, at the age of twenty-eight, a relatively experienced soldier. He had seen service in Ireland, South Africa and India and must have seemed surprisingly intelligent and well educated to those around him. Certainly there can be no doubt about his intellect; his early letters give a strong indication of the clarity and agility of his mind and one imagines that, had officers been submitted to intelligence tests in Edwardian times, Fuller would have emerged with an extremely high IQ. About the education there is need for some qualification; he read widely and searchingly, and was intellectual as well as intelligent, but he was essentially self-taught. He left school before reaching the age of seventeen and it is doubtful if either Jimmy's or Sandhurst added a great deal to his educational development. The fact that he was never subjected to any rigorous tutorial or group criticism as a young man may go some way towards accounting for both the originality and waywardness of various of his later views.

The new adjutant was also not the most moderate, modest or tolerant of men. He often embraced the extreme, though logical, view; he certainly despised fools and he was very capable of causing offence through a mixture of integrity and somewhat insensitive adherence to the truth. He had once told his mother a story about a captain and a midshipman with the second of whom one feels he readily identified. '"Well, youngster",' the story went, '"so you've come to join—eh?" "Yes, if you please, sir", meekly responded the midshipman. "What is it—the same old yarn? Send the fool of the family to sea—eh?" "No, sir," ingenuously replied the youngster. "Oh no, things have changed since your time, sir."'[2] He told his mother that the midshipman was four foot eight and the captain six foot four, and one feels that this also made the story an important one for Fuller. He was always conscious of his shortness of stature, and this may have been a contributory factor in the development of the aggressive side of his personality.

It is also true that he was very conscious at this time of his financial as well as his physical limitations. Captain and Mrs Fuller lived on Fuller's pay and his small allowance in modest circumstances at 89 Overstrand Mansions, Prince of Wales Drive, Battersea, a rather sombre block of apartments, in a row of such blocks overlooking Battersea Park, on the south, and wrong, side of the river. Sonia's influence drew him yet farther away from the norms of the mess, to reinforce both a virtually innate pro-Germanism and a developing belief in authority. As early as 1899 he had believed that Carlyle was the greatest English prose-writer[3] and his views about 'simpering counter-jumpers' and 'toe-nail-clipping Gauls' were of a piece. Even when he praised democracy it was from an unusual standpoint, while his growing involvement with the occult was also perhaps an attempt to understand the meaning of life, in the traditional explanations of which his sharp eyes had detected cracks and inconsistencies.

But above all, the most important characteristic of the new adjutant was his ability to devote himself with single-minded application to an intellectual cause. When he took up his new job he was actually most heavily involved in an attempt to create what he called 'a new spirituality' on the basis of the criticism of conventional religion. This was where Crowley and the *Agnostic Journal* came in, and Fuller's own studies of Indian philosophy and religion. It was also at this time that he first met Meredith Starr, a mystic, writer, poet, herbalist, homoeopath and self-described 'constructive psychologist' with whom he was to have a close and life-long friendship quite outside his military life; Starr's father had been a colonel but he was otherwise an unmilitary figure.[4] Fuller himself sharpened his critical teeth on religion, but once he ceased to see the value in that, since rational attack on human irrationality was pointless, and once he became interested in his job, he substituted war for religion as the object of his criticism.[5] He tells us in his *Memoirs* that he took 'no interest whatever in things military' before about the year 1910 and that this was fortunate because his 'brain was not lumbered up with conventional military doctrines'.[6] Certainly his brain was not so encumbered but there is more than a touch of disingenuousness in his claim that he had taken no interest in military matters before his move to London. His views on the Boer War, written at the time, are proof enough of that. It certainly is true that his military interests were unconventional and not those of the average young officer. It was after his friendship with Crowley broke down, and as a result of the satisfaction he obtained from his new job and, later, from his studies for the Staff College examination, that he began to develop a sense of professional dedication, the fruitfulness and intensity of which were a product of his critical, intellectual single-mindedness.

Throughout his time with the Middlesex his interest in the occult must have clashed with his growing preoccupation with the problems of military training and morale. Indeed it is difficult at first sight to imagine any two more distinct interests, although, it could be argued that a common factor imbued Fuller's attack upon both and that was his anxiety to see behind the outward appearance of things; in later life, he succeeded in rationalizing magic and war in a way which he found satisfying. In 1907 he published his first book, a slender pamphlet called 'The Star in the West—a Critical Essay upon the Works of Aleister Crowley', the cover of which—a symbolic drawing—he designed himself.[7] In the same year he went to a summer camp on Salisbury Plain, the last the Volunteers ever held, for in 1908 The Volunteer Forces became the Territorial Force and the 2nd South Middlesex was amalgamated with another battalion. Fuller became one of two adjutants, one of whom was obviously redundant; but the day was saved for him because the War Office suggested that, if the men could be recruited by a certain date, another Middlesex Battalion might be formed. Consequently Fuller and two ex-Volunteer officers found a retired Grenadier Guardsman as Commanding Officer and enlisted some 400 men by the due date. In his own words: 'As we were not allowed to recruit in London, and as eighty per cent of the men we knew lived and worked there, the problem was solved by collecting them in Putney, taking them out to the first lamp-post in the County of Middlesex, and attesting them under its glimmering light.'[8] He put a great deal of effort into the musketry training of the new battalion, the 10th Middlesex, and the next year, in 1909, it came top in musketry in competition against all Territorial Battalions in the country. His attitude to his men, all of whom were part-time volunteers, was sympathetic and practical and he found time to deal with both employers and girl friends.[9] Perhaps today his values and his methods would be unkindly labelled paternalistic, but in Edwardian London they were enlightened and effective. He found success pleasing and enjoyed himself immensely; also he enjoyed having plenty of spare time, much of which he undoubtedly employed in activities in association with Crowley and Starr, one which was involved in the writing and editing of an occult journal called *Equinox*. He also appears to have been subsidizing Crowley to a small extent,[10] and Crowley in his turn asked Fuller to lunch with Colonel F. N. Maude—the editor, in 1908, of Colonel J. J. Graham's 1873 translation of Clausewitz. It may have been this meeting which aroused Fuller's interest in the author of *On War*, with whom he was subsequently to be compared, since he later claimed that he first read Clausewitz at about this time.[11] In 1909 and also in 1911 he found time to take Sonia to Germany for a holiday. In 1911 his friend-

ship with Crowley came to an embittered end after a quarrel
about *Equinox* and Crowley's refusal to undertake a libel action
against those who had criticized him. Crowley was to try to take
up the threads of their association again in later years but without
success. [12]

On a hot summer day in 1911, while on a visit to Folkestone,
Fuller chanced to see the Second Battalion of his own regular
Regiment marching along 'in full war paint. Somehow the sight
of those decked-out, sweating men horrified me. Mentally I
looked round for some avenue of escape, and in an instant I
decided to work for the Staff College.' [13] Times have changed; the
Staff College is not now an escape from regimental soldiering, or
rather only a temporary one, since although attendance at that
august institution will almost certainly result in a number of staff
appointments, it is only through Staff College that the majority
of officers can now hope to achieve command of their regiments,
or indeed promotion of any sort beyond the rank of major. Fuller,
however, like so many officers today, had a not very serious trial
run at the Staff College examination in 1912 and failed by a
narrow margin. [14] In consequence he had to rejoin his Regiment as
a company commander, a post held then by a captain. He moved
from Battersea to Aldershot where he also acted as Rail
Transport Officer (RTO) to Aldershot Command before and after
the Army manoeuvres in both 1912 and 1913. In 1913 he acted as
Brigade Machine Gun Officer to the 5th Infantry Brigade. In fact
his experiences between 1907 and 1913 were singularly, if fortuitously, appropriate in the light of the coming war in which the
training of non-regular soldiers, the use of railways and the
impact of machine guns were to be of overwhelming importance.

It was during his time with the 10th Middlesex, and subsequently in Aldershot, that he began to write seriously and
professionally for publication. His early works, articles and
pamphlets, were in general concerned with the practical problems
of training and morale which faced him as a territorial adjutant.
His very first military publication was 'Hints on Training
Territorial Infantry' [15] which was written between 1907 and 1912
and published in 1913. This pamphlet, based on his own experiences, contains a great deal of practical and sympathetic advice
to unit commanders, showing imagination and understanding of
men, and including sections on employers and girl friends. At the

same time he also wrote a pamphlet, not published until 1914, called 'Training Soldiers for War'.[16] He admitted that this had been begun as a treatise on moral training for the Regular Army and Territorial Force but by the time of publication, was offered to the New Army to help in fashioning it into a formidable weapon of war. It is a well-structured essay on training, based on psychological and educational principles, and contains chapters on confidence, discipline, initiative, lectures, PT, combat drill, musketry and field training. In it Fuller drew on many French writers, including Grandmaison and Le Bon. The preface, dated October 1914, contains an echo of Foch which Fuller no doubt much regretted in later years. 'Once man's heart is won,' he wrote 'men may be slaughtered, they may be annihilated, but they will not be conquered and to will success is all but equivalent to victory.' When, nearly fifty years later, in *The Conduct of War*, Fuller made fun of Foch's famous statement that, 'a battle won is a battle in which one will not confess oneself beaten', he pointed out that morale does not render the assailants bullet-proof, but he omitted to make any reference to his earlier and Foch-like views.[17]

Next, and while at Aldershot in 1912–13, he wrote two articles for *The Army Review*, one called 'The Mobilization of a Territorial Infantry Battalion'[18] and the other, 'Notes on the Entrainment of Troops to and from Manoeuvres'.[19] The former contains a simple and well-considered mobilization plan, while the latter concentrates on practical problems and was to be instrumental in August 1914 in getting its author appointed as a DADRT or Deputy Assistant Director of Railway Transport— another very grand-sounding staff appointment for a captain. About this time also Fuller produced an undated paper, now in the Liddell Hart Archives, entitled 'Notes on Infantry Tactics',[20] in which he asked how discipline could be improved, and concluded that improvement would come from the reduction of friction which itself stems from inefficiency. He likened a disciplined body of men to a pack of hounds rather than a troupe of performing dogs. He also found time to write another article in 1913. This was published in the journal of an institution which was to play a not inconsiderable part in his life—the Royal United Service Institution (RUSI), called 'The Revival and Training of Light Infantry in the British Army, 1757–1806'[21] which analyses Sir John Moore's training system. Colonel G. F. R. Henderson,[22] perhaps the most well-known of Camberley's Victorian instructors, had preceded Fuller in recommending this system, but Fuller started where Henderson left off and in the next ten years was to devote many bottles of ink to Moore's activities at Shorncliffe Camp. Fuller himself, however, was proudest of 'The Three Flag System of Instructing Infantry in Fire Tactics',[23] and 'The Procedure of the Infantry Attack, a Synthesis from a Psychological Standpoint.'[24] In the first of these articles Fuller evolved a system of using fire effect in training, but in the second he spread his net much wider and began to use concepts with which his readers were to become very familiar in later years. The second article begins by reducing war to the simplest element, the two methods of waging it. These are by the use of missiles from a distance or shock weapons at close quarters. To these the shield may be added, not made of leather or steel any more, but in the form of ground or fire cover. Here, however, Fuller added a pregnant footnote: 'The reappearance of the shield proper in modern warfare, now used by artillery, is interesting, and may lead to a further reintroduction of this essentially defensive weapon.'[25] However, he went on to put forward the more traditional view that the close-quarter fight is in the end the act of decision, 'the shock, which crowns the victory'. Although bullet and shell might be superior to bayonet and sword, the former were 'mere forerunners, servants of the master blow, the fight at close quarters'.[26] Fuller divided the attack into four phases—approach, demoralization (attack at a distance), decision (close quarters) and annihilation (pursuit). He recognized that the approach would be under fire, although he did not mention defensive machine-gun fire, the effectiveness of which had already been shown in the Russo-Japanese war. He stated that superiority over defensive fire must be obtained in order to advance and that such offensive fire must be achieved by the fire of men lying down in the rear or on a flank. The advancing infantry should proceed in single file rather than in section lines but there finally had to be a traditional assault, the instinctive surge forward which 'cannot be taught, for it alone can be experienced',[27] followed by a pursuit by fresh troops, but not by cavalry which can no longer 'take part in the act of decision'.[28] The psychological standpoint of the title is that the nature of this act of decision makes moral forces all-important in the infantry attack but that forces based on education (religion, patriotism, esprit de corps, discipline) are artificial and will evaporate in battle. What remains is the instinct of self-preservation leading to a desire either to close or to flee, the outcome depending on habit acquisition stemming from training or way of life. When he wrote this article Fuller certainly saw many of the problems which were soon to face Europe's armies but apart from his pointer towards the shield his solutions were not original or satisfactory. Henderson, in particular, at the turn of the century, had advocated thin lines of skirmishers and tactics based on fire and movement,[29] and had also at the same time dismissed the further usefulness of cavalry as shock troops.[30] The truth was that movement under enemy fire had, by reason of the technology of the breech-loading magazine rifle and the machine gun, become a suicidal undertaking. Until a new turn of the technological wheel gave soldiers some protection from the hail of bullets about to sweep the fields of Flanders and Northern France, the psychological insights of the young Fuller or the ageing Foch were unlikely to provide a solution, although, of course, Fuller's writings on training and morale were extremely relevant in terms of the necessity to withstand the horrors of the forthcoming stalemate. Technology, however, and not psychology, was to provide the battlefield solution, as far as it was provided in the First World War; the good, lousy, stinking, rancid Saxon or Goth and the hair-combing, toe-nail-clipping Gaul were all equally vulnerable to the bullet.

In 1913 he succeeded in his second attempt at the Staff College examination, and on New Year's Eve, 1913, he and Sonia moved to Camberley. In those days Staff College was a two-year course but Fuller's sojourn there was to be suddenly and rudely truncated by the outbreak of war. Once again, and through no fault of his own, he was not to remain for long *in statu pupillari*. His own memory of his few months at Camberley was of being the recipient of a great deal of staff displeasure. This appears to have been generated initially by a paper which Fuller wrote called 'The Tactics of Penetration: A Counterblast to German Numerical Superiority', which was later published in the *RUSI Journal* of November 1914.[31] There is a copy of a reprint of this paper in the Liddell Hart Archives and on it Fuller has noted that the

Commandant of the Staff College considered it lacking in
military judgment. This was Brigadier General L. E. Kiggell, later
Director of Military Training at the War Office and then Haig's
Chief of Staff, but a man of little character. His reaction, however, was not in the least surprising since military doctrine at the
time was based upon the tactics of envelopment, not penetration.
In 1902 Henderson had written that frontal assault against good
troops had become suicidal[32] and had therefore advocated
envelopment; indeed he believed that the new strength of the
defensive paradoxically led to a strengthening of the offensive
because it released troops from the line who could then be used in
the attack. The tactics of Field Service Regulation, 1909, had
been based on the proposition that the decisive attack was best
directed at one or other of the enemy's flanks. 'The moral effect
of an envelopment which threatens an enemy's line of retreat, and
enfilades his front is always great.'[33] Fuller's thesis, which ran
head-on into this teaching, was that the quick-firing field gun and
the machine gun had changed all this. The former was now the
master missile-throwing weapon and would lead to the substitution of penetration for envelopment because guns commanding a
weak or decisive point would in future be able to so deluge it with
shells as 'to enable the decisive attack to proceed against it'. The
problem became one of bringing up sufficient artillery ammunition, and this could be solved by the use of motor transport. The
machine gun was a 'terror-spreading' weapon which could be
used to precede or flank attacks. This paper was certainly heter-
odox and pointed to future reality in the sense that it dwelt on
the problem and necessity of penetration. But Fuller was advancing the wrong reasons and advocating an ineffective solution.
Penetration became necessary principally because in the conditions of the First World War on the Western Front envelopment
became impossible. Once the Schlieffen Plan had misfired the
front lines stretched unbroken as far as they could go, and the
mass armies, themselves the consequence of technological and
political change, were faced with the necessity of attempting to
roll back or penetrate each other's fronts. Rolling back was to
cause unimaginable casualties, or rather imagined only by such as
I. S. Block, a Polish banker, who forecast a bloody and
entrenched military stalemate in any future war in a book written
in 1897.[34] Penetration, massive attack on a narrow front in order

to create a flank, and that paradoxically in the rear, was really the only answer. In 1914 Fuller wanted to penetrate by using artillery but Henderson had seen the future more clearly when he concluded in 1903 that artillery was impotent against well-constructed entrenchments.[35] In another paper written at Camberley, and based on a visit to an artillery practice camp at Larkhill in May, Fuller developed his views about the importance of artillery; putting forward the heresy that artillery had become the superior arm, he wrote that infantry would have to co-operate with artillery as often as artillery co-operated with infantry. The demoralizing fire of artillery would have to precede infantry assault; wire and field works would limit manoeuvre and again lead to the substitution of penetration for envelopment.[36] In his *Memoirs* Fuller admits that in his pre-war thinking about penetration he 'miscalculated the holding power of the enemy';[37] it is, of course, also ironic that a few years later he was obliged to fight a crusade against methodical artillery barrages on the grounds that surprise was lost by them and the ground rendered impassable to mechanical transport. In spite of the understandable mistiness in early 1914 of his view of the future battlefield, his perception of the importance of using new or improved weapons to achieve surprise was a valuable one.

At Camberley he also began to develop his thinking along another path which was to be prominent in his writing. In 1911 he had come to the conclusion that a European war might be imminent. This had stimulated his interest in military history and caused him to turn to *Field Service Regulations* in order to prepare himself.[38] There he had found that: 'The fundamental principles of war are neither very numerous nor in themselves very abstruse.'[39] This had not satisfied him because he did not know and had not been told what the principles were. He had therefore read the *Correspondence of Napoleon* and in 1912 had come to the conclusiion that Napoleon's guiding principles had been Objective, Mass, Offensive, Security, Surprise and Movement. He had enunciated these principles in 'Training Soldiers for War' but at Camberley he began to apply them to the study of military history. He found them helpful but was reprimanded for attempting to amend rather than study *Field Service Regulations*. He must have been an irritating and disturbing student, particularly as by this time he had several publications to his credit. It was perhaps fortunate for Fuller that he was not obliged to remain for two years at Camberley! His last few months were disturbed by the reverberation of the clash of loyalties which the Ulster question presented to the British army officer of those days, but as July drew on, war drew nearer. Students were ordered to parade their horses for sale to the Government. All leave was cancelled and each officer received his mobilization instructions. Fuller's instructed him to report, if war were declared, as an Assistant Embarkation Staff Officer at Southampton. On August 4th war was declared and on the 5th the staff course dispersed. By evening, and after a bicycle ride with Sonia to Farnborough station, Fuller was established in the South Western Hotel in Southampton, Sonia having been temporarily left behind at Aldershot. She joined him a few days later in rooms in Southampton.

It is very probable that, had Fuller not been posted to Southampton in 1914, he would have failed to survive the war since the casualty rate, even for staff officers, was very high in France in the first months of fighting. Moreover it was not until almost a year after the outbreak of war that he arrived in France or saw active service. Perhaps this gave him the chance to think through the consequences of the events which he observed at first from a safe distance. There was not, however, much time for thought in Southampton. 'Notes on the Entrainment of Troops to and from Manoeuvres' having acquired for him the post of DADRT, he was immediately thrust into the fray of preparing to receive, detrain and embark a large part of the British Expeditionary Force.

The hastily assembled Embarkation Staff at Southampton was largely made up of Staff College students, like Fuller, and of numbers of recalled retired officers, known in those days as 'dugouts'. One of these, a retired infantry major, was appointed as Fuller's assistant. The two of them were faced with the task of organizing the movement of troop trains from the station to the docks, at peak periods at the rate of one train every four minutes. This operation was made more difficult by the fact that there was only one set of tracks between the station and the docks and each empty train had to be removed before a new full train could make the journey. By a strange coincidence, and to help in this work, Fuller was provided with a sorting device of movable strips of

wood representing trains, which had actually been invented by a
neighbour of his at Camberley, and which he knew how to work.
The rush began on the 9th and throughout the remainder of
August he was kept very busy manipulating the sorting device,
plotting the allocation of train-loads to wharves and preventing
other military agencies from upsetting the good relations he had
established with the railway officials. By the end of the month six
divisions had passed through his hands. Included amongst these
formations were the Oxfordshire Hussars, a Yeomanry, or part-
time, unit, whose officers caused Fuller both amusement and
annoyance by demanding to take a very large quantity of personal
baggage with them, and by complaining about the absence of
notepaper in the requisitioned cattle-ship on which they were to
make the crossing to France. Fuller also claimed that he solved a
stevedores' strike by appealing to the vanity of the Chief
Wharfinger and persuading him that his reputation and authority
depended upon his getting the men back to work.

The pace quickened again in October when Fuller was temporarily sent to Devonport to supervise the disembarkation of the
Canadian Expeditionary Force. In Devonport he experienced
considerable inter-Service difficulty, because the docks there were
under naval control. The Canadians added to his problems as they
had a propensity to get very drunk and disorderly while marching
through the town to Friary Station. However it was the Canadian
officers against whom he generated the greatest feeling. In the
middle of October he could not prevent himself from telling his
mother in a letter that the Canadian soldiers would be good
enough after six months' training 'if the officers could be all
shot'.[40] Even such an unconventional soldier as Fuller found
white colonial armies a little difficult to take in 1914.

At the end of October he returned to Southampton and began
to campaign for a staff appointment in France. The other Staff
College students had been disappearing one by one since
September, and Fuller was eventually the last remaining. He had
to wait a long time for a posting and when it came in December it
proved magnificently Pyrrhic, a posting not to the Front but as a
General Staff Officer, Third Grade, or GSO 3, to HQ Second
Army, Central Force, Home Forces in Tunbridge Wells.

He arrived in Tunbridge Wells with Sonia on December 15th,
which happened to be Sonia's birthday. They established them-

selves in a hotel but this was undoubtedly the 'nadir' so far of his military career. Not only was he uninvolved in the cataclysmic events which were taking place across the Channel but the job he was given, organizing training for the Territorial battalions of which Second Army consisted, was entirely spurious because his new master, Brigadier General H. J. du Cane, would hardly ever let him leave the office. Fuller organized the filing system and became involved in paper exercises, stemming from the invasion threat, concerned with evacuating sheep from Sussex, Kent and Surrey to Salisbury Plain, and with deciding whether or not to destroy all intoxicants in public-houses when the enemy landed. These activities apart, he spent his time writing a book which he called *Notes on the Training of the New Armies, 1797–1805*. This work was a development of his earlier *RUSI* article on the subject and led to another article which was published in the *RUSI Journal* in November 1916.[41] After the war he published the full work as two separate books.

In March 1915 he began a further campaign for an overseas posting but got nowhere until in May he managed to have a full-blooded row with du Cane during which he told him what he thought of him and his work. This resulted in du Cane saying to Fuller: 'If that is what you think, I will have you sent to France.'[42] In this way Fuller achieved his objective. He was posted as GSO 3 to VII Corps and on July 19th Sonia saw him off at Folkestone.

It is not easy, after the bombing offensives of the Second World War, the devastation of Hiroshima and the dangers and tensions of insurgency and guerilla warfare, to visualize the conditions of warfare in France in 1915, particularly the paradox of murderous and muddy spasms of slaughter along a narrow linear front while safety and good living were only a few miles back on either side of it. Indeed for generals and their staffs, once the early mobile operations were over, this may have been the safest war of all time, while simultaneously being the most dangerous for regimentally employed officers and men. Fuller's new life was then a far cry from the hard-riding, sharp-shooting existence he had led in South Africa, and he was never actually personally involved in front-line fighting at all throughout the war. At first, the differences between Tunbridge Wells and Marieux, a village near Doullens some ten miles behind the Front, where he found

HQ VII Corps just before lunch on the 20th, must have seemed minimal. He met the Corps Commander and his chief staff officer, the Brigadier General Staff and was allocated to the GSO 2 Operations as an assistant. His job was to help plan operations but he soon found, however, that he had little real work to do. The entrenched stalemate made operations, apart from patrolling and suicidal set-piece frontal assaults, impossible, at least if carried out in accordance with the precepts of contemporary tactical thought. The stalemate had developed, of course, as a consequence both of the magazine rifle and machine gun and of the impossibility of outflanking movement around a front which now stretched from the sea to Switzerland. It was the scenario of Fuller's own pre-war thinking about penetration but the problem was that penetration by artillery did not work.

Fuller visited the trenches along VII Corps' six-mile front and began to do some hard thinking. He told his mother that the German trenches were quite as strong, or stronger than the British,[43] that a million and a half more men were required in France[44] and that, although trenches could be captured by infantry after artillery bombardment, the infantry could not then exploit its success because the bombardment had to be lifted for fear of killing one's own troops. His own solution was a massive increase in machine guns which could take up where the artillery left off. 'Whichever side,' he wrote, 'can throw the greatest number of projectiles against the other is the side which has the greatest chances of winning.'[45] Unfortunately both sides were able to throw enough at the other to prevent either achieving victory. Sufficiency even then made nonsense of superiority.

In September 1915 Fuller spent a great deal of his spare time writing an article on 'The Principles of War with Reference to the Campaigns of 1914–1915', and this was anonymously published in the *RUSI Journal* in February 1916.[46] The principles had their origins in 'Training Soldiers for War' and in his studies at Camberley and were to be an absorbing and at times obsessive interest for him for the next ten years, representing as they did the tip of an iceberg in his thinking, an iceberg labelled Science of War. The article begins with an attack on the 1909 edition of *Field Service Regulations*, which he had first inveighed against at Camberley. He ridiculed the dismissal of the principles of war as the compilation of a grammar without an alphabet. He continued:

Do not let my opponents castigate me with the blather that
Waterloo was won on the playfields of Eton, for the fact
remains geographically, historically and tactically, whether
the Great Duke uttered such undiluted nonsense or not, that
it was won on fields in Belgium by carrying out a fundamental principle of war, the principle of mass; in other words by
marching on to those fields three Englishmen, Germans or
Belgians to every two Frenchmen.

The principles had now expanded to eight by the addition of
economy of force and co-operation, a significant comment on
what Fuller had seen of the war. Operations ought to be conducted by harmonizing the principles and applying them against
the background of conditions—time, space, ground, weather,
numbers, morale, communication, supply and armament. In tactics the principles of demoralization, endurance and shock also
applied. To any army officer, and not only British, there will be a
familiar ring about much of this since it was in Fuller's thinking
that much principles-of-war doctrine had its origins. In the
remainder of the article Fuller applied his principles to the current situation in France and recommended a dual attack to nip
off the German salient between Arras and Rheims by a converg-
ing offensive aimed at Namur. He argued that the primary tactical objective in penetration was the capture or forced withdrawal of the enemy's artillery position because the gun was the
master weapon and infantry would be forced to retire with it. To
achieve this objective, however, it would be necessary also to
capture a variety of infantry positions. The secondary tactical
objective was to prevent the enemy occupying a prepared rear
defensive line since this would nullify penetration. To achieve the
primary objective an advance of 3–5,000 yards or more was
necessary and to achieve the secondary, the capture of the
enemy's first-line system and line of defended posts and villages
was required. A limited objective was necessary to avoid the
creation of exposed flanks. In trench warfare the approach was
already completed. Demoralization was the function of the artillery supported by rifle and machine-gun fire. The rifleman was no
longer the true demoralizer but merely the escort of other arms
until the act of decision began. The act of annihilation would
have to be carried out by a new force. All this is really an

application of 'The Tactics of Penetration' to the military situation at the end of 1915. The problem was that artillery was not the master weapon; small-arms fire was still dominant.

On the final page of the article Fuller wrote: 'Germany, and the destruction of Germany, of her military might, and of her national resources, of her arrogance, of her materialism, her servility and barbarity is our one and only objective; and every seduction which distracts us from the straight path must be banished by the sigil of victory. In her destruction is success, in her destruction is death to her allies.' This appeal to the heart was no doubt primarily directed against the Easterners, those who wanted to impose strategies of indirect approach on the war. However, in view of Fuller's origins and marriage, one cannot avoid the suspicion that he felt a need in 1915 to demonstrate his loyalties. In this connection it is not insignificant that he dropped the practice of signing his letters home 'Fritz' after his arrival in France and the subjection of his correspondence to censorship.[47] However, his patriotism did not inhibit him from describing the Government as 'the presiding rabble' in a letter to his father at the beginning of 1916.[48]

It was while he was serving at HQ VII Corps that he was promoted Major and that he was invited to work out a syllabus for a Third Army refresher course for officers and NCOs. This invitation arose from the fact that Major-General A. L. Lynden-Bell, the senior staff officer in Third Army, had read 'Training Soldiers for War'. He asked Fuller to command the school set up to run these courses but Fuller wisely declined on the grounds that he had not had enough experience in France. He did, however, produce the syllabus. Sometime later he took a week's leave in England and in the New Year, on February 4th, 1916, was posted to 37 Division as a GSO 2.

HQ 37 Division, which was part of VII Corps, was commanded by Major-General Count Gleichen and its headquarters was located a few miles north of Marieux in a small château built in imitation of Versailles. As a result of a French withdrawal the headquarters was soon moved into a modern house at Bavincourt. As a GSO 2, Fuller's work was much the same as it had been as a GSO 3. The division consisted of three brigades and the brigadiers were an independent lot who would not have taken kindly to overmuch interference from a major at divisional headquarters.

In April Fuller was ordered to the Third Army School he had helped to found the previous year and asked to run a series of one-week Commanding Officers' Conferences for groups of twenty to thirty lieutenant-colonels and senior majors withdrawn from the line. This was an awe-inspiring task because the students were all senior to him and incensed at having to return to school. However, he put one or two of them in their place and made the conference a highly successful affair. After Fuller had run five they were renamed Senior Officers' Courses and transferred to Aldershot. After the war they became the Senior Officers' School which flourished for many years in Aldershot and, later, in Wiltshire. Perhaps the success went a little to Fuller's head because it was at this time that he told his father that he considered it 'an extraordinary thing whilst every science is run on a few definite principles, war today should be run on the dice-box of luck. . . . We can predict certain events in war as surely as Darwin could in life directly he grasped the fundamental principles of evolution. However we have no military Darwin as yet, let us hope the Germans will not discover one.'[49] One cannot avoid the suspicion that even in 1916 he had a premonition that perhaps the name of the military Darwin might be J. F. C. Fuller.

In May he returned to 37 Division and wrote a paper on 'The Principles of Defence as applied to Trench Warfare'.[50] The War Office refused permission for the RUSI to publish this on the grounds that it might be of value to the enemy. In it Fuller argued for a more rational attitude to trench warfare, and for the capture or retention of ground to be regarded as a means to victory rather than as an end in itself. He made a typically logical and unconventional suggestion that wire entanglements should be erected behind rather than in front of the front line trenches or forward slopes so that, when attacked, troops could retire securely behind them. The erection of entanglements in no-man's-land was, after all, a hazardous occupation and drew fire on to our own trenches. Most of the paper is, however, devoted to an application of the principles of war to the conditions of defence in mid-1916.

Fuller's service with 37 Division came to an end with the outbreak of the Franco–British Somme offensive. On June 20th he wrote to his father and told him that if Lloyd George 'were only a gentleman he might do well enough, but he is such a little bounder that I am afraid he will be rather out of his depth'.[51] The 'little bounder', however, had to agree to the Somme and at 7.30 a.m. on July 1st Fuller watched part of the attack in front of the village of Fonquevillers, or at least he saw a little through the smoke and dust. The offensive lasted for five months at the cost of enormous casualties. 37 Division was in reserve and on July 5th, the day Kitchener was drowned off the Orkneys, was broken up to relieve brigades in other divisions. Having thereby lost his job, Fuller was found a new GSO 2 appointment on July 17th in Third Army Headquarters at St Pol, where he was congratulated by his GSO 1, Colonel 'Tom' Hollond, upon rejoining the British Army. This, of course, was a reference to the Germanic name of the Commander, 37 Division.

The new job had a little more status than either of the previous ones, being in a higher formation headquarters, and Hollond was a master at obtaining support from friends in other Army Headquarters in order to achieve some desired decision from GHQ—a technique which Fuller could perhaps have adopted with profit later in his career. Also in the headquarters, on the Q side, was a Captain T. J. Uzielli who was shortly to play a vital part in the development of Fuller's career. It was, however, a sapper officer, Captain F. H. E. Townshend, who pointed Fuller's thinking in a significant direction in early August. This officer showed Fuller a paper he had written, 'The Ms in Red Ink', in which he developed the idea that all that was needed to win the war was to penetrate in a few hours the thin enemy front, 500 miles long but only five miles deep, with an advance of five miles on a front of a hundred. Townshend did not say how this was to be done but he did indicate that the first step towards doing it was to see the problem clearly in the abstract.[52] In fact Townshend was one of a number of younger staff officers in Third Army who had been thinking very deeply about the future of the war.[53] His views naturally interested Fuller since they reinforced his own belief in penetration.

In mid-August rumours began to circulate about the existence of a new weapon of war. Townshend told Fuller that the weapon was an armoured and tracked car and they obtained permission to see a number of them at Yvrench on the afternoon of August 20th. As they drew near in their car they encountered more and more sightseers. In Fuller's own words: 'Everyone was talking and chatting, when slowly came into sight the first tank I ever saw. Not a monster, but a very graceful machine, with beautiful lines, lozenge-shaped, but with two clumsy-looking wheels behind it.' Fuller and Townshend looked at each other and exclaimed: 'What price "The Ms in Red Ink?" '[54] Here was the missing tool of penetration, the answer to the dominance on the battlefield of small-arms fire.

For the remainder of the year Fuller had nothing to do with tanks. Rather he was concerned with attempting to change the doctrine on minor infantry tactics, arguing for single-file rather than wave or line formations in attack. While he was so involved, however, and while the Battle of the Somme continued its bloody raging, Lieutenant-Colonel H. J. Elles was appointed Colonel Commanding the Heavy Branch of the Machine Gun Corps, the name given to the embryo Tank Corps. Uzielli was transferred to the Heavy Branch Headquarters at Bermicourt on October 8th and it was he who recommended Fuller for a new GSO 2 post which was created there in December. On Boxing Day Fuller arrived at Bermicourt to meet the immense challenge of opportunity which his new post presented. With hindsight it is possible to see what a magnificent apprenticeship his professional thinking and writing had been for the grasping of this particular opportunity. His interest in morale, psychology and training was obviously invaluable for one concerned with the production of an entirely novel fighting arm, using, however, entirely familiar human material; his theory of penetration had suddenly been made workable; his belief in the science of war and in the value of principles of war fitted him admirably for devising the tactics and strategy of the tank. A few days after his arrival, on New Year's Day 1917, his name was listed in the London Gazette as one of those many awarded the DSO.

3. Enter the Tank— 1917–18

The world is now so familiar with the tank, that groaning, clattering, turreted apparition in so many television news bulletins, that it has become for us the very symbol of war. For soldiers in the First World War, however, the tank was new, original, strange, even hilarious, and either comforting or terrifying, depending upon your relationship with its inmates. The first tanks were very slow, very cumbersome and looked very large. After the war, ironically, they were used to adorn many British parks and children played on them happily. So do we reduce our more destructive and murderous artefacts to an acceptable role. And then, in 1940, we melted those tamed engines of war down, along with the park railings, to make new weapons. Fuller would probably have argued that the first tanks were the reverse of destructive and murderous in their total effect because they preserved their crews and were capable of bringing about an early end to the war. Analogous arguments are advanced today about the deterrent effect of nuclear weapons. The maintenance of peace through armament is certainly a rational and workable policy and one to which most regular soldiers are professionally dedicated. In 1916, however, it was not a question of maintaining peace through armament but of achieving it, of winning the war.

It is possible to trace the origins of the tank, or at least of the armoured vehicle, back into history, as Fuller himself later did in *Tanks in the Great War* and *Armament and History*. Both the original British and French tanks were derived from the Holt caterpillar tractor,[1] and the man with perhaps the greatest claim to have been their originator was Sir Ernest Swinton, at one time a sapper officer and at others assistant secretary of the Committee of Imperial Defence (the CID) and Chichele Professor of Military History at Oxford. Fuller came into the tank business after the tank had been invented, after its first use in September 1916 and also after a lot of thought had been given to its design and tactical deployment. Two such thinkers were the banker, Lieutenant-Colonel Albert Stern, who was for some time Director-General of Mechanical Warfare Supply in the Ministry of Munitions, and Eustace d'Eyncourt, who acted as Chief Technical Adviser and was by profession a naval designer. Others, of course, had also played major parts and these included Winston Churchill. French development owed much to the then Colonel J. E. Estienne.

Swinton claimed that he conceived the germ of the tank idea in October 1914. It was to be the antidote to machine guns and wire, 'a power-driven, bullet-proof, armed engine, capable of destroying machine guns, of crossing country and trenches, of breaking through entanglements, and of climbing earthworks'. And while driving from St Omer to Calais on October 19th, 1914, Swinton suddenly realized that the key to the problem lay in using the caterpillar track already used on agricultural tractors.[2] The use of such tracks had already been recommended to Swinton for military transport purposes by a mining engineer called H. F. Marriott in July 1914,[3] and numbers of other inventors had designed or made armoured track-laying vehicles as far back as 1855.[4] Swinton made numbers of attempts to interest GHQ, the War Office and others in his ideas between October 1914 and June 1915. The very first of these initiatives, the explanation of his ideas to Hankey, the Secretary of the Committee of Imperial Defence, led eventually to Churchill's famous letter to Asquith, of January 5th, 1915, proposing, inter alia, steam-driven tractors on the caterpillar system, armoured and carrying men and machine guns. This in turn led to the setting up of the Landships Committee to investigate armoured cross-country vehicles. This was a purely naval committee and stemmed from the previous involvement of the Navy in the use of armoured cars by units of the Royal Naval Air Service operating in France. Churchill's original letter to Asquith contains the seeds of much future tank/infantry doctrine since tanks are seen as *points d'appui* on which supporting infantry could rally,[5] a concept which Fuller accepted at least as late as 1920. A later initiative from Swinton took place on June 1st, 1915, when he handed a paper to the Sub-Chief of the GHQ Staff entitled 'The Necessity for

Machine-Gun Destroyers'. This paper, which Swinton claims formulated 'the conditions upon which the Tank was eventually developed'.[6] stressed the strength of linear defensive in depth using machine guns, trenches, wire, gas etc., and upheld the view that machine guns would stop all offensive efforts unless penetration was achieved through artillery bombardment or some other means of destroying machine guns or neutralizing their effect on infantry.[7] 'The first alternative,' Swinton wrote, 'is not at present within our power. ... The second is believed to be possible through the employment of "Armoured Machine Gun Destroyers" which will enable us to engage guns on an equality.' In the paper Swinton described these as 'petrol tractors on the caterpillar principle, of a type which can travel up to four miles an hour on the flat, can cross a ditch up to four feet in width ... armoured with hardened steel plate proof against the German steel-cored, armour-piercing and reversed bullets and armed with—say—two Maxim 2-pounder guns'.[8]

He went on to suggest that the tanks should be saved up for a surprise assault on a large scale and should not be used initially in small numbers because of the loss of surprise which would result. In the attack, which would only be preceded by an artillery bombardment early the night before to cut the enemy wire, with subsequently only occasional bursts of rifle fire to prevent repair, the destroyers would advance to the enemy trenches, crush his machine-gun emplacements or destroy them with 2-pounders, and enfilade his trenches with Maxim fire. This action would draw the bulk of the enemy's fire and the infantry would be able to assault practically unscathed. Moreover, once surprise was over, the artillery would shell the enemy's artillery. The destroyers would move through the enemy defensive zone and then turn right and left, thus taking the flank trenches in the rear. And finally destroyers and infantry would proceed forwards, possibly getting within rifle range of the enemy guns. In defence the destroyers would act as mobile strong points or anti-aircraft artillery. They would also be useful where gas was used.[9] It is obvious from the contents of this paper that Swinton's claim was justified and indeed his tactical thinking foreshadowed much of what actually took place, and at least a substantial part of Fuller's own thinking in the war. D'Eyncourt and Stern held similar views about the necessity to save up tanks for a massive surprise attack.[10]

Although the paper did not meet with a sympathetic reception from the Engineer-in-Chief, eventually, on June 22nd, 1915, it was sent by the Commander-in-Chief for consideration to the War Office, where Swinton himself followed a month later. Meanwhile, on June 30th, the War Office sent Swinton's specifications for a machine-gun destroyer to the Admiralty's Landships Committee and from this followed the chain of events which led to the trial and acceptance of 'Mother' at Hatfield on February 2nd, 1916. Some very interesting comments on Swinton's paper, which must be mentioned, are those of Lord Cavan, then commanding 4th Guards Brigade in France, and a future enemy of Fuller's as Chief of the Imperial General Staff in the 20s. He wrote to Swinton on June 12th, 1915, expressing great interest in the destroyers but warning Swinton that the scheme to use them would only work once or twice in his part of the line in the summer, and never in the winter because of the boggy ground. Cavan also believed that infantry could actually travel on the destroyers during the assault.[11] Swinton himself worried about the effects on the destroyers of German field guns and, particularly, of guns mounted in armoured cupolas, unless the destroyers were armoured against shell as well as shot.[12]

Obviously, therefore, Fuller was in no way involved in the invention of the tank. He was also by no means the first officer to write about its tactics. Of course Swinton had touched on tactics in his June 1915 paper but in October 1915 he began to write a paper on tank tactics, which was completed in February 1916, and sent to the War Office and GHQ in March. Its contents were unknown in what became Tank Corps Headquarters in France until early 1918, and hence to Fuller, and they could not, as Swinton admits, have been responsible for the conduct of the Battle of Cambrai. Fuller said that he first saw the paper in February 1918 and this more or less coincides with Swinton's memories.[13] 'Notes on the Employment of Tanks' is nevertheless of considerable interest because it again pre-dates Fuller's own thinking. The 'Notes' begin by defining the tank as 'primarily a machine-gun destroyer, which can be employed as an auxiliary to an infantry assault'. Next Swinton dealt with the characteristics of the tank then being produced and detailed its offensive systems—machine guns and case shot from 6-pounders against personnel and its own weight and the 6-pounders against machine guns and artillery. As regards passive defence, the tank's armour would give complete protection against shrapnel balls, almost complete protection against rifle and machine gun fire and considerable protection against HE splinters. He then suggested that one in ten tanks should carry wireless sets while others should be capable of laying line. Visual signalling by balloon and smoke would also be possible. Even more interesting is a section on 'Vulnerability' in which he admitted that howitzers, field guns, high-velocity, small-calibre, quick-firing guns and mines were all capable in varying degrees of putting tanks out of action. This was the chief weakness of the tank but could be lessened by the use of counter-bombardment. Next there is a repetition of his earlier point about surprise. He now stated categorically: 'these machines should not be used in driblets (for instance, as they may be produced), but that the fact of their existence should be kept as secret as possible until the whole are ready to be launched, together with the infantry assault, in one great combined operation.'[14]

The next sections of the 'Notes' deal with various measures of preparation, rather than tactics, but Swinton did imply in a footnote something very like Fuller's later concept of 'morcellated' attack or multiple penetration in order to take linear defences in the rear. There follows a final section on tactics in which Swinton dismissed the possibility of night attack and recommended attack by tanks just before dawn, followed, once the tanks are three-quarters of the way across no-man's-land, by commencement of the infantry charge. He argued strongly against keeping the tanks in reserve to be used if the infantry got 'bogged down', mainly because this would increase casualties, possibly result in the tank being caught in heavy shell-fire, and lessen the possibility of quick, deep penetration. Once the enemy's front line is crossed, the tanks should enfilade it with fire while waiting for the infantry and then proceed 'straight ahead at full speed for the Germans' second line',[15] using machine-gun fire to deal with German reinforcements coming up and 6-pounders, or the crushing technique, to deal with second-line machine guns. Swinton then went on to discuss whether or not tank attacks should be step-by-step affairs, with each step preceded by artillery preparation or whether a violent effort should be made 'to burst right through the enemy's defensive zone in one great rush'.[16] This, he held, depended on the Commander-in-Chief and the particular strategic situation but he made out a strong case for attempts at one-day breakthrough. He emphasized that tanks cannot win battles by themselves. 'They are purely auxiliary to the infantry, and are intended to sweep away the obstructions which have hitherto stopped the advance of our infantry beyond the German's first line and cannot with certainty be disposed of by shell-fire.' [17] Since the greatest danger to the tank was the field gun, artillery during the attack should be used principally to silence these and not to damage machine guns, earthworks and wire behind the enemy's first line, since the tanks themselves can cope with these. Before the attack there should be normal artillery preparation, to avoid arousing suspicion, but special efforts should be made to knock out enemy light guns in the defensive zone. Aeroplanes should also be used in an anti-artillery role. Some tanks should be used after the assault to clear away obstacles in order to facilitate the passage of reinforcements or a mass cavalry burst-through.

It has been necessary to quote Swinton's views at length both in order to fit the new tank staff officer into his context and because Fuller's later thinking in the First World War was, consciously or unconsciously, very much a development of Swinton's. Where Fuller later departed most from Swinton was over the question of artillery preparation, which Fuller considered should be discontinued, both in order to achieve the very surprise Swinton sought by retaining it, and to prevent the ground being made impassable to tanks through shell-fire. However, even in *Tanks in the Great War*, published in 1920, Fuller still agreed with Swinton that tanks were auxiliary to infantry, [18] although he was soon to change his views.

French developments were independent until Estienne, who had had a somewhat similar idea to Swinton's—but a little later—visited England in June 1916. As a result he suggested that France should concentrate on light models, and this was done, the earlier heavier models being dropped. Estienne pleaded unsuccessfully for delaying use until the French were ready. French tanks, the early heavy ones, were first used on April 16th, 1917, but it can fairly be said that Britain led the field both technically and tactically in tanks in the First World War, particularly as the Americans and Germans were not really in the race at all.

Another officer who wrote about tanks before Fuller arrived at

Bermicourt was the future Lieutenant-General Sir Gifford Le Q. Martel, who was serving as a captain there before Fuller's arrival. He was known at the time to his friends as 'The Slosher', 'a famous boxer' who 'cultivated adventures as a milder person might cultivate roses'.[19] He had been sent home in mid-1916 to help Swinton prepare a tank training area,[20] and in November 1916 wrote a paper called 'A Tank Army', 'so as to clear my mind as to the eventual possibilities with tanks'. This paper, Martel admitted, 'was worded as a prophecy of what would happen and is written with the confidence with which one writes in one's early years'.[21] In it Martel argued that since no contemporary army could fight against an army containing 2,000 tanks, all large continental armies would have to have tank armies in future; these would replace unprotected soldiers except in woods and mountains, and most wars would start with duels between tank armies. Tanks would operate from tank bases defended by impassable trenches, mines and stakes or concrete pillars, fixed armaments and a garrison. In operations tank armies would aim at the destruction of the enemy's tanks. There would be three main types of tank, apart from specialist and supply tanks. First, there would be destroyer tanks which would replace the infantry and cavalry, destroy the enemy's small tanks, deal with his men, bases and stores, defend one's communications and bases and protect one's own battle tanks against the enemy's torpedo tanks. Destroyers would be fast (20 mph on level ground) with a large radius of action, lightly armoured ($\frac{1}{2}$-inch plate) and armed with machine guns and a 1-pounder gun. Next would come light, medium and heavy battle tanks using direct fire, except in the case of the heavy, to destroy enemy tanks and cover one's own destroyers. The light tanks would have $1\frac{1}{2}$-inch plate, 3-inch and 1-pounders and a speed of 4 to 5 mph. The heavies would have 12-inch howitzers, very thin armour and travel at 2 mph. Finally there would be torpedo tanks to destroy the enemy's battle tanks; these would fire 100 lb. torpedoes, carry a machine gun, travel at 30 mph and have only $\frac{1}{2}$-inch armour. They would advance at night or behind smoke, and fire their torpedoes from a range of about 500 yards. Martel foresaw such tank armies, each with its integral specialist branches, manoeuvring for position with the destroyers of each side making contact and fighting each other with light tank support. Next the mediums would engage. When one side gained an advantage the torpedo tanks would be launched through the broken destroyer screen at the enemy's battle tanks. When the enemy retired to his base the heavies would arrive to reduce him. In a final paragraph Martel suggested that all tanks should be amphibious.[22]

Martel stated later in *Our Armoured Forces* that all this was only 'a moderate prophecy' but he also pointed out that 'A Tank Army' was 'the first paper ever written predicting mechanized armies making full use of tanks', and also that the paper foreshadowed many of the armoured weapon and equipment system developments of the future.[23] This later point is certainly true but the most remarkable feature of the paper is the way in which it anticipated a lot of the so-called 'all-armoured' thinking of Fuller and others in the twenties, and anticipated also implicitly Fuller's use of the naval warfare analogy in attempting to think through warfare between mechanized armies. It could also, of course, be argued that Martel's torpedo tanks bear some relationship to mounted anti-tank guided weapons while his heavies are very like self-propelled artillery. Martel himself, and the Royal Armoured Corps, turned their faces against 'all-armoured' thinking in the Second World War and went for co-operation between the arms. In spite of this, the 'all-tank' trend of the twenties has been attributed to Martel's paper.[24]

It must therefore be remembered that Fuller took up his new appointment and began to think about tanks, not only in the light of his own previous military experience and thought, but also in the footsteps of Swinton and Martel, as well as in the footsteps of all those, both military and civilian, who had been concerned with the invention, development, production and use of tanks up to December 26th, 1916. In spite of pleas from both French and British quarters that tanks should be first used in a mass assault they were in fact initially used in driblets to support the British offensive on the Somme in September 1916. In the first action, on the 16th, forty-nine tanks were used but only thirty-two reached the start-line; nine of these broke down, five ditched, ten were hit and seven more were slightly damaged. The tanks were used in twos and threes to attack strong points and aimed to arrive five minutes before the infantry along free lanes left in the artillery barrage.[25] This action was not a great success. Ten days later tanks were used again, this time only thirteen, of which nine got stuck in shell holes. One tank, however, took 1,500 feet of trench; eight German officers and 362 men were captured, as well as many killed, at the cost of five British casualties.[26] Here was an indication of the possibilities. In mid-November eight tanks were used in another action but this time without spectacular results. There was obviously great need for a tank tactician to draw some immediate lessons from these actions and apply them. The machine was basically sound, although it required some mechanical improvements, but it had not been given a fair trial. As Fuller wrote later, it had been used in the wrong conditions, its commanders had little idea of tank tactics and its crews had not been properly trained.[27] Moreover it had been used in driblets to support infantry and major surprise had been lost once and for all.

The Heavy Branch Headquarters at Bermicourt, which lies between Etaples and Arras, and not far from Agincourt, was housed in a small château, two storeys high, one room deep and cold in winter. Here Fuller met Colonel Hugh Elles, whom he had known slightly at Camberley; although Elles was slightly younger than Fuller, he had been a year ahead of him at the Staff College. Elles was a sapper who eventually became a member of the Army Council but did not share Fuller's later visions about armoured warfare. He was a gallant and tough officer, boyish and even reckless, a leader with flair, élan, charisma—not primarily a man of ideas, but one who was able to take advice from those who were. He must have found his new, voluble and intellectual GSO 2 difficult to argue with. Indeed we know that this is so since Captain the Hon. Evan Charteris tells us in his privately printed, 'HQ Tanks 1917–18', that Elles used often to say: ' "No, Boney, you are wrong. You are wrong, Boney", an assertion which he had difficulty in supporting.'[28] Under Elles was Uzielli on the 'Q' or supply side and Fuller on the 'G' or General Staff side. Fuller's main responsibilities were training, intelligence and operations, and to assist him he had Martel and another captain, F. E. Hotblack. In theory the Heavy Branch was responsible to the War Office through GHQ but no officer had any comprehensive responsibility for it in either place. Swinton had gone back to the CID and the appointment of Brigadier-General F. G. Anley as Administrative Commander of the Heavy Branch, with an office in London, did not much help matters, although it was he who

founded the Tank Camp at Wool in Dorset, now the
Headquarters of the Royal Armoured Corps. Tanks had no real
identity within the War Office until August 1918, a fact which is
not at all surprising considering their novelty and their use as
infantry support, but which does to some extent explain why they
were so often misused and why the Bermicourt Headquarters had
to spend rather more of its energies in fighting GHQ and London
than it did in fighting the Germans.

Fuller must have greatly enjoyed life at Bermicourt. At last he
had an opportunity to use his brains professionally at a satisfying
level. It is fortunate that the same Captain Charteris who wrote
about Fuller's arguments with Elles also left a pen-picture of
Fuller at Bermicourt:

> A little man with a bald head, and a sharp face and a nose of
> Napoleonic cast, his general appearance, stature and feature
> earning him the title of Boney. He stood out at once as a
> totally unconventional soldier, prolific in ideas, fluent in
> expression, at daggers drawn with received opinion, author-
> ity and tradition. In the mess his attacks on the red-tabbed
> hierarchy were viewed in the spirit of a rat-hunt; a spirit he
> responded to with much vivacity, and no little wit. But he
> could talk amusingly and paradoxically on any subject. His
> specialities were Eastern religion, about which he could be
> bewildering, spiritualism, occultism, military history and
> the theory of war ... [he] had dabbled in philosophy of
> which he could handle elementary statements to the com-
> plete confounding and obfuscation of the mess. He was an
> inexhaustible writer, and from his office issued reams on
> reams about training, plans of campaign, organization and
> schemes for the use of tanks. ... He was neither an admini-
> strator nor probably a good commander, but just what a
> staff officer ought to be, evolving sound ideas and leaving
> their execution to others. He was well up in Napoleonic
> lore, and had all the maxims at his finger ends.[29]

This description is so accurate and telling in relation to all that
one knows about Fuller that one can fairly assume that Charteris
has given us an authentic glimpse of 'Boney' in 1917. Charteris
had been brought out to France by Elles at Fuller's instigation,

The future scourge of the Cavalry. Fritz Fuller in the nursery

Fuller as a Sandhurst cadet in 1897

A cross-country supply train in the Boer War. An early version of the road transport which Fuller regarded as an essential in mechanised war

Tank Headquarters, Bermicourt, 1917

from an exquisite maisonette in Mount Street, to keep the Heavy
Branch records and write a history, and this he was obviously
very competent to do, even to the point of hinting that his
master's philosophical education had not been as rigorous as it
might have been.

Fuller wrote himself in 1920 that before the Great War he had
been 'an 1870 soldier. My sojourn in the Tank Corps' (as the
Heavy Branch became at the end of July) 'has dissipated these
ideas. Today I am a believer in war mechanics, that is in a
mechanical army which requires few men and powerful machines.'[30] This sojourn was soon to become very exciting and re-
warding but it is nevertheless necessary to note that in his letters
home in the first half of 1917 he complained several times about
being jockeyed into a GSO 2 post with tanks on the promise of
promotion which did not materialize. As late as July he showed
no realization of his extraordinary luck in going to the Tanks.[31]
Hindsight must not so much cloud the vision as to allow us to see
in Fuller any perception, in the early months at Bermicourt, that
he had found his flood tide. That perception came as, partly
through his own efforts, tanks began to show their enormous
potential—and, frustratingly, never quite to achieve it.

In February he produced 'Training Note No. 16'. This was a
pamphlet on tank tactics, 'the first training manual of its kind'.[32]
In *Tanks in the Great War* he stated that the chief factor he bore
in mind in working out tank tactics was 'penetration with security',[33] and this, of course, echoed his earlier views on penetration.
In 'Training Note No. 16' he defined the tank as a 'mobile
fortress' intended to escort infantry in the attack, pre-eminently
an offensive weapon, to be used in mass and in circumstances of
'surprise' and therefore to be preceded by an artillery bombardment not exceeding forty-eight hours in length.[34]

On April 1st, 1917, he was finally appointed GSO 1 and
promoted Lieutenant-Colonel but this was still only a temporary
rank. In fact he remained a substantive Major until he was
promoted to the rank of Brevet Lieutenant-Colonel on January
1st, 1918, and Brevet Colonel on January 1st, 1919. He did not
become a substantive Colonel until August 31st, 1920. This is
perhaps not surprising considering that he was still only forty-
one at that time. What is surprising is the very modest rank held
by so many of the tank pioneers. Stern, for instance, was in

charge of tank supply as a Lieutenant-Colonel and wrote direct to the Prime Minister nevertheless. Stern must have got his dates or ranks wrong because he noted in his diary on April 14th, 1917, that during a visit to Bermicourt, 'Major Fuller gave a lecture on what the Tanks had done, and illustrated his remarks on a blackboard.'[35] Just prior to this, in March, Martel had shown Fuller his paper, 'A Tank Army'. According to Martel, Fuller questioned Martel's thesis because he felt that tanks would always be a form of infantry support rather than an independent arm.[36] However Fuller himself in his *Memoirs* makes no such criticism of Martel's paper.

Fuller's first tank operation, the Battle of Arras, began on April 9th, 1917. Detailed tank planning had been going on since January and Hotblack went out every day collecting intelligence. The intention was to use the new Mark IV machines, but none of these arrived in France until the battle was nearly over. A German line-straightening withdrawal in February upset the preliminary planning but eventually GHQ decided to push three Cavalry Divisions through a Third Army attack in front of Arras in order to penetrate the German second-line defences and take the main Hindenburg line to the south in the rear. The First Army were to provide support on the left and the Fifth Army on the right. The Heavy Branch managed to collect sixty reconditioned Marks I and II tanks but Fuller's advice was ignored, that they should all be used 'en masse' in the south around Bullecourt over unshelled hardgoing in order to penetrate the German left flank. The tanks were split up along the First, Third and Fifth Army fronts. Between April 2nd and 6th it snowed, thus making tank movement difficult to conceal. The 8th was fine, however, and Elles and Fuller drove to Arras to see the preparations for themselves. They discovered six bogged tanks near Achicourt and two hours before zero hour it began to rain.

Tanks played little part in the first two days of the battle. First Army swept up the Vimy Ridge but the eight tanks allotted to it were soon ditched. In front of Arras advances of 3–4,000 yards were made in which tanks took some small part but, as was inevitable, the artillery assault, which made the infantry advance possible, destroyed the ground over which the guns would have to be brought up in order to press forward the attack. As a result no decisive results were achieved and the cavalry were unable to exploit the initial success. Fuller claimed that he had foreseen this, which was why he had wanted all the tanks used in the south in a Fifth Army assault following on after the Third Army stalemate. On the 11th he drove to Arras again and explored the battlefield to the east. Here he saw a tank 'standing out of a trench with its tail end resting on the bottom of it. On looking through the sponson door, I saw the driver sitting upright in his seat, but he was beheaded. A shell had entered his driving window, decapitated him and had passed through the roof of the tank, apparently without exploding.'[37] To the east of this some tanks had helped the infantry clear the village of Monchy-le-Preux, but it was in the south, with Fifth Army in front of Bullecourt, that eleven tanks, without a preliminary artillery bombardment, had led the Australians through the wire and over the trenches of the Hindenburg Line. Unfortunately the Australians had been driven back to their original line in a counter-attack at noon that same day but the initial success demonstrated to Fuller's satisfaction that were tanks used in mass, over unshelled ground, and were they also supported by supply tanks, a great victory could be achieved.

Elles was promoted Brigadier-General on May 1st but tanks were not used again until June, in the Battle of Messines near the Channel coast. By this time numbers of Mark IVs were available and also old Mark Is and IIs converted for use as supply tanks. At Messines there was a tremendous preliminary bombardment lasting ten days, part of which Fuller went up to witness and for which purpose he was issued with a special pass, like a Cup Final ticket. The battle itself began on June 7th and was primarily an infantry affair, although seventy-two tanks were in support plus fourteen reserve and supply tanks. The Mark IV's armour proved effective against the armour-piercing rifles which the Germans were using in an anti-tank role.

After Messines, on June 10th and 11th, Fuller wrote a paper called 'Projected Bases for the Tactical Employment of Tanks in 1918'. It was this paper which led to the tactics used at the Battle of Cambrai in November 1917 because, although Swinton had expressed similar views back in February 1916, Fuller had not read them, and it was Fuller, not Swinton, who planned the use of tanks at Cambrai. In his paper Fuller argued that shallow linear fronts could be defeated by an infantry advance of a few thousand yards; guns could no longer facilitate such an advance because of deep entrenchments, but tanks could. Since 1916 the Germans had begun to deploy their defences in more depth and so the attacker had first to exhaust the German reserves. This could be done either by hitting him at a point he dare not abandon or at one where he did not expect an attack. The Germans, however, were likely to draw back their guns in order to make them safe from counter-bombardment but they would still be able to lay down heavy fire on any attacker who broke through their first-line defences. Once the attacker's guns advanced into counter-bombardment range, the Germans could quietly withdraw to a new defensive position. In the actual assault, because the German guns would be farther back, the chief danger lay from machine guns; hence the value of the tank, particularly as it could provide its own artillery barrage once the limit of the attacker's guns' range was reached. Once the enemy's defences in front of his guns had been captured, medium tanks and infantry should attack the guns, and, subsequently every medium tank available, independent of guns and infantry, should clear the area to the rear of the guns to facilitate pursuit by armoured cars, cavalry and tractor-drawn infantry. Such operations would require very large numbers of tanks and the ground chosen would have to be suitable for tanks. 'The tank must no longer be looked upon as a spare wheel to the car, in order to meet an unforeseen puncture in our operations, but as the motive force of the car itself, the infantry being no more than its armed occupants, without which the car is valueless.' The infantryman, with machine gun and bayonet, was still at this time for Fuller the decider of the battle. Envelopment and penetration were 'the two grand-tactical acts of battle' but in the 'present' war the latter was the prelude to the first since it would lead to the creation of flanks. But even the lack of flanks was not the main difficulty, which was the impossibility of secrecy because of the immensity of preparations. The tank could regain surprise for the attack and could achieve break-through if used in such a way as to draw in the enemy reserves before the surprise decisive attack was launched. 'The one thing to realize is,' Fuller concluded, 'that mechanical warfare is going to supersede muscular warfare. . . . The tank today carries forward the riflemen of the future . . . we should forthwith prepare to raise the mechanical army we shall require.'[38]

There are echoes in this paper of Fuller's earlier thinking about penetration just as there are also similarities with Swinton and Martel; it also points the way towards 'Plan 1919', which Fuller was to devise the next year, and in his *Memoirs* he stated that the writing of the paper led him to see more clearly that the decisive attack 'should be directed against the enemy's rear in order to strike at the foundations of fighting power'.[39] The paper was shown to Major-General Sir John Capper, who had taken over as Administrative Commandant of the Heavy Branch on May 1st, 1917, and who approved and developed it but failed to have the basic ideas accepted by GHQ. Capper, an Engineer who had once commanded the Balloon School, was more effective than his predecessor and eventually became Colonel Commandant of the Tank Corps. Both he and Fuller became more and more worried about the effects of preliminary bombardment on the ground which the tanks had to cross in the attack, particularly as in Flanders shelling destroyed the drainage system and waterlogged the land. In spite of the advice of the tank men the next operation, the third battle of Ypres, or Passchendaele as it was later called, was fought between July 31st and November 10th, 1917, as an artillery-prepared, infantry battle and, as Fuller had predicted, the Germans withdrew their guns so that they covered the attackers' second and third objectives without themselves being vulnerable to counter-bombardment or capture. Tanks were used but mud, water and faulty tactics prevented any substantial tank success. Before the battle Martel had opened an Advanced Heavy Branch Headquarters at Poperinghe, famous for the foundation there in 1915 of Talbot House, a canteen and church from which grew the Toc H organization dedicated to friendship, community and religious comfort. For the Headquarters, however, there was to be no immediate comfort and it was soon moved two miles north to Lovie Château where it was established on sodden ground in a collection of huts and bell tents. The Tank Corps, as it became on July 28th, committed three Tank Brigades, a total of 120 tanks plus sixty reserves, to the fighting. There was a twelve-day preliminary bombardment and the grandiose plan, aimed ultimately at capturing Bruges, totally misfired. The C-in-C, Sir Douglas Haig, could only foresee victory through attrition, and of this there was a fearsome quantity around Passchendaele that summer and autumn. Fuller himself paid a short official visit to

England from September 11th–14th and then withdrew to
Bermicourt since there was no operational planning for him to do
at Lovie Château. Here he took part in entertaining a variety of
visitors which ranged from Churchill (then Minister of
Munitions), and the Chinese C-in-C, to George Bernard Shaw and
Horatio Bottomley.

For some weeks before this Fuller had begun to campaign for
the opening up of a tank battle south of Cambrai and on August
8th he had sent a paper on 'Tank Raids' to GHQ. This called for a
short, demoralizing and destructive raid with some tanks going
straight for the German guns and others enfilading his trenches
and destroying his strong points. What Fuller wanted was a series
of such raids leading to a decisive battle in 1918. His paper called
for air support, and later the Tank Corps sappers produced the
idea of getting tanks across trenches too wide for them by
carrying, on the nose of each, a great bundle of brushwood to
form a fascine, which could be dropped into the trench and used
as a bridge. Eventually the raid materialized as the Battle of
Cambrai but GHQ tried to turn it into a decisive battle without
ensuring that there were sufficient tank reserves to exploit any
initial success. 376 fighting tanks were involved together with
ninety-eight administrative tanks. On November 3rd Tank Corps
Advanced HQ was established in a mouldering cabaret in Albert.
Tactics were worked out in detail for tank–infantry co-operation.
On the 18th Fuller closed his office and went forward to visit the
tank units on the ground. On the 19th, the day before the battle,
Elles asked Fuller to draft a Special Order but, after making an
attempt, Fuller asked Elles if he would do it as he was better at
that sort of thing. Elles then sat down and produced one of the
most famous orders of the First World War. It began:
'Tomorrow the Tank Corps will have the chance for which it has
been waiting for many months—to operate on good going in the
van of the battle.' Its last paragraph read: 'I propose leading the
attack of the centre division.'[40] In such words does great military
leadership find its expression. Fuller remonstrated with his
General but the latter had his way and spent the next day leading
the battle line in tank 'Hilda'.

There was no preliminary bombardment but at 6.20 a.m. the
air was rent with a dull and rhythmic roaring, pierced by the
shrieking of shells. This barrage jumped forward as the tanks,

looking like 'small dull-coloured huts endowed with movement',[41] relentlessly advanced. The Hindenburg line was pierced and in all a penetration of some 10,000 yards was achieved in less than twelve hours. Fuller felt that the battle should then have been closed down since the cavalry, partly due to the location of its Corps HQ six miles behind the front, failed to take the opportunity for exploitation provided for it by the tanks. The battle dragged on for days but on the 28th the Tank Corps Units were withdrawn. On the 30th the Germans counter-attacked and tanks were hastily gathered together to assist in restoring the line. Cambrai showed conclusively what tanks could do, but because it did not lead to a decisive victory neither the C-in-C nor the CIGS, Sir William Robertson, were convinced of their value and both believed that the Tank Corps should not be permitted to consume human and material resources which might have gone to the infantry.

Now began for Fuller a period of intense activity during which he mounted many attacks, not on the Germans, but on GHQ and the War Office. He made several visits to England. On the first of these visits, on December 9th, he discovered Sonia working in the Grosvenor Hut, a Services canteen opposite Victoria Station. It was this which finally decided him to fight for what he believed in instead of arguing over what he thought was wrong. If unpaid women could work for soldiers without unending conferences so could he. In this crusading mood, and set upon opening the eyes of those who held the levers of power, he saw Churchill a number of times and began to inundate the in-trays of both soldiers and politicians with notes and papers on the need for anti-tank measures and for carrier, smoke, mortar and exploitation tanks. He fought hard to achieve an increase in the establishment of the Tank Corps, or at least to prevent a decrease, and pointed out that once tank met tank the opportunity for decisive action would have disappeared. At the end of January 1918, he came reluctantly to the conclusion that the decisive attack would have to be postponed until 1919 and that the Allies would then require 12,000 tanks to carry it out. He told GHQ that military success must be given to the politicians otherwise the outcry against the military of the 'ignorant and discontented proletariat'[42] would not be stopped. He was unsuccessful at first in preventing Haig from ordering the reduction of the Tank Corps by 8,000 men and unsuccessful also in preventing Haig from relegating tanks to a defensive role, in line with his overall defensive policy for 1918. Tanks were to be strung out in a sixty-mile cordon along the front in the role of Martello Towers or 'savage rabbits'. The latter concept consisted of digging large dugouts as tank lairs where 'this beast would squat and slumber until the enemy advanced, when it would make war-like noises and pounce upon him'.[43] As Fuller pointed out, tanks are essentially offensive machines and to degrade them into pill boxes is to waste almost all their very expensive potential.

And then, quite suddenly on March 21st, it happened. The Germans, relieved after the signing on March 3rd of the Treaty of Brest–Litovsk of any substantial involvement on the Eastern Front, and not yet faced by a large number of American troops in the west, mounted a massive attack at the juncture of the British and French armies and, without tanks, in a week drove the British Fifth Army back forty miles to a little east of Amiens. British tanks were used, more or less piecemeal, from their 'savage rabbit' posture, to help stem the German advance but by the 23rd the normal command structure in Fifth Army had ceased to function. In the end the attack petered out, not because it had been defeated but because the Germans ran out of supplies. Medium A tanks, or Whippets, which would travel at 8 mph and were armed with three machine guns, were first used in this battle, the Second Battle of the Somme. As a consequence of the staggering defeat, in First World War terms, which the Germans had inflicted on the Allies, General Foch was appointed Allied Commander-in-Chief.

On April 2nd Fuller again put pen to paper and produced a report which he called 'The Basic Causes of the Present Defeat'. In his view these were the lack of a strategic policy for winning the war, the incapacity of senior officers, the loss of morale among the troops and the adoption of a system of passive defence. This paper was sent to GHQ and its gist was communicated to Churchill when Uzielli chanced to meet him that day in Doullens and brought him in to dine at the Bermicourt Château. It was on this occasion that Churchill, prophetically one feels in relation to his own more famous version somewhat later, quoted Clemenceau's words of March 25th:

We will fight before Amiens and in Amiens.
We will fight if necessary behind Amiens.
We will fight before Paris, and we will fight in the streets of Paris.
We will fight if need be upon the sea-shore.

Fuller claimed that he rather spoilt the occasion by exclaming: 'Well, our Generals will get us to the sea-shore all right; have no doubts as to that.'[44]

On April 9th the Germans launched another offensive around Armentières on the River Lys and again the British were forced back. It was in this battle that the first tank-versus-tank action took place. Fuller nearly missed the opening of this offensive, which lasted until the 26th, because he was in London on the 5th and 6th seeing General Capper and calling, without specific invitation, on Sir Henry Wilson, the new CIGS whom he later characterized as a born actor, a Harlequin of the Mephistophelean type. However, Mark V tanks had begun to arrive in France and an Inter-Allied Tank Committee had been formed of which Fuller was to be a member. On May 7th he was not surprised to be told that he was to be replaced as a member by General Capper. On the 6th the War Office ended a long battle about tank reductions by telling Haig that the target of eighteen tank battalions, agreed in January, would stand. Meanwhile Capper persuaded the Inter-Allied Committee to recommend a target of 13,000 tanks for 1919 and eventually agreement for five Tank Brigades was given. Prior to this, in February, Lieutenant-Colonel F. Searle, the Tank Corps' Chief Engineer, had produced an experimental tank which had reached a speed of 20 mph and which Fuller believed would revolutionize warfare. There were, however, two problems: the development and production of the tank and the obstructive attitudes of GHQ. The solution of the first problem was begun by holding a conference at Bermicourt on April 28th out of which the Medium D concept emerged, a 20 mph machine with a 150–200 mile radius of action. Also it was decided at the same conference to send Lieutenant-Colonel P. Johnson, of Searle's staff, to London to design the tank. He eventually became head of the first government Tank Design Department which remained in existence up to 1923. A solution to the second problem was evolved at about the same time which involved transferring tank control from GHQ to the War Office and taking

Fuller from France back to London. In fact Stern believed that this decision was made in mid-April and stated that General Harrington, the DCIGS, told him then that 'the Tank Corps was now to be brought into the Army Organization, with the tactical side under the War Office branches concerned. Colonel Fuller was to be appointed to take charge of Tanks in the Department of the General Staff.'[45] Before he returned to England, however, Fuller was to have what he, and many others, have thought his greatest idea, and one that was, at least indirectly, to have far-reaching consequences in the Second World War and, later still, in the Arab–Israeli Wars—an idea that obviously stemmed from morale, penetration and the science of war, but one which was born out of Fuller's and others' experiences in the First World War. This was 'Plan 1919', a proposal for winning the war with tanks in 1919 by using them in mass and in new tactical and strategic ways.

Fuller has stated in a number of places that he conceived the basic concept which underlay 'Plan 1919' sitting on the top of Mont St Quentin, a little hill not far from Peronne, while he was watching the retreat of British troops in March 1918.[46] This basic concept was derived from the question, 'Why were our troops retreating?' and the answer, 'Because our command was paralysed.'[47] The concept was 'strategic paralysis', to be brought about by attacking and cutting off the enemy's brains, in other words his field headquarters, from his fighting troops. 'Plan 1919' was originally called 'The Tactics of the Medium D Tank', but before becoming 'Plan 1919' became 'Strategical Paralysis as the Object of the Attack'.[48] According to Fuller himself the idea was 'a psycho-tactical one',[49] but he used 'strategical' rather than 'tactical' in conjunction with paralysis because 'the primary aim of the attack was to paralyse the enemy's command and not his fighting forces . . . that is his strategical brain and not his fighting body'.[50]

'Plan 1919' was actually written on May 24th, 1918. Douglas Orgill, as recently as 1970, described it as 'one of the most remarkable documents in the history of war' but commented that its ideas were similar to those of Foch and Wilson.[51] Wilson had, indeed, advised the War Cabinet on March 19th that a break-through on a broad front was the only way of winning the war by 1919 and that this breakthrough would only be militarily possible by employing a large number of tanks, about 8,000, in a Cambrai-type attack. Infantry assaults had failed, he believed, because artillery preparation eliminated surprise, destroyed ground and enabled the enemy to withdraw his guns and reorganize.[52] Moreover on May 28th, 1918, Wilson agreed that preparations for an offensive with large-scale tank co-operation in June 1919 were to be made and this offensive was to be based on break-through by tanks with infantry in carriers, supported subsequently by foot infantry and supply tanks.[53] Foch's pro-tank views became apparent in July.[54]

It must also be recognized that Stephen Foot claimed that, when serving as a GSO 2 in the War Office Tank Directorate under Capper, he conceived the idea of using tractors to bring up supplies for the advancing tank forces. This idea he incorporated in a memorandum called 'A Mobile Army' dated April 24th, 1919, which was shown by Capper to the DCIGS and from which Foot believed 'was evolved the whole plan of campaign for 1919'.[55] The details of Foot's paper are as follows. Victory would be achieved by deep penetration but the recent German advance stopped because the infantry became tired and supplies could not keep up with the advance, particularly when roads and railways had been destroyed. The answer, according to Foot, lay in substituting tank tractors, or cross-country motor lorries, capable of carrying, or hauling on a sledge, a 3-ton load. This would also obviate the requirement for bringing forward fodder, petrol being much less of a problem. The mobile army thus formed would be preceded in its penetration by light tanks in place of cavalry and supported by heavies. Centres of resistance could be by-passed because the mobile army would have no supply lines to protect continuously. French, American and British should all have mobile armies designed to advance sixty miles in six days, but such advances should come after an initial attack by other troops and large numbers of tanks on a front of thirty miles or more and on the Cambrai model.[56]

As will be seen there are some similarities between this paper and 'Plan 1919' but the former lacks the concept of 'strategical paralysis', suffers from a step-by-step approach and is by no means original as regards tank tractors. Martel, for instance, recommended the use of supply tanks in his November 1916 paper,[57] and they were used for refuelling tanks at the Battle of

Messines on June 7th, 1917. What he was really suggesting was exploitation by tractor-supplied foot-infantry after a major tank–infantry assault on the line and this was something very different to Fuller's armoured breakthrough to the rear prior to any attempt to reduce the front line. No doubt Foot's paper had some influence on Capper but by the time the latter put his paper, 'Armoured Striking Force for 1919' to the CIGS on July 1st, 1919, he had seen Fuller's 'Plan 1919'. Indeed Fuller claimed that Capper's paper was the 'GS' edition of 'Plan 1919'.[58]

'Plan 1919' begins with a definition of tactics as 'the art of moving armed men on the battlefield'. Tactics change as weapons and means of transport change. The tank has revolutionized the art of war because of its increased mobility, protection and offensive power. It enables men to fire on the move while under protection, and so 'superimpose naval upon land tactics'.[59] Fuller actually prefaced this statement with the words, 'whilst securing a man dynamically, it enables him to fight statically', an example of the difficult style he found himself increasingly unable to avoid in analysis of this nature, perhaps because he was so often trying to see the deeper, or occult, meaning behind the surface of things. 'Plan 1919', however, continues with the claim that the tank has also revolutionized strategy, which is based on communication. The use of cross-country vehicles makes the earth 'as easily transversible as the sea'. Thus the side which mechanizes will win, 'for the highest form of machinery must win, because it saves time and is the controlling factor in war'. Up to the present, tanks have been used to support infantry and artillery tactics but they will eventually destroy the system on to which they have been grafted. The infantry will become a subsidiary and then useless arm on ground over which tanks can move. Nevertheless strategic principles do not change and the primary one calls for the destruction of the enemy's fighting strength. This can be achieved principally by destroying the military organization either by wearing it down, through fighting his soldiers (body warfare), or by rendering it inoperative by putting his power of command out of action (brain warfare). The latter method would involve an attack on the German Army, Corps and Divisional Headquarters which would result in the collapse of the front line, particularly if the German supply system were also dislocated. The former method would require more tanks than could be produced by 1919; the latter would require fewer and its strength lay in the initial attack going in on the Headquarters rather than the front line.

After this introduction Fuller examined the problem of actually getting at the command structure, located, as it was, in an eighteen-mile belt behind the defended line. Either aeroplanes or tanks could cross this line, the former by flying over it and the latter by penetrating it. But aeroplanes would have to land and the troops in them would then merely be infantry. The difficulty of using tanks was that no suitable tank existed, but a plan for one did and it could be produced in time. This was the Medium D which, as we have seen, was to have a maximum speed of 20 mph, and a range of 150–200 miles. It would also require the capability of crossing a 13- to 14-foot gap and be sufficiently light to use on ordinary roads and bridges. The tactics of the Medium D would be based on the achievement of surprise and on the disorganization of the enemy's massed reserves before breakthrough. A front of about ninety miles would be selected and a force of four or five German armies collected as a response to visible preparations. The primary objective would be the area between the German Divisional and Army headquarters while the area between his front line and his guns would be the secondary objective. This was a reversal of previous practice and the foundation of surprise. Once preparations were complete and without tactical warning the Medium Ds would proceed at top speed by day or night to the primary objectives, these being marked by aeroplane or artillery. This would take about two hours. Meanwhile supply and road centres would be bombed but signal communications would be left alone in order to assist the spread of panic. Once all this was having its effect, a tank, infantry and artillery attack would be mounted on the secondary objective. Penetration having been effected, a pursuing force of Medium Ds, other Medium tanks and lorried infantry would be launched into the rear to deal with Army Group headquarters and remaining hostile troops. The German Western GHQ would be bombed. A ninety-mile front would be possible because the attack would be 'morcellated'; that is, sections of the front only would be penetrated in the attack on the secondary objective, the unattacked sections being enveloped subsequently.

In conclusion Fuller pointed out that the use of Medium Ds

would render foot infantry useless except in gaining the secondary objective, and that they would require mechanization if they were to keep up with the new tanks. In future their use would be restricted to assisting with tactical penetration, occupation, protection of rear services and operation over ground unsuitable for tanks. Their tactics would be defensive and the machine gun would be their chief weapon. In 'Plan 1919' Fuller wrote that cavalry would be invaluable in the pursuit if they could keep up with the Medium Ds, but he claimed in his *Memoirs* that this point 'was inserted to propitiate the horse-worshippers. Tractor-drawn light infantry would have been more effective'.[60] Field artillery would have to be tractor-drawn. The RAF would have to protect, guide, supply and assist Medium Ds while the Royal Engineers and Army Service Corps would have their tasks much increased. Moreover, Medium Ds would enable attacks to become methodical until the enemy could meet the Medium D with a similar or superior weapon. Strategy would 'practically cease for that side which pits muscular endurance against mechanical energy'. Naval tactics would be applied to land warfare. Medium Ds would save time but if insufficient were produced by 1919 the Germans might have a better machine in 1920. 'To use a new machine in driblets is to make the enemy a patentee in the design . . . as yet no weapon has been produced which time has not rendered obsolete. The number of Medium D tanks required by May 1919 is 2,000, and with this number there is every prospect of ending the war.'

In an appendix Fuller listed his detailed requirements. These were:

1. A disorganizing Force for the attack on the primary objective of 790 Medium Ds.
2. A Breaking Force of 2,592 Heavy Tanks and 390 Medium Ds for the secondary objective.
3. A Pursuing Force of 820 Medium Ds and 400 Medium Cs.

Such was 'Plan 1919'. A few days after writing it Fuller heard from Foot in London that the War Office was thinking of tanks as a way of winning the war. He therefore set off again for London, leaving Bermicourt at noon on the 28th and arriving at Victoria at 6.30 that same evening. He went straight to Foot's

office at 1, Regent Street where he was shown what must have
been the 'Mobile Army' paper. Next day he saw Capper and Stern,
and the latter undertook to send a copy of 'Plan 1919' to
Churchill. On the 31st he spent two hours with General
Harington who asked him to write a paper on the reorganization
of the Tank Corps and to come on posting to the War Office. He
left a copy of 'Plan 1919' with Harington and returned to France
the next day, where he discovered that the Germans had mounted
a third great attack, the third Battle of the Aisne, and had pushed
the French back thirty miles to Château-Thierry on the Marne,
uncomfortably close to Paris. At Bermicourt, however, Fuller and
Uzielli got down to the reorganization of the Tank Corps and, on
June 6th, sent off a scheme to Harington which proposed the
establishment of a Tank General Staff Section in the War Office,
the addition of a Tank Staff Officer to GHQ and the establishment of Tank Group Commanders to act as advisers to Army
Commanders. These proposals in fact were intended to give the
Tank Corps the same sort of organization as the Cavalry and
Artillery.

On the 25th Fuller travelled to England again to attend with
Elles an imposing War Office Conference which included
Churchill, Harington and Capper. Future tank policy was
discussed but little was decided except that the setting up of
Fuller's future War Office section was confirmed. Before Fuller
returned to France on July 3rd, however, Capper had submitted
his version of 'Plan 1919' to Harington, 'Armoured Striking
Force for 1919'. This paper called for 12,516 tanks.

Fuller arrived back in France in time to be on hand during the
remarkable Battle of Hamel on July 4th. He had been concerned
with planning this battle, a relatively small affair, with General
Rawlinson, the Fourth Army Commander, and had persuaded
Rawlinson to allow the new Mark Vs to play a decisive part,
although he had failed to gain agreement that tanks should
precede infantry. Hamel was a small village a few miles east of
Amiens. The objective of the attack was to advance 2,500 yards
on a front of 6,000 expanding to 7,500 yards using ten battalions
of infantry, sixty fighting tanks and four supply tanks. This
represented an enormously increased frontage for each infantry
battalion compared with the battles of 1917. There was no
preliminary bombardment. The tanks started 1,200 yards behind

the infantry but soon caught up and in most cases overtook them, thus reversing the Army Commander's instructions. The battle was fought in less than two hours, between 3.10 and 5.00 a.m. and was a complete success. No Tank Corps personnel were killed and fifty-eight of the sixty fighting tanks reached their objective. The supply tanks brought up 50,000 lb. of infantry supplies a few minutes after 5.00 a.m. in the way Foot had suggested in his paper. It was this battle, more than any other, which justified the tactics developed by the Tank Corps and its GSO 1. As he wrote home after Hamel, 'it is impossible for men clothed in wool to beat men clothed in steel',[61]—or at least so it seemed at the time.

On the 5th, the Secretary of State for War, Lord Milner, visited Bermicourt. Fuller had met him once before, in Government House in Cape Town in 1900. He now set about preparing for him 'Notes on Tank Economics', much of which has a very modern ring about it. He compared the effectiveness of cavalry and tank formations, the cost of ammunition expended in various battles and the relative expense, in production man-hours, of the shells fired at Arras and tanks lost at Cambrai; he emphasized the saving in weight when petrol is substituted for forage and the way in which tanks saved men and hence time, because it took a much shorter time to produce a tank than a man.

On the 14th he visited England again and saw General Lynden-Bell, now the Director of Staff Duties (DSD), in order to make arrangements about the staffing of his new War Office branch. DSD was then responsible for all general staff work, including training, except operations and intelligence, with particular emphasis on establishments, manpower and organization. There was therefore a slight intake of breath when he discovered that Fuller proposed that all but one of his staff officers should be non-regulars, but he got his way. The next day he saw General Harington and advocated that Foch should be converted to the 'Plan 1919' concept. Harington wrote to Foch on July 20th advocating an attack on the enemy's brain and stomach concurrently or in advance of an attack on his body, and enclosing a copy of a paper entitled 'Memorandum on the Requirements for an Armoured Striking Force for an Offensive in 1919'. This Memorandum was based on Capper's paper of July 1st, which was derived from 'Plan 1919'. The object of the striking force was given as: 'To strike at the brain of the enemy by attacking his Headquarters and communications and so paralyse his action.' The method proposed was an attack on a 160-kilometre front with penetration over 80 kilometres by means of a large number of fast tanks either crossing trenches themselves or in the wake of bridge-laying heavy tanks. This force was likened to armoured independent cavalry and was to be supported subsequently by cavalry. Its function was to attack German Divisional Corps and Army Headquarters and destroy communications. At the same time the German GHQ and Army and Corps Headquarters would be bombed. Coincidental with this attack (although the paper does refer to the possibility of it taking place subsequently) the main infantry attack, supported by heavy and light tanks and aeroplanes, would go in. Behind this clearing and pursuing forces were to follow through. The whole force was to be designed for rapid advance, independent of roads and railways, and this would necessitate the provision of large numbers of cross-country mechanical vehicles for supply and the movement of guns. 10,500 tanks would be needed by the Allies and over 7,000 cross-country tractors for the British element alone.[62]

There is a great deal of Fuller's thinking in this Memorandum but there are also echoes of Foot's emphasis on cross-country mechanical supply. Fuller admitted in his *Memoirs* that the Memorandum did not entirely follow his proposals in that he had 'wanted the attack on the primary objective to take place before the attack on the secondary was launched'. Indeed it must be emphasized that this was the whole point of the attack on the German HQs. Secondly Fuller pointed out that he had not wanted the destruction of communications.

On July 21st the same sort of proposals and a copy of the Memorandum were sent to Haig, while, on the 25th, the CIGS produced a paper for the War Cabinet on 'British Military Policy 1918–19'. In this he admitted that the principal factor in victory was the development of American military power and the growing shortage of French and English manpower. War-weariness would oblige England to strike in 1919 or stop the war. 'It must be realized,' the paper continues, 'that all enthusiasm for the war is dead.' The culminating attack had to come by mid-1919. 'As our resources in man-power diminish it is surely prudent to economize what remains by endowing them to the fullest extent with the most effective man-killing equipment—such as machine guns, tanks and aeroplanes.' One cavalry division should be disbanded, the CIGS went on, and the manpower utilized for machine guns or tanks. Marshal Foch had been asked to approve an Allied tank attack in a fifty-mile front supported by 10,500 tanks of which some 3,000 would be British with 7,300 tractors in support.

Foch agreed the main principles of the Memorandum on August 6th. 'Tanks are indispensable for clearing the way and supporting the rapid advance of the infantry. They must be used in as large numbers as possible.' Haig and others saw the danger that increases in the Tank Corps would lead to further reductions in the cavalry. Be that as it may, it can be stated with confidence that had the war lasted another year there would certainly have been a massive allied tank offensive.[63] Meanwhile Fuller returned to France on July 17th to find himself involved on the 21st in a conference at Fourth Army HQ about an attack which General Rawlinson proposed to make in front of Amiens. The Army Commander wanted to use as many tanks as possible and had requested six battalions for the attack and two Whippet (Medium A) battalions for exploitation. Fuller suggested that the whole of the available Tank Corps should be employed, the attack made more decisive, and the Whippets used to carry out a right-hook exploitation behind the Germans facing the French south of Amiens in order to open up a twenty-mile gap in the enemy lines. Rawlinson did not accept this latter proposal and the proposed attack remained a limited operation. Nevertheless the number of Tank battalions committed was raised to twelve, two Whippet, eight Mark V and two Mark V One Star and, together with supply tanks, the total number of tanks involved was 580. The attack was to be led by tanks without preliminary artillery bombardment.

Elles had gone to England on the 19th and when he returned on the 28th he was surprised to find preparations for a major battle in full swing. Fuller briefed him and then left for London again on the 31st to open his new War Office branch, Staff Duties 7 (SD7) under Lynden-Bell. This he did at 10 a.m. on August 1st at the top of the National Liberal Club, which had been converted into a War Office Annexe. What happened there to the newly created DDSD (Tanks) must come later, since Fuller's French experiences would not be complete without reference to the fact

that on August 6th, now temporary Colonel, he returned to
Bermicourt, and thence to Tank Corps Advanced Headquarters
at L'Etoile, near Fourth Army Headquarters at Flixecourt, in
order to supervise the activities of his successor, Colonel H.
Karslake. Whether this officer enjoyed the experience is not
recorded. However, Fuller discovered at once that GHQ had
extended the scope of the battle, making it virtually unlimited as
regards exploitation. The Whippets were to be tied to the cavalry
and 324 fighting tanks were to be launched on a front of 22,500
yards. This was very condensed compared with Hamel, and Fuller
believed that many more tanks and infantry could have been kept
in reserve. An armoured-car battalion was also to be used.

The battle began on the 8th and Fuller was up early that day at
L'Etoile to wait for the messages. Most of these were dropped by
aeroplane. It soon became apparent that the initial attack was an
overwhelming success and there was a swift and general advance
of 14,000 yards. The Whippets, however, were impeded by the
cavalry, who could not keep up in the face of enemy fire, but the
armoured cars actually overran two German Corps Headquarters
while one particular Whippet, which got detached from the
cavalry, wrought great havoc behind the lines. Day One was a
great success, but, because there were insufficient reserves, only
two miles were gained on Day Two. On the 10th it was only
possible to put sixty-seven tanks into action and Elles decided to
try to persuade Fourth Army to close the battle down which was
done on August 17th. Fuller wrote a report on the battle on the
10th, spent a final night in Bermicourt and returned to London
the next day. In spite of the fact that Amiens was not immediately decisive, it was a major victory and was followed by a
series of Allied successes in which tanks played a prominent part
and which led to the Armistice of November 11th. Fuller
claimed: 'The battle of Amiens was the strategical end of the war,
a second Waterloo; the rest was minor tactics.'[64] Certainly a
general advance in one day of eight miles, in the face of strong
opposition, on a front of seventeen miles, was a remarkable
achievement although it must of course be set against advances
which the Germans, virtually without tanks, had made earlier in
the year.

This is an appropriate point at which to leave Fuller to settle
into the War Office and consider briefly his contribution to the

allied cause, and to military theory and practice in the second half
of the First World War. There was no trace of his earlier, or later,
pro-German attitudes; his concerns were entirely professional
and patriotic, and his views about Churchill, for instance, were
strikingly different from those which he publicized later, both
during and after the Second World War, although his deep-seated
distrust of democracy was sometimes apparent.

There is no doubt whatever that Fuller's was the driving
intellectual force behind the development of the tactics and
organization of the Heavy Branch and the Tank Corps in France
in 1917 and 1918, often in the face of strong military opposition;
there is also no doubt that his influence soon spread back across
the Channel into the fastnesses of Whitehall at a very high level
indeed—particularly so for a mere temporary lieutenant-colonel
at a time when the bearers of that rank were legion. Stephen
Foot's tribute to Fuller gives us a close-range view:

> At the Staff College before the war, Fuller was nicknamed
> 'Boney'; the events of 1914 to 1918 justified the title. To
> General Swinton and Mr Winston Churchill must be at-
> tributed the credit for the fact that the new weapon, the
> Tank, ever came into existence; to General Elles and his
> power of picking men was due the inspiration that made the
> Tank Corps such a splendid fighting force; to Colonel Uzielli
> we owe recognition of great organizing ability that enabled
> the Tank Corps to function effectively; but the brains
> behind it all were Fuller's. A flash of inspiration combined
> with faith may be responsible for initiating an invention,
> skilled hands may forge it into a weapon, gallant-hearted
> men may be ready to use it, careful arrangements may bring
> the man and weapon to the scene of action—all this is
> useless without the brains that direct the weapon's use and
> that was Fuller's contribution.
>
> For their success Tanks require tactics no less than petrol;
> Fuller devised them. Before an attack can be launched there
> must be a plan; Fuller made it. After an attack, lessons must be
> learnt both from success and failure; Fuller absorbed them.
> And, sad to relate, in the case of the Tanks a constant war had
> to be waged against the apathy, incredulity and shortsighted-
> ness of GHQ; Fuller fought that war, and won.[65]

Charteris, another first-hand witness, as has already been stated, also called Fuller the Tank Corps' brain. Stern, however, coupled Fuller with Elles, when writing in 1919 about the responsibility for 'the tactics, efficiency and magnificent *esprit de corps* of the Tank Corps'.[66] Modern war is a corporate business and it is only at the highest levels of command that soldiers can change the course of history, and even then their success, or failure, also depends upon political, technological, economic, even geographical and meteorological factors, as well as upon their strategic sweep, tactical grasp or charismatic qualities. Fuller was not alone in developing the tactics of the tanks, in operational planning, in military or political influence, in organizing the new Corps. Many of his initiatives were stimulated by events and by discussion with others. Nevertheless he, of all the Tank Corps officers in the First World War, provided the cerebration and the intellectual energy.

Next one must ask how original were Fuller's developing ideas about armoured warfare, especially those embodied in 'Plan 1919'. Originality is a difficult concept to apply across the board of human thought and endeavour. Even the most seemingly startling of ideas often have their roots in the work of others. Fuller himself wrote: 'Ideas are frequently stillborn, but they are seldom or ever spontaneously generated. Either they are the mental effect of some outward cause or the children of reflection.'[67] Sir Basil Liddell Hart believed that Fuller was an original thinker but he also stated that he and Fuller were both working along the same line when they first met after the war.[68] This is the point. In the strategic and tactical stalemate of the First World War, there were numbers of men in whom events, brains and motivation generated thought about armoured warfare. No one man can justly claim, on his own, to have invented the tank or to have developed the most suitable tactics for its use, or strategy into which to fit those tactics.

'Plan 1919' was not wholly original in the sense that some works of art are, or appear to be. Compared with the thinking of officers like Haig, 'Plan 1919' was original. Compared with the thinking of Swinton, Martel and Foot, or Foch and even Pétain, it was only partially original. Foch had believed as early as October 1917 that a mechanical attack was essential, and he and Pétain had agreed by April 1918 that tanks were the functional equivalent of infantry and were required in large numbers. Swinton, as we have seen, was at the very centre of the generation of the tank concept, and believed in and advocated penetration, surprise, large-scale pre-dawn use in advance of the infantry, enfilading fire, gas, counter-bombardment, the 'morcellated attack', burst-through, air support and the anti-tank danger from field guns; Martel saw tank armies replacing infantry, tank bases, tank army fighting tank army in a very naval style, and different types of tank, including the sort of fast destroyers which Sir William Tritton had first recommended on October 3rd, 1916.[69] Lord Cavan was concerned about loss of surprise and saw infantry riding on tanks; Foot wanted cross-country supply and gun-towing vehicles. Some of these ideas went even further than Fuller did in 'Plan 1919', particularly Martel's tank army concept, and many of them, sometimes adapted, formed part of Fuller's 'Plan 1919' thinking. D'Eyncourt had suggested the formation of three tank armies immediately after Cambrai, and the General Staff, in commenting, had put forward the view that the 'advent of the tank has in reality given us a new arm'.[70]

Nevertheless there are parts of 'Plan 1919' which do appear to be original. Fuller's insistence on a total absence of tactical artillery preparation is one, but this is obviously designed to preserve the ground for tanks rather than maintain strategic surprise, since 'Plan 1919' is based on gathering in the German reserves by visible Allied preparation; tactical surprise, however, could obviously be aimed at. Even Swinton wanted normal artillery preparation. Fuller's use of fast tanks, very like Martel's destroyers, for an attack on the enemy command structure prior to a major assault on his front line was extremely original, at least as a modern objective, although the monarch and his standard bearer had in the past often been the centre of gravity of the battle. Martel himself wrote later that it was indeed Fuller who had the idea of using fast tanks by themselves against the enemy's HQ and communications.[71] Many military thinkers from Clausewitz onwards had emphasized the importance of attacking the enemy with immense strength at the decisive point and this had normally been regarded as his military concentration. Fuller, seeing the very great difficulty of defeating the enemy concentration because of the mass army and advances in military technology, was in 1918 advocating an attack on the brain, not the body, so that the body would then collapse or succumb more easily to a traditional assault. There are relations between this method of attack and Douhet's air power strategic bombing theories, since both regard the opposing linear conventional armies as being of little account. In a letter written in 1949 Liddell Hart stated that whereas Fuller propounded deep tactical penetration, he, Liddell Hart, propounded deep strategical penetration by the expanding torrent method.[72] This criticism of Fuller will not, I think, stand up. 'Plan 1919' was certainly strategic in the sense that it was directly aimed at the use of military force to achieve a political goal, that is, the end of the war: German surrender. Attack on the brain was certainly original in the context of the First World War and, linked with the armoured fighting vehicle, led to some of the most original strands in the strategic thinking and actual warfare of the next fifty years.

It is also necessary, finally, to consider how valid Fuller's proposals were as a solution to the military problems of the First World War. 'Plan 1919' was never used and so there can never be any proof. The chief difficulty of the generals on both sides in France was that infantry—artillery attacks, after initial success if put in with enough strength, always petered out in the end because there were never enough reserves left over for exploitation, and because supplies could not easily be brought up over ground destroyed by intensive shell-fire. Another problem was the enormous number of casualties which resulted from an infantry attack, although this problem was not allowed to inhibit strategy except perhaps in the winter of 1917–18. The strategy of armoured penetration to destroy command and control so that the enemy's first-line defences could be reduced more easily later was obviously politically and militarily appropriate for 1919, although it could be argued, both that the injection of American manpower had eased the pressure on human resources, and that it was very unlikely, as Martel had pointed out, that the Medium D could have been developed and produced in sufficient quantities to implement Fuller's plan by the middle of 1919.

Perhaps, given strong military and political backing, it is just possible that something approaching Fuller's plan could have been implemented by the autumn. As has been seen his clear, rational and unconventional concepts were usually watered down, distorted, or cut down to size by the Staff, and this would no doubt have happened again. This must be a serious factor in making an evaluation of 'Plan 1919'. New weapon systems, or revolutionary tactics or strategies, would often be overwhelmingly effective if they were employed massively or with complete rationality or at least complete surprise. Instead, tanks were asked to co-operate with cavalry. Tanks did not achieve victory in 1916, 1917 or 1918, although after Amiens they led to it; the Germans achieved some staggering successes in 1918 virtually without tanks. Indeed, even the *Official History of the Great War* in a volume published as late as 1947, but completed early in the Second World War, plays down the role of tanks from August 1918 onwards and attributes their reputation to the need of the Germans to find a scapegoat for their defeat.[73] Liddell Hart challenged this interpretation[74] and it does seem on balance that tanks had a very considerable tactical influence on the battles of the autumn of 1918, as well as the moral effects the *Official History* admits. Only through the use of masses of tanks was a purely military conclusion to the stalemate in north-east France possible, and Fuller's proposed way of using masses of tanks was brilliant in conception. In the event the war was not brought to an end in November 1918 by purely military means. Nevertheless 'Plan 1919' was a most remarkable document and would probably have led, given the preservation of its basic elements, a sufficiency of Medium Ds, and the absence of any developed and effective anti-tank counter on the German side, to a swift and resounding military victory had the war continued. Had Fuller thus emerged as the architect of such a victory his subsequent career might have been very different.

4. *The Reformer of War—* 1918–22

When he moved into the War Office, Fuller was thirty-nine years old and a Brevet Lieutenant-Colonel, a relatively junior officer and not one to come out of the war, like Elles for instance, with an exalted temporary rank. Part of the problem was that he had not had the good fortune to command. Ironside, for instance, although two years his junior, commanded a brigade and became a temporary major-general in 1918. However Fuller's reputation and influence were a great deal higher than his rank and it was certainly easier in those days than it is in our hierarchical meritocracy for men of ability and energy to reach the ear and presence of the mighty. One of the penalties society pays for social democracy is a more rigid stratification by rank or level of job than obtained when it was social origins which divided us up.

At this time his diminutive stature, prematurely balding head, and deep-set, piercing eyes must have marked him out from his brother staff officers, as did, for those who knew him more intimately, the fact that his wife had a German accent and was regarded by many as an extremely abrasive and difficult person.

Fuller's mother and father still lived at Sydenham, where Fuller and Sonia used to visit them, although Sonia was undoubtedly something of a trial to the family. Thelma tolerated her daughter-in-law reluctantly, but Fuller was very loyal to his wife and never went farther in public than squeezing her hand in order to try to restrain her. Sonia quarrelled with Walter, Fuller's brother, who was a lawyer but had served in the Infantry during the war until he was gassed and disabled. One of the quarrels was related to Sonia's complaints that the ageing clergyman would not increase his eldest son's allowance. In the end the brothers had to stop visiting Sydenham together.[1] Perhaps at least part of the trouble was that Fuller's marriage was childless.

His return from France to London was, for Fuller, the end of a great adventure—the greatest adventure of his life, experienced against a background of increasingly cataclysmic events and out of which his most original and valuable thinking grew. He seemed well able, throughout his life, to divorce his private affairs from his public life. Had he stayed in France it is probable that he would have become a temporary brigadier. That he chose to accept the invitation to come home is an indication of his stern sense of duty for he believed, while the war lasted, that his influence in London would be more valuable to the cause of the tank than his continued presence in Bermicourt. He knew when he made the move that he was giving up a post so interesting that 'were I to live a hundred years I should never hold another equal to it'.[2] Later, when the war ended, he seriously considered resignation because he began to feel out of sympathy with the Government's conduct of the peace negotiations, unhappy about the influence of the United States on these and convinced that the Army would rapidly slip back into its 1914 mould. He had become a radical in both his political and military thinking; not in any sense, at least as yet, a man of right or left, but a hard, rational thinker who followed his reasoning right along to the end of the road. Infantry, the League of nations, the outlawing of war, vacillation in Ireland—all these matters, and many others, he swept imperiously aside in his writing and conversation. Just after the Armistice he went to see Elles in France to discuss the future. Out of this visit, and Fuller's own experiences by then in the War Office, there emerged the requirement that kept him in the Army. This was the necessity for the Tank Corps to have a defender at court and a propagandist outside it. It was, in turn, out of these activities that more grandiose schemes and concepts began to flourish in Fuller's mind, schemes for reforming and mechanizing the Army, and also concepts for the reform of war, for the establishment of a science of war, and for a consequently necessary reform of the nation itself, and of man. It was eventually the frustration he underwent as reformer which soured his military career and drove him politically off the rails.

Fuller's first tour in the War Office, from August 1918 until July 1922, can be divided into two parts. The first is the period up to November 1918 when he was most concerned with attempting to make something like 'Plan 1919' a possibility, and the second is the period from the Armistice until his next posting, during which he was most involved with the defence of the Tank Corps and with military reform. These were the years in which he tried to achieve his aim from within the bureaucracy but during which he also began to sound a shriller and shriller trumpet to audiences, both military and civilian, outside the War Office. It must also be remembered that it was a period in which the structure of the nineteenth-century world was changing and dissolving with a rapidity which was too great for the perception of many people in high places. In Britain Lloyd George remained Prime Minister but his days were numbered and there was soon to be a short-lived Labour Administration. In Versailles new nation states were created out of old empires; Germany was squeezed as hard as the French could engineer while the major powers renounced war as an instrument of policy except in common defence against an aggressor. Disarmament was a fashionable policy, particularly as it satisfied both the world's need to do something about its revulsion from the bloodshed of trench warfare and the necessity many states soon encountered for financial retrenchment. America turned its back on Europe. Ireland festered, nationalism began to ferment in India, while in Russia the Bolsheviks won the Civil War, a victory which British military aid and intervention was powerless to stop. In the years 1918–22 almost all the seeds of change, whose luxuriant growth we see today, were germinating vigorously, if sometimes unseen. Nevertheless Britain was still apparently almost as powerful as ever; her military forces were stationed or campaigned across very large areas of the globe, from Shanghai to the West Indies, while in the two years after the war she even had a strong naval presence in the Black Sea and gave naval and military aid to the counter-revolutionary forces in the area. In Batum, in Georgia, today firmly a part of the Soviet Union, there was for some time a British garrison commanded by a brigadier-general who administered the place by martial law and had a British magistrate and chief of police to assist him.[3] It is against this background that one must consider Fuller's work and aspirations, and not against the shrunken horizons visible from Whitehall today; one must also remember how very new an invention the petrol engine was and how very deeply ingrained in the popular and military minds was the concept that foot soldiers won wars with rifles and bayonets, that mobility and dash were provided by men on horses and that apart from these the only other land fighting arm of any significance was the artillery. Change which may sometimes be acceptable in the heat of necessity generally becomes repugnant when that necessity is apparently removed, particularly when the existing order has been institutionalized into a social structure.

At first, as head of SD7, where he was responsible for the organization and establishments of the Tank Corps, Fuller was mostly involved in overcoming obstructions which were placed in the way of the provision of adequate manpower and accommodation for the corps in preparation for the 1919 campaign. Over these problems he saw the CIGS and the Secretary of State, over the head of his immediate superior, DSD (Lynden-Bell), and obtained what he wanted. The War Office system under which matters had to progress slowly up the hierarchical ladder, or become subject to horizontal consultation, was far too slow and cumbersome for Fuller, as was the system of financial control. The passing of minutes from branch to branch he regarded principally as a means of avoiding the making of decisions; committees were similar devices, while the Army Council itself, being a committee, was an entirely inappropriate tool of command and control. For the energetic and able officer it is always possible to bypass obstruction; but if he utterly omits to reduce it, it may well be his undoing in the end.

For a time, however, all went well. He became a member of the new Tank Board which had the responsibility for production under the Ministry of Munitions. Doubts began to arise about the time-scale of production for the Medium D so Fuller forced a decision through the Tank Board to press on, for the time being, with production of the Medium C instead. It was only half as fast as the D but it was tested and reliable. Similarly the Mark VIII was proving to be too heavy and Fuller therefore persuaded the board to increase the production of Mark Vs instead. He visited Bermicourt again in September but on his return to London discovered that GHQ were proposing to split the Tank Corps up into Groups and spread it amongst the Armies in France with a virtually powerless Director-General spanning the gap between GHQ and the War Office. Fuller wanted a Corps Commander, rather than a Director-General, so that the Tank Corps would be capable of independent operations. He organized DSD into going yet again to France and on October 3rd there was a conference at GHQ. Fuller got nowhere on this occasion, although Haig was not present, because the latter's view, that if tanks were not infantry or cavalry they must be an auxiliary arm, inhibited any concessions. Elles became Director-General and could only command the GHQ tank reserve. GHQ stated that they did not want any tank expansion and would not facilitate it; eighteen tank battalions was enough. Fuller was convinced that these attitudes were the product of intrigue and influence by the 'shadowy cavalry cabinet'[4] around Haig. He paid yet another visit to France a week later to attend a meeting of the Inter-Allied Tank Committee in Versailles.

On October 17th the King became Colonel-in-Chief of the Tank Corps, which was a helpful development for its future, and on the 25th he visited the Training Centre at Wool. Fuller and Lynden-Bell met him there and afterwards travelled back to London in the royal train and lunched with him. Prior to this, on the 21st, it had been agreed at a War Office conference that the Tank Corps should receive 30,000 additional men. On the 28th, in Fuller's absence, Foot, now his assistant in SD7, went to see a very senior officer to arrange for the necessary drafts to be sent to Wool for training. He was told that the Prime Minister had decided at a Paris Conference the previous week that there would be no expansion of the Tank Corps. Foot did not believe that this was the truth and became very angry. He immediately sent a note of the conversation to DCIGS and the drafts did go to Wool the next day.[5] This was not the end of the matter and there was more obstruction from GHQ in early November. It was essentially now a contest for the survival and supremacy of the cavalry in the order of battle; in battle itself their vulnerability and restricted role had been amply demonstrated for years. In the end the cavalry was saved as an institution by the bell which sounded a few days later on November 11th.

For the next three and a half years Fuller soldiered on in a War Office which became increasingly distasteful to him, at first in SD7 and then, on the abolition of that branch, as head of SD4 where he was responsible for all forms of training throughout the army. As the chief spokesman of the Tank Corps within the War Office he was faced with a threefold problem—the need to establish the Corps on a peace footing and provide it with officers and men, the need to iron out a policy on the design and procurement of tanks, and the need to procure and find acceptance for a tank organization and tank tactics which would fit the army system.

He tackled these problems in two ways, by working within the bureaucracy and by propaganda and persuasion outside it, the inner and outer spheres of action [6] as he called them. In the inner sphere success ultimately crowned his almost missionary efforts to establish the Tank Corps but not until thirteen months after he left the War Office. Prior to this, wordy battles ranged about whether the Tank Corps should have officers of its own or whether they should be seconded to it or be drawn exclusively from the RE. There was also conflict about the desirability of having two Corps, one independent and the other for infantry support. Fuller himself proposed that surplus cavalry regiments might be converted into tank battalions. In the end the Tank Corps was permanently established as a separate arm of five battalions on September 1st, 1923, and was granted the 'Royal' prefix on October 18th that year. Undoubtedly Fuller was one of the most prominent architects of this new structure and Lynden-Bell gave him due credit for this and also praised his energy and brain power. [7] It must also be noted, however, that Capper became the first Colonel-Commandant and that Elles, until given an infantry brigade in October 1923, ran the Bovington Centre and in May 1923 was appointed Inspector of the Tank Corps. [8] On the other two sides of the inner problem Fuller was not successful. To deny that there ought to be a few tanks in the peacetime army could be demonstrated to be a perverse and irrational view; to obstruct tank procurement and to argue that armoured machines were still a subordinate element in warfare could be made to appear much more respectable. Immediately the war ended work on all tanks except the Medium Cs and Ds was stopped and some months later Fuller gave up the C in order to preserve the D. He also encouraged Johnson in his design of a Light Infantry Tank. The first D trial took place on May 29th, 1919, and an average speed of 23 mph was achieved. In March 1922 the Light Infantry Tank achieved a speed of 30 mph. Much development work, however, was obviously necessary and the Master-General of Ordnance's Department, concerned about the unreliability of these machines, and also about making the best use of scarce financial resources, was not happy with Johnson's tank design department. Fuller discovered in December 1921 that a new medium tank had been built by Vickers on the orders of the MGO's department without his knowledge or agreement. Eventually Johnson's department was closed down, work on his tanks was discontinued and the Vickers medium tank was issued to the Army. This was a reliable but unrevolutionary machine which was not replaced for sixteen years.[9] The scrapping of the Medium D was a tragedy but an almost inevitable one. On Fuller's instructions Johnson had given it an amphibious capability and had designed a steel cable suspension system. Here, however unreliable, was the prototype machine of blitzkrieg and mechanized warfare. As regards the third aspect of the problem, Fuller's failure to convince the military that a new tactical doctrine was necessary was virtually complete. He wanted first to motorize the supply services, and second, to reorganize the Infantry Division by including a company of tanks in each infantry battalion and two squadrons of tanks in each cavalry brigade. He also suggested officially the formation of an experimental force and this was done. A New Model Brigade was set up in Aldershot in 1921. It carried out exercises in that year and the next, when it died away having achieved almost nothing except a demonstration of the fact that military experiments, like many others, can be made to prove almost anything depending upon the aims and prejudices of the chief experimenter, in this case General R. H. K. Butler, the Commander of 2 Division and Haig's former DCGS. Fuller did his best; for instance, in the *Army Quarterly* of January 1922, he wrote that to be a member of an experimental brigade was 'an honour which in peace time cannot be equalled'.[10] As he was soon to find out it is very difficult for a serving officer, except in times of grave national or military crisis, to bring about swift and radical changes of view within the military establishment, particularly when these changes would strike at the very fabric of the military organization.

It was at least partly because of his lack of success in the inner sphere that Fuller began to operate so extensively in the outer. Also he obviously enjoyed writing and lecturing. His aim was to supplement and bolster up his efforts at reform from within, by advertisement and by the stimulation of controversy outside. 'If we want progress we must seek opposition', he wrote in 1920,[11] and in 1923, 'it is by exaggeration that man's mind is aroused'.[12]

He certainly aroused opposition by his writings and he developed a black-and-white style which missed no tricks. Boney was an adept at stirring things up.

His first venture was the initiation of a newspaper which was called *Weekly Tank Notes*.[13] Foot was told off to edit this and the first copy was circulated to thirty War Office branches on August 10th, 1918. The circulation quickly increased and in the end both the King and the Prime Minister received copies, and the *Notes* were published regularly until February 1920. While the war and its immediate aftermath lasted they formed an excellent platform for Fuller's propaganda, although no doubt they earned him the reputation of being a troublesome and earnest fellow. The early numbers deal, inter alia, with German anti-tank rifles and mines, with the 'Whippet', Medium A tank or new 'mechanical cavalry', with aeroplane co-operation, infantry–tank co-operation and with the German view, published in the *Neue Freie Presse* on September 15th, that 'the best means of fighting Tanks are undoubtedly Tanks', an opinion which is only today being seriously challenged. The very last wartime number contained an article, almost certainly written by Fuller himself, which upheld the view that in the end the ideal army would become 'one invulnerable man, a kind of Achilles with an armoured heel', that 'man himself is an encumbrance on the battlefield'. This was Fuller at his most controversial, exaggerated and prophetic best. After the war the *Notes* continued from time to time to contain articles of this nature on such subjects as the influence of petrol and gas on war, the applicability of naval tactics to land tank warfare, the requirement for cross-country tractors, the tank as a 'mechanical policeman' and the theory behind 'Plan 1919'. Memorable sentences abound of which perhaps the two most striking are: 'tools or weapons, if only the right ones can be discovered, form ninety-nine per cent of victory', and 'strategy . . . will practically cease for that side which pits muscular endurance against mechanical energy'.

On February 11th, 1920, Fuller gave a lecture to the RUSI on 'The Development of Sea Warfare on Land and Its Influence on Future Naval Operations'.[14] Capper was in the chair and he generously introduced Fuller as the man 'very largely responsible for getting out the tactics of the tanks'.[15] The audience was then treated to one of the most enlivening and far-seeing perform-

The Brain Barn: Fuller's offices at Bermicourt, 1917

Fuller, Elles and Uzielli (*from the left in the front row*) and others at Bermicourt. (See page 49 et seq.)

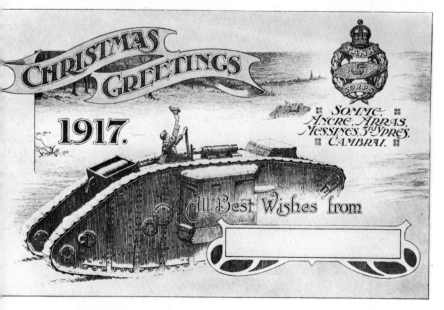

The Cambrai Christmas card. The tank seen in a very un-Fuller-like context

Sonia in the First World War

ances which can ever have been delivered in that institute. Fuller began by defining his subject as land sea-warfare and with the statement that 'science has gripped the fighting services and is shaking them closer and closer together'.[16] He went on to show that naval conditions were superior to land because at sea muscle had been replaced by machinery and skin by armour. Naval tactics were dynamic and could be superimposed on land warfare through the use of tanks, or landships, particularly if these were made amphibious for river-crossing and for launching from naval vessels, or from submarines at sea. Fuller then got out his crystal ball:

Let us now become clairvoyant as regards the future. The professional seer looks inside your hat before she tells you your fortune. A very sensible act. She consults the past, gauges your value by the name of the shop you bought your hat at, and then spins you the story on at least one sound foundation—your probable income.

I have shown you the inside of the Tank hat, and I hope you will agree with me from what you have seen that it was good enough value for money spent to permit me spinning you a story.

I see a fleet operating against a fleet not at sea but on land: cruisers and battleships and destroyers. My astral form follows one side and I notice that it is in difficulty; it cannot see; there appears an aeroplane and gives it sight. It says by wireless telegraphy the enemy are yonder. The approach march begins. I see a man in one of the aeroplanes whose head is swollen with the future; he is the Commander-in-Chief of the land fleet I am following. Suddenly I see the fleet is moving a few points north-east; the Commander-in-Chief has spoken to it by wireless telephony. I sniff the air; it seems impure. Is it gas? The Tanks submerge; that is to say, batten down their hatches. The battle begins.

Out go the mine-sweepers; we are in the enemy's land. A series of detonations show that the act was not executed a moment too soon.

The enemy's fleet concentrate their fire on the gaps made. The Commander-in-Chief is again talking. A small squadron moves to the north, tacks east, and huge clouds of smoke pour across the sky. New gaps are made and the fleet moves through.

Then I see the old scene re-enacted—the contest between armour, gun-fire and mobility.

The enemy is disorganized, demoralized; his flag aero-plane has been brought down; his brains are paralysed; it is now the pursuit.

A great river winds across the picture. I put spurs to my astral shell; the enemy must either drown or be pulverized. I rub my etheric eyes; his machines are rushing down the banks, and, plunging into the water, they churn it to foam as they swim through it. Ours follow suit; it is now a race for mobility.

A little later in the lecture he continued:

We see a stretch of weary sand—it is the Baltic coast. We see curious ships racing through the Skaggerrak. They are now standing out a mile or more from the coast, for the water is shallow. There is a rumbling sound, then from their prows squat objects splash into the water—they are moving rapidly towards the shore line; from the water they crawl on to the sands; they are Tanks, and Warnemünde, 150 miles from Berlin, is ours. We materialize and find some commotion going on amongst the enemy's armies on the Western Front.

From the surface Tank carrier the next step is the sub-marine Tank carrier—a kind of sea serpent which spews monsters on to the beach. What would Olaus Magnus think of this, he who wrote of sea serpents fashioned of skin and blood?

Think now what such possibilities mean to us islanders. No longer will our sailors belong to the Great Silent Fleet but to a fleet which belches war on every strand, which vomits forth armies as never did the horse of Troy, and which will swallow them up again if the land appears unpropitious and carry them safely home beneath the ocean.

Think of the naval bases seized and the landing places protected. Think of the Channel which separates us from Europe. It has been called a 'ditch'—it may become a veri-table tube railway for hostile armies.

Munchausen! Munchausen! Perhaps; but do not let us disparage our inventive genius like a certain Italian alchemist did his own at the beginning of the sixteenth century. He promised to fly from the walls of Stirling Castle to France. He attempted to do so and, falling, broke a leg. He attributed his failure to the fact that he used for his wings feathers of fowls which, he said, had an affinity for the dung-hill!

It was not his feathers which had an affinity for this unpleasant heap, but his brains. He had been thinking backward of Icarus; he should have been thinking forward in terms of the Wright Brothers.

A lesson. Do not let us now, in 1920, only look backwards to 1914. Let us think forwards to 1930, or we shall become pillars of salt in an arid and unproductive wilderness. Let us look ahead; the world is getting small, but science is vastly huge. Every rational thought is a true thought which may lead to realizable effect. There is nothing too wonderful for science—we of the fighting services must grasp the wand of this magician and compel the future to obey us.[17]

In the ensuing discussion the only hint of opposition came from Dr Miller Maguire who sounded a note of warning about anti-tank developments. 'What one man can do,' he said, 'another man can do. The brain of humanity is always changing and working as against other human beings whether on the land, in the air, or under the sea.'[18] Swinton commented that it was strange that a machine invented as a cure for machine guns and wire should now be held up as the means by which the whole nature of war would be changed. But he supported Fuller and pointed out that the tank would be useful against gas and ray warfare, but not against germs. 'With regard to the lecture generally, I consider that it has been the best exposition, the clearest vision, of what warfare is likely to become that I have heard.'[19] Tennyson d'Eyncourt also spoke about the tremendous economy of the tank for any army. That February afternoon was in many ways the peak of Fuller's influence and acceptability. But the opposition, if muted and perhaps not well represented in the audience, was soon to gather strength and break like an angry wave upon the Whitehall beach.

First, however, came *Tanks in the Great War*, Fuller's first full-length book. This was based on information collected officially by SD7 from the tank battalions as part of the Elles–Fuller campaign to preserve the Tank Corps. The book was easy to read and not quite as advanced in its views as the RUSI lecture. It was well received in the press and even merited editorial comment in the *Daily Mail*. 'Young men who dream dreams and realize them in action,' the editor wrote, 'are a precious asset to any nation. Therefore we hope that War Office will pay proper attention to the striking theories on the future of mechanical war which Colonel Fuller ... enunciates in his book.'[20] The *Observer* called it 'an example of clear thinking, free of cant, and a reasoned exhortation to progress'.[21] The only warning note sounded in the national papers was that Fuller's view that war would be eliminated by weapons ignored the influence of the dictates of morality.[22] The *Daily Herald* quoted an MP's view that 'the policy of attempting to secure peace by preparing for war was madness'.[23] However, the *RUSI Journal* contained a different warning. Its review was quite favourable but accused Fuller of being an enthusiast and of exaggerating the hope that tanks would reduce the numbers of combatant soldiers required in an army.[24] In the book tanks are portrayed as the answer to the 1914–16 stalemate and as an auxiliary to infantry in the 1920 context. Fuller gave an account of the use of tanks in the war, including their first use in Sinai in 1917. He claimed that 300 more medium tanks in 1918 would have led to a decisive victory and an unconditional surrender. In the future he saw infantry becoming the armed occupants of tanks and he saw armies and weapons themselves as the principal means of preventing or eliminating war. 'To limit the evolution of weapons is therefore to limit the period of peace.'[25] He ended the book with one of his near-prophetic utterances, this time about deterrence: 'If the civilian population of a country know that should they demand war they may be killed in a few minutes by tens of thousands, they will not only cease to demand it but see beforehand that they are well prepared by superiority of weapons to terrify their neighbour out of declaring war against them.'[26]

The occasion of the breaking of the wave, however, was the publication of Fuller's winning RUSI Gold Medal Military Prize Essay for 1919. The subject was 'The Application of Recent

Developments in Mechanics and Other Scientific Knowledge to Preparation and Training for Future War on Land'. Fuller's entry was anonymous but he was lucky that Swinton was one of the judges.[27] He won first prize, £30, the medal, and his identity was revealed. Congratulations followed from a member of the Army Council and then the essay was published in the May 1920 issue of the *RUSI Journal*.[28] Immediately the climate changed, for the essay was found to be what Fuller himself called 'violent military Bolshevism'. General Lynden-Bell rushed round to his room and exlaimed: 'Boney! Boney! What *have* you done?'[29] What Fuller had done was to crystallize, in thirty-five pages, his reflection on his experience of the war in the light of all his previous military thinking.

He began with the proposition that it was necessary to think about war, which was both a science and an art, scientifically. Armies were combinations of men, movement, weapons and protection, and petrol had changed movement. As regards men, soldiers had souls, educated men were easier to train and so the Army should become a People's University! The tank had superimposed naval tactics on land warfare and the enemy's brain paralysis could be achieved through the use of high-speed tanks. 'The idea,' he wrote, 'underlying these tactics was but an extension of a system of tactical penetration written prior to the Great War and propounded by a writer [i.e. Fuller] in the *Journal* of the RUSI of November 1914.'[30] Tanks could be made gas-proof. Tools were very important and we should therefore invest money in military mechanical progress. In the future battles it was machine fighting-power we should need, not mere superiority in numbers of men. Indeed one man would form an ideal army if he could release millions of gas cylinders. Wars would no longer be declared because the 'first shot may well prove the last shot'.[31] Gas inundations would protect mobilizing armies and by 1960 there might only be one arm using a fighting machine which could operate on land, sea or air. Mobility and not size was important for the New Model Army which might be most concerned with the prevention of war. A 'thinking' General Staff was a necessity with a single Ministry of Defence and C-in-C instead of an Army Council. Above all, Fuller believed that the requirement was for a mechanical army, scientifically trained, in which tanks would eventually replace infantry, artillery and cavalry. Aeroplanes would co-operate with tanks and all supply vehicles would be mechanized. The evolution of this sort of army would take ten years. At first there should be special corps for the new arms, with gradual reductions in the old, and experimental units and formations. Supply should be mechanized first, then the fighting services and finally everything. In the end three main types of fighting vehicles were likely to emerge—fast destroyers or mechanical infantry, fast battle cruisers or mechanical cavalry and heavy-gunned battleships or mechanical artillery. In the Empire there would be mechanical police. At home there would have to be national registration for speedy mobilization and standardization of factories for easy conversion to war production. Above all, economic and manpower resources would have to be used with the greatest attention to economy, or what later became called cost-effectiveness.

This was indeed violent military Bolshevism in terms of the climate of thought prevailing in 1920, but almost all of it was rational and developed from Fuller's earlier views and his work with tanks, and in retrospect his recommendations seem restrained and evolutionary. Liddell Hart believed that he was not trying to provoke, but rather to allay, conservative fears.

This he signally failed to do. Articles appeared in the *RUSI Journal* pouring scorn on Fuller's prophecies and particularly on his suggestion that the cavalry would be displaced by tanks. In Paris, however, they were impressed, and the essay was issued to all French battalion commanders.[32] Fuller was made 'Officier d'Académie', a distinction which he was denied permission either to accept or refuse! In the end, two years later, the French Assistant Military Attaché, when tidying up on posting, found the decoration in his safe and rushed round to Fuller's office and presented him with it.[33] From mid-1920 onwards he was publicly identified as a military radical and the chief enemy of the cavalry establishment and all forms of military conservatism. Before this reaction set in strongly he was invited to Belgium and lectured to the officers of the Brussels Garrison on tanks. He delivered the lecture in French and was given an interview by the Belgian King.[34]

In 1920 Fuller also contributed three lengthy articles on 'The Influence of Tanks on Cavalry Tactics' to the *Cavalry Journal*.[35] This was subversive work and treated as such. The first article began with the statement that the whole study was aimed at arriving 'at some common basis of understanding on the subject of tank and cavalry co-operation and the part that these two arms may play should they be called upon to fight side by side within the next few years'.[36] The cavalry 'idea', Fuller continued, is not necessarily part of an obsolete doctrine and the study of cavalry and tank achievements in the recent war was necessary in order to see 'how far mechanically moved weapons can re-establish the cavalry "idea" which carries with it the decision of the battle'.[37] After this stealthy and devastating introduction which forced the cavalryman to defend his horse rather than his function in battle, Fuller went on to analyse tactics into the three powers of hitting, guarding and moving (the modern triad of fire-power, protection and mobility), battle into the three parts of assembly, approach and attack, and attack, into the three acts of demoralization, decision and annihilation. An obsession with threes appears to have taken root in Fuller's mind at this time. Tactical organization, however, was based on two essentials, mobility and stability, and these were the essence of the cavalry 'idea'. In the first cycle of cavalry tactics the cavalryman fought with the *arme blanche* but eventually unarmoured horsemen turned into armoured knights; in the second cycle armour became too heavy and ineffective and cavalry were used for shock until even that role was taken from them through the invention of the breech-loaded rifle. Cavalry then became tactically useless, except as mounted infantry, although still of strategic importance, for instance in reconnaissance or finding a flank. The machine gun, magazine rifle and field gun then rendered infantry and cavalry immobile, and in France from 1915 onwards there were no flanks to find. A new means of implementing the cavalry 'idea', of annihilating the enemy, had to be found. The tank idea was not new but in 1916–1917 it made possible the reinstitution of the charge against infantry. The knight in armour had reappeared. Light and heavy tanks were really light and heavy cavalry, but the tank was superior to the horse except in certain respects such as speed, radius of action, endurance, flotation, forest fighting and visibility; and in time these deficiencies, except forest fighting, could be overcome. Until they were, tank–cavalry co-operation was necessary; once they were, the tank could replace the horse.

Fuller then dealt with the difficulties of co-operation. In what he called internal defence and small wars it was possible. In great wars cavalry would still exist if one broke out before 1925 and the war would probably pass through an initial mobile phase in which cavalry could be used, a secondary static phase in which horses would be chiefly useful for machine gun transportation, and a tertiary mechanized phase in which cavalry would either mechanize, or become battle-field police until replaced by cross-country motor-bicycles. In any phase the mixing of horses and tanks in action was of doubtful effectiveness because the mobility of tanks was thereby reduced. The cavalryman provided improved vision, but the aeroplane could do even better.

The third article concludes with the view that scientific progress is inevitable and that the cavalry, as men on horseback, is doomed. This was the third cycle in cavalry tactics. The equipment, not the idea, was obsolete. Firepower and gas would also lead to the disappearance of the infantry soldier. The future mechanical army would probably contain super-heavy, mechanical cavalry replacing artillery, and heavy and light mechanical cavalry replacing the present infantry and cavalry. In the battle of the future the new light cavalry would manoeuvre for flanks and rear, helped by the independent cavalry (aeroplanes); pursuit would once again be possible and the act of annihilation would be accomplished. 'There is something magnificent and awe-inspiring in this picture,' Fuller wrote, with for once a very narrow vision, 'of the triumph of the brain of man above all material difficulties.'[38] In order to achieve this state of affairs free thought was essential to combat inertia and 'our strivings must be backed by an invincible courage for truth. Many men are capable of winning the VC on the battle-field but there are few who can write a truthful minute to a conservative officer'.[39] Fuller then appealed to the cavalry leaders to choose the right direction themselves.

One doubts if he was very much surprised that numbers of such leaders dipped their pens angrily and wrote at once to the *Journal* after reading the first article. Lieutenant-Colonel Howard-Vyse rose to the defence of the *arme blanche* as obsolete but more effective than dismounting behind the first fire-swept ridge. However, he sold the pass by admitting that if the absence of flanks and large reserves was to be a normal feature of future war then it was not the *arme blanche* but cavalry as a whole which should be abolished.[40] Major-General W. D. Bird was more effective and made a plea for gradual rather than sudden change which Fuller echoed in the last article. Bird agreed that one day the warhorse might disappear, but wondered if the moment had arrived. He also thought that in peace there was the danger of setting up an arms race and that it was 'not improbable that in military affairs the ascendancy of Conservative stupidity is, on the whole, less mischievous than that of Radical folly'.[41] Brigadier-General G. A. Weir was furious with Fuller for not giving enough weight to the Palestine campaign and argued that, when circumstances were right, cavalry could still charge infantry.[42] An anonymous Indian cavalry officer wrote after the second article and advanced the view that tanks might eventually become susceptible to a new sort of bullet and that the horse was not as vulnerable as people thought.[43] The arguments Fuller's opponents put up against him, although sometimes containing some validity, were on the whole rationalizations of the fear, which many regular officers felt, that their way of life was threatened. A smelly, cumbersome, groaning assortment of armoured vehicles was no proper substitute for a troop of chargers, and there was a world of difference between the social context of the stable and the garage.

Fuller's next venture was to enter for the 1920 RUSI Naval Prize Essay competition with an entry on 'Changes in Naval Construction and Tactics'. He won first prize but when the RUSI discovered that the winning author was both a soldier, and an officer called Fuller, the Gold Medal was not awarded and publication in the *RUSI Journal* was refused. Eventually the essay was published in *The Naval Review*.[44] It was not as revolutionary as some of Fuller's work at the time, and in some respects his vision of the future was distorted. He confined himself to the next decade and advocated the retention of battleships and destroyers. All other vessels would, he believed, submerge. Aircraft would not threaten battleships but were required at sea for information-gathering purposes. Submarines would be required to land amphibious mechanized forces.

Besides all this he wrote other articles which were part of his propaganda campaign in the outer sphere of action and these were published in such journals as the *Army Quarterly*, *RE Journal* and *Nineteenth Century and After*. The most significant event, however, in his life at this time was the beginning of his association and friendship with the then Captain Basil Liddell Hart—and this was as significant for Liddell Hart as it was for

Fuller. They first met in June 1920[45] and their friendship continued, with one notable break in the late thirties and early forties, until Fuller's death nearly forty-six years later. As has been noted earlier, Liddell Hart claimed later in his life that he and Fuller were both working along the same lines when they met[46] and this was undeniably true in the sense that both were developing ideas for the reform of war in the aftermath of the bloodshed and stalemate of the First World War. Both were Light Infantry officers but Fuller, the Regular, was much older and more experienced than Liddell Hart, the war-time volunteer (who had been gassed in France). In 1920 Liddell Hart was temporarily attached to the Army Education Scheme, but was actually working for General Sir Ivor Maxse, GOC Northern Command, on a redraft of the *Infantry Training* manual, while serving as a Brigade Education Officer in Lichfield. It would be very difficult to judge who in the end contributed more to this friendship; certainly Fuller had the sharper and more agile brain while Liddell Hart had more humanity, tact and political judgment. They made an excellent partnership to which they brought complementary attributes. In the early days Fuller naturally made the major contribution and Liddell Hart accepted this. In early June 1920 he sent Fuller his draft of the sections in Volume II of *Infantry Training* on infantry–tank co-operation and Fuller agreed with them. In the same letter he enclosed a draft of an article he had written on his 'Expanding Torrent System of Attack'. Fuller believed that Liddell Hart's idea would work well but thought he had made too much of the 'Fog of War', 'by converting it into a pitch darkness'.[47] Later, in 1928, Liddell Hart accepted that Fuller was the mechanized pioneer and that his own conversion was not complete until 1921.[48] After the Second World War the issue re-emerged in correspondence between them, and Fuller's recollection then of their first meeting was that Liddell Hart had said: 'I have come from General Maxse to put forward an infantry tactics which will defeat the tank.'[49] Liddell Hart questioned Fuller's memory and believed that what he had said in 1920 was: 'I feel quite certain that the tank will very soon become the sole arm of importance.' It was in 1922, he claimed, that he wrote the remark about infantry because he was then making as good a case as he could for an article on infantry in the *Encyclopaedia Britannica*.[50] Perhaps it is only in the 1970s that we are seeing an infantry tactics and technology capable of defeating the tank. The validity of tactical and strategic thinking relates closely to the political and technological context of such thought. Fuller and Liddell Hart were both original military thinkers, separated by a gap of seventeen years in their ages and experience. In 1920 Fuller was the more original and it was he who in a sense educated Liddell Hart and helped his individual genius to flower. Neither, it must be remembered, had the benefit of a full university education; although Liddell Hart had read History at Cambridge for a time before the war.

In the twenties the two corresponded voluminously and met frequently. Fuller's letters and copies of Liddell Hart's replies are preserved in the Liddell Hart Archives in States House, Medmenham. While Fuller remained at the War Office the correspondence centred on the tank itself, and it is interesting to note the way in which the pair of them batted back and forth the ball of argument to their mutual benefit in a sort of epistolary Socratic dialogue. Liddell Hart, for instance, claimed that in spite of the fact that tanks were the weapon of the immediate future 'man as an individual fighter may be resurrected' because the infantryman is 'the smallest target and the most universally mobile of all weapon carriers'.[51] Fuller replied that gas was likely to knock the bottom out of the small target theory, that the antidote to an armour-piercing ray is more likely to be carried by a tank than a man.[52] Three weeks later he added that if a means of penetrating armour were devised, armour would become obsolete but the tank's mobility would remain.[53] In 1922 their friendship became so close that Fuller became godfather to Liddell Hart's son, Adrian, who was born on August 24th that year.[54] And at the end of the year Fuller asked Liddell Hart why the latter had joined the Army Education Corps, 'for it is a blind-end'.[55] So it would have been for Liddell Hart had he stayed in it at that time.

Towards the end of his tour in SD4 Fuller began to write *The Reformation of War*. The majority of this was written in April 1922 between nine and ten-thirty in the evenings and on occasional Saturday afternoons and Sundays.[56] He described the book to Liddell Hart, perhaps a little disingenuously, as 'simply a pot boiler or rather a means of advertisement'.[57] It was a lot more than that. After being notified that his next appointment was to be as a Chief Instructor at the Staff College, and this was at the special request of General Sir Edmund Ironside, the Commandant, he left the War Office on July 31st, 1922. Ironside, as has already been noted, was two years younger than Fuller and had become a major-general in 1918. He was a gunner officer and had had some notable adventures in South-West Africa after the Boer War, where he posed as a Boer driver in order to obtain information about German activities. It was this escapade which suggested the character of Richard Hannay to John Buchan. Later he went to the Staff College as a student and was in the Senior Division when Fuller attended in 1914. Fuller's new post was not vacant until January 1923 and so he had to go on half-pay until then. In consequence he decided to take Sonia away for a long Continental holiday. He wanted to escape from his tribulations and exertions in the War Office and wanted also to finish *Reformation*; Sonia was always delighted to be taken to more congenial environments. He first and on his own visited a French division on manoeuvres at Valdahon, which he found extremely dull, and then travelled to Basle by train, changing, much to his disgust, at Besançon and Belfort. He was met at Basle by Starr who was staying near there in some form of religious institution at Dornach. Sonia joined him at the end of the month and they stayed at the Park Hotel before going on to Austria, where the book was finished 'in about a dozen hotels each with a jazz band'.[58] They left Austria on November 21st and began the journey home via Munich, Leipzig, Hamburg and Cologne. The War Office had made a fuss about an earlier draft of the book but had ultimately, 'said I could publish it but recommended me not to do so'. Undeterred he sent the new draft off to Hutchinson's before leaving Salzburg.[59]

Reformation is prefaced with a section in which Fuller opened the windows of his soul so that we can see the shadows of both his past and future aberrations. The irrational rationality which characterized his worst writing and thinking is discernible in such statements as that, 'to anathematize war is to gibber like a fool, and to declare it to be unreasonable, is to twaddle like a pedant',[60] or 'without war there would be no driving out of the money-lenders from the temple of human existence',[61] or again, 'the true purpose of war is to create and not to destroy'.[62] 'I may be a heretic a military Luther,'[63] he wrote—and this is how he was beginning to see himself; his introspection would have been the clearer, however, had he compared himself with Calvin rather than the less radical Luther.

The book itself covers much of the ground, but more comprehensively, which he had already covered in his essays, lectures and articles. What is new is the introduction of more politics, psychology and philosophy. War is described as 'the god of creative destruction, that grim synthetic iconoclast'.[64] Armies are barbaric if they are separated in intellect from the nation to which they belong and will in these circumstances be better at causing wars than fighting them. War has economic causes but is concerned with race survival. 'Great nations are born in war, because war is the focal point of national concentration; great nations decay in peace'.[65] States should not assist their weaker citizens but help the strongest to develop. Wars are inevitable but war is a science aimed at the imposition of your will on the enemy through the destruction of his physical or moral strength. In studying war one must therefore begin by studying man and his ability to move, to use weapons and to protect himself. The laws of this science are the principles of war, still in Fuller's view the eight he used in his 1915 article in the *RUSI Journal*— objective, offensive, security, concentration, economy of force, movement, surprise and co-operation. His commentary on them now, however, included definition of the nation's political object in war as being the imposition of 'its will with the least possible ethical and economic loss not only to itself, but to its enemies and to the world at large'[66]—the less the loss the greater the victory. The defensive is not the strongest form of war as Clausewitz believed but a prelude to the offensive. Superiority of numbers is not an overriding consideration and the principle of co-operation makes it necessary for one master mind to control the whole national machinery.

After this beginning Fuller went on to deal with the psychological side of war—particularly the psychologically decisive point which was the enemy's command system—and with the ethics of war. In this latter area his views about war enhancing national character sound an unattractive note today. On the subject of peacetime armies he wrote with feeling that they had little to do with preparedness for war but were principally concerned with maintaining their tradition. Neutrals he described as 'weedlings' and non-lethal gas, he believed, could humanize war.

Aeroplanes would enable greater use to be made of gas. 'Tactically the soldier is simply a weapon mounting of about one-eighth hp energy'[67] who moves in one dimension; air warfare was three-dimensional, and in future wars there would be a struggle for capture of the air. In land warfare the plane would eventually be replaced by something new. Soldiers would be protected against gas, planes would have to fly lower and use bullets, and so soldiers and planes would have to be armoured. The force of gravity would in the end give victory to the tank, not the plane.

As regards naval warfare Fuller went farther than he had done in his 1920 essay and advanced the view that the 'age of the present naval Brontosaur is nearing its end'.[68] A submarine invasion force could avoid a surface fleet and by means of a pre-emptive gas strike, without benefit of a declaration of war, directly attack and overwhelm the enemy's will. In imperial defence he advocated that in wars against uncivilized nations the form of warfare should depend upon the culture existing in the land. Mechanization was vital in such wars, but air attack had limitations because of the limited development of the enemy's nervous system.

Reformation also contains pleas for Service unification and tri-Service strategy, for cost-effectiveness in defence management, for an imperial Generalissimo, for another experimental brigade, and for the 'mechanicalizing' of transport, artillery and infantry within twenty years. And finally, for good measure, Fuller attacked parliamentary government, socialism, the Armistice, Wilson's Fourteen Points, the League of Nations and, somewhat illogically in this context, the concept that soldiers should have political influence. 'To create or change a policy is neither the right nor the duty of the soldier, for the sword is the instrument of policy and not its fashioner.'[69]

While the printers were producing this book, Fuller, still travelling, was sketching out and writing a series of fifty lectures on 'The Sciences of War' and 'The Analysis of War' which he proposed to deliver to his students at the staff college.[70] At the end of the year Sonia and he arrived home and he took up his appointment at Camberley in January 1923.

5. The Science of War— 1923-5

'When sunset gilds the Surrey pines', John Betjeman wrote in 1932, 'The fam'ly usually dines.'[1] The family, that is, of Colonel Kittiwake, obviously a retired officer, who lived in a cosy little bungalow, named Coolgreena, on the outskirts of Camberley. For most British army officers, serving or retired, the area on either side of the A30 south-west of Bagshot has a welcoming and comfortable familiarity. There the Royal Military Academy, Sandhurst and the Staff College share the same grounds, while all around, some in what Betjeman called 'roads "not adopted" ' and 'woodlanded ways'.[2] but others increasingly in quite ordinary thoroughfares, are still to be found many military generations, from potential cadet, home from prep school, to parchment-faced, octogenarian major or major-general.

Fuller, however, although he had lived there twice before, as a student at Sandhurst, and at the Staff College, was able to look at Camberley without much sentiment. His sojourn as an instructor at the Staff College was merely an episode in the wandering life which began for him when he left SD4 and which was to continue until his retirement at the end of 1933, 'a period of such little importance, that so far as I myself am concerned, I should have done far better to have lapsed into civil life'.[3] These words, of course, were written in 1935 at the time of Fuller's greatest disillusionment with the Army. In January 1923, although not filled with feelings of homecoming, and certainly with Sonia's heart back on the Continent, he must have cherished considerable hopes that he would be able to continue as a teacher and a writer what he had only partially succeeded in doing as an administrator; that is, to reform war and to reshape the armed forces.

At the age of forty-four he could look back with pride on his activities in the War Office, since he had certainly been one of

those principally responsible for the saving of the Tank Corps
and for its permanent establishment on a peacetime footing. This
was a notable achievement and one made in the teeth of
entrenched and often irrational opposition. But that was virtually
all of outstanding importance that Fuller, the military bureaucrat,
had achieved; his views and proposals on tank development,
organization and tactics had been obstructed and ignored; his
propaganda had amused or irritated but seldom had it had a real
influence on military decision-making. The reasons for his failure
to bring about reform from within were many. The First World
War had been so bloody an affair, for most soldiers at least, that
the whole climate of educated opinion turned for a while either to
constraining war back to something reasonably sporting and
acceptable, or to outlawing it altogether. A serious and scientific
study of war was only acceptable in those countries whose
policies actively threatened peace.[4] The concept of using armed
forces in a preventive or deterrent role was imperfectly understood,[5] if perceived at all, while financial retrenchment and economic disorder made it virtually impossible to gain agreement to
any new expenditure. Expenditure, moreover, on tanks
threatened the continued existence of the cavalry and, perhaps,
even of the infantry, and it was Fuller himself who drew attention to this and so provided a rallying cry for military and social
vested interest. As John Wheldon has written, 'lacking patronage,
would-be reformers had to preach directly to the multitude, and
so become not reformers but rebels'.[6] This was true of Fuller
whose partial failure in the inner sphere led to increasing
stridency in the outer. Here he was flying in the face of the fact
that in British political life, military policy, especially technological policy, is almost always made within the establishment,
which appears to be largely impervious to popular or political
clamour except through the influence of political parties in
Parliament or Government. Military reform is always a political
matter and Fuller's activities became increasingly quasi-political
from the moment he left the War Office. In this sense it would
have been more appropriate, and perhaps more effective, had he
been a civilian. Certainly the techniques of exaggeration and
extremism which he used would have generated less fury had he
not been a serving officer. That his intemperate language was
tolerated speaks much for the latitude of the Army Council and

the independent status of the army officer in the twenties. But it is doubtful if Fuller's abrasive style did much to help his cause. It achieved the object of advertising his message but not of selling it. In 1918 this message had been a clear and simple one: victory through strategic paralysis achieved by breakthrough with massive numbers of medium and heavy tanks on a narrow front, followed by the destruction of both formation headquarters and front line defences; by 1923 the message had become more complex, more comprehensive, more political and less apparently appropriate to the international situation. But just as 'Plan 1919' was a true development of Fuller's earlier thought and experiences, so his message in the early twenties was rationally derived from his 1918 position.

Penetration through mechanization was the essence of 'Plan 1919' and mechanization, or mechanicalization as Fuller often called it at this time, was the starting point of the 1923 message. But the message, as Fuller's writings already quoted have shown, now also embraced the views that war was a science as well as an art, and ought to be studied scientifically, and that technology was more important than man on the battlefield and therefore the future lay with small, professional armies. It also included the perception that when mechanized armies fought each other there would develop a sort of naval war on land, that when the tank's armour became penetrable this would lead, not to the obsolescence of the tank, but to a greater emphasis upon mobility and firepower at the expense of protection, and that radical military reform both of organization and training was essential. The aim of military forces should be to achieve victory at the least cost both to oneself and one's enemies, or even to prevent, or deter, war altogether. By 1923, however, a shriller note had also begun to appear, a note of discordance brought about by frustration and disillusion, and this was Fuller's view that since war was in the last resort related to racial survival, and since existing systems of government did not seem to be willing or effective instruments of military reform, then it might be necessary to substitute more authoritarian systems in order to achieve it. The end of present-day democracy was in sight, he believed. The whole of this message, no doubt regarded by many as Boney's Gospel, and the ways in which it was delivered, were almost entirely consistent with the characteristics he had displayed as a young officer and with the tenor and direction of his early writings. There was, of course, no pro-German sentiment in his writing immediately after the war, but even this was to re-emerge before long. Fritz became Boney but Boney did not forget Fritz.

How did the message compare with other military thinking at the time and with the political climate? That it was totally out of tune with the latter needs little elaboration. British politicians wanted peace, and expected it, and were seeking financial savings and the avoidance of military involvement on the Continent. Military thought was more divided. The emotional cavalry and infantry reaction against mechanization has already been described. Even men like Major-General Sir Louis Jackson, who had helped with tank development in the war, turned against it subsequently on the grounds that it was only needed in trench warfare which was unlikely to occur again. 'The tank proper was a freak,' he said at the RUSI in November 1919. 'The circumstances which called it into existence were exceptional and not likely to recur. If they do, they can be dealt with by other means.'[8] He went on to speak in favour of cross-country mechanical transport to carry guns, supplies and men, and of armoured cars, machine-gunners on motor cycles and lorried infantry; but his simple condemnation of the tank was seized upon by all its opponents. Another officer, a certain Major T. E. Compton, who contributed to the same issue of the *RUSI Journal* in which Jackson's lecture was published, believed that the appointment of Foch as Generalissimo had been more important than tanks in the final victory and pointed out that the Germans had broken the Allied front twice without using tanks.[9] Admiral Sir Reginald Custance published his thinking in a book in 1924[10] which contrasts strikingly with Fuller. Custance's military thought stems from Clausewitz, whose thinking he understood whereas Fuller was always criticizing Clausewitz without demonstrating convincingly that he had grasped the subtlety of what he was attempting to destroy. Nevertheless Custance's book, *A Study of War*, was old-fashioned, almost totally devoid of technological considerations and contained very little appreciation of the ways in which war had expanded or doubt about its traditional place in the nature of things. It must be admitted, however, that Custance was over thirty years older than Fuller and had been retired in 1912.

General Sir Ian Hamilton, who had commanded the Gallipoli expedition and was described by Fuller years later as being 'in spite of his poetic imagination ... a thoroughly orthodox general',[11] published *The Soul and Body of An Army* in 1921. This was entirely different and contained such statements as: 'Cavalry has been dead as the dodo for twenty long years'; 'numbers and blind obedience are going to have less and less of an innings against science and efficiency';[12] 'there will be no infantry except escorts in cars: tank followers';[13] 'Consider then the tank; consider it well; for I say unto you that Solomon in all his wisdom hit upon no happier device';[14] 'In the future let us be famous for tanks.... The tank is a warship on wheels. The tank marks as great a revolution in land warfare as an armoured steamship would have marked had it appeared amongst the toilsome triremes at Actium.'[15] Hamilton's generalship in the field may not have pleased Fuller but his views on the tank were similarly revolutionary although he rather devalued his coinage at the end by proposing that both aeroplanes and tanks should be brought 'into the regimental framework' and that each infantry battalion should be issued with two tanks rather than that separate tank battalions be formed. Like Fuller, however, Hamilton could be prophetic. 'If we are going to be as cautious as in 1917, we may live to see the disinherited children of our brains marching against us in strange uniforms, commanded perhaps by those Asiatics who can copy and fight, though, thank God, they cannot invent.'[16] The strange uniforms were to be German and Japanese and it would not be unfair to regard Hitler's tanks and Hirohito's aeroplanes as disinherited children. Hamilton also believed that 'uncomfortable fellows who press for progress have a bad time of it in London'.[17] One wonders if he had Fuller in mind, who is not otherwise mentioned in the book. Lieutenant W. S. King-Hall went farther than Hamilton and saw tanks eventually doing all the fighting, saw naval tactics obtaining in tank-versus-tank battles and prophesied that once tanks had gained command on land, gas would be used against the civil population.[18] Lieutenant-Colonel W. D. Croft, who was runner-up to Fuller in the 1919 Gold Medal Essay Competition, went even farther than the winner in arguing for an all-tank army, and although his essay lacked Fuller's breadth of vision it contained such revolutionary statements as that 'everything, including transport, will be converted to tanks'.[19] These are but a few examples of military thought more or less contemporary with Fuller's in 1923. They serve to show that Fuller was not unique in his belief in mechanization and his analysis of its consequences. His thinking was, however, the most comprehensive and rationally structured corpus of military and political theory on the subject at the time.

Soon after his arrival at Camberley, as has already been told, his most important work to date, *The Reformation of War*, was published. It received not unfriendly reviews, which is an indication that at this time Fuller's message still fell, at least in some circles, on receptive ears. The *RUSI Journal* thought the book stimulating and original, the *Tank Corps Journal* recommended every thinking man to read it, while the *Army Quarterly* was benevolently critical, and this was to be the last time for many years that Fuller encountered benevolence in professional circles. 'Colonel Fuller', the *Army Quarterly*'s reviewer wrote,

> is our one and only military prophet and like most prophets has little enough honour in his own country—save that of being misunderstood. . . . He maintains, however, that the true and logical developments of war in the immediate future should trend not towards increased slaughter and destruction, but towards greater humanity, and security both of human lives and economic resources. . . . He avers that the true purpose of a general in the field should be . . . subjection of the enemy's will by the most effective and rapid means available. . . . Colonel Fuller is not an easy writer to read or an easy thinker to follow; like all prophets he is often obscure, not seldom inconsequent, too often biased. But what would you? We have only one military prophet; and in as much as the time has not yet come to build his sepulchre, it is perhaps ungracious to cast too many stones at him.

The review concluded by advising its readers to purchase the book which if rightly used would 'be more fertile in professional and intellectual benefit than . . . the works of the dry and pedantic Clausewitz, the somewhat geometrically minded Hamley, or even the brilliant and suggestive (but pre-war) Foch'. All this may have been an attempt to cut the author down to size by the application of some belittling, humorous patronage but, nevertheless, the reader could still feel that Fuller lived inside the military Pale. The *Sunday Times* and the *New York Times* were also very complimentary, as were numbers of the more respectable weekly magazines. Criticism centred on his support of the use of gas, and in the *New Statesman* on the way in which his original and acute ideas were embedded in a lot of 'the most intolerable verbiage'. Nevertheless *Reformation* rapidly became a best-seller.[20]

At the Staff College Fuller's fellow instructors included the future Field-Marshal Viscount Alanbroke and Lieutenant-General Sir Ronald Adam, the former a lieutenant-colonel and the latter a major. Among his students were the future lieutenant-generals Irwin, Norrie, Nye, Pope, Pownall and Tuker, together with numerous future major-generals. Fuller began by refusing to take over from his predecessor. Having spent most of the second half of 1922 in writing his lectures, he wanted to make a completely fresh start and this is precisely what he did. He walked into his office, rang the bell for the chief clerk and told him to burn all the existing schemes and documents. He expressed the hope in his *Memoirs* that his successor did the same,[21] but obviously that officer did not have Fuller's courage and the files at Camberley still contain the instructions Fuller issued and the lectures he delivered. Students were told at once that, 'in submitting work the ideal to aim at is that it should be easily, and quickly grasped by the reader'.[22] This was an admonition of which Fuller himself increasingly should have taken heed. Students were also informed that the new Chief Instructor would be setting papers on Sir John Moore and Xenophon's *Cyropaedia* and required them to tackle a reading list which included Gustave le Bon's *The Crowd, a Study of the Popular Mind*. One can imagine the surprise and even, perhaps, hilarity to which these instructions must have given rise. The regular army captain in the twenties, who had probably seen service in the First World War, and whose social instincts would not have led him to believe in the importance of the popular mind, no doubt took a great deal of convincing that Napoleonic warfare, ancient Greek military training, and crowd psychology were relevant and appropriate subjects of professional study.

The lectures themselves, which some of Fuller's students found far above their heads, are remarkable for their educational, rather than training, orientation. The first was on 'The Science of War', and was a stirring declaration of intent which began with the transformation into a scientific law of the author's view that victory should be obtained at the smallest cost—the law of the conservation of military energy. It continued with a complaint that there was a lack of scientific study of war and ended with the promise that Fuller intended to deal in subsequent lectures with the elements, principles and conditions of war. The lectures also covered such matters as military psychology, tanks, analysis of tactics and strategy in the First World War in the light of the principles of war, and warfare in the ancient Hellenic world. From them all, it is possible to see that Fuller was attempting to distil from *a priori* reasoning a series of prescriptions or hypotheses for success in war, and to test these out by applying them to the history of warfare, while not always resisting the temptation to test the generals against the principles, rather than the principles against the generals. It must, for those able or professional enough to take it seriously, have been a stimulating lecture course, and one which Fuller developed and repeated for the three years he taught at Camberley with the result that many of the more progressive officers who studied under him came for a while to look up to him as the Army's great brain;[23] for the less able and less motivated it no doubt induced not a little sleep and subsequent ill-informed ridicule; no doubt, also, this ridicule was tempered by some knowledge of Fuller's record and probable future.

Lecturing and instructing at Camberley did not fully occupy him and even though he loyally turned out to watch games and sporting events in which he was very little interested; there was time to write numerous articles and to have them published in various military and civilian journals. He also lectured outside Camberley and, for instance, in June 1923 addressed the RAF Staff College on 'The Development of Scientific Warfare'.[25] There was time, at last, for him to revise and arrange for the publication, in two separate books, of the work on British military training in the Napoleonic Wars which he had written while stationed in Tunbridge Wells in 1915. *Sir John Moore's System of Training* was published in 1924 and *British Light Infantry in the Eighteenth Century* the next year. Besides being historical works these two had another purpose.

What, then, must we do [Fuller wrote at the end of the first] if the spirit of Sir John Moore is to live in us?

We must first remember that man remains man and that his heart does not change. Secondly, we must remember that the means of war do change and that the intelligence of man must keep pace with these changes. We must keep our minds subtle and active, and never let outselves be hypnotized by traditions; we must criticize ourselves, and criticize our criticisms; we must experiment and explore.

What we require today is a second Shorncliffe Camp, another Experimental Brigade, in which not only new weapons of war will be tried out and new tactics elaborated, but new methods of discipline will be tested; for though the heart of man does not change, or so slightly as to be imperceptible, his intelligence must expand as war becomes more scientific, and, consequently, the discipline of his mind must change with his tactics.[26]

And in the second he produced the following conclusion:

I will now turn to the present and look at the future, for unless history can teach us how to look at the future, the history of war is but a bloody romance.

Today we are faced with a new tactics, a tactics of armoured machines. These new tactics will demand a new discipline, as highly intellectual as Moore's was highly moral and Frederick's highly brutal. This is not the place to describe what it should be, but the fact remains that a change will take place, must take place, and the army which grasps this change first is the army which stands to win.[27]

The campaign for an experimental brigade with Fuller in command was getting under way. As the *Daily Telegraph* reviewer said of *British Light Infantry in the Eighteenth Century*, Fuller was at this time 'less a pure historian than a prophet with an historical text'.

In one sense the publication of these two books, which were well received in the national press, compensated Fuller for the ban which was placed on the publication of the book he most wanted to see in print. This was to consist of a selection of his

Camberley lectures entitled *The Foundations of the Science of War*. At the end of 1923 he asked the War Office for permission to publish and this was refused on the grounds that the new CIGS, Lord Cavan, objected to the writing of books by staff officers. Fuller asked for, and obtained, an interview with the CIGS which took place, fortuitously but memorably, on November 5th. Lord Cavan was an ex-Grenadier and an Irish peer who had held many distinguished military appointments and was eventually to command the troops at the Coronation of King George VI. He told Fuller that it was contrary to discipline for serving officers to publish books because these might call into question the validity of the Manuals. 'On principle I consider that no officer on the active list should be permitted to publish any book on a military subject. I cannot enforce this as regards the Army generally, but as regards General Staff officers I intend to do so, and whilst you are at the Staff College I cannot give you permission to bring this book out.'[28] It was useless to argue so in due course he merely asked to have his tenure of appointment at Camberley reduced from four to three years.

In February 1924 he lectured on 'Tanks' at King's College, London, under the auspices of the University of London's Military Education Committee. Swinton was in the chair.[29] In August he went to America to visit US industry. He travelled out on the *Berengaria* which he described as 'not a floating palace, but a floating ghetto'.[30] In November he lectured once more at the RUSI. Swinton was again in the chair and he introduced Fuller as 'a thinker on war, a writer on the military art, and an apostle of progress, whose attitude, or "general idea" can be best expressed in the words "Quo Vadis". This afternoon his special idea will best be conveyed by the words "Quomodo Vadis".'[31] Fuller's subject was 'Progress in the Mechanicalization of Modern Armies' and the most significant statement he made that afternoon was that he had 'been requested by the War Office to say that the views expressed in this lecture are not necessarily those of the General Staff'.[32] In the lecture he stressed the importance of protected mobility and called for the development of battleship, cruiser and destroyer tanks, together with a tactics to fit them and an industrial base to produce them. In question-time, Liddell Hart, by now on half-pay and freelancing as a sporting and military journalist, suggested the formation of an experimental mechanized formation. In fact Fuller had asked him to do this in a letter written some days beforehand.[33] Fuller, somewhat disingenuously, replied that he had been forbidden to mention this issue but suggested that Liddell Hart write an article about it for the *Morning Post*. In conclusion Swinton agreed that infantry were useless against tanks and suggested that the answer to tanks was the tank itself or the anti-tank gun.

In quite extraordinary contrast to all this professional activity, but of direct relevance to the nature of much of what was eventually to be included in *Foundations*, were Fuller's revived and continuing interest in and contact with the world and underworld of the occult at this time in his life. Between 1921 and 1924 Crowley pestered him with letters and blandishments all of which Fuller outwardly resisted. But his interest in the occult remained strong. In April 1923 he published an article in *The Occult Review* on 'The Black Arts' in which he put forward the view that in the heart of unknowable things the black arts are really white, 'lucid and limpid, capricious will o' the wisps which beckon us over heath and through hut, throng, cathedral, city and study'.[34] Two years later he actually published a very learned little book on *Yoga* which he defined as leading to mastery over the Unknowable.[35] He regarded himself as a working yogi, he told Starr at the time, a searcher after Truth which, like an onion, had many layers. All roads led to Truth and he had chosen War simply because he was a soldier. It was in *Foundations* that the marriage of his military and occult studies was to see the light of day. This, he told Starr, was a 'big book on war'; the work he had put into it had not got him military advancement but it had got him closer to Truth.[36]

His first published work on the concept of a science of war had been an article in the *Army Quarterly* in October 1920 actually entitled 'The Foundations of the Science of War'.[37] In this he had claimed that 'war is as much a science as any other human activity' because it was built of facts.[38] First you had to sort them out and then you could both analyse military history, build up theories and solve military problems. The real point about this was that Clausewitz had believed that there was 'no human affair which stands so constantly and so generally in close connection with chance as war.'[39] Even Henderson was only really prepared to state that military organization had become a science, not war.

Fuller never denied that the practice of war was an art, but he claimed that the art ought to be based on a science and the science must begin with the description, and classification of the facts of war. Napoleon, in his insistence on the value of military history and in his perception of military principles was obviously one of the sources of Fuller's inspiration. Clausewitz, however, Fuller once told Liddell Hart, 'was a pre-Darwinian'.[40]

In the article he began the process of description and classification. He identified the elements of war as being men, movement, weapons and protection. Each element has a positive and negative sphere of action; thus movement can be protective or offensive, weapons are shock or missile in nature, and protection is either direct like armour or indirect like the use of firepower. Man himself has two spheres of action, the moral and the physical. The best ways of using these elements can be deduced from consideration of the duel and are the principles of war, still eight in number as in 1916, but with concentration significantly substituted for mass. All the principles are of equal value but must be harmonized and weighed against the conditions of war. The conditions are the factors of time, space, ground, weather, numbers, morale, communications, supply, armament etc., which affect the elements. Each condition can either increase the endurance of the attacker or the resistance of the defender. The commander has either to avoid, break down or turn to advantage each condition; in battle he has to apply the conditions to the principles and evolve a plan using the elements. 'Such is battle and such is war—a science based on sure foundations, rooted first in the past with its boughs and leaves moving this way and that above and around us according to the conditions of the moment but governed by the laws of existence—action and inertia.'[41]

All this was reasonably easy to follow and represented a highly original attempt to impose some order on the study of war and on the process of appreciating and solving military problems. The principles of war themselves had attracted official attention even before the publication of the 1920 article. In 1919 Fuller had sat on a committee concerned with the revision of the Staff College Entrance Examination and had then pointed out, as he had done as a student at the Staff College and even earlier, that *Field Service Regulations* contained no definition of the principles of war. The CIGS had decided that definition was necessary and the chairman of the committee responsible for revising the *FSR* had asked Fuller for a copy of a lecture based on his 1916 article which he had given at the Commanding Officers' School in Aldershot. The result was that two fundamental principles were included in the draft revised 'FSR': (1) Infantry never relinquishes captured ground, (2) Infantry is never exhausted. Eventually the draft was taken up by the Staff College, where Dill, who was to become CIGS in 1940–1, was a Chief Instructor. Mainly due to the efforts of the future General Sir Bernard Paget, Fuller's principles, in a slightly modified form, were included in *FSR*. Since then they have found their way into the military textbooks and regulations of many armies.[42] Six of the principles came from Napoleon; nevertheless Fuller was responsible for their definition and updating and for their almost universal acceptance. In 1929, for instance, Major-General Sir Frederick Maurice, most famous for his enforced retirement from the Army after his letter to *The Times* in May 1918 about the inaccuracy of Lloyd George's statement on the strength of Haig's army, and by 1929 Professor of Military Studies at London University, wrote a book on *British Strategy*. This was almost entirely devoted to a consideration of Fuller's principles of war. Even today cadets in military academies and students in staff colleges will find the principles very familiar. Whether by successfully disseminating them Fuller performed a military service, or succeeded in further stultifying and inhibiting the very sort of thinking he wished to encourage, that is, common sense or thinking adapted to circumstances, is a point which must be considered later.

In *Reformation* Fuller had expanded what he had begun to call the system and dealt at length with the psychological side of war. In *Foundations* the system reached the peak of luxuriant growth. The book was a most remarkable achievement, full of learning and thought, spanning a field covering philosophy, psychology, history, politics, economics, technology, strategy and tactics, and all constrained into a rigorous and more or less consistent and coherent conceptual framework, a framework which is sustained on every page. It is a book which was obviously aimed, in spite of subsequent occasional disclaimers, at that shelf in the bookcase where one might keep *On War, The Origin of Species* and *Principia Mathematica*. Indeed Fuller wrote in the Preface: 'In a small way I am trying to do for war what Copernicus did for astronomy, Newton for physics, and Darwin for natural history.'[43] Admittedly he had told Liddell Hart as early as 1923 that the book was only the first of ten he wished to write, the others covering such subjects as 'The Foundations of the Art of War', 'The Foundations of War Training', 'The Foundations of Grand Strategy'. 'When these are written I will then write my one and only book on war. I write these things to educate myself not others.'[44] And just before publication he told Liddell Hart that he would 'give it about five years before I rewrite it; as it stands it is only a draft'.[45] Such modesty serves only to emphasize the fact that the book was for Fuller at the time a magnum opus, a weighty and original, if not definitive, contribution to knowledge and the genesis of a new science.

One of the troubles was that the book did not, and still does not, read attractively. It is patently a collection of lectures, edited for publication, and it is unremittingly didactic with little of the literary elegance or imagery of Clausewitz and with much less of the salty flavour and choleric views of much of Fuller's early and later writing. It is difficult to read and pitched at a level of abstraction which makes comprehension a slow and arduous business for the reader. Such passages as the following abound:

> we apply to these conditions the principles of war—this is analysis, which will enable us to discover which conditions will assist us and resist us. This leads to transformation, and through transformation to hypothesis. Thirdly, having ascertained the military values of the conditions, bearing the hypothesis in mind, we equate these values with the elements of war and discover how these elements will be affected. Then, bearing in mind our object, guided by the principles of war, we arrange these elements and set them together in a plan—this is synthesis.[46]

The level of much of the argument is also extremely elevated, and readers, whom Fuller calls students, are advised in one footnote to study Herbert Spencer's *First Principles* and the four volumes of David Hume's works. He does concede, however, that 'if these be found too long, then Thomas Huxley's essay on "Hume", which is a masterpiece of clear thinking'[47] would suffice. One wonders if Fuller had an accurate enough perception of the educational level and motivation of either the Staff College student or the general reader. Another problem, at least today, is that much of Fuller's thinking was based on philosophical writing which would now be regarded as merely of historical interest. No doubt it was some of these considerations which led Sir Archibald Montgomery-Massingberd to abuse 'Fuller's latest book' to Liddell Hart. Montgomery-Massingberd was a very ambitious man, once Chief of Staff in Rawlinson's 4th Army on the Somme and later to be CIGS at a crucial point in Fuller's career. The fact that he denied having read the book and stated that he probably never would because it would only annoy him, makes one wonder if perhaps there was some sort of deliberately engineered whispering campaign, the instigators of which seized upon the less felicitous aspects of the book in order to discredit the author.[48] Perhaps it was the sheer effrontery of a mere Colonel, somewhat 'déclassé' through his association with the greasy, noisy and smelly machines of Royal Tank Corps, setting himself up as a competitor of Clausewitz and Foch, which caused so much anger. This time it cannot have been principally a reaction against mechanization because the book does not deal in depth with anything so ephemeral as that. Montgomery-Massingberd's dislike of Fuller in any case probably stretched back to 1914 when he had been an instructor at the Staff College.

The book begins with an analysis of the present absence of scientific method in the study and practice of war, the former of which Fuller classified as alchemy rather than science. Scientific knowledge of war is required in order to avoid the repetition of mistakes, to make prediction possible and to form the basis of the art of war. The science obviously cannot be exact. All this was merely giving the substance of his 1920 article a respectable introduction. However, Fuller then introduced the concept of the threefold order which he considered a universal foundation 'axiomatic to knowledge in all its forms'.[49] Here was something new; in the 1920 article he had seemed impressed with the duality of things, the positive and negative, the moral and the physical, but in the book he showed himself obsessed, no lesser word can describe it, with trinities. He told Liddell Hart that the threefold order was the key.[50] In the book he attempted to explain the theory of the relational nature of knowledge, that it is a record of the interplay between oneself and the universe, between inertia and change, and that this trinity 'surrounds us at every turn'.[51] As

Professor Luvaas has pointed out this owes a lot to Hegel's view that all knowledge is relational between the person and the object, and this is a debt which Fuller did not acknowledge.[52] It is also an extremely metaphysical concept which Fuller then applied to everything in the universe, both abstract and concrete. Time he divided into past, present and future, force into energy, motion and mass, mind into knowledge, faith and belief, nature into earth, water and air, mankind into men, women and children, matter into solids, liquids and gases. Knowledge, he argued, must be subjected to system and this should be based on man—mind, soul and body. The body itself has a threefold organization— structure, control and maintenance—and three elements— stability (which is negative), activity (which is positive), and co-operation (which is relative). Wars are matters of men, and the three modes of force in war, mental, moral and physical, are based on the mind, soul and body of man. Similarly, national power is ethical, political and economic while military forces are divided into the Navy, Army and Air Force. And so on——! In seeking to classify the phenomena of war Fuller endeavoured, with a mind accustomed to the arcane, the occult, and the mystical symbolism of number, to perceive a universal law governing knowledge itself, and although he specifically refused to claim that the threefold order was such a universal law, he stated that it formed the norm of his entire system for the study and practice of war.[53] The tragedy for Fuller was that the three-fold order is entirely irrelevant to the system, which can be understood without it, as we shall see. He was certainly philoso-phically learned but his learning was untutored and his enthusiasms outside his own military, and later historical, provinces were apt to cloud his judgment. The threefold order was a regrettable aberration; it would have been perfectly pos-sible to have divided things into fours—corners, wheels, gospels— or sevens—ages of man, sisters—or twos—arms, legs, eyes, computer language. But it was not really necessary to divide things into numerical groups at all; such obsession with division had more to do with the world of Crowley than the science of war, and it gave Fuller's enemies a lot of ammunition.

The remainder of the book is an expansion of the 1920 article with the addition of trinities, some analysis of the causes, objects and instruments of war, a fundamental law and a chapter on the applications of the system. The causes of war, Fuller believed, were biological and national and in both cases stemmed from the right of survival. Political questions between nations cannot be settled by a court; 'Leagues of Nations are leagues of nonsense, as they cannot control the causes of war.'[54] The objects of war are related to the causes and can be the achievement of national security, ethical objectives such as liberty, or economic prosperity—existence, honourable existence and profitable existence. Wars with an ethical objective are the most ferocious; the others are best won with the least cost to all, victors and vanquished alike. In fact, the political object in peace and war is a more perfect peace and therefore the power to wage war should be regarded as a creative force. 'War, and not peace, is the true condition which gives expression to nationalism'.[55] All this has evident rationality but is violently emotive in its impact, today as in 1926. It also is obviously related to geopolitics and easy to regard as very close to Nazi doctrine. As regards the object of war being a more perfect peace it should not be forgotten that Clausewitz, living as he did in the shadow of Napoleon, had written almost a hundred years earlier: 'A conqueror is always a lover of peace (as Buonaparte always asserted of himself); he would like to make his entry into our state unopposed.'[56]

Fuller next dealt with the instrument of war which could be economic, moral or military force. He dealt only with the last in detail and for several pages reduced such matters as the fighting arms, the fighting and maintenance functions, the need for a Ministry of Defence and study of the enemy, to the threefold order, and called for a generalissimo to control the three Services. The instrument of war included, he claimed, three forces, mental, moral and physical. Each type of force had three elements: mental force had reason, imagination and will; moral force had fear, morale[57] and courage; while physical force had weapons, protection and movement. It is through the study of the enemy's physical elements that we learn to understand him, for 'the physical sphere is, in fact, the alphabet of war'.[58] Fuller went far beyond this alphabet in his attempt to classify the constituent elements of military force, and in this technological age his analysis of the mental and moral elements is difficult to accept. Nevertheless, in the sphere of nuclear deterrence, for instance, it is possible to see mental, moral and physical elements in a credible posture, elements we today call strategy, intention and capability. However, he wrote eighty-two difficult pages on the elements, and this was many pages too many for the average military reader, as the lectures on which they were based were for the average Staff College student.

Every possible cause which can produce an effect in the instrument of war is a condition of war and Fuller next studied these, which can be infinite in number. He identified a trinity of conditions, military space, force and time. The general avoids, resists or turns to advantage the conditions in which he operates while the staff examines the conditions for him. Many battles are lost because no one realizes that the conditions have changed. With his Camberley lectures in front of him and their reference to a law of the conservation of military energy, Fuller next asked if any general principle governed the way in which the conditions affect the elements or forces of the instrument of war and concluded, in a very difficult philosophical passage, that there was such a principle or law and that this could be derived from the proposition that force endures whatever use may be made of it. Fuller's law of economy of force is historically demonstrable, he claimed, in that the 'side which could best economize its force, and which in consequence, could expend its force more remuneratively, has been the side which has always won'.[59] It is regrettably usually only possible to induce laws from the study of human behaviour at a very high level of generality, so high that the law has almost no useful meaning. This is true of Fuller's law; it is tautological; it merely states that the side which fights most effectively wins, and this means nothing since victory is the only valid criterion of the effectiveness of fighting.

Fuller admitted that his law was too abstract to be a useful guide on the battlefield; instead he extracted from the law nine general expressions of the tensions created by the interaction of the conditions and elements of war; these were the principles of war already familiar to the reader. They were the same as the principles of the 1920 article except that direction was substituted for objective, distribution for economy of force, now of course a law, and co-operation dropped for endurance and determination. Significantly this made nine principles, which could be divided into threes, both between the mental, moral and physical spheres, and between the functions of control (direction, deter-

A Medium A or Whippet tank

Crushing enemy wire

Fascines, or bundles of brushwood which could be dropped into trenches too wide for tanks to cross and used as bridges. (See page 56.)

A Mark V Male tank

mination and mobility), pressure (concentration, surprise and offensive action) and resistance (distribution, endurance and security). Almost a hundred pages are then devoted to an analysis of these principles.

The book ends with a chapter on 'The Application of the Science of War'. First Fuller summarized his system which he described as 'an attempt to establish the theory and practice of war on a scientific footing by applying the method of science to the study of war',[60] because war must be reduced to a science before it can be practised correctly as an art. He then considered the problems of evidence and atmosphere inherent in the study of military history and put forward the view that its one true value was that it prepared us for the next war, as the one true value of history itself was its usefulness in the future. He then claimed that the system could be applied with profit by the military historian who should use its framework by ascertaining the causes of the war he is studying, the object of the belligerents and the military objects of the generals. He should then evaluate the instruments of war in physical, moral and mental order in order to obtain a tactical picture, cultural and racial understanding and understanding of the military leaders. Next he should examine the conditions in which the war was fought and the actions of the participants in the light of the principles of war and the law of economy of force. Finally he should project his deductions into the future and consider them in the light of probable future conditions. The system, he concluded, could also be applied to the fighting of wars, or rather to the construction of military plans and the solution of military problems. In this case the soldier must make certain he understands the object, must evaluate the elements of force in both his and the enemy's instruments of war, must examine the conditions, and how to deal with them, must regard the enemy as capable of using his means intelligently, must apply the principles of war to the enemy's means as influenced by the conditions, must work out a plan for the enemy, must apply the principles to his own means in the same way and work out a plan to defeat the enemy or frustrate him, should he gain the initiative, and must finally decide on his distribution of force. And then, at the very end of this weighty book Fuller advised those military readers who did not understand his system simply to follow the great maxim, 'when in doubt, hit out',[61] With such a very unscientific and monosyllabic recommendation does the book end.

As a result of Lord Cavan's interdiction, *The Foundations of the Science of War* was not published until after Fuller had left the Staff College. Before examining the hysterical reaction it provoked in some quarters it would be worthwhile to evaluate the book briefly in a calmer context since, for Fuller, himself, at the time, *Foundations* meant so much. As has already been stated the threefold order was at least a military aberration, the analysis of the causes of war verged on fascist geopolitics, and the law of economy of force was tautological. The principles were in many ways valid inductions from the study of military history and military practice but they are so generalized as to be poor guides to action except at the very highest level of command, and they often conflict with each other in practice—surprise with concentration for instance, and endurance with mobility. Fuller certainly failed to reduce war to a science; it may not one day be impossible to do so, but it was impossible in the state of knowledge which obtained in 1926, and it still is impossible today. For war to be a science it would be necessary for the scientists of war to be aware of all the factors which are involved, or might become involved, in the outcome of any war, and the ways in which they would interact and change as the war progressed. In the United States of America recently a number of military thinkers have tried to use the methods of science in order to predict the outcome of military engagements and have developed RICE, the Relative Index of Combat Effectiveness. This is an immensely long formula which attempts to quantify the various elements of military effectiveness on both sides (Fuller's elements of the instrument of war) in order to determine which will win. This sort of thinking is, consciously or unconsciously, a development of Fuller's own; one only has to look at the complexity of the formula, and the fragility of the assumptions on which it is based, to realize that man is not yet omniscient enough for such calculations.

Clausewitz, Fuller's 'pre-Darwinian' devotee of chance, believed that war was neither a science nor an art. He questioned the distinction between art, as doing, and science, as knowing, but concluded that war belonged 'not to the province of arts and sciences, but to the province of social life'.[62] War, he believed, was not a science because it was a matter of action, and not an art because it did not exert itself upon inanimate or passive human material but upon reacting, living force. Fuller specifically challenged Clausewitz on these points. He did not claim that war was an exact science, because it dealt with numbers of unknowns, but he believed that chance rules where ignorance abounds and, although ignorance cannot be completely eradicated by knowledge, 'the more we realize that war is the province of law and not of chance the more we shall grow to understand its changes, and, as we understand them, learn how best to economize and expend our force'.[63] Obviously the more we know of the factors which influence victory or defeat in war the less will the outcome appear to depend on chance, and yet to eliminate chance altogether the generals would have to be omnipotent as well as omniscient, in the sense of controlling all the consequences of all the actions and reactions they initiate, and also in the sense of being able to control acts of God. The argument is essentially sterile and metaphysical. For all practical purposes war is war, a human activity; its practice should be based on knowledge, but its practitioners must use the tools and methods knowledge gives them as best they can amidst the fog and heat which will surround them. Fuller's challenge to Clausewitz did not, and does not, stand up.

Foundations, however, was a noble try. The system of considering objects, elements, principles and conditions when making a plan is a good one, if not too rigidly applied, and this same system applied to the study of military history yields excellent results, as it did later for Fuller.

Throughout his time at Camberley Fuller's intimacy with Liddell Hart was growing. They corresponded and met and Fuller exposed the principles of war and the threefold order to Liddell Hart's critical analysis. He told Liddell Hart that the threefold order could be applied to industry where management could be divided into direction, concentration and distribution. Earlier, in 1923, he helped Liddell Hart to a vacancy in the Royal Tank Corps but this came to nothing because Liddell Hart was not regarded as medically fit; he also backed Liddell Hart's application to take a Ph.D. at Cambridge but this again did not materialize. Liddell Hart was invalided out of the Army in 1924 and Fuller attempted to cheer up Mrs Liddell Hart by asking her husband to tell her that leaving the Army was the equivalent of being released from prison.[64]

Liddell Hart was rather more successful in his efforts on Fuller's behalf. In July 1925, he published *Paris, or the Future of War* in which he attacked the doctrine he ascribed to Napoleon (through Clausewitz) of numerically superior, frontal assault and called for the imposition of will at the least cost as the object of war. He recommended moral and economic objectives as well as military ones and advocated air power and the use of gas; he thought that infantry might survive for a time because some terrain was tank-proof but he saw infantry becoming tank marines and artillery becoming self-propelled. Tank-versus-tank battles would be naval in style and even military objectives might be moral, as were the objectives of 'Plan 1919'. *Paris* owed a lot to the Fuller–Liddell Hart dialogues but it also brought Liddell Hart into discussion with General Sir George Milne in the Norfolk Arms at Arundel in August 1925. Milne, who had been selected to become the next CIGS, asked Liddell Hart how he thought the mechanization of the Army might be carried out and was told that a special operational research or 'thinking ahead' organ should be created as well as an experimental mechanized formation. Milne objected that the creation of new War Office branches was financially difficult and that the only post which did not have onerous current business was that of Military Assistant to the CIGS. Liddell Hart immediately jumped in and suggested that this post should be used for 'thinking ahead' and that Fuller should fill it.[65] On August 24th Fuller received a 'rather apologetic letter from the DSD' asking whether he 'would favourably consider the appointment of Military Assistant to the CIGS'.[66] Fuller stated in his *Memoirs* that he could not imagine why the letter was apologetic; this is a little disingenuous since such posts are normally filled by more junior officers and his predecessor had been a Brevet Lieutenant-Colonel.

During the Army Manoeuvres in September he met Milne for the first time although the latter had commanded the artillery at the Larkhill Practice Camp in 1913 which had inspired Fuller's heretical Staff College essay on the importance of artillery. They were both looking at an experimental self-propelled gun and Milne remarked that it was needed. Fuller agreed but suggested that it should be armoured. Milne recommended caution 'otherwise you will frighten people'.[67] Undeterred, Fuller wrote to Liddell Hart: 'the first day we meet officially, I intend putting a written policy before him. He will have to get down to it, he hints at caution, but what we want is audacity. If he is not too old, he will see the wisdom of this.'[68] They met once again before Fuller moved to the War Office when Milne recommended him to read an anonymous article on the manoeuvres in the *Sunday Times* which Fuller himself had written.[69] It is extremely probable that the new CIGS did not know what Liddell Hart had let him in for—and similarly probable that the Army took Fuller's appointment as both a promise and a threat.

The Commandant was sorry to see Fuller leave Camberley[70] and the Christmas edition of the Staff College magazine *Owl Pie* noted his departure with a mixture of affection and respect. 'Although it is not our role to comment on the changes of the changing year, perhaps it may be permitted to congratulate the Army on the appointment of Colonel Fuller as Assistant to the new CIGS. Too many generations of students owe too much to "Boney" for us to say less—or more. The good horse Mobility (by Audacity out of Surprise) should be closely watched for the Empire Stakes.'[71] And so his years as an educator and a philosopher of the science of war came to an auspicious end, and yet in the omens there were portents of danger. There was the cautious Milne himself and the nature of the book which was about to burst upon the military world. As he left Camberley for London he carried with him the seeds of disaster.

6. The Tidworth Affair— 1926–7

'Colonel J. F. C. Fuller DSO, who has just been appointed military assistant to the new Chief of the Imperial General Staff, is probably by far the cleverest man in the Army.'

It was in this way that the *Sunday Express* announced Fuller's new appointment and it is a notable tribute to his fame, if not notoriety, that so relatively lowly an appointment should have been commented on at all in the press. Whether the *Sunday Express* was doing him a service in drawing attention to the fact that he was probably 'the cleverest man in the Army' is arguable.

On February 19th, 1926 General Milne, at the age of sixty, and Colonel Fuller, aged forty-seven, entered the War Office together, and the fact that they did was the responsibility of Captain Basil Liddell Hart, then only thirty years old.[1] It seemed as if the two most important military intellectuals of the twentieth century had brought off a magnificent coup which would result in the mechanization and modernization of the British Army. At this stage Liddell Hart was the catalyst; the opportunities lay with the CIGS and his MA and in their characters lay also the problems. Fuller was dedicated to mechanization, hyper-intelligent, astringent, uncompromising, somewhat fanatical; Milne was also intelligent but sensitive to climate, aware of opposition, prepared to compromise. Fuller was a man of ideas but Milne was a man of the world. In his first few minutes in the office Milne, who had commanded all the British forces in the Macedonian campaign, discovered that Lord Cavan, his predecessor, had exercised very little control over his Major-Generals, the Directors of Staff Duties (DSD) and Military Operations and Intelligence (DMO and I). He made a splendid impression initially by asking DMO and I, Major-General Sir John (Jock) Burnett-Stuart, who had been one of Haig's senior staff officers in GHQ when Fuller was head of SD7 in 1918: 'Who is the General Staff?' This question was caused by Stuart's repeated reference to the 'General Staff' in his conversation with Milne. 'I am the General Staff,' Milne answered his own question or as Fuller put it, 'L'état c'est moi.' And that seemed to be that. But it was not, for as Fuller himself later commented, Milne invariably started audaciously and ended cautiously. 'Could one have turned him mentally upside down, what a superb CIGS he would have made'.[2] How many men are similarly constructed? It is one thing to make ambitious plans in the study, but quite another to see them through in the teeth of lack of interest, irrational opposition and appeals to a sense of group solidarity. Of course, Milne, unlike most people, had little to lose, having reached the pinnacle of his profession. Perhaps for that very reason it must have been particularly irritating to have an assistant who was more evangelical, more determined, more prepared to make a sacrifice of himself, than one was oneself. Fuller was a hard taskmaster, too hard for Milne, and this was undoubtedly one of the many reasons which led to the unpreparedness of the British Army in 1938, and perhaps also to the relative preparedness of the Germans. But this is running ahead.

Up until its disappearance in the 1960s the War Office had at its head an Army Council chaired by the Secretary of State for War. On the military side it was composed, until VCIGS was added in 1942, of the CIGS, the Adjutant-General (AG), Quartermaster-General (QMG) and Master-General of Ordnance (MGO). This council was the supreme authority, under the Cabinet, for army matters. The CIGS, although the senior Military Member, was only *primus inter pares* and not Commander-in-Chief. After his victory over Stuart, Milne so far forgot this as to ask Fuller to draft a memorandum to the Secretary of State, Sir Laming Worthington-Evans, asking the Cabinet to lay down the purposes for which the Army existed. Fuller knew that such a direct address to the Minister would cause a row but he does not appear to have advised Milne against it because he thought Milne would respond to any opposition from the other Military Members by bringing about their removal. However when QMG protested with the words 'As Member of Council . . .', Milne took the hint and did nothing, probably taking refuge in the thought that he would be able to replace at least two of the other three with his own nominees when they retired in less than a year.

It verges on the tragic that Fuller's last chance to reform the Army from within had to be through the medium of an instrument which at times could be so very pliant. For those few months in Whitehall Fuller had the opportunity to mould events and institutions again, but only through the CIGS and not in his own right; he was, however, once more an integral part of the military machine at the highest level, poised to act the soldier visionary, to rub the Army's face in the inevitability of penetration through mechanization, and its consequence once mechanized armies fought each other, of mechanical mutual envelopment, naval warfare on land. His position seemed strong but Milne's disenchantment and irritation grew day by day, and Fuller was soon exposed and isolated because he was really nothing more than a private secretary who could easily be encapsulated in his own lack of base or executive authority; to be merely a private secretary at the age of forty-seven, and after fighting in two wars and acquiring worldwide fame as a military thinker, was not much of a reward even if it did give him a bird's-eye view of the General Strike. Indeed he appears to have spent a considerable amount of time dealing with the register of confidential letters and obtaining, with great difficulty, such small items of office equipment as pairs of dividers for his master. At one time he suggested to Milne that what the CIGS really needed was a deputy rather than a military assistant, but this suggestion got nowhere and the major-generals, whose papers to the CIGS all passed through Fuller's hands, were obviously tempted to suspect that it was the MA, not the CIGS, who was making policy decisions. This was not a healthy situation, but on top of this his credibility, and his stature in Milne's eyes, were not improved by the reception given by both the military and the civilian reviewers to the publication of *Foundations* in the spring.

Fuller himself admitted that *Foundations* was only a draft and would require complete revision in about five years.[3] In spite of this the book got a balanced review in the *Observer* whose reviewer called it 'arresting, vivid, powerful, original, and the work of the most thinking soldier of our time', although he accused Fuller of imagining that other soldiers could not think at all and mocked both his Copernican and Darwinian self-comparisons and his 'mystic conglomerations of circles and triangles with abstract titles' in the book's diagrams. The *Spectator*'s man wrote that Fuller's searchlight was 'brilliant, far-reaching and well-directed'. *The Times* called it 'the work of one whose enthusiasm and intellectual boldness will assuredly not go to loss in his profession'; but took Fuller gently to task for being too abstruse and for expressing 'in runes arguments not difficult to follow if expressed shortly in English'; the *Referee* was prepared to class it with Clausewitz's *On War* and the *Civil and Military Gazette* prophesied that it would become 'a text book, for the serious study of every officer who takes his profession seriously'. The *Saturday Review*, however, thought it 'a very curious piece of work' and the *Manchester Guardian* called it 'most disappointing'.[4] But it was the *Army Quarterly*'s reviewer who, Brutus-like, plunged a dagger into Fuller's reputation, and yet the *Army Quarterly* was the same journal in which six years previously Fuller had published the article from which *Foundations* grew. Indeed in the very number containing the review, Fuller had an article on 'Major-General Henry Lloyd, Adventurer and Military Philosopher' in which he praised Lloyd's quality of supreme common sense.[5]

The anonymous reviewer, who may well have been the same man who the year before had attacked Liddell Hart's views in 'Paris' on armoured attacks on rear headquarters and whom Fuller believed was Brigadier-General J. E. Edmonds, the official historian of the First World War, announced his baneful assault with the gibe: 'he who can, does; he who cannot, teaches'.[6] This referred, of course, to Fuller's employment at the Staff College and the fact that the book was based on his lectures there. The reviewer told his readers that he had given *Foundations* to a recently joined officer who had passed high out of Sandhurst. ' "Poor fellow", was the verdict. "No more than that?" And the answer came: "Do the Staff College teachers black their faces as well as ink their fingers, and does Colonel Fuller rattle a couple of bones when he lectures?" ' In a footnote this allusion was explained. It came from 'The Hunting of the Snark':

> Chanted in mimsiest tones
> Words whose utter inanity proved his insanity,
> While he rattled a couple of bones.

The reviewer himself believed that 'the danger of such a book is that the young should take it seriously'. He burst into someone else's verse again on the same page with a quotation from Sir Macklin in *Bab Ballads* which he thought would have made an excellent review. Sir Macklin:

> Argued high and argued low;
> He argued also round about him.
> . . .
> The hundred and eleventh head
> The priest [Col.] completed of his structure.
> 'Oh bosh!' the worthy bishop [General] said,
> And walked him off as in the picture.

In less poetic vein, the reviewer then essayed a more serious comment. 'As in most of his published work, he is irremediably bound to the past, can at best only think in terms of the last war, and that he seems to have misunderstood, regarding it as a case of normal warfare, whereas, from first to last, it was a siege.' 'Threes', of course, come in for adverse comment as did Fuller's reading:

> Colonel Fuller has read much in the last fifteen years, and thought more. The pity is that he seems to have read some of the wrong sort of books, obscure and forgotten authors rather than masters—he thinks poorly of Clausewitz, Dragomirov, Foch and Co. The result, as so often is the case with self-centred thinkers, is that he has produced, and clothed in cabbalistic language, old ideas, believing them, in their fantastic forms, to be original. He thinks that he has discovered new principles, which, if he will read, say the works of Colonel (now General) Mordacq—not to mention Goltz and other Germans—have been already formulated and clearly formulated.

Fuller, the reviewer concluded, had written 'common nonsense'. 'His ideas will not help a soldier to feed himself or slay an enemy.'

This was venomous stuff. To accuse Fuller of being a teacher because he was incompetent to do anything else was wildly unjust; to accuse him of being tied to the past was insane. This sally stemmed from the view that trench warfare was an aberration and the tank, as General Jackson had said in 1919, was therefore a freak; it was in this sense, the reviewer believed, that

Fuller had misunderstood the last war, but the criticism ignored
the futurism of so much of Fuller's work. To accuse him of
merely dressing up old ideas in new clothes missed the whole
point of Fuller's attempt to draw so many threads together into a
coherent structure; to accuse him of using cabbalistic language
was perhaps nearer the mark. Certainly Fuller's ideas were not
primarily dedicated to helping soldiers to supply themselves or
kill enemies but the reviewer's very phraseology revealed the level
of his thinking—and his undeclared and wistful regret for the conditions of a past much farther back in history than the First World
War. The review was based on a distillation of the attitudes of
those sections of the officer corps which wanted warfare to revert
to happier times, the N. W. Frontier perhaps, or the Peninsular
campaign, or even to an imagined Golden Age which had never
existed. What these sections of the officer corps rejected and
disliked above all else was peacetime professionalism. For them the
officer was a gentleman who properly did half a day's work for half a
day's pay and left most military matters to the sergeant-major. It
was a posture Fuller had affected in Ireland at the very end of the
nineteenth century but one which he had left behind him long
before he became a Staff College student. In spite of his gallantry
in South Africa and his fame in the Tank Corps in 1917 and 1918
he had this time offended against the ark of the social and
military covenant. There would be, many felt, no quarter. Boney
had been too clever.

On April 7th Fuller wrote to Liddell Hart and asked him to
read the review which he described as 'a string of hostile abuse.
. . . If our leading military journal can subscribe to such twaddle, I
cannot help feeling I am right in attacking the traditional
school'.[7] On the same day, either before or after receiving Fuller's
letter, Liddell Hart sent a letter to Lieutenant-Colonel C. M. Headlam, the editor of the *Army Quarterly*. 'I have no brief for Fuller's
writing,' he wrote. 'We often disagree, and I think that in many
places he might be both simpler and clearer—but to treat him as
a literary mountebank, ignoring the profound influence he has
exerted on military thought here and abroad, is a silliness which
can only recoil on the reviewer. . . . In view of Fuller's responsibility for the Cambrai plan of 1917, for the Allied plan of 1919, the
progressive way he has won over the high military authorities to
his view, and his present post—the silliness of such comments is

apparent.'[8] Headlam was not converted; on April 12th he replied[9] and told Liddell Hart that the reviewer found the book contained nothing original and was tedious to read. Headlam agreed with him.

The next number of the *Army Quarterly*, issued in July, contained an anonymous defence of *Foundations*, actually written by Liddell Hart, called 'The Value and Originality of *The Foundations of the Science of War*[10] and an editorial on the subject by Headlam.[11] Liddell Hart condemned the violent language of the review which he categorized as a personal attack, perhaps brought about by Fuller's references to Darwin. He satisfactorily demolished the reviewer's points and referred to the acclaim which Fuller's Gold Medal essay had received as 'an exact vision of the future'. He quoted numbers of much more favourable reviews and listed three matters on which he thought Fuller original. They were, first, the application of scientific method to the study of war, a compliment which he qualified by admitting that Fuller was a clearer thinker than he was a writer; second, the attempt to organize a method of military thinking; third, the concept of the three spheres of war—mental, moral and physical. Praise was also heaped on Fuller's influence since 1920 on mechanization. 'His views have permeated and transformed military thought.' Methods of thought were also vital because of the modern speed of change which necessitated intellectual means of recomposing military values. The threefold order, however, Liddell Hart called 'too symmetrical' for his taste but submitted that it at least provided a 'mental weighing machine by which we can balance and co-ordinate our thought upon war'. Headlam's editorial, on the other hand, while attempting balance, lent support to the reviewer.

> Colonel Fuller [Headlam wrote] has the knack of making simple things appear difficult, and the ordinary man has neither the time nor the patience to puzzle his brain in extracting the obvious from the complicated. Colonel Fuller, in addition to being one of our most thoughtful and progressive soldiers, is an officer, as the writer of the article in this number points out, who has proved his capacity as a staff officer in the field, but there is no doubt that if his written work on military subjects is to be of real value to

practical soldiers, he should endeavour to cultivate a simpler and less diffuse style of writing. ... That [men of action] would do well to read Colonel Fuller's latest work is possible; that they will read it, is improbable.

This editorial was in no sense an apology and made no attempt to answer Liddell Hart's point that the reviewer had mounted a personal attack in violent language. Indeed Headlam's reference to Fuller's service as 'a staff officer in the field' could itself be construed as venomous.

On July 9th Fuller wrote and thanked Liddell Hart for his counter-blast in the *Army Quarterly*. It was, he wrote, 'a noble effort to support a friend'.[12] Unfortunately the damage was done. The undoubted weaknesses of *Foundations* were seized upon by Fuller's enemies and exploited mercilessly; Milne's confidence in the intellectual brilliance of his MA was undermined as his irritation with him grew. Meanwhile Fuller was once again decorated, this time with the CBE, no doubt in recognition of his years at Camberley.

In August 1925, it will be remembered, Liddell Hart had discussed the formation of an experimental mechanized force with Milne in the Norfolk Arms in Arundel. In March 1926 the Secretary of State announced in his speech on the Army Estimates that such a force was to be created. In April the CIGS put an outline plan to the Secretary of State which called for the creation at Tidworth—a military cantonment in the heart of Salisbury Plain—of a force comprising a tank battalion, an armoured car company, some mechanical gunners and sappers, a signals unit and three mechanical infantry battalions, two re-equipped with machine guns. Mechanical meant carried in motor vehicles. The Secretary of State agreed in principle on April 20th and the next month the CIGS asked Fuller to find out what could be assembled on Salisbury Plain, and to draw together views on the subject. Fuller suggested that what was most needed was a group consisting of a tank battalion, an armoured car company and a battery of self-propelled guns. In addition a mechanized infantry battalion, a mechanized machine-gun battalion and some dragon-drawn guns, cavalry and motorized RE would be desirable. He thought that the proposed three infantry battalions would be redundant and that the Brigadier who commanded the force would not be able to supervise the training of these three battalions. Sir John Moore, he pointed out, got rid of every redundant officer and man from his Model Brigade in 1803. Similar action was now required, or at least the Brigadier should be given a Second-in-Command to supervise the redundant infantry. Moreover no units in the force should be called upon to send drafts overseas. Milne accepted Fuller's first group, postponed consideration of the second and ruled that the three infantry battalions would not be required.[13] It should be noted, however, that there was confusion here because Milne's original proposal, although containing three infantry battalions, called for them all to be mechanical and two to be machine-gun units.

DSD was then asked to produce a paper on the subject. This his staff did with considerable speed and it was submitted to Milne on May 17th. The paper recommended Tidworth once again and continued that the 7th Infantry Brigade, which had four infantry battalions in station, was based on Tidworth and could be used as the basis for the force but should be renamed HQ Experimental Mechanized Force. Its commander would need a motor car, DSD argued somewhat oddly, and the force itself should consist of a tank battalion, two armoured-car companies, a special reconnaissance company, a field and an ordinary RA brigade, three infantry battalions, an RE and a signals unit. One of the infantry battalions should be converted to machine guns and mounted in 1 ton Morris vehicles.[14] At first sight the views of DSD and the MA to CIGS did not seem all that far apart except on the question of infantry battalions.

DSD also forwarded the views of the then Colonel G. M. Lindsay, the Inspector Royal Tank Corps. Lindsay thought that there were too many infantry battalions to motorize and too many machine guns in relation to the number of fighting vehicles. He opposed the rearming of existing units and the perpetuation of the regimental system, and he did not want any distribution of mechanized fighting vehicles outside the RTC for the time being except for artillery tanks; he believed also that the conversion of the cavalry should be delayed.[15] The CIGS responded in a minute to DSD signed on June 1st. 'I do not propose,' he wrote, 'that the Tank Corps should swallow the Army, but as this Corps is the only one which at present possesses trained personnel, we must draw on it in order to initiate the Experimental Unit. What the future has in store I do not know.' He also ruled: 'To begin with, no infantry will be required in the Experimental Unit. The object is not the creation of a light division on the French model; in place it should be looked upon as the embryo of a new mechanized fighting force.' The machine-gun battalion, he instructed, should be formed as soon as possible but: 'There is no necessity to alter the 7th Infantry Brigade at present.' 'I consider Colonel Lindsay's ideas very sound,' he concluded. 'And though at the present moment they are too ambitious, I want everything done to put them into effect as soon as possible.'[16] The influence of Fuller is obvious in this reply, but that influence had its limits. While he had succeeded in persuading Milne that conventional infantry were not required, he had obviously failed to convince him that the 7th Infantry Brigade needed a new structure or a new name. In fact in this respect the CIGS was being less adventurous than his DSD. On June 11th the latter replied and told the CIGS that he intended to appoint a Colonel Commandant to 7th Infantry Brigade to command for purposes of combined training a field artillery brigade, a pack artillery battery, a medium artillery brigade, three infantry battalions, a tank battalion (or battalions; this is not clear) and two armoured-car companies. The CIGS's instructions that infantry would not be required appears to have been ignored although it was probably intended that one or more of the infantry battalions would be motorized or converted to a machine-gun role. The GOC 3 Division was to supervise but the various Arms were to remain under their own commanders for training other than that of a combined nature. The CIGS approved these proposals though with some misgivings.[17] All these minutes must have passed through Fuller's hands.

In July a financial obstacle arose. Sanction for the money required for the erection of the buildings the force would require was difficult to obtain. There were also difficulties about converting one of the chosen infantry battalions, the Somerset Light Infantry, to machine guns because it was due to relieve its sister battalion in Egypt.[18] The August holidays followed; General Burnett-Stuart, by now commanding 3 Division, was told by DSD that the force would come under his direction, but he was given no clear objectives for which he was driven, one imagines unsuccessfully, to ask. In his letter to DSD he pointed out that infantry would not be able to keep pace with the rest of the force unless mounted in armoured cross-country vehicles. He also stated that it would be useless handing over the force to an ordinary officer like himself; experts and visionaries were required with 'a touch of the divine fire'.[19] September followed without any final resolution of the financial problem. Fuller told Liddell Hart that he thought Experimental Brigade was a better term than Mechanical Force which reminded him of Archimedes or Henry Ford.[20] That same month Milne suddenly said to Fuller: 'I am going to send you to India.'[21] This was a bombshell. Admittedly it was only to be a visit but it would mean that Fuller would be unable to exert any further influence on the negotiations leading up to the creation of the Experimental Force until his return. He had known for some time that Milne was worried about India; indeed modernization of the British Army depended at least in part on modernization of the Army in India since the one was the base for the other. He had also known that Milne was contemplating sending an officer to Delhi but Fuller had suggested Lindsay. As he wrote in his *Memoirs*: 'I was to be the victim.'[22] It is impossible now to know exactly why Milne sent Fuller to India when he did. Perhaps he was tired of his presence. Perhaps he placed India high in his hierarchy of military priorities and thought Fuller was the best man to tackle it; certainly there was growing concern about the Russian threat to India in the event of war with that country, although Indian military matters were the responsibility of the India Office and not the War Office.[23] Perhaps he had been impressed by Fuller's knowledge of India, by 1926, of course, two decades out of date. Perhaps he had been shown an advance copy of the book Fuller published on October 19th, *Imperial Defence, 1588–1914*, in which in a rather slim volume, Fuller, with great clarity, considerable historical perception and no cabbalistic language whatever, argued against the League of Nations and advocated instead a League of British Nations, held together by both fear and affection and guarded by a strong defensive organization. Perhaps a combination of all these played its part. When Fuller asked what Milne wanted him to do in India, Milne said he was too busy to tell him and even the day before he went he was told: 'You know all my ideas, so carry on.'[24] This attitude could have stemmed either from great confidence in Fuller or lack of any real interest in his mission.

Finance, however, were interested when Fuller, told that there would be difficulty in getting a berth on a troopship at such short notice, asked for authorization to travel by Pullman, civilian ferry and Blue Train to Marseilles and thence first class on the P & O *Kaiser-i-Hind* to India. The official so tackled demurred but agreed to co-operate when it was suggested to him that he should explain his decision to the CIGS. This small difficulty surmounted, Fuller made his farewells to Sonia and left London on October 7th.

His arrival in Delhi just over two weeks later was somewhat marred by the fact that the C-in-C, Field Marshal Birdwood, although warned of his coming, had gone off on leave to Assam. The Chief of Staff, Lieutenant-General Sir Andrew Skeen, arrived from Simla a day later. Fuller found him to be a man of great charm 'and as a Crusader he would have looked superb in chain armour'.[25] Skeen, however, was so immersed in the problems of mountain warfare that Fuller decided he would have to tour the Frontier before he could hold any useful discussions with him. Accordingly he set off on October 31st and spent a month travelling by car in the Peshawar and Quetta areas of the border with Afghanistan. This expedition he thoroughly enjoyed and it confirmed his view that the fundamental military problem was one of communications. Once good motor roads had been driven into the mountains, lorried columns could supply the frontier troops quickly and easily, and except on supply days the roads needed only to be patrolled by armoured cars. Off the roads light tanks could operate up the 'nullahs' or river beds. Such a scheme would be more effective than the use of aircraft. He also became convinced that the military problem itself was not the fundamental one; this was economic and would only be solved by trade and prosperity leading to the civilization of the tribesmen.[26] On his return to Delhi at the end of November he expounded these ideas to Skeen. Back in London a fortnight later he submitted a long written report to Milne but although this was considered a most 'insubordinate document'[27] little action resulted. Indeed no major attempt to reorganize the Army in India took place until Hore-Belisha intervened in 1937. However, the trip did lead to the publication of an article by Fuller in the *USI of India Journal* in October 1927 entitled 'Tanks in India'[28] in which he advocated light tanks transported in six-wheeled lorries as both the tactical answer to the Frontier problem and the organizational answer to the problem created by the existence of different sorts of armies in the UK and in India. It also led to the writing and publication, in 1931, of *India in Revolt* in which the whole Indian question is considered much more comprehensively and politically.

In 1926 Fuller also published two more books, both very short. One was called, *Atlantis–America and the Future*, and in this Fuller expressed his concern about the future nature of the United States once her population had grown to equal that of China; the other was entitled, *Pegasus-Problem of Transportation* in which he advocated roadless commercial vehicles and wanted to help to solve the problem of unemployment by peopling the Empire with British stock. He was becoming a prolific writer and must have devoted most of his spare time to the pen, a devotion with which his childless marriage obviously did not interfere. Articles by Fuller continued to crop up frequently in the journals, and two published in 1926 in the *RA Journal* must be mentioned. One, called 'Tactics of Penetration',[29] is evidence that he still believed in penetration but also felt that envelopment would again be possible when armies mechanized. The other, 'The Ideal Army of the Artillery Cycle' set out Fuller's latest thinking on mechanized warfare.[30] The army of 1946, he thought, would contain heavy, light and pursuit divisions. The heavy division would comprise scout, assault and destroyer tanks, self-propelled guns and tank-infantrymen in cross-country vehicles; the light divisions, scout and destroyer tanks only; and the pursuit divisions, pursuit tanks only. This would mean a small, professional army and an army which was entirely armoured. Artillery would have become the principal arm but its vehicles would look like tanks; its guns would be small calibre, high velocity and designed to shoot tanks, not infantry. The assault tanks would do the job done in the past by infantry. Also some tanks would have three spare crews, carried in cross-country vehicles, and trained to fight as infantry. There would necessarily be a change from linear to area strategy, rear attack would become a normal operation of war and bases therefore must be able to protect themselves. This article, it could be argued, called for an all-tank army and justified Milne's fears about the RTC swallowing the Army. Actually Fuller's views were more subtle than his detractors gave him credit for and, although he doubted the use of infantry in the offensive—and here Liddell Hart disagreed with him—his real position was based on an unwillingness to accept that foot infantry could fight alongside, and keep up with, tanks. In this connection it is important to remember that the first tanks did indeed perform an infantry function; the need for bigger guns only grew from the need for tank to fight tank; the need for speed for exploitation and strategical paralysis grew out of the siege-breaking success of the machine itself and the vulnerability of horsed cavalry. The confusion between the functions of armoured fighting vehicles, rifle infantry and horsed cavalry was compounded by the existence of human institutions labelled infantry, cavalry and tanks, each of which had innumerable vested interests often unrelated to any contemporary military function. However these articles and the thoughts they provoke hint at Fuller's future preoccupations. For the time being he was still at the centre of a stage about to see a simple trial of a very simple mechanized brigade. It was a trial which would give scope to Fuller's continuing interest in penetration and envelopment, in training and in the application of scientific method to the solution of military problems; but it was also to be an affair in which Fuller's almost fanatical sense of dedication, and his confidence in his own cleverness, were to trip him up.

From India he had written significantly to Liddell Hart: 'There are two classes of human beings, those who are destined to succeed sorrowfully and those who are destined to fail joyfully . . . I belong to the second class.'[31] Unfortunately the joyfulness of failure is an emotion most easily discerned and savoured in retrospect. There was not to be much joy for Fuller in the next few months. While he was still in India the financial problem with the Experimental Mechanized Force had been resolved, and on November 1st Milne told the Secretary of State that it was to be set up.[32] Prior to that, however, in October, General Sir David Campbell, the Military Secretary, who had been selected by Milne as GOC in C Aldershot Command, had put forward his views on mechanization to the CIGS. These were extremely advanced and gave cavalry only a short lease of life while at the same time giving infantry a much lower priority than tanks. In India, he felt tanks could replace infantry. Milne had surprised Campbell by making a very cautious response.[33] This was the more surprising as, again during Fuller's absence, Milne staged a display of mechanized vehicles at Camberley on November 13th for the Dominion Prime Minister's Conference at which the new 'Independent' tank prototype was disclosed for the first time and a miniature 'Blitzkrieg', complete with air support, was mounted on the spectators whose ardour, however, was symbolically quenched by an incessant downpour of rain. The 'Independent', a 31 ton giant capable of 20 mph, was never developed.

On December 18th Milne told Fuller that he had selected him to command the Experimental Force.[34] Fuller later expressed surprise that he had become the chosen one because he was quite content to be MA to the CIGS. This was false modesty. Milne, in spite of his natural caution, would have found it extremely difficult to choose anyone else. Perhaps also Fuller's absence in India had convinced him that his office would be a more comfortable place were Boney not to sit just outside the door. This apart, it would have been unjust and stupid to give the force to another officer; Fuller had lived with tank tactics and strategy since December 1916. It was entirely appropriate that he should be called upon to examine their future and the future of mechanized warfare. On December 18th, 1926 he reached the pinnacle of his military career; few professional soldiers have such an opportunity in peacetime as Fuller faced then. The military world was at his feet. On Christmas Eve, he received the then customary letter, offering him the appointment, from the Military Secretary, still Sir David Campbell. In this he discovered that he had been appointed to command, not an Experimental Mechanized Force, but the 7th Infantry Brigade. He thought this was a mistake, and accepted the post, but he soon discovered that it was not, and that as the Mechanized Force was merely a temporary formation his appointment had to be linked to something more permanent. On the 31st he was instructed to take over at Tidworth on May 1st, 1927.

It was over this question of the name and scope of his appointment that tensions and misunderstandings developed to such a pitch that in the end Fuller cast himself down from his pinnacle into the outer darkness. In the first place, just as he should not have been surprised at his selection, he should also not have been surprised that it was to command 7th Infantry Brigade. After all, it was Milne himself who had told DSD not to change the name of its HQ to HQ Experimental Mechanized Force and who had agreed to the inclusion of three infantry battalions; Fuller must have seen the papers which passed between them on this subject. Secondly, it was, and is, an honour and a high military achievement to be given command of a brigade. This was not enough for Fuller. He felt that the duties of a brigade commander would impinge too heavily on the priorities of an experimenter in mechanized warfare. For some weeks he turned the matter over in his mind and even told Liddell Hart that he was not overjoyed and regretted leaving the War Office where he felt that he was needed. 'I like this monastery,' he wrote, 'it is so peaceful and absurd.'[35] On February 5th he went down to Tidworth to see for himself what command of the brigade amounted to, and he took Sonia with him.

To the British Army of the twentieth century the words 'Tidworth' and 'Catterick' have a flavour to them which, next to 'Aldershot', conjures up most pungently the atmosphere of service in a military cantonment at home. In 1895 North and South Tidworth were very small and sleepy villages on the edge of Salisbury Plain. In that year, however, the War Office decided to purchase parts of the Plain to accommodate new ranges and training areas and to establish permanent barracks. By 1900 over 43,000 acres had been acquired and barracks were being rapidly erected. Tidworth Garrison itself developed very much on the Indian pattern, a fact which was emphasized by the lush and delightfully incongruous names given to the barracks and still used today. Jellalabad, Aliwal, Candahar, Bhurtpore, Lucknow, Mooltan—what un-Tidworth-like visions do these red-brick Edwardian buildings evoke? After the First World War more land was acquired and the training areas proved ideal for tanks. Even today Tidworth has a raw and frontier look about it, except for those deliciously named barracks, and when Fuller went down in 1927 it must have seemed even more incongruous than it does today. Tidworth can grow on its residents but at first sight it does not attract.

It certainly did not attract Fuller, although one assumes he was not affected by the look of the place; Sonia may have been. He saw the Brigade Commander, Colonel G. H. N. Jackson (promotion to brigadier was not then automatic and immediate for brigade commanders), and discovered that it would not only be a question of commanding a brigade, and using parts of it, together with other temporarily allocated units, as an Experimental Force, but also of commanding Tidworth Garrison. This appears to have been too much for Fuller. On the way back to London he called at the Staff College and discussed the matter with the future General Sir Bernard Paget, who had been associated with the 1921 Experimental Brigade. Paget then wrote him a letter which he received on the 7th and which encouraged Fuller at least to ask for an Area Commandant to look after the Garrison, and a Staff Captain and shorthand-typist to assist him in running the Experimental Force.[36] The same day Fuller also saw Liddell Hart at the War Office, and although there is no record of what advice Liddell Hart proffered he never claimed subsequently that he tried to dissuade Fuller from complaining to the CIGS.

On the 8th Fuller spoke to Milne about what must have appeared to him as the unwanted threefold nature of his future command. He pointed out that only one of the infantry battalions in 7 Brigade was to be converted into a mechanized machine-gun battalion and that in consequence he would be commanding two separate formations, an 'ad hoc' experimental one, and a conventional one. On top of this he had to consider the requirements of the post of Garrison Commander. If he failed to carry out the mechanized experiment successfully then every soldier opposed to it would regard it as a failure of the newer arms. It was as important to convert the Army as it was to experiment and neither could be done with the existing staff and multiplicity of duties. He continued:

> I do not pretend to be a Sir John Moore, who . . . got rid of all unnecessary officers and men, and . . . established an organization through which he could rapidly and economically convert ideas into actions. If Moore considered this necessary, it surely is still more so in my case.[37]

Having delivered himself of this carefully constructed declaration he proceeded to ask Milne for permission to hand over three of the infantry battalions to another officer, either a 2 IC or a battalion commander, and Tidworth Garrison to the Commander of the Tidworth Cavalry Brigade. He ended by asking for a permanent Staff Captain and a shorthand typist. The CIGS told him not to be silly, and in view of the fact that it was Milne himself who had previously decided not to alter 7 Brigade this was no doubt in Milne's view a mild response. Undoubtedly the arrangements which Fuller had a hand in making in the summer had been somewhat distorted in the final outcome but the distortion was not really all that dramatic. The proposals the CIGS had originally agreed excluded the three unmechanized infantry battalions; these had crept back into the plot, however, by the middle of June, long before Fuller was sent to India. The situation was a fluid one and could almost certainly have been sorted out on the spot by an officer as experienced, able, energetic and forceful as Fuller. Indeed, it would have been within his own power to delegate control of the three battalions to another officer within the brigade. It is certainly possible to regard the whole affair as a storm in a teacup and it is clear that the CIGS so regarded it; Fuller's priorities, however, were intellectual and organizational, as well as personal, and he felt impelled to seek a perfect set of conditions for the initiation of his experiments. Moreover he felt confident in the strength of his own position, as he had cause to do. He handed the CIGS his suggestions in writing; these were placed in a desk drawer without being read. Significantly the written suggestions contained a request for a small entertainment allowance for as long as he had to deal with the large number of units envisaged in the current proposals. This request he did not mention in his *Memoirs*. It is apparent from the paper that the real sticking-points for Fuller were not the infantry battalions or the allowance, but the Garrison command, the staff captain and the shorthand typist.[38]

Fuller waited for a week before broaching the subject again. He felt that the CIGS was jeopardizing his whole policy of modernization by refusing to undo the bungling of DSD's department. In fact, as one can now see, this was too black-and-white a view of the situation. It was Milne's own cautiousness which Fuller was assaulting and it is surprising that he did not realize this at the time, and appears never to have done so subsequently, in spite of the fact that he was made well aware in the end of the reality of Milne's lack of practical, as distinct from theoretical, audacity. On the 15th he asked if his paper had been read and on being given a negative reply he wrote to General Burnett-Stuart, the GOC 3 Div who had asked for a 'visionary' to command the Experimental Force, in the hope that he would intervene with the CIGS. Burnett-Stuart, however, was put out by Fuller's desire to be freed from routine duties and the command of infantry units which he must have seen as a bid for independence from divisional control. He replied on the 18th and Fuller took his letter as a rebuff. It is true that he told Fuller that he had been invited to become one of his brigade commanders, not to produce 'a new military heaven and earth';[39] he also warned Fuller against trying to reorganize his division which he preferred to run himself, and against losing his sense of proportion. But these criticisms were balanced by the expression of pleasure that Fuller was coming to work with him, by recognition, both that he did have that spark of divine fire Burnett-Stuart had previously mentioned to DSD, and that Fuller's anxieties were due to concern lest he should not be able to live up to what he thought was expected of him.[40] Fuller, however, was upset and two days later he spoke to Liddell Hart to tell him that he was thinking of presenting an ultimatum to Milne.

For a fortnight Fuller's future hung in the balance of his mind. Then on March 3rd the Secretary of State announced: 'Arrangements have been made to assemble in the Salisbury Plain area an experimental mechanical force, composed of entirely mechanized units ... whose primary function will be to study the tactical employment and the organization of a highly mobile force of this nature.' This statement and Burnett-Stuart's letter precipitated Fuller into his next action which was to tackle the CIGS again and to ask him if he had given any thought to his suggestions. Milne told him that he had not and that he did not know where they were. Even when Fuller told him in which drawer of his desk they could be found, Milne still refused to consider them. Fuller then left the room and wrote out his resignation, because 'it would have been a fraudulent act on my part to fill an appointment which in no way resembled the one made public by the Secretary of State';[41] nobody told the latter about this resignation because he repeated his previous statement in the Commons on March 7th and added: 'This force will be placed under the command of an officer who has made a special study of mechanical warfare'. That officer was obviously Fuller.

Middle-ranking officers in the British Armed Services do not often resign on matters of principle; indeed resignation on such grounds is almost as rare amongst very senior officers. Officers accept that their position is subordinate to that of their political and civilian masters and so are unlikely to leave over matters of political principle. Technological, strategic or tactical affairs, on the other hand, rarely reach such white heat, at least in peacetime; when they do, of course, great personal stresses and conflicts of loyalty can be created. Fuller believed that the causes of his resignation were matters of enormous technological, strategic and tactical importance; to many of his brother officers, however, it must have appeared that he had chosen to make a fuss over a very minor matter. He had been given the Experimental Force. What did the name matter, or the minutiae of control and composition? There had to be garrison commanders, and establishments, anyway, were notoriously difficult to change. If Fuller wanted to alter the arrangements the best way, the usual way, the easy way, was to do so quietly on the ground. The resignation, also, came as a great surprise. In Fuller's own words it, 'fell like an exploding bomb—the War Office was upheaved';[42] in Liddell Hart's words it became 'more difficult for the opponents of progress to ascribe his refusal of the appointment to low motives—for most ambitious men would have been more likely to swallow their doubts than to sacrifice their career to a scruple.'[43] Fuller claimed that his action was in no way disloyal, and yet this is just what many officers thought it was. In being true to himself and his principles, Fuller was being disloyal to the group and, of course, most important of all, to his master, the CIGS. When the MA to the CIGS resigns on a matter of principle it is obvious to all that the two cannot agree, and when the MA is someone as well known, and as committed to mechanization as Fuller was in 1927, then the conclusion will inevitably be drawn that the CIGS and his MA are parting on that issue.

General Campbell, who had just given up the post of Military Secretary, wrote immediately to Fuller from Aldershot and begged him to withdraw his resignation. His letter arrived on the 7th, the very day the Secretary of State was making his announcement about Fuller in the Commons. He wrote:

> I have heard with absolute consternation that you have sent your papers in, and I am writing to beg you to withdraw them—and you are the only man in the whole Army to whom I would make this request. Your going would not only be an irreparable loss to the Army in itself—greater

than anyone else's going would be—but I am quite certain it will also do the CIGS a great deal of harm among the younger and the progressive school in the Army. In my opinion, if you have any affection for the Army, which I know you have, you should put yourself without reserve at the disposal of the CIGS, and carry on for at least a year in whatever billet he wants for you; after that you can reconsider the whole matter. We cannot afford to lose men like you. Do think this over.[44]

On the 8th Fuller received another letter, this time from Burnett-Stuart, in which the GOC 3 Div told Fuller that he was distressed at his resignation and hoped that his previous letter had not contributed to the decision.[45] It had, of course, done precisely that.

Fuller wrote a letter of explanation to Campbell who agreed in his reply that Fuller could not accept the 7th Infantry Brigade, feeling as he did, but again asked him to withdraw his resignation. He saw Fuller on the 17th and tried to see him a second time on the 18th, failed and wrote again. 'The Chief,' he told Fuller, '... feels ... that he can do *nothing* as long as a pistol (in the shape of your application to retire) is presented at his head.'[46] He also pointed out that Fuller had been offered the job, not ordered to take it.[47] This letter finally made Fuller change his mind. He saw Milne and told him that he had not realized that his resignation would be regarded as a threat. He had applied to retire because he disapproved of the way the Experimental Force was being set up and that this was all he could do, without appearing to bargain. It is difficult to accept that Fuller's actions at this time were dictated by nothing more than a desire to disassociate himself from a course of action of which he disagreed. On the one hand he must surely have believed that his resignation would cause the CIGS to change his own mind and accept his suggestions about the Tidworth Force. Indeed the resignation itself was a direct and immediate consequence of Fuller's failing, by ordinary means, to persuade Milne to make changes. On the other hand he may have had more personal reasons for turning down the Tidworth job. It was probably Sonia who argued against accepting it on the grounds that there would not have been enough money for the entertainment involved. This latter factor seems extraordinary in the circumstances, but lesser reasons have had greater consequences.[48] It is more likely that Sonia's unwillingness to go to Tidworth as the Garrison Commander's wife, or even her unsuitability for that role, were merely additional factors which helped push Fuller into putting his papers in. Whether this was entirely a moral gesture, or whether it was also a threat intended to compel Milne to make changes and to lead to Fuller becoming Commander of an Experimental Force rather than an infantry brigade and a garrison are questions to which we can never obtain a complete answer. It would, however, be very surprising and entirely out of character if Fuller had not nurtured the hope that his resignation might serve to put matters right to his own, and the Army's, advantage. Of course he saw these as synonymous. Even in this more or less final interview with Milne he continued to bargain and told him that he would withdraw his resignation if Milne assured him that it was his intention to modernize the Army and that he would not insist on his going to Tidworth. The CIGS gave him these assurances and Fuller withdrew his resignation.

By these actions Fuller gained nothing for himself. Liddell Hart believed that Fuller should not have withdrawn his resignation having once offered it because this weakened his stand without any concrete guarantee, and this is certainly true. However, one must bear in mind when making a judgment that Generals Campbell and Burnett-Stuart, and no doubt others, had brought some very strong and telling 'military' pressures and arguments to bear on a man who had been a regular officer all his adult life. Liddell Hart also believed that Milne, had he been more magnanimous, could have preserved 'Fuller's services for the great experiment, and at the same time put the experimental force on a proper basis'.[49] This is difficult to accept. Fuller specifically asked not to be given the Tidworth job and would only have accepted it on his terms,[50] what Liddell Hart called 'a proper basis'. Milne could not have agreed to such changes in Fuller's favour once it became known, as it was inside the military establishment, that he was making changes he personally thought unnecessary or unwise because his MA would otherwise resign. Fuller's application to resign was probably the worst decision of his life. If it was in any way a threat it was based on a gross overestimation of the strength of his own position; if it was not then it was a very selfish act, fundamentally based on a Pilate-like washing of hands. Fuller was not a Pilate and there must have been an element of threat in what he did. He, himself, called it a 'really stupid affair'[51] and so it was, or rather an affair of pride, rigidity, misjudgment, missed opportunity and great emotion. The heart of the tragedy, however, lay in the fact that there was really so little difference between what Fuller was offered and what he went to the wall for. In the last analysis it boiled down to authority to delegate responsibilities which he could almost cer-tainly have delegated once arrived in Tidworth, authority to hand over the duties of Tidworth Garrison Commander, which need have occupied him for no more than a day a week, and authority to employ a Staff Captain and a shorthand typist, both of whom he could probably have acquired in due course on the ground. It was really no wonder that the CIGS had said, 'Don't be silly.' It must be concluded that Fuller can have had no inkling at the time that these modest demands would lead inexorably to his resigna-tion. It had always been his practice to make such demands; in the past they had usually been met but unfortunately this time his fraying relationship with Milne would not stand the strain. 'Boney' had been too clever again and was now to reap the harvest of the asperity and the unacceptable brilliance he had been sowing for years.

It was next decided that Colonel Jack Collins should be trans-ferred from command of the 9th to that of the 7th Infantry Brigade. Fuller could not stay in the War Office because a replacement as MA had already been nominated, this time a Lieutenant-Colonel. However General Ironside, now moved from the Staff College to command the 2nd Division at Aldershot, asked for Fuller as his GSO I, and on April 9th his appointment to Tidworth was formally cancelled. On April 21st it was an-nounced in the Press that Collins was to be transferred from 9 Brigade to 7 Brigade. This was too much, in turn, for Liddell Hart. Fuller had not told him about his resignation until April 1st in the hope that Milne would take adequate steps to fulfil his assurance that he was intent on modernization. Even when in the picture, Liddell Hart refrained from public comment, but when the bare announcement of Collins' appointment convinced him that nothing was going to be done to put right the inadequacies in the control or composition of the Experimental Force, he wrote an article for the next day's *Daily Telegraph* under the heading: 'An Army Mystery—Is There a Mechanical Force?' This caused another great explosion in the War Office and the Secretary of State complained that he had been misled into believing that a properly constituted mechanical force was to be set up, not an infantry brigade with some mechanized units added on from time to time. Milne put the blame on Burnett-Stuart for failing to work things out satisfactorily with Fuller. On the 22nd the *Westminster Gazette* came out with an article much like Liddell Hart's but under the more sensational headline: 'Mystery of the Mechanical Army'. This was sold, suitably advertised by a poster, outside the War Office door.

As a result of this Press campaign the War Office was obliged to repeat the Secretary of State's announcement of March 3rd. The *Daily Telegraph* commented that this was a pledge that a new mechanized formation was being set up 'and not merely tacking on a number of mechanical units to an infantry brigade. ... We shall watch with heightened interest for this force to begin its training, and, as a foretaste, for the wording of the *London Gazette*, in which Colonel Collins's appointment and the fresh appointment to command the 7th Infantry Brigade are announced.'[52] As Fuller told Liddell Hart, the *Daily Telegraph* could not fail either to win the game or call the War Office bluff. In the event the *Daily Telegraph* took nearly all the tricks. On May 12th Collins was gazetted as 'to command the Experimental Mechanized Force and the 7th Infantry Brigade' and he was subsequently given ample staff assistance and allowed to assign the unmechanized infantry battalions to other brigades for training. The only one of Fuller's conditions not met was that Collins had to act as Tidworth Garrison Commander, but he actually became, as a priority, Commander Experimental Mechanized Force and this was more than Fuller had even asked for.

Although Fuller's application to resign achieved nothing in itself, it must be admitted that Liddell Hart's journalism certainly did. It resulted in a restriction being placed by the Secretary of State on Liddell Hart's access to the War Office but it also put back the Experimental Force into something like the shape Fuller thought it ought to have had in May 1926. But, of course, it was at the expense of Fuller's leadership and one cannot but believe that the changes in organization and composition achieved in

May 1927 were of little importance compared with the loss of Fuller to the force. So little effect did the experiments have that the future Field-Marshal Montgomery–Massingberd was still talking about the necessity of using tanks to support cavalry at the end of 1928.[53] For Fuller it was undoubtedly the virtual end of his military career and of a road he had trod since December 1916 when he had first been posted to the Heavy Branch. That road had led to Cambrai, to 'Plan 1919', to the Gold Medal Essay, to fame and to the establishment of the Royal Tank Corps. Henceforth Fuller was never again to be given the command of mechanized units, and had in fact only some three and a half years of employed service in front of him. The military establishment did not find it easy to forgive either his insults or his brilliance and enthusiasm, and the ridicule to which *Foundations* had given rise undoubtedly undermined his position. Had he gone to Tidworth it might have led to the development of a mechanized army capable of saving Western Europe from Hitler in 1940. But perhaps, given the political and economic climate of the time that is unlikely, and for success, it would have been necessary for similar developments to have taken place in France. Perhaps, at least, the British Army would have used its armour differently and more effectively in the later stages of the Second World War; perhaps the Allies would have got to Berlin first. Who knows? These are merely unprovable speculations. Certainly the Experimental Force of 1927–8 achieved very little of substance and this was undoubtedly partly due to Collins's caution and lack of mechanical vision and enthusiasm. However it was because Fuller's active military career came to such an end that he was able, and was obliged, to devote his brilliance and his energies to the pen.

On April 30th he left the War Office, as an inmate, for the last time and in May established himself, until he found a house, in the Officer's Club at Aldershot. From there, later in the month, he wrote to Starr complaining that people were so stupid. 'We, first of all,' he wrote, 'have got to get power.'[54] Power was to elude him.

7. *A Vision of the Future of War—1927-33*

For the next six years, until his retirement at the end of 1933, Fuller, although still a serving officer, was consigned, politely but effectively, to the military outer darkness, and the fact that this consignment took him to such extremely soldierly-sounding locations as Aldershot, Rhine Army and Catterick, and translated him from Colonel to Major-General, made it very difficult for him to complain, particularly after the Tidworth episode. But following Tank Corps Headquarters, DSD's Department, Camberley and the CIGS's office, it was just as much an exile as Ovid's Black Sea coast; and Bombay, had he gone there as a Major-General when the post was offered in 1931, would have been the ultimate in hot Siberias.

There is no doubt that *Foundations* did Fuller harm at a most crucial point in the development of the British Army. As he wrote to Liddell Hart in 1949: 'except for a mine-exploder, we had in being in the year 1926 all the makings of an armoured fighting force. But after I left Milne in the spring of 1927 the whole thing was gradually dropped.'[1] And Fuller's leaving greatly facilitated the dropping. Moreover the slings and arrows with which he was assaulted in the *Army Quarterly* were not confined to that journal. In the second half of 1927, after Fuller had taken up his post in 2 Division and moved into a house in Farnborough, V. W. Germains, who normally and significantly wrote under the pseudonym 'A Rifleman', produced a very readable book entitled *The 'Mechanization' of War*[2] which comprised a major assault on Fuller's theories. The book began with a foreword by Major-General Sir Frederick Maurice, Professor of Military Studies in the University of London. Maurice put on record the fact that he was disposed to attach greater importance than Germains did to the part played by tanks in the First World War but he agreed that tanks were dependent on other arms for their greatest effect and were not, in the contemporary state of the art, either independent or invulnerable. Tank enthusiasts who talked of revolutionizing war and of doing away with infantry and cavalry had to have their claims very carefully examined.[3] He went on to doubt if any weapon had ever revolutionized war. Railways had probably effected more change than weapons, and aircraft might eventually do the same, but these changes did not alter the fundamental principles of strategy and to date the study of military history from August 8th, 1918 was ridiculous.[4] Maurice also felt moved to comment on the fact that some of the tank enthusiasts were attempting to create a so-called science of war. Maurice did not believe that commanders who attempted to imitate the scientists and confined themselves to a cautious process from ascertained fact to ascertained fact would get very far. The commander normally had 'to deal with the unexpected . . . upon incomplete data. He must, therefore, be an artist, not a scientist.'[5] He concluded the foreword by pointing to the danger that concern with technique would lead younger students of war to forget the art. Reliance upon one particular weapon, of which we had only limited experience, was a dangerous process even if made attractive by the probability that casualties would therefore be reduced. The CIGS had promised to restore mobility to our Regular Army. That was where mechanization was important, and important also for the Reserves who in the event of mobilization would not be fit enough to march.[6]

Professor Maurice's comments were undoubtedly aimed principally at Fuller but were moderate and rational, at least for the most part. 'All-tank' armies, in the sense of armies consisting entirely of mechanically propelled, armoured, tracked, direct-fire, weapon platforms, would have been a false start. It is arguable, of course, that Fuller and his followers never advocated such a development, that they only sought to abolish foot infantry and horsed cavalry. Nevertheless it is demonstrable that Fuller in the twenties was sceptical of everything except tanks, but that he later changed his mind. There may have been a time when tanks as an independent arm could win wars in certain places, at least under air superiority, and the Sinai may have been such a place in 1967, but the Yom Kippur War showed recently that that time has gone. The principles of war, or strategy, if they can be said to

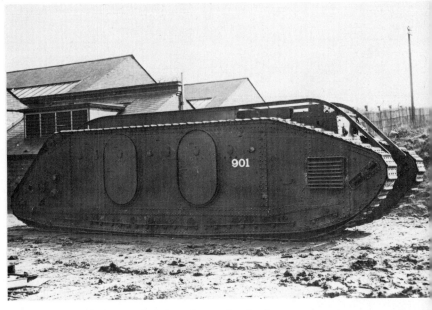

An armoured infantry carrier of 1918: one for the future

The Medium D tank (without armament, showing the front on the right):
the instrument of victory?

Fuller as a colonel *circa* 1919

have any validity at all, have an unchanging one, as Fuller would have been the first to agree. Maurice's views about weapons were very similar to Fuller's own; weapon changes altered the instrument, not the principles, of war. Maurice's criticisms of the science of war were reasonable, although Fuller himself did not deny the importance of the art, provided it was based on the science. Modern developments tend to justify Fuller rather than Maurice; generals today are extremely ill-advised if they do not proceed cautiously from ascertained fact to ascertained fact. The concept, perpetuated by Maurice, that wire and machine guns only 'threatened' to destroy the army's mobility, was more irrational, of course, since wire and machine guns had destroyed the mobility of unmechanized armies more than a decade before. It was the relation between the penetrability of wool and steel which had been central to Fuller's thinking since 1916, but which had still perhaps not been entirely accepted by Maurice. Until very recent times there has been a military trauma about mechanization. On the one hand almost all officers saw the efficacy of tanks but on the other they felt an emotional attachment to the older arms. The ultimate solution has been the retention of the arms, except that all travel and generally fight inside vehicles which look like tanks. Anti-tank guided missiles, and guerilla warfare, have now arrived to complicate the issue and perhaps complete a full circle of the wheel. All this, however, is far removed from 1927 and from Germains' more extreme views for which Maurice's foreword was only a softening prelude.

Germains argued that there was a technique, not a science, of war and that the postulation of laws of war was absurd; he also pointed out that mechanization was not a process confined to the introduction of tanks and cross-country tractors, since guns, aeroplanes, lorries, trains, steamships and telegraphs were all mechanical inventions. However, he then argued that the popular theory that the deadlock on the Western Front was only finally solved by tanks was insupportable from the facts. The deadlock was a consequence of balanced military resources and standardized methods and was broken by the entry of America into the war. He castigated Fuller for dwelling 'upon the glamour and glory of the great Break-Through of August 8th, 1918' rather than thinking 'over the Tank fiasco of March 21st'.[7] He questioned the effectiveness of tanks in the defensive and further pointed out that German attacks without tanks were just as successful as Allied attacks with tanks. If the Germans had been able to attack in strength in 1917 they might well have won the war without tanks at all. There were many other factors leading to victory in July and August 1918 than a few hundred tanks. Much of this is reasonable enough argument but the full emotional flavour of Germains' writing comes through in a passage in which he tried to contend that Fuller and his friends must be wrong because Haig, Foch and Ludendorff did not have faith in tanks as substitutes for guns, infantry or even cavalry. 'Can we seriously believe,' he wrote, 'that the vision of all these men, the chosen leaders of the greatest nations in the world engaged in the greatest struggle known to history, was so over-clouded by tradition that, in the elegant phrase of one of our "scientific" writers, they "saw things as cows see them"?'[8] This kind of *argumentum ad hominem* falls abrasively on the modern ear at a time when the people are quite prepared to believe that their leaders are fools, and if middle-aged or older, blinkered and inhibited by tradition. Fuller's reference to the bovine nature of military vision had come in *Foundations* when he was commenting on the inability of soldiers in the pre-war decade to accept the views of Bloch about the military stalemate that would develop in any future war.[9]

A considerable portion of Germains' book was devoted to a consideration of the problem of tank design. He had obviously studied this in some depth and he pointed out, without reference to underwater weapons, that it was more difficult to armour a tank than a warship because the tank's entire bulk was exposed. The tank was a compromise between armour, armament, speed and endurance. But any gain in one element had to be offset by sacrifice in others unless overall size was increased, and this conflicted with the need to present a small target, since tanks could never be proof against artillery and would always have vulnerable tracks. Tank guns would never be very accurate because of the irregular motions of the gun platform. These inherent problems of tank design were exacerbated by the fact that tanks would never again achieve substantial surprise, to which their early successes were mainly due, and it was therefore cheaper to build anti-tank weapons than to build tanks. A great deal of what Germains had to say about tank design was based on sound thinking and thinking which Fuller himself had done or was about to do. Fuller knew well that there would one day be an effective counter to the tank; indeed once tank fought tank that counter could be said to exist. Germains' technique, however, was to exaggerate the stance of the protaganists of mechanized warfare. Thus he asked his readers to take the *Royal Sovereign*:

> mount her on caterpillar tracks, and you surely have the very apotheosis of the land-warship. You have a mighty vessel, 580 feet long, towering upwards of one hundred feet above the ground, her bowels protected by thirteen-inch armour, her main gun-turrets by eleven-inch, and bristling with a formidable array of eight 15-inch and fourteen 6-inch guns. There are small calibres to deal with aircraft, and the entire structure, assuming no loss on the designed speed, can move across country at a rate of some 26 land miles an hour. It will be hopeless, you may think, for infantry and guns to stand up to the attack of so formidable a monster. Think the matter over.[10]

A very little thought will show that it would be absurd to build such supertanks. Of course no tank protagonist had ever suggested that they should be built but Germains argued that the *Royal Sovereign* concept illustrated the problem inherent in all

The phrase 'saw things as cows see them' must have particularly offended Germains because he returned to charge this particular windmill halfway through the book:

> It is emotionalism, not 'science', to talk about 'Witches' Sabbaths', 'Black Masses', and the rest of it. And it is impertinence to talk of the soldiers who 'saw things as cows see them'. Among these soldiers were men such as Schlieffen, Hindenburg, Joffre, Foch, Roberts, Kitchener, and that brilliant military historian, Col. G. F. R. Henderson. Are we seriously to believe that among all these men who had led abstemious lives, lives of study and research, such as forms a worthy comparison with the very best work done by leaders of thought in any other branch of human activity, there was to be found no man who really understood his business or who was able to shake himself free

from the 'miasma of military traditions'? Surely it requires
mental arrogance of no common degree, and a very actual
ignorance of facts in the writer who dares to put forward so
preposterous an assertion? [11]

Towards the end of the book Germains attacked Fuller's con-
tention in *Tanks in the Great War* that, in future mechanical war,
battles will become more and more like naval actions. This, he
argued, was 'to take a very hasty and superficial view of a many-
sided and complex problem. There are at sea no such things as
railways, roads, great cities, forests or swamps. To get a naval
analogy . . . we must conceive ships manoeuvring in waters filled
with treacherous shoals and shallows, pitted with jagged rocks,
sown with mines, yet threaded by passages known to the enemy,
and which enable him to concentrate at will.' [12] Again history
would support Fuller, at least as regards great differences between Flanders 1915–18 and the campaigns in France in 1940, in
the Western Desert in 1941–2 and in Sinai in 1967. Linear
entrenchment was greatly lessened as a permanent condition of
major war by the invention and development of the tank,
although the land sea certainly contained more surprises and
difficulties than Fuller envisaged. Germains was on surer ground,
however, when he wrote: 'The net result of "mechanization" is
not to eliminate the man, but to enhance his power.' The
infantryman of the future will be transported and supported by
vehicles but 'will play a part as essential in war as that of the
artisan in peace'. [13] His final advice could be summed as being to
go easy on tank building for fear of starting an arms race or
becoming over-dependent on petrol which was only obtainable
abroad. Cavalry, moreover, never formed more than one-sixth of
Napoleonic armies, neither should mechanized columns. A
national army, based on conscription, would always be essential
in war, and the small, professional, mechanized army would
merely be a valuable adjunct to it. It is only through a large
national army that we could escape deadlock and trench-warfare.
These sentiments appeared to have turned the Fuller thesis on its
head. Fuller was arguing that only armour could break the
stalemate and obviate trench warfare. Germains was arguing that
conscript infantry armies were required because small mechanical
armies could not defeat them. Germains was wrong. He over-

emphasized the value of size and underestimated the effectiveness of armour. But he made two very perceptive and prophetic points when he drew attention to the dangers of arms races and of dependence on overseas oil. *The 'Mechanization' of War* represented the educated, journalistic reply to Fuller. To have a book of 250 pages written primarily in order to attack your views was a sign both of the hostility those views aroused, but also of the importance which at least some members of the educated public put upon them.

Another sort of response flowed from the pen of Lieutenant-Colonel H. V. S. Charrington of the 12th Royal Lancers and a colleague of Fuller's at Camberley in 1925—a very educated, restrained and balanced military response. In 1927 this officer published *Where Cavalry Stands To-Day*,[14] a slender and sensible apologia for the cavalry. He admitted the limitations of cavalry on the western front, agreed that the absence of flanks prevented it making effective use of its mobility and accepted that aircraft were superior to cavalry for long-distance reconnaissance. He also agreed that, in conditions of trench warfare, cavalry must not be sent forward until the enemy's resistance had been completely broken in the portion of the front selected for their advance! Had cavalry been used in this way at Cambrai, he argued, the breach made by the tanks could have been exploited as it was at Amiens. In open warfare, or against an inferior enemy, the cavalry could still play a full part as Allenby had showed in Palestine. These were modest claims. Charrington concluded that if land forces were completely mechanized there would be no place for cavalry. Certainly some mechanization would take place and this process should be applied to most forms of horse-drawn transport. However there were disadvantages in complete mechanization. The world's petrol supply might fail, natural obstacles were not easily surmountable by mechanical vehicles, anti-tank obstacles could be created and neither tanks nor aeroplanes were suitable for police duties overseas. Drivers, moreover, easily became strained, particularly at night, mechanized units were difficult to transport by sea, and opposed mechanized landings were hazardous. A completely mechanized force would have great possibilities in suitable country but mechanical fighting vehicles would never be more than essential support to troops less constrained in their movements and could never entirely replace them.[15] Tactics therefore demanded the retention of a large proportion of infantry in the British Army and rapid movement of this arm would make it possible to retain cavalry who could be used for tactical reconnaissance, were not liable to mechanical breakdown and did not require heavy logistic support or extensive maintenance. Cavalry were also necessary in terrain which was unsuitable for tanks. Charrington here unhappily used the Ardennes as one example of such terrain! Co-operation with armoured fighting vehicles was, however, essential, although opportunities for the use of a steel weapon by mounted horsemen would still occur.

There is a feeling of sadness, an atmosphere of a reluctant concession, a sense of clutching at wispy straws pervading Charrington's book. He, and many other intelligent cavalry officers, knew that the day of the mounted soldier was over; their arguments were faint and doomed. It was not the tank which swept cavalry from the battlefield but rather the saturation of all open ground by accurate small arms fire; indeed the power of the mounted warrior had been in decline since the fourteenth century. Wherein lay the justification for the retention of an arm, except perhaps in the colonies and in small numbers, which apart from employment in forests, mountains, swamps and against very inferior opponents, could only be used when the enemy's resistance had been completely broken? Mechanized armour was in its infancy but energy would have been better spent in overcoming its teething problems than in using them to justify the retention of the horse. In much of his writing in the next few years Fuller continued to toil at the solution of these problems, particularly the problems of mechanized tactical doctrine, but he also began to stretch the parameters of discussion by developing the concepts he had originally constructed at the end of the war and in the early twenties about warfare between mechanized forces, rather than between mechanized and unmechanized. Germains and Charrington were really only concerned to argue for the retention of a balance of arms; indeed Charrington saw but shied away from the prospect of completely mechanized forces. Fuller's increasingly insistent and strident questions were to become: What will happen when armoured formation meets armoured formation? What will happen when air forces come of age? At the same time also he began to ask more questions about the causes of war itself, and about the effect of social, political and economic change on the prevalence and nature of war. His belief in small, professional mechanized armed forces, his feelings of distaste for democracy, his natural authoritarianism, his career frustration and the lack of appreciation from the military with which his books were met, began to ferment together and produce the makings of a heady and dangerous brew. The death of his father in this year at the age of ninety-five may also have removed an inhibiting influence, for one gains the impression that Fuller was always in awe of that rather stern and traditional clergyman. His mother, the cosmopolitan and intelligent Thelma, who was to live until 1940, was much more indulgent and accommodating.

As GSO1 2 Division Fuller was under-employed. There were two brigades of the division in Aldershot but these were commanded by officers senior to Fuller whom he appears, uncharacteristically, to have left to their own devices; there were in addition a Guards Brigade in London and some artillery in Brighton and Catterick. Nothing of very much importance, at least on Fuller's scale of values, took place, and what did occur ran smoothly and filled up the days of those who wished to concern themselves with peacetime military routine. It was, Fuller claimed, a relief after the stress and upheaval of the War Office and he was able to spend his mornings either peacefully in the office or on horseback, riding around the barracks. Fuller and peace of this sort, however, were unaccustomed bedfellows. Unable to stir pots in Whitehall or Tidworth, he spent much of his afternoons and evenings blowing up the fires under the very considerable cauldron of his own mind. The two years he spent at Aldershot were extremely prolific in terms of articles, lectures and books. He lectured and wrote about mechanized warfare, and about the causes and nature of war, and he began to research and write books that at least appeared historical. Occasionally, he applied his imaginative gifts to divisional training schemes and injected some unconventional surprises into them. He once, for instance, invented a C-in-C who gave an inchoate briefing to a brigade commander before suddenly dying of apoplexy; elucidation thereby became impossible, and muddle, the normal wartime condition, was enthroned from the start.[16]

The quiet afternoons and evenings at Aldershot, untouched by television, enabled Fuller to devote his time and energies to numbers of manuscripts which were to be printed between 1927 and 1933. In these years, and while still in the Army, he published no less than nine books, a most remarkable literary achievement, particularly since some of them required historical research and all of them a deal of original thought. Of course, he had devoted much of his life to thinking about war, and much of his published work at this time was based on ideas he had produced and research he had begun in the previous decade. But Fuller's thought processes were developing throughout his long life; he was a living example of *l'éducation permanente* and if sometimes in these middle years his thinking was slipshod or incomplete, or his exposition hurried, the sheer quantity of his writing is explanation, if not excuse, enough. As he told Starr at the time: 'To stand erect a man must learn to abandon the support of others.' [17] Fuller was now very much on his own. Even Sonia, one feels, who appears never to have read his books, did not enjoy much domestic conversation.

Many of the articles Fuller published while he was stationed at Aldershot were popularizations of themes in his earlier books. In *The Nineteenth Century and After* in May 1927 he wrote on the theme of the principles and conditions of war; [18] in October that year he published two articles, one in *The Fighting Forces* on the well-worn theme of bullets and steel plate [19] and the other in *The Journal of the Royal Artillery* on 'The Problems of Air Warfare'. [20] This latter article is full of interest both from the 1927 viewpoint and with hindsight. Aircraft, he held, had enormous advantages of speed and movement but they had no protection against missiles (in the sense of shells or bullets), could not remain at rest in the air and needed to return frequently to the earth. In internal security operations in primitive countries aircraft could be used to deliver gas attacks, 'a flying anaesthetist followed by a winged Black Maria'; in small wars in primitive countries soldiers were more use then aeroplanes since air attack on tribesmen on hill-tops was as sensible as hunting fleas with dogs; in bigger wars aircraft would be used to terrorize the civilian population, and it would be better to use gas and chemicals which were less destructive; in anti-naval warfare anti-aircraft guns would gain the upper hand but planes could be used to disorganize fleets so that submarines could attack them; in major land wars the real answer was not an air umbrella, but mechanization since aircraft would not so much abolish armies as compel them to mechanize. Some of these prophecies were pointed in false directions, especially recommendation of gas and chemicals and dismissal of the direct value of aircraft against ships; the air umbrella has proved essential even after mechanization. The emphasis on terror bombing, however, and on the value of land forces in small wars in primitive countries were clear and accurate predictions as the Second World War and the US campaign against the Vietcong have shown. Fuller's writings had always contained numbers of such predictions but they were to grow in quantity as he grew older. Prophecy is the wrong word to describe his foresights; prediction is nearer the mark since predictions can be based on scientific method, on rational thought, as Fuller's generally were, whereas prophecies are inspired by the Gods, or based on what Fuller would have called alchemy. In November he lectured at the School of Military Engineering, Chatham, on 'The Influence of Mechanical Arms on Field Engineering[21] and put forward the view that mobile warfare was just a phase. In January 1928 he published an article on his old favourite 'Science and War'.[22] In November another followed on 'The Elimination of War',[23] an eventuality which would only come to pass when war lost its utility.

In the same year a number of his lectures and articles, going back to 1919, were gathered together and published in book form as *On Future Warfare*. This book, being much less pretentious and much easier to follow, probably had far greater influence than the metaphysical *Foundations*. It was, for instance, translated into Spanish and published in Madrid, in 1929[24] and was given two reviews in the *RUSI Journal*, one somewhat abusive and full of ridicule of 'strategical paralysis' and 'area warfare', but the other more considerate and understanding. It was published, however, at a time when the conditions, as Fuller would have called them, were stony soil for warlike principles. It was in 1928 for instance, that the Cabinet affirmed that the Ten Year Rule, under which it had been assumed that no major war would break out for ten years, was to be regarded as a rolling rule so that at any time war would be at least ten years ahead. Future war was, therefore, in 1928, a distant prospect.

It was in 1928 also that Fuller had his first serious row with Liddell Hart. This stemmed from a request from the latter the previous August for an article on 'War' for the *Encyclopaedia*

Britannica at four guineas a page. Liddell Hart was acting in an editorial capacity for the Editor-in-Chief J. L. Garvin, and had told Fuller that he wanted a 'study of the natural history of war through the ages'.[25] Fuller had discussed the article with Liddell Hart [26] and had submitted it to Garvin on December 10th. However on March 9th Liddell Hart, on instructions from Garvin, told Fuller that the article could not be published because it 'contained many generalizations contrary to the verdict of historians who carried more weight'.[27] Fuller was quite naturally hurt and when the Fullers and Liddell Harts met on the 10th Sonia let it be known she thought Liddell Hart responsible for the shabby treatment she considered had been meted out to her husband. Liddell Hart thought Fuller probably agreed with her and, in order to clear the air, he wrote him a long letter on the 11th in which he tried to record the basis of their relationship. The *Encyclopaedia Britannica* rejection, he wrote, had hurt him as much as Fuller, but Fuller had not given Liddell Hart his first step up; this had been done by Maxse. Fuller had backed Liddell Hart's applications for the RTC and for Cambridge but neither of these had got anywhere. Liddell Hart had paid higher tributes to Fuller than vice versa and he agreed that Fuller was the mechanized pioneer. Liddell Hart's conversion had not been complete until 1921. However, while Fuller had pioneered the concept of armoured forces, cross-country movement and the attack on command and control, Liddell Hart had been the pioneer on questioning whether the enemy armed forces ought always to be the military objective, on using the defensive power of the machine gun as the staple argument for mechanization and the ancient horse-archer analogy as the historical argument. He brought this extraordinarily frank evaluation to an end by admitting that his friend had 'the profoundest intellect which had been applied to military thought in this century and so far as comparison is allowable in any century'. He recognized Fuller's superiority and argued that Fuller's conceptions were less due to logical process than to inspiration and 'that you are apt to use the former in a subsequent stage to explain the latter'. Fuller was not always right, although a genius, and his thought was on a higher plane than his exposition, which varied in his written work between 'dazzling brilliance and a certain mistiness'. Fuller was impervious to argument, lacked receptiveness and his historical knowledge was uneven. He was sometimes too bold but 'the creative imagination is often more likely to arrive at historical truths than the pedantic burrower in documents'.[28]

On receipt of this remarkably magnanimous document Sonia went in to bat again and wrote a petulant letter to Liddell Hart in which she stated: 'Boney has never for one moment grudged you anything, because he is far too unselfish.'[29] Fuller replied also the next day but with more calm and reserve. 'What an epistle,' he wrote; 'surely this is a storm in a tea cup. I don't think I am jealous of you, or even that we are rivals, I welcome criticism of myself, but generally take little notice of it, and I have always valued your support.'[30] A few weeks later he wrote: 'I am still much bewildered—you see I am not the genius you proclaim me.'[31] Liddell Hart had probably tried to get too close; Fuller, in spite of all his correspondence, and his active and varied life, was a very private man. The friendship, however, survived.

At the end of 1928 Ironside was posted to India and Major-General T. A. Cubbitt became Fuller's new Commander. Cubbitt was a direct-speaking, fighting soldier and Fuller got on well with him. Both Ironside and Cubbitt recommended Fuller for further promotion,[32] and the former wrote Fuller regular letters from India in which their intimacy is apparent, as is also Ironside's preoccupation with speculations about who was going to be posted or promoted amongst the upper echelons of the officer corps.[33] Such speculation is, however, endemic in the military profession, as in others. At this time, also, Fuller corresponded with Churchill and lunched with him once at 11, Downing Street.[34] He also corresponded with Milne, who appears to have been prepared to forget the Tidworth incident, or to have purged any guilt he may have felt by being nice to Fuller. Milne arranged for him to help Lord Birkenhead with some articles on war a hundred years hence and Fuller lunched with Birkenhead at the India Office. 'Don't,' Milne wrote '. . . go further than one hundred years.'[35] Fuller had also begun to collect material for his future work on decisive battles, and one of his 1914 fellow-students from Camberley, who was serving with the Iraq levies, sent him a sketch of the battlefield of Arbela which is still preserved in Rutgers Library in New Brunswick. Arbela was to figure in Fuller's thinking as the classic example of attack by penetration.

On December 13th, 1928 Fuller sent Liddell Hart typescripts

entitled '100 Problems on Mechanization' and 'The Importance of Military Invention'. Both were subsequently published in the *Army Quarterly*.[36] In April 1928 he published an article in *The Journal of the Royal Artillery* on 'The Natural History of War'. These three pieces of work are important, both in themselves and as a means of understanding the thrust of Fuller's thinking in the thirties. The '100 Problems' illustrated Fuller's maturing views, not so much on tanks, as on warfare between mechanized armies. When forwarding the articles to Liddell Hart he pointed out that any attempt to change the mental attitudes of officers had to be backed up with an official sanction if it was to be successful. There was, therefore, need for an official book on future warfare, a third volume of *Field Service Regulations*: 'speculative tactics of armies in all the circumstances in which we are likely to use them'. The article itself attempted to bridge the gap between semi-mechanization and mechanization and was the forerunner of the books on *FSR II* and *FSR III* which Fuller was to publish in 1931 and 1932. 'The Importance of Military Inventions' was more academic in nature and attempted analysis of the relations between technology and war. It pointed forward to *Armament and History* published in 1946. 'The Natural History of War' was quite different; it had its origins in the ill-fated *Encyclopaedia Britannica* article, and it dealt, not with the conduct or technology of war, but with the causes of war, which lay, Fuller believed, in culture and civilization. 'The Natural History of War' points towards Fuller's polemical and political period, towards the extremity of view which was to warp and twist much of his thinking in the years between his retirement and the Second World War when, having failed from within to change military mental attitudes sufficiently to bring about the full and rapid mechanization of the army and its tactics, he sought other external and more dangerous means of doing so. 'The Importance of Military Inventions' was the third shot in Fuller's locker, the pursuit of more academic analysis to which he would eventually turn when both mechanical reform and political adventure failed him. It is ironic that just at this time, in March 1929, the 'Purple Primer' a manual on *Mechanized and Armoured Formations* was issued by the Army Council.[37] This was imbued with much of Fuller's thinking and excluded infantry from both light and medium armoured brigades. The problem for some years, however, was going to be lack of money for defence spending and lack of any widespread acceptance in many regiments that the days of the horse and of marching infantry were over and numbered respectively.

In July 1929 Fuller was promoted Brigadier and posted to Germany for a four-year tour as Commander of 2 Rhine Brigade. This was located at Wiesbaden, some two hundred miles east of Cambrai and Bermicourt, the scenes of Fuller's previous military activities on the Continent, and here he arrived on July 23rd. It was eleven years since he had left France for the War Office, and in all that time he had not served outside England, but the prognosis for this first version of Rhine Army was not good—a fact which may or may not have been apparent to those who sent him there. In the event Fuller's command of 2 Rhine Brigade lasted three months and he came home in October when Rhine Army was evacuated, this time to command 13 Infantry Brigade in Catterick. In the short time he was in Wiesbaden he was not able to do much work; he spent the first weeks attending horse shows and other similar events and organized ten days of section and platoon training. He introduced the three flag system during this training and got into trouble with the Divisional Commander, Major-General Thwaites, whom he called a 'gingerbread General'; he could not understand the three flags, and thought the system absurd and contrary to regulations. Fuller, who, it appears, had determined to seize the first opportunity of clearing the air between them, inquired of Thwaites who was commanding the brigade and pointed out that unless brigadiers were permitted to exercise their imaginations he had no place on the Rhine. Fuller told Liddell Hart that after this they became 'quite good friends'.[38]

Before going to Wiesbaden Fuller had completed the draft of a book on 'The Generalship of Ulysses S. Grant' and had sent a copy to Liddell Hart for his views. These he had received at considerable length and just before leaving had returned a letter which began:

> Dear Lord God Almighty!
> I value your criticisms and have accepted about 50% of them; but, in spite of your omniscience, I cannot accept them all, unless you provide better evidence....[39]

'Grant' was history but it was polemic at the same time. It was a study of Grant's role in the American Civil War and of that war as one of the first which had roots in the Industrial Revolution, but it was also full of rather vague political recommendations for the 1930s based on the lessons which could be drawn from a study of Grant. The whole work was founded on the system developed by Fuller in *Foundations* and was aimed at accuracy of spirit as well as of fact.[40] It begins with an analysis of the 'natural history' of the war, its origins and results, then of its strategy, tactics, and technology, and thirdly there follows a narrative of Grant's campaigns. The fourth part of the book is called 'The Generalship of Peace' which is where the lessons and the polemic principally come in. Here Fuller developed the views that war had creative power and value, that destruction was not necessarily evil and might be essential in order to make it possible to create something better, that war could only be avoided by removing its causes—internal discontent and external economic friction. The former, he believed, could be cured through order, discipline, scientific management and common sense, and the latter through scientific statesmanship and the establishment of universal free trade. All this was a long way from Vicksburg and Chattanooga but perhaps not so very far from Hitler and Mussolini, although at the end of the book Fuller makes no attempt, when describing the new autocrats, to identify himself with them; indeed he categorizes them as Russian in essence, for they ruled by force whether anti-democratic or anti-aristocratic.

By the end of October, Sonia and he were in Catterick, which Fuller described as 'the end of the World, at least of the intellectual world, all people can do here is to kill things—it is just a blasted moor'.[41] There are echoes of his early views on service in Ireland in this. He also described the camp as being 'like a mining settlement'. One cannot help concluding that even Tidworth might have been an improvement! In mid-November Liddell Hart wrote to him on the subject of *Grant* again. Catterick could not have improved Fuller's tolerance because he replied in blistering vein: 'Your letter ... is one of the most extraordinary examples of self adoration I have cast eye on for a long time. One day like Narcissus you will fall into the pond. You talk of "your corrections" as if you were a schoolmaster and I a little boy.'[42] Liddell Hart demonstrated greater tolerance. They made it up and *Grant* received a quite kindly review from Liddell Hart's pen in the *Daily Telegraph*.[43] *Grant* was a vehicle for all Fuller's current interests—in history, in mechanized war, in the causes of war and in technology and war; it was, as history alone, somewhat impure.

In Catterick he continued to correspond with Meredith Starr and in one long letter told him that the first step to take in the present machine age was to destroy the 'Christian World Ideal'— the slave's ideal based on fear.[44] He also continued to write articles. His arrival coincided with the publication of a limpid little piece in *The Army, Navy and Air Force Gazette* on 'The last 800 Yards' about the problem of assaulting on to the objective in the face of modern small-arms fire and the necessity for armoured fighting vehicles.[45] Next spring the same journal published an article by him on 'The Rise of the Artillery Cycle and Certain Speculations'.[46] These speculations were that the elimination of war would come from the ridiculous nature of a soulless battle in which mutual weapon-power improvement, tactical perfection, rendered fighting pointless. Fuller himself continued to do his job and to train soldiers for war. He complained to Liddell Hart that he was beginning to believe he was a crank because as a Brigadier he actually made out his own exercises,[47] and in the winter of 1929 he gave all his officers a series of lectures on *Field Service Regulations*, Volume Two, keeping them awake with the occasional difficult question. His stay in Catterick was not, however, to be much longer than in Wiesbaden. On September 14th, 1930, he was promoted Major-General and at the beginning of October received a letter from the War Office putting him on half-pay from December 14th.[48] On November 1st he and Sonia left the cold and mud of Catterick for Farnborough. They had no permanent home of their own and they decided to go to Switzerland to ski and await events. It was therefore in the Bernese Oberland, at the Regina Palace Hotel in Beatenberg, that he received a letter from the Military Secretary's Branch dated February 2nd, 1931,[49] in which he was informed that he had been selected for command of a Second-Class District in India, provided that the Government of India agreed. The vacancy was for four years and would occur at the end of November, but Fuller was required to reach India and take over by the end of July. He was requested to inform the writer confidentially whether or not it was agreeable to him to accept the post but to

give his reasons if he wished to refuse. This news dashed the
hopes Fuller must have entertained that he would be given a
responsible position at the centre again, or that he would be able
to regrasp the nettle of mechanization. After all, he had worked
his passage back in Aldershot; he had been given two appointments in command of regular brigades, however short-lived one
of them might have been; he had not published anything to give
rise to great ire or ridicule since *Foundations*; he had the entrée
to high places; the political climate was moving, if ever so
slightly, away from disarmament. He told his mother: 'It was the
worst command they could offer me, and it was offered me as an
insult.'[50] Only a few weeks beforehand Ironside had speculated in
a letter from Meerut District, itself in India, as to whether Fuller
might get the post of DSD.[51] At this remove in time the differences in importance between an Indian District and a Director's
desk in Whitehall are not as apparent as they were in 1931. It is
all too easy now to look back at Indian military appointments and
envy their somewhat pro-consular-like incumbents; moreover the
East and counter-insurgency have for many years been the focus
of military attention and training. To Fuller, Bombay, as he soon
worked out from the *Army List* the District must be, would have
seemed an exile and a disgrace; his command would have consisted of two batteries of guns, an infantry battalion and an
RAMC company. However, he wrote in his *Memoirs* that it was
not India, or the worst District in India to which he objected; it
was to serving under a Government of India whose actions he
could not approve and to be given a job with nothing to do.[52] On
February 11th he wrote to the War Office declining to accept the
post. He gave his reasons as follows: 'As presumably most of my
duties will be connected with communal riots and boycott disturb-
ances, and as I have no confidence in the Government of India,
which, in my opinion, through weakness and lack of foresight are
largely responsible for the present turmoil, I do not consider that
I am a suitable officer to serve in that country. Further, from a
purely military point of view, I consider such an appointment a
pure waste of time'.[53] In all this there was considerable validity
particularly as Fuller had last visited India only just over four
years previously as the personal emissary of the CIGS, and had
written an insubordinate report on Indian military policies, and
as, of all officers in the British Army, it was most inappropriate

that he should have no mechanized units at all under his command. However, the Army Council, of which Milne was still the
senior Military Member, was utterly unprepared to change its
mind. A reply was sent to Fuller at the end of the month which
expressed the Council's surprise 'that an officer of your seniority
should have given political reasons for declining a military appointment in the service of the Crown'. The letter also pointed
out that 'the selection of officers for higher military appointments is made by the Secretary of State, in the light of advice
received from the Selection Board, who take into consideration
the military qualifications of the various officers eligible for such
appointments'.[54] Fuller certainly had sinned against the principles
of military professionalism in refusing an appointment on
political grounds. He considered that he had been asked for his
reasons and had merely given the true ones. 'King's Regulations'
he felt, did not forbid officers to hold political opinions, and he
did not want to be put in the position in which General Dyer had
found himself in 1919 at the time of the Amritsar riots and
massacre.[55] This reasoning was a little disingenuous. In giving
political reasons for refusal, he had made a tactical mistake. Had
he given other reasons, that the post was in his opinion a deliberate insult and that he would have been of more use in almost any
other major-general's appointment in the British Army, he could
not have fared worse. Undoubtedly Fuller made a mistake in not
going to Tidworth; his decision to turn down Bombay was much
more understandable, whatever reasons he actually gave for it.
With hindsight, though, it is possible to speculate that had he
given less political reasons, or had he gone into exile for four
years, his forthcoming association with fascism might not have
taken place and his services might then have been acceptable in an
active capacity in the years immediately before the Second World
War and in the war itself. Those services might have been more
valuable to Britain than the books he wrote in the next ten years,
with the exception of *Lectures on FSR II* and *Lectures on FSR III*
which he could have published anyway, or than the political
activities in which he became caught up. But this is mere idle
speculation. Ironside was distressed and thought the offer of
Bombay was stupid and insulting. He hoped Fuller would not
retire and asked him to think seriously before he made up his
mind.[56] Sonia, when she later met the officer who actually went

to Bombay, is reputed to have remarked: 'I hear you have accepted Boney's job. It's only suitable for a nit-wit like you.'[57]

For the next three years Fuller became a wanderer, living on
his half-pay, his royalties from books and articles, published both
at home and abroad, and, increasingly, on income from free-lance
journalism. Sonia and he travelled widely in Europe and, when
they returned to England, lived in temporary accommodation in
Farnborough or Chelsea. In the first two years of this odyssey,
1931 and 1932, Fuller published no fewer than five books, *India in
Revolt* in 1931 and *Lectures on FSR II*, *Lectures on FSR III*, *The
Dragon's Teeth* and *War and Western Civilization*, in 1932.
Although much of the writing of these books had been begun
prior to 1931—*India in Revolt*, for instance, stemmed from his
visit to India in 1926, and *Lectures on FSR II* was based on his
winter lectures in Catterick—and although the ideas in themselves were developments of ideas he had been working on or
thinking about for many years, the publication of five serious
works in so short a time-span was a considerable achievement.
The books may be grouped into two distinct sets: first *Lectures
on FSR II* and *Lectures on FSR III* which deal with mechanized
warfare, and the tactical and technological future of war, and
represent the apogee of Fuller's career as a military theorist;
second the other three in which, following up his article on 'The
Natural History of War', he addressed himself to the problem of
the relations between war and culture or civilization, in both a
European and a colonial context. It was partly this latter problem
and the mode of thinking which it generated which, in the face of
his inability to obtain acceptance for his military theories, was to
lead him, all his life a disbeliever in democracy, lemming-like into
the fascist sea.

Lectures on FSR II were written in the form of a commentary
on *Field Service Regulations*, Vol. II, and therefore deal with
contemporary warfare. *Lectures on FSR III* are commentaries on
a hypothetical volume of FSR, unwritten, unpublished, and dealing with future warfare, with 'Operations between Mechanized
Forces' as the book is in fact subtitled. Much of the detail of these
books, as of *On War*, has been rendered obsolete by technological
and political change but the thesis underlying them is of startling
clarity, and very considerable interest even today. Up until this
time Fuller had adapted his theories of penetration to changing

circumstances, had seen the tank justify and facilitate them and had accepted that tank warfare could lead to the creation of flanks and hence to envelopment rather than penetration. His writing had contained many indications about the future, about the use of naval tactics on land, about airpower, gas, and the elimination of war through weapon power. In the new books he structured and systematized his military thinking and presented the whole in a very modest little package, two slender volumes which caused little stir at home, and were translated only into Spanish[58] and Czech[59] at the time, but which certainly deserved far more attention and acclaim than they received. Fuller later claimed that they were published in the Soviet Union in 1932 but this appears doubtful as will be explained later.[60] Guderian, however, read Fuller's books in the thirties and these probably included *Lectures on FSR III*.[61]

Fuller's thesis was that as armies were mechanized, warfare would pass through an asymmetrical and a symmetrical stage; he does not use these latter phrases but they provide a short-cut to understanding his concept. In the asymmetrical stage the mechanization of opposing armed forces is unbalanced, perhaps a mechanized force faces an unmechanized or partially mechanized one; in the symmetrical stage partially or fully mechanized forces face each other. In any situation of asymmetrical mechanization the tables are greatly loaded in favour of the more highly mechanized force. Thus, even in the conditions of 1931 in Europe, infantry, Fuller held, could no longer close with the enemy and destroy him, until he was virtually destroyed himself,[62] and the infantry role was to form the base of tank action, to move it forward, to hold by fire and occupy by movement.[63] The answer to the tank was the tank, or rather the tank protected by the anti-tank gun and the machine gun. As Fuller told Liddell Hart after the war: 'The real change in my outlook of the early twenties and in the early thirties came with the advent of an effective anti-tank weapon, and in my *Lectures on FSR III* I built my ideas round tank and anti-tank.'[64] He also believed that future armies would be surrounded by swarms of 'motorized guerillas',[65] irregular or regular troops making use of the multitude of civilian motor-cars which would be available. Rivers would become important tank obstacles and defence in depth would become essential. Cavalry would have little place in war even in this asymmetrical stage. 'Cavalry, we are told, "should be concentrated in a position which will give them full scope for co-operation in the decisive phase of the battle". What is this position? I cannot say, unless it is the entrance of a railway tunnel, unknown to the enemy, which will enable them to pass beneath the battlefield and attack the enemy in the rear.'[66] However, in the event that defence proved successful, the tank was stopped and a front could not be broken, the true battle would be shifted to the industrial areas and bombing and submarine warfare would become all-important.[67] This is reaching into a symmetrical context, of course. The important point Fuller was making was that mechanized armies could easily defeat unmechanized[68] but that once both sides mechanized, and particularly when some form of effective technological and tactical counter to the tank was found, then the immense advantages the Tank Corps possessed, but was not allowed to exploit, in 1917–18, would evaporate, and one would return to a situation of potential stalemate on land, and so must resort to the air and the sea. Douhet, an Italian brigadier, had come to a somewhat similar conclusion earlier when he recommended that the decisive victory should be ach-ieved through gaining command of the air and attacking civilian targets with bombers. In the outcome, as Fuller was to discover, bombing—at least, conventional bombing—did not achieve vic-tory, which had to be achieved by sheer overwhelming weight of land forces, often transported and supported by air or sea, but still fighting on the ground. The motorized guerilla concept was also over-theoretical in the context of war between armies; roads can be blocked, even Continental ones without fences and ditches,[69] and certainly they can be mined or attacked from the air, while unarmoured cars are as vulnerable to small-arms fire as the horse. In insurgencies or internal security operations it is, of course, different, and the motor-car has proved a most effective weapon platform, or weapon itself, in Northern Ireland.

In the symmetrical stage, that is in warfare between partially or fully mechanized forces where technological and tactical development is roughly balanced, Fuller held that aircraft might eventually 'render armies and navies useless'[70] and that industry would become the controlling factor in war.[71] Guerilla warfare was likely to be revived and cost would limit the size of mechanized armies which would have to be fully mobilized in peacetime in order to prevent the enemy winning with a rapid thrust. Small, highly trained professional armies would be required; conscripts would become merely supportive.[72] The new order of battle would consist, not of cavalry, artillery and infantry, but of motorized guerillas, a mechanized first line and an unarmoured but partially motorized second line, plus an air force.[73] Land warfare would become like naval warfare[74] (this point goes right back to the Gold Medal essay) but the principles of war would remain valid.[75] Infantry and tanks should operate in different roles, and infantry should not be used where they could be attacked by tanks.[76] Mechanized armies should be organized into two wings—an offensive tank force and a protective anti-tank force—and they should travel together like fleets, taking their own harbours round with them like modern wagon laagers.[77] In these circumstances infantry would only be useful for mountain or forest warfare, or occupation duties[78] while cavalry 'will die a lingering though natural death', although the cavalry idea would live on in the motorized and mechanized trooper.[79] The armoured units themselves would require reconnaissance, artillery and combat tanks and numbers of specialized machines for water-crossing, assault, supply, bridging, gas, min-laying and mine-sweeping.[80] Aeroplanes and tanks were complementary to each other, although one day a 'manless flying machine' might alter the whole form of war.[81] As in the asymmetrical stage, the tank could only be defeated by the tank, because it had to be penetrated by a shell, and the shell had to be fired from a mobile armoured gun, that is, a tank. 'Therefore, the answer to the tank is the tank; therefore, the present-day infantry battles will be replaced by mobile armoured artillery battles, and though in these battles the armour used may be no protection against the shells fired, it will have to be maintained in order to prevent the bullet coming back into its own.'[82] The aims of these mechanized armies should be directed more towards denying the enemy petrol, than to destroying him.[83] When the tank offensive is countered armies will once again face siege warfare.[84] Assaults on these bastions would have to be carried out by tanks followed up perhaps by 'infantry in armoured carriers'.[85] Should these assaults fail then an air attack on the civil will would be inevitable.[86] In small wars in undeveloped countries Fuller also recommended the use of military technology, particularly aeroplanes, light tanks and non-lethal gas. He wrote about the latter:

Ever since the World War we have possessed a toxic smoke which will cause acute toothache in every tooth lasting for a number of hours. Given this chemical and not high explosive, here is the picture:

War is declared and the warriors bid farewell to their wives and children. They swarm up the hill sides and lie in wait for the tail end of the punitive column. No column appears, instead a solitary bombing machine loaded with half a ton of toothache mixture sails over their village, noses for wind and drops its goods on its windward side. Growing hungry the warriors return for their evening meal; but no curried goat and chupatties await them, in place a howling mob of women and children who hurl expletives at their heads, words which have more effect on their morale than ever had bullet or T.N.T. After six such vocal bombardments the war is off. Three tons of toxic smoke and a little petrol costing perhaps a hundred pounds has accomplished in a few days what a two million pounds punitive column has frequently failed to accomplish in three months.[87]

It would be unfair to leave these two books, however, on this note. In them Fuller distilled a very great deal of practical military wisdom. In many passages he was decades ahead of his time. Motorized guerillas were a false start, except perhaps for the German motorcyclists in 1940; the logistic problems of armoured forces have tended to inhibit them from emulating fleets, except in the Western Desert in 1941–2 and more recently in Sinai and Egypt; foot infantry have proved a tougher species than Fuller imagined and the line stretches as far as the 1970s Arab soldier with his suitcase anti-tank missile. But the vision which Fuller had of armoured warfare was a remarkably far-sighted one, so far-sighted that it was rarely realized in the Second World War, and has perhaps only begun now to focus— and, of course, in a war, the Yom Kippur War, between small nations armed by others with advanced technology but to whom nuclear weapons were unavailable. For it was the invention of the atom bomb which finally put paid to Fuller's dream, the dream of professional mechanized warfare between major states, since recourse to the nuclear weapon would be open to the side which thought itself about to lose, and it could hope to stave off its own utter destruction by using such weapons in a battlefield role. At least that is the presently accepted theory. In other non-visionary respects Fuller was also breaking relatively new ground. His cool and rational defence of the tank, even when penetrable, has recently had to be re-argued in the face of the threat presented by ATGW, and his attempt to substitute functions for the traditional Arms has an ultra-modern ring about it.

These books were Fuller's best effort in the field of military theory, a fitting summation to his professional career. Had soldiers and governments in Britain followed his advice in the thirties we should have been a great deal better prepared for the Second World War, although the army might have been an unbalanced force, too stuffed with tanks. He was writing, however, at the predictive as well as the prescriptive level. He prescribed an armoured remedy but he predicted that when both antagonists in a war had taken the remedy, it would no longer be effective; the mechanized enemy would become resistant to the mechanized attack. The consequence was that he was proposing ultimately a situation of mechanical absolute war, a technological rush to extremes, which would achieve no political goals and would lead to attacks on the civil will. However we have now discovered that attacks on the civil will by HE bombing from the air tend not to destroy it, while the prospect of mutual assured destruction inhibits nuclear bombing. Fuller's vision of the perfection of mechanized warfare points then to deterrence at the conventional, as well as the nuclear, level. The architect of Cambrai and Amiens, the inventor of strategic paralysis, saw that, in a symmetrical mode, war would become unwinnable but that the way to avoid it was to be militarily prepared for it. However the author of the second set of books, the authoritarian, the frustrated, disappointed and embittered professional, appeared at times to see in war a creativity essential to mankind. His different views were undoubtedly contradictory but Clausewitz himself had been similarly ambivalent about his own theoretical model, the concept of the perfection of war, absolute war. It is possible for professionals to develop an affection for war, or for a concept of war, while at the same time deploring its consequences. Clausewitz and Fuller both did so; Liddell Hart appears to have successfully resisted the temptation, perhaps because he found human beings as acceptable and likeable as he did ideas, whereas Fuller, certainly, was much more at home with concepts than with fallible and emotional men.

This second set of books foreshadowed many of the themes he was to develop, in books and in journalism, in the remainder of his life. In all three books the themes of anti-democracy, of the creativity of war, and of the necessity for a strong, united Europe occur and recur. In all three also Fuller developed his pathological view of history and of the causes of war, which led him eventually to the belief that there were two such causes, the economic and the biological. The economic cause stemmed from economic disequilibrium between states, the biological cause was a product of the fight for racial survival and expansion.[88]

India in Revolt, published in 1931, was a very perceptive, in some respects prophetic, book. Fuller saw that the East could not just take over the history of the West. He argued that only colonial despotism prevented Hindu–Muslim troubles, and believed also that Britain, in Westernizing the Indian intelligentsia, had sown a whirlwind in the shape of democracy which would necessarily be anti-British. Fuller's solution was a return to princely rule or a franchise based on village headmen but he feared breakdown and partition. 'We have poured the new wine of democracy with all its strange fermentations into the ancient bottles of Indian theocracy and are now hoping for the best.'[89]

In this book his dislike and distrust of democracy was given forcible expression. Democracy was 'a disease'[90] and had 'feet of clay'.[91] 'Government of the people by the people for the people' was 'twaddle'.[92] 'In democracy, as it is conceived today, we reach the age of the political saurians—a maximum of body and a minimum of brain.'[93] War was the greatest of all creative activities[94] and normally accomplished its end which was 'the creation of a better form of peacefulness'.[95] 'Authority' was the word missing today from the world's social vocabulary. 'It implies the control of the majority by the minority, because intelligence is a rare and stupidity a plentiful quality in humankind. The masses must be controlled by some myth, some ideal which enslaves their animal instincts and emotions . . . which creates order, and which restricts their natural appetites. . . . The masses must have a religion, that is a mythology, a Holy Grail.'[96] Obviously the book was not all about India, but a great deal of it was. There is an interesting chapter on Gandhi—'a saint who for love of God has sinned against humanity, and on the tomb of his memory will the words "Non pacem sed gladium" be inscribed in letters of blood.'[97] *India in Revolt* makes lively reading even today.

At the end of 1931 Fuller wrote to Liddell Hart from Switzerland, where he was again on holiday at the Regina Palace Hotel in Beatenberg: 'My next book, which I hope will be out in February, I am calling "The Dragon's Teeth". It ought to bite someone, and I am not at all sure it will not bite myself.'[98] He acknowledged, it is fairly certain, that in attacking the causes of war more directly, as he did in this book, he was moving yet farther away from the accepted path of the professional soldier. His aims in the book were to demonstrate the nature of those causes, that they lay in peace not war, and that the elimination of war could only be brought about by changing peace, that is by radically altering the social order.[99] He was advocating, therefore, drastic political change—and not only in order that armies might be reformed, but also in order that the causes of war might be eradicated. The existence of slums he regarded as a cause of war.[100] 'War is ... an economic question';[101] and 'the fundamental cause of war is discontent with the existing peacefulness';[102] 'war in itself is not a disease, but the result, or outward manifestation, of a disease, a sickness incubated in peace and hatched out in war-time'.[103] Democracy, he considered, stemmed, like socialism, from the Christian ideal of equality in which ignorance was apotheosized and the efficient paid for the inefficient. 'Democracy may therefore be considered a Satanic instrument; for it is in conflict with God or Nature.'[104] The First World War was the first of the great democratic wars, a war of the 'hoi polloi ... the canaille';[105] 'democracies should not indulge in wars, as they are totally incapable of terminating them honourably'.[106] Since war had as its object the improvement of peace, the abolition of war might lead to the destruction rather than the preservation of mankind. 'Pax Perpetua is a fitting motto for a churchyard'.[107] The book also contains a fair amount of history of warfare and an exposition of a law and a factor which were developed from 'Weekly Tank Notes' and *Foundations* and were to figure prominently in his later writing. The law of military development stated that armies must adapt to changing environment in order to remain fitted for war[108] while the constant tactical factor was concerned with the action–reaction phenomenon between technological change in offence and defence—military inventions tend to lead to the production of their counters and so on and on.[109] He also yet again advocated the use of gas and made the unhappy prophecy that its use in the next war was a certainty.[110] Another prophecy was nearer the mark, however, since he foresaw that the use of chemically-propelled, electrically-directed weapons which would shift the object of battle from the destruction of soldiers to the killing of civil will.[111] The elimination of war, he reiterated, would come through the new instruments, rather than through a demand for their abolition.

War and Western Civilization, published later in the same year, was the forerunner of *The Conduct of War*, published many years later at the end of his life and perhaps now his most well-known work. The object of the book was: 'To reflect on the experiences of the last 100 years in order that we may fashion a little candle which will light our way through the next 100.'[112] It contains again a great deal of historical matter, much of it from secondary sources, on war in the nineteenth and twentieth centuries, and was dedicated to his father, perhaps because that long-lived clergyman had been born himself in 1832 and had nearly survived the century. Fuller linked the nineteenth-century expansion and brutalization of war with the rise of democracy and nationalism, and contended that scientific and industrial development had 'delivered into the hands of the masses more and more deadly means of destruction'.[113] He wondered if modern democracy was worth while in view of the number of wars which had taken place since 1832. Clausewitz did not escape stricture. 'What Clausewitz really did was to democratize war, and when the spirit of his doctrines was coupled with that of Darwin's *The Origin of Species* (1859), they produced the Prussian Military System; and when with that of Karl Marx's *Das Kapital* (1867), they produced the Russian Revolutionary System. All three writers based their theories upon "mass struggle"—in war, in life and in economics.'[114] These bizarre views were, no doubt, fashionable in the 1930s; in fact in *On War* Clausewitz merely analysed the relations between war and policy and certainly made no proposals to 'democratize' it except in relation to what we would now call resistance movements. He did, of course, with qualification, recommend the use of superior numbers, and it is from this purely military consideration that much misunderstanding sprang. In *The Conduct of War* Fuller was kinder to his illustrious predecessor.

Later in the book Fuller praised Moltke for his perception of the impact of small arms on the battlefield in the US Civil War, that it led to the desirability of combining a tactical defensive into a strategic offensive. On the other hand, in a brilliant passage, he totally demolished Foch's pre-1914 argument that improvement in firearms added strength to the offensive. Foch had contended that if you increased the rate of rifle fire you increased the advantage of an attack mounted by two battalions on one. Fuller commented: 'Is not this complete lunacy? To mention one factor only . . . as the defender offers but one-eighth of the target that the attacker does, the assailants' hits must be reduced by seven-eighths.'[115] The result then, Fuller easily demonstrated, was the opposite of that which Foch drew. An increased rate of rifle fire decreased enormously the advantage of the attackers. Of course Foch had been writing before the 1914–18 War, so Fuller could be accused of taking unfair advantage of hindsight!

As regards the future of war Fuller dwelt on rear attack, on the rise of Asian nationalism and on the nonsense of disarmament. He believed that for industrial reasons wars would probably be waged by alliances rather than single states. 'What will future warfare then be like?' he asked.

It will include many strange contradictions, so strange that unless we have thought them out beforehand we shall be utterly surprised. War will be absolute in the extreme, for whole nations will be besieged; yet there will be no front of operations, fronts will be everywhere. Again, there will not be one war but two wars, the first waged against the enemy's armies, and the second against his civil population; the former becoming more and more humane and the latter more and more brutal, as happened in the Middle Ages.

It is at the moral and industrial centres that the main blows will be struck, and not so much at military power itself, because military power is founded upon the civil will and upon civil industry, and to attack an army at its foundations is a more certain way of destroying its power than by removing its roof tile by tile. Cities and towns will consequently have to be protected and defended as they were in the Middle Ages, and the people disciplined for war in order to shield themselves against the main weapon of the attacker— their own panic. They must not only be physically disciplined as soldiers are in order to maintain order during a crisis, but mentally disciplined so that they may withstand the corrosive effects of propaganda; for every human achievement will be distorted by the enemy to further his war ends. Wars will in fact largely become armed propaganda, steel-girt lies, demor- alizing shells and stink bombs aimed to shatter the enemy's will, every effort being simultaneously made to render one's own side explosive with fury, scorn, cruelty and hatred for the enemy, his people and his cause—such are the motive forces in democratic wars.

The main military weapon of attack will, I consider, be gas, not because it is so deadly but because it is so terrifying. Yet, possibly, it will be abandoned, for in the minds of a demented and thoroughly animalized people it may be con- sidered too humane. Nevertheless its power to surprise and above all the cheapness of its production should appeal to democracies.

Finally, paradox again, the longer the war the greater will be the improvement in weapons; armies, instead of deterior- ating, as they have done in the past, will progressively grow more efficient, whilst civilians will become more and more demoralized, until terror coagulates into solid panic which the slightest moral shock will detonate into explosion. The final wars of the democratic age, the age of economic nationalism and of nations in arms, will be as unchivalrous as they are scientific; they will not be pleasant affairs, or profitable ones.[116]

Detailed comment is superfluous. In many ways this was a clear vision, but such distortion as there was comes, surprisingly, from an overestimation of the effects of bombing and of gas, the one discovered after the Second World War and the other before it, since ineffectiveness was undoubtedly the major consideration weighing against the use of gas in that war. On Europe's future plight, however, Fuller's views were better founded, in that he saw her wedged between the jaws of the Russo-American nutcracker. He called therefore, at the end of the book, for a sort of united Europe with a Continental army based on Berlin. He did not lay down his pen, however, before producing a peroration in praise of war itself, a surgical instrument as it were, which has cut the living flesh free from the dead flesh'.[117] 'War,' he concluded, 'is a God-appointed instrument to teach wisdom to the foolish and righteousness to the evil-minded.'[118] In retrospect one cannot but be struck by the yawning differences between the ways in which we look at war today and the ways Fuller, and many others, did in 1932, a difference which is only partially explained by the invention of nuclear weapons. One is also struck by the ambivalence and contradictions in his position. His analysis of the causes of war has some validity; his attempt to relate changes in war and warfare to political and technological change has even more; his views on the elimination of war are very arguable. But his growing hatred for democracy and his praise of war itself are alien to our age.

In these years he saw Liddell Hart quite often in England[119] and Sonia and he went to visit him in Geneva in February 1932 from their holiday retreat in Beatenberg. Liddell Hart was attending the Disarmament Conference, a subject on which Fuller's views were extreme; but Karl Radek, the Editor of *Izvestiya*, told Liddell Hart that he would much like to meet Fuller and they all lunched together for three hours. On arrival Radek flattered them both somewhat outrageously with the words: 'What a coincidence—the military brains of Great Britain together in one room.' In *Izvestiya* Radek later called Fuller and Liddell Hart 'the pioneers of a revolution in warfare'.[120] It was one of the first of such congratulatory couplings which were to become a feature of most of the post-war comment on the two of them. Radek also appears to have told Fuller that over 100,000 copies of a Russian edition of *On Future Warfare* had been sold, and it was as a result of this that Fuller came to believe that Radek had been referring to *Lectures on FSR III*, an error which Liddell Hart pointed out years later while emphasizing the incontrovertible fact that *Lectures on FSR III* had not been published until five months after the meeting with Radek.[121]

Troubles with the War Office continued. In 1929 he had been taken to task about some of the contents of the draft of an article on 'Generalship'.[122] At the end of 1932 he received a letter from the Permanent Under-Secretary asking for his comments on a passage in *War and Western Civilization* in which he had accused the British Government of engineering the Opium War in order to acquire Hong Kong in 1842 and throw open numbers of Chinese ports to foreigners.[123] 'This most iniquitous piece of banditry,' Fuller had written, 'laid the foundations of the present Civil War in China.' Fuller justified himself on the grounds of historic truth[124] but in January 1933 the Permanent Under Secretary wrote to him conveying to him the displeasure of the Army Council and asking him to take greater care in future. Whether or not the opinions expressed by Fuller were correct, the Army Council believed their publication highly improper since it gave 'to those who seek to undermine the prestige of the British Empire, an opportunity which might have most unfortunate results'.[125] None of this deterred Fuller in the least from the use of his pen. On January 9th, 1933, he wrote significantly to his mother:

> When I was offered Bombay I knew perfectly well if I refused it I should not be employed again. It was the worst command they could offer me, and it was offered me as an insult. As far as I am concerned they may keep their appointments, I do not seek them; what I should like is some civil employment. . . . I have fallen back on the pen and intend to use it whether the War Office like it or not. What I write is neither scurrilous or libellous or even personal, and as an officer on half-pay can write what he likes I see no reason why I should discontinue doing so . . . with one or two exceptions, any appointment which could be offered me would be ruinously expensive, as it is, had I never taken up writing I should have had to leave the Army long ago. The higher appointments are only for comparatively well-off men, and I much doubt whether there is another major-general in the Army who is trying to carry on an appointment solely on his pay.[126]

It is obviously important, in connection with Fuller's writings from the time he went on half-pay onwards, to remember that he was concerned to supplement his pay, and subsequently his pension, from royalties and fees. He continued to publish articles in the *Army Quarterly*. In January 1933, for instance, there was an article on 'Military Inventions; Their Antiquity and Influence on War' in which he put forward yet again the view that military technology lessened the horrors of war while the Geneva Disarmament Conference would result in the re-establishment of siege warfare (which technology had overcome) 'in all its Satanic glory of 1914–18'.[127] In July the *Army Quarterly* carried another article by Fuller, this time on 'The Place of the American Civil War in the Evolution of War'.[128] Straightforward commercial journalism is, however, more profitable than writing for professional magazines and in 1932 Fuller had begun to write, for *Everyman*, articles with such titles as 'Is Geneva an International Lunatic Asylum?';[129] 'Is the British Army Any Use?';[130] and 'The Way to a Cheaper and More Efficient Army'.[131] In 1933 he began to write for the newspapers, but not until he was on the point of retirement. In December, for instance, the *Daily Mail* carried a piece by him entitled 'Britain's Out-of-Date Defence Forces' and the *Daily Mirror* another on 'Our Inefficient Army—Criminally Obsolete'.[132] The author of staid works on training and deeply thoughtful and erudite volumes on military theory and philosophy discovered in himself the ability to write colourfully, trenchantly and intelligibly for the masses he appeared, or affected, to despise. This ability should come as no surprise, for the pungency and wit of his letters, and of the less pretentious of his books, had only to be used at the right level for him to become a famous journalist overnight. It is worth wondering what might have been the fate of his more theoretical works had they been composed in language as intelligible to a military audience as the language of Fuller's journalism was to the ordinary newspaper reader.

In 1933 he also published yet two more books, *Grant and Lee: A study in personality and generalship* and *Generalship, Its Diseases and Their Cure: A study of the personal factor in command*. Both were based on earlier work. It is apparent from their subtitles that both represent, from different standpoints, the same phase in the development of Fuller's thinking, a phase no doubt at least partially inspired by his own frustrating elevation to two-star rank. In *Grant and Lee* he set out to analyse two personalities against the background of the Civil War, and he came to the conclusion that the traditional view of Grant as a butcher and Lee as a great general was incorrect, that Grant was a great general and Lee in some ways a very bad one. He was annoyed when Liddell Hart brought out a reissue of one of his own books at the same time that *Grant and Lee* was published and told his mother that 'Liddell Hart could not keep out of the picture'.[133]

Generalship was a stimulating and on the whole sensible little thesis which was founded, somewhat surprisingly, on Clausewitz and showed Fuller at his practical best. He summarized the essentials of generalship as being courage, creative intelligence and physical fitness—the attributes of youth—and he attacked the power of the General Staff to control the General, and the age and mentality of the generals of the day. The remedies he proposed were drastic. He wanted young generals in wartime, and he wanted them trained and tested, without staff assistance, in peacetime. He attacked the army's anti-professionalism and he wanted individuality developed, not suppressed. Every general should have a real second-in-command who could replace him, not a chief-of-staff. Above all he wanted to abolish the General Staff, replace it with a General's Staff, not to advise him, but to see his orders carried out; and he wanted to give generals armies small enough to command, mechanized armies with the general back on the battlefield in the tank, like Elles, one supposes, at Cambrai. Naturally enough much of this went down extremely ill with most senior officers, even with such enlightened ones as Dill and Swinton.[134] As Liddell Hart put it: 'If you say to Smith, "Mrs Brown has a pimple on her nose," he simply takes it as a statement of fact: but if you say it to Mrs Brown she takes it as an insult.'[135]

In February 1933 Milne retired from the post of CIGS which he had held for seven years. General Sir Archibald Montgomery-Massingberd succeeded him and, as Liddell Hart wrote in his *Memoirs*, 'With his entry into office Fuller's fate was sealed.'[136] The new CIGS detested Fuller and had made no secret of the fact. He refused to read Fuller's books for fear they would make him angry and, although he accepted the fact that Fuller had brains, he believed that he lacked loyalty and was only admired by those who opposed the establishment in order to seek their own advancement.[137] When Montgomery-Massingberd discovered in June that Fuller's *Grant and Lee* and Liddell Hart's *Sherman* had been prescribed as set reading for the officers' promotion examination he had the subject they supported, the American Civil War, cancelled in the new issue of Army Orders, so determined was he that such heretical authors should not be honoured in this way.[138] And when, in December, Fuller completed three years on the unemployed list, the opportunity was taken to have him retired. Accordingly Fuller was informed that he would be placed on the retired list on December 14th and this fact was published in the *London Gazette* on the 16th. And so ended, at the age of fifty-five, and a few years before what will almost certainly prove to have been the largest and longest mechanized war of all time, the military career of Britain's most experienced and able tank officer, the victim of his own brilliance and energy, and of his own inability to trim his words and his actions to the winds of political reality and human frailty. During his service career he had undoubtedly made a major impact on thinking inside the Army about mechanization, and this was to bear fruit after the opposition it aroused died down and was overtaken by events; he had also stirred up the public mind on the same subject; he had a similar, and in many ways more immediate effect on armies and governments abroad, notably in Germany, Spain, Czechoslovakia and the Soviet Union. His more political thinking about the causes of war and the failings of democracy really had very little consequence at home, and were redundant in those countries where they fell on more sympathetic ears. He was, on balance, too clever, too rigid, too intellectually arrogant and self-reliant to be highly successful in a military career—at least in peacetime. All his life he had been a private man—his own best friend and worst enemy. He was now to have an opportunity to go it entirely alone, outside the more and more uncomfortable and unacceptable scaffolding of the military institution.

8. The Dark Years— 1934-9

It is not remarkable today for retired generals to take up second careers; in 1934 it was more unusual. Fuller, having been on his own admission an unconventional soldier, next became an unconventional journalist.[1] It was in part financial necessity which drove him into the columns of the popular Press, but he was also increasingly motivated by the urge to find a popular rather than a professional or educated forum for his military and political views; he was, as he himself admitted, motivated both by a need for bread and butter and a desire for propaganda.[2] At first he wrote principally for the *Evening Standard*, but he also contributed to the *Daily Mail*, the *Daily Mirror*, the *Sunday Dispatch* and the *Manchester Evening Chronicle*. A selection of his titles will illustrate what he was about: 'We Need One Brain for Our Fighting Forces';[3] 'Playing at Soldiers';[4] 'England Can Keep the Peace—Between Germany and France';[5] 'Let us Rearm Wisely and Save Money';[6] 'Our Air Force Needs a Motorized Army';[7] 'They Now Move Tanks by Numbers';[8] 'Too Many Old Men in the Army',[9] 'Wolf into Poodle. The Farce of this Week's Manoeuvres'.[10] Such titles had a dramatic and immediate appeal at a time when rearmament and the growing military threat were beginning to arouse much passion—on one side or another.

Throughout the early years of his retirement up until 1939 the Fullers lived in Chelsea, at first in Beaufort Gardens, and from mid-1934 onwards at 37 Cheyne Court Mansions. It was while they were living there, on June 7th, 1934, that Sir Oswald Mosley, a mile and a half away in Olympia, held his most famous meeting from which large numbers of hecklers were vigorously and none too gently evicted by Mosley's stewards. Mosley was strongly criticized from many quarters for his methods and it was from this point in time that the support he had from the right wing o the Conservative Party virtually evaporated. To very large sections of the British electorate and establishment he appeared to have been exposed as the satanic harbinger of a Continental-style regime based on violence and stormtroopers.[11] It was characteristic of Fuller, who believed that mass reactions were almost always wrong, that he should have chosen Olympia as the occasion for joining Mosley. The two men had met before but, after Olympia, Fuller wrote to Mosley and asked if he could join his organization. 'The time to join a man is at his worst moment' were the crucial words in his letter.[12]

It would be a great mistake to underplay the importance or seriousness of this move or its consequences. There is ample evidence in Fuller's previous life and writings to show that joining the British Union of Fascists was in many ways a natural development of his previous political thinking and beliefs; his letters to Starr in particular show that in the early thirties he believed that the Western political system needed to be scrapped rather than repaired and that war might be a force in its reconstruction. They also reveal that he was interested in the 'New Britain' movement but concluded that it lacked organization; fascism, on the other hand, he concluded as early as February 1934, had 'come to stay'.[13] It is important not to judge his action by standards derived from feelings of revulsion engendered by events which took place after June 1934. It is also reasonable to conclude that he saw in fascism a way of implementing the military reforms he thought essential for purely patriotic reasons, reforms which he had largely failed to have adopted from within the military machine. There is also ample evidence, as will later become apparent, to show that any chances he might have had, in the thirties or forties, for military re-employment, or for a really significant and permanent civilian job, were destroyed by his overt membership of the BUF and his fascist writings. Becoming a fascist did Fuller almost as little good as it did Mosley.

For some years the two were close. Mosley thought Fuller brilliant and incisive but impatient. He was certainly admitted to Mosley's inner councils and would have been made Minister of Defence had Mosley come to power.[14] In August Fuller received a long letter from Mosley, on BUF paper, in which he was asked to draw up a clear-cut policy on the co-ordination of defence. 'You can help immensely, not only in our Organization, but in the development of our policy, and I would very much like to have your detailed criticism of it.'[15] Mosley also gave him the BUF rule book for comment; Fuller thought it too bureaucratic and, typically, advised scrapping the lot, a recommendation which Mosley did not follow up.[16] From this time also Fuller began to adopt the fascist attitude to the Jews. He had always found it easy to make sweeping racial generalizations, as his early views about Kaffirs and Frenchmen illustrated, but he now began to parrot the shrill and irrational condemnations of the growing anti-Semitic stereotype. It is difficult to understand how brilliant men of extreme rationality can associate themselves with anti-Semitic or other unpleasant racialist views and yet it could be argued that it is just such men who sometimes seem most prone to fall victim to irrationality of this sort. Late in his life Fuller complained that his political outlook had been misunderstood.

> I am not opposed to democracy [he claimed in 1963] in which the electorate is responsible and well informed—a selected or educated democracy. What I object to is a mass electorate, because it is always irresponsible and ill-informed. It was for this reason that I supported Sir Oswald Mosley. He adopted the fascist theory of the Corporate State, according with which the electors are organized into vocational groups instead of being divided into districts. I saw in this a possibility of introducing responsibility in a mass democracy... Unfortunately Mosley mixed this up with Black Shirts and other rubbish. Also I supported him because he advocated a fully mechanized army.[17]

This justification, nearly thirty years after the event, certainly hits one of the nails on the head in its last sentence but otherwise it is a very imperfect recollection. Fuller was opposed to democracy because democracy, at least of the Western variety, must mean in the last resort that the people's will, however imperfect or ill-informed, should prevail, and this he could not accept. His whole interpretation of history was based on belief in the influence of great men, not of the people. The corporate state was a means, not of making mass democracy responsible, but of removing power and influence from the masses while still paying lip service to their sovereignty; the communist state is very similar. Mosley's predilection for Black Shirts was one which Fuller was prepared publicly to accept at the time although he privately found it rather funny. 'Other rubbish' may refer to anti-Semitism and Fuller cannot escape the very serious charge that he actively put forward extreme anti-Semitic views. The conclusion must be that, since Fuller publicly embraced fascism for at least five years and held a high place in its British hierarchy, his political views at that time have not been misunderstood, and he must bear responsibility for them.

It was also in 1934 that Fuller began to put a considerable effort into another ill-starred venture. This was attack by illumination, the concept that tanks fitted with powerful flickering light-projectors could carry out successfully night attacks by illuminating and dazzling the defender. Such tanks were code-named CDL, or 'Canal Defence Lights'. In 1933 Fuller had joined the de Thoren Syndicate which was named after Commander Oscar de Thoren, RN, who had suggested the weapon in 1915, but was headed by a man called Mitzakis and was dedicated to the production of the projectors. Fuller was to devote much ink and effort to the subject of CDL in the next fifteen years.[18] In a similar context he saw himself for a while as the right man to become a national arms salesman and believed that a growing market existed amongst the rising nations of Asia.[19]

1934 also saw the publication of *Empire Unity and Defence*. This was, for the most part, a well-structured plea for a revival and reconstruction of the British Empire in order that it could bring peace and stability to the world,[20] and for greater co-operation between the imperial nations and between the three Services in each nation.[21] He pointed out that the only existing imperial institution was the War Graves Commission[22] and called for the establishment of an Imperial Council and a Ministry of National Defence.[23] He made his usual fun of the League[24] and of disarmament[25] and pointed out that because economic attack was now the stronger form of war, Britain was in peculiar danger.[26] On Europe he was particularly shrewd. Britain is part of Europe but the Empire's centre of gravity lies in the oceans. We cannot cut ourselves off from Europe, but if we cut ourselves off from the Dominions and the Empire we shall be shifted from the European centre to the European circumference. Therefore we need a closer imperial union even if Canada leaves. As to Europe we

should withdraw all our guarantees and only intervene in a
European war if we must, to strike at the culprit; we should leave
Hitler and his like alone. The sacrifice of British lives 'because
some ridiculous Pole has knifed some ridiculous German' did not
appeal to Fuller. However, he was pessimistic about the future
because Britain's statesmen were incapable of taking the necessary action.[27] All this was an arguable, if extreme, position.
Fascism, however, also peeped through the rationality. In one
place he held that dictatorship ran counter to the Anglo-Saxon
ideal;[28] in another he admitted that the strange forms of
Mussolini, Hitler and Lenin were proclaimed foul but 'perhaps,
less than a generation hence we shall call them divine'.[29] Worse
still, he raised the bogey of the threat of a world oligarchy of
Jews[30] and called the League a bastard, 'pink Jew-Bolshevik
baby'.[31]

By the end of 1934 he was beginning to contribute to fascist
journals. In November he published an article in *Blackshirt* under
the stirring title 'Earl Haig—The Man of Bronze. The Man is
Dead: We salute him, but his spirit must be buried. An archaic
political system that crashed into war'.[32] In December he paid a
visit to Germany and met Hitler whom he found easy to talk to.[33]
In the New Year, he published an article on the Jews in the first
issue of the *Fascist Quarterly*. He called the article, ominously,
'The Cancer of Europe'[34] and it was later published in *Weltpost*
under the title 'General Fuller über die Juden'.[35] The Nazis were
to make considerable mileage out of Fuller's writings in the next
few years. From Cheyne Court Mansions, he set out in January to
visit Germany again, and this time he saw Ribbentrop and Hess.[36]
In England he attended many Blackshirt meetings but also continued to contribute articles to the daily newspapers and nearly
succeeded, with Liddell Hart's help,[37] in getting himself made the
latter's successor as military correspondent of the *Daily
Telegraph*. However, his 'Cancer of Europe' article offended its
proprietors and he was not appointed.[38]

In February, yet another Fuller book was published. This was
The Army in My Time, one of a series in which other titles were
Literature in My Time by Compton Mackenzie and *Marriage in
My Time* by Marie Stopes. Fuller told Liddell Hart that his own
contribution was spiritually in the potboiler class[39] but Swinton
thought it contained a lot of truth unfortunately expressed in a

way calculated to exasperate the reader.[40] The *National Review* thought that Fuller had 'developed into a clear and amusing writer'.[41] In parts the book was certainly not much more than journalism and there were touches of a rather cheap bitterness in such statements as, 'our Army is a national institution maintained to amuse the people who love displays'.[42] A conscious populism seems to be behind another passage which concludes with the words: 'the soldier is now plagued by a super-abundance of education in place of beer'.[43] The book is divided into four sections—the pre-Boer War era, the Boer War, the World War and the future. It contains a castigation of the Cardwell reforms, the failure to see the relevance of mounted infantry and entrenchment early in the Boer War, and the failure of European armies to learn from the lessons of the Boer and Russo-Japanese Wars and to realize the future potency of the bullet. Fuller drew many lessons from the World War, the more interesting of which were that: since the aim of wars of industrial attrition was defeat of the enemy nation rather than its army, the reinstatement of prosperous peace was impossible; non-industrial nations could no longer be free and independent in the old sense; tanks formed the basis of air strikes at the enemy's moral foundations and so wars would become area or even cubic rather than linear; the civil population would become the main target in future war the tactical object of which would become demoralization rather than destruction; and land and air warfare needed to be combined with the object of imposing one's 'will on the enemy with the least possible destruction of life and property on both sides, so that the final object of war—a more contented form of peace—may be established'.[44] 'To win a war and lose the peace which should follow it, is the action of an intoxicated fool,'[45] Fuller concluded.

Looking into the future he repeated, in a popularized form, the message of *Lectures on FSR III*: the requirement for a small, mechanized army. He now believed that in war our problems were to secure the UK base, to establish overseas bases and to operate forward from them. The first was an RN–RAF affair, the second was tri-Service and called for amphibious tanks in opposed landings, while the third called for a mobile army capable of protecting air forces on the ground. In future war distribution of force would replace concentration of force as the fundamental principle as a result of the growth of air power; zones of moving 'fortresses' or tank and anti-tank formations would replace trench systems and would protect air power on the ground. Air forces would operate against each other from these bases and against enemy civilian centres. It can be argued that throughout *The Army in My Time* Fuller was an unrepentant 'all-tank' man. He argued once more against mixing infantry and tanks,[46] and called for the separation of the 'gendarmerie' and army functions as mechanization proceeded. Planes would become the dominant offensive arm and their bases had to be protected by the dominant land weapon, the tank. Infantry should not be bolstered up by protecting them with tanks because this destroyed the offensive power of tanks. Instead tanks should be protected by troops capable of beating back an armoured attack, that is by tanks themselves and by troops in partially armoured vehicles using land mines and anti-tank machine guns and cannon.[47] It can, therefore, also be argued that Fuller did not believe that all fighting should be done by tanks, that he envisaged armoured gun-carriers and personnel carriers. The conclusion from this somewhat sterile argument must flow from one's definition of a tank. The argument generated a lot of heat in the thirties. Infantry still exist as offensive troops today so Fuller must have been wrong in claiming that they were offensively useless forty years ago, the argument could run on. But today's infantry are not foot soldiers and they travel and often fight in armoured fighting-vehicles. Also they have now been given a weapon with which they can defeat tanks, the guided missile. The emphasis which Fuller placed on the defence of grounded air-power was in the event unwarranted as regards strategic bombers because the aeroplane's increasing range made it unnecessary to locate such machines in the fighting zone.

There are no fascist undertones in *The Army in My Time* but in March he burst forth into fascist print again, first in the *Daily Mirror* with an article on 'How I Would Run the Country'.[48] Fuller's recipe was the handing over of the Government to Mosley 'on condition he made me his Minister of Defence'. To Mosley he would suggest passing over 'the care of our lunatics to the Hon. Sir Richard Stafford Cripps', considered, of course, by others to be the intellectual giant of the Labour movement. In April there followed an article in the second issue of the *Fascist Quarterly* on 'Fascism and War' in which he argued that the fascist countries were more able to make quick and efficient decisions in the face of the threats of war which must result from the pressures of overpopulation and economic nationalism.[49] These threats were of course derived from his own perception of the biological and economic causes of war.

Elles, now a Lieutenant-General and Master-General of Ordnance, wrote to him three times in April about the de Thoren lamp.[50] The two main events of the year for Fuller, however, were his visits to Hitler's manoeuvres in September and to the war in Abyssinia from October onwards. He was the sole foreign journalist present at the manoeuvres on Luneberg Heath, site of Germany's ultimate surrender, and his reports in the *Daily Mail* are evidence of how impressive he found the German military machine even at that date.[51] How much influence his writings, and the verbal advice he gave on his many visits to Germany, had had on its development is difficult to quantify. German generals were later to testify that much heed had been paid to his words, but he claimed he never corresponded with any of them, or with the Nazis, in the thirties.[52] It may have been during the September visit that he made his unheralded inspection of Dachau and later reported to Mosley that he 'saw prisoners but no evidence in those pre-war days of any ill-treatment, beyond the usual rough jail standards'.[53]

The Italian conquest of Abyssinia brought about Fuller's longest and most adventurous journey since Milne had sent him to India in 1926. At first Britain had taken a strong line at Geneva, and Fuller had campaigned against this particularly in an article in *Blackshirt* in August in which he opposed sanctions against Italy and prophesied that another world war would result in 'plague and anarchy'.[54] In September he was appointed by Lord Rothermere as the *Daily Mail*'s special war correspondent, and he left Victoria Station at two o'clock on the afternoon of October 3rd, seen off by Sonia and bound for Rome and Africa.[55] He thought Sonia took the parting bravely and sweetly and his 'heart went out to her, for to her it means so much to be left alone'. After crossing the Channel he caught the Rome Express at Calais, reached Paris at 8.45 p.m. and Rome at 7.20 p.m. the next day. On the 5th he visited the Forum and on the 7th, after sightseeing in St Peter's, had an interview with Mussolini at 5.0 p.m. in his study in the Palazzo Venezia. He found him as easy to talk to as he had found Hitler. Mussolini arranged his passage to Abyssinia by sea. He questioned Fuller about British attitudes to the League crisis he had precipitated and said that he could not understand the hostility of the British Press. Fuller explained that Jewish influence was the reason. He suggested that Italy ought to fight a short war because her weakness was her staying power. As he left the room his impression was of a man of Napoleonic proportions advised, unfortunately, by sycophants. The Italian people, Fuller had concluded, regarded the war as Mussolini's private affair. He stayed for two more days in Rome and then went to Naples where he boarded the *Biancomano* without a ticket as the guest of 'Il Duce'.

There were 3,600 troops on board, many of them what Fuller called 'armed colonists' or 'Blackshirt volunteers', as well as six other correspondents, two American, two French and two Italian. On the 14th they reached Port Said and were given a great welcome by the Italian community as they sailed through the Canal. They arrived at Massawa on the 17th. Fuller disembarked the next day and went immediately by rail to Asmara, the capital of Italian Eritrea. From here the Commander-in-Chief, General de Bono, had set out on October 2nd to lead an army of 110,000 across the river Mareb into Abyssinia without benefit even of a declaration of war. In Asmara, Fuller had a long talk with Count Ciano, who seemed afraid of what England might do. Next day the *Daily Mail* photographer, who had also been sent to Asmara, bought an old Fiat lorry and on May 20th they used it to visit de Bono's HQ in Coatit, a little on the Eritrean side of the frontier. De Bono was an old man, too old for the job, Fuller thought as he returned to Asmara and spent the next few days in writing four articles. He had decided to concentrate on articles rather than news because the news agencies were given transmission priority over newspaper correspondents like himself. On the 24th he set off on a trip towards the front but returned to Asmara on the 27th. On November 3rd he went in a bus with eleven other journalists to Adigrat, an Abyssinian town which had been occupied by de Bono some weeks before. There was a thunderstorm, his kit was soaked and he had some difficulty in finding a tent. The *Natal Advertiser* reported later that at one time he had been put in a tent with the mess servants[56] and it may have been on this visit to Adigrat. Generals who become journalists may

have to pay a social penalty! Next day, resilient as ever, he was
attached to some Blackshirt troops, 'the armed colonist' variety
no doubt. They looked like brigands, Fuller thought and enjoyed
looking like that, 'a kind of Pirates of Penzance business'. 'Some
wore as badges skulls with daggers in their teeth, others flashes of
lightning etc. etc.'. Their discipline, he concluded, was nil. His
subsequent article in the *Daily Mail* was more complimentary. 'A
kinder, more considerate, and more generous-minded body of
men I have yet to meet.'[57] This trip was quite a lengthy one and
he did not get back to Asmara until November 11th.

Sanctions were imposed by the League on the 18th and
Mussolini immediately replaced de Bono with Badoglio, Italy's
most distinguished soldier. On the 20th Fuller sent a cable to
Swinton to be read out at the Cambrai dinner. Badoglio landed at
Massawa on the 28th and imposed a rigorous censorship on
foreign journalists. Fuller tried to visit the front again but was
stopped at Adigrat. He had met Badoglio on the *Biancomano*
when the Marshal was paying a visit to the campaign so he now
requested an interview, and got one, in Asmara, on December
10th. The interview was pleasant enough but restrictions were
not lifted and journalists were confined to Asmara. Fuller hung
on hopefully for a while but after Christmas he decided that there
was no point in staying and on January 7th, 1936, he left for
Khartoum and a plane home to Croydon. The war, after passing
through the guerilla stage, moved, prematurely for the Emperor,
but as a consequence of his own actions, into the decisive battle
phase, and ended in June with an Italian victory.

Back in London, and reunited with Sonia after an absence of
three and a half months, he was invited to an informal meeting
with Churchill, Duff Cooper, now Secretary of State for War,
Liddell Hart and Trenchard at Buck's Club on January 14th, at
which he was given an opportunity to air his views on Abyssinia,
the iniquities of the Cardwell system and Defence reorganization.[58] In January the *Army Quarterly* carried a Fuller article
entitled 'Is War More Horrible?'[59] in which he argued for fascism
on the grounds that war was becoming more psychologically
horrible for civilians and it was, therefore, necessary to abolish
democracy in order to protect the population from terror
through the imposition of discipline. In the end, he concluded,
terror might itself restrain mankind from attempting periodic

suicide, which is of course our situation today.

In the spring Nicholson and Watson published *Memoirs of an Unconventional Soldier* in a handsome binding. Fuller had had to leave much of the proof-reading to a certain Captain J. Russell Kennedy, who had, in fact, been with Sonia when she saw him off in October at Victoria, but he had received a copy himself in Asmara on December 31st and had hastily read it through on the flight to Croydon. Almost the whole of the book is devoted to an exhaustive account of his military career, to the virtual exclusion of any detail of his private life or of his non-military activities. As he told Starr, 'if you want to live a full life . . . you must live with your occupation as if it were your wife.'[60] His experiences in South Africa are also only briefly summarized because he had already written, and intended to publish, a separate account of them. In spite, or even perhaps because of this, the first 451 pages of the book provide a stimulating and immensely valuable, if caustic, account of the development of the British Army in the first three and a half decades of the twentieth century as seen by one of its most thoughtful, able and controversial officers. On almost every page Fuller demonstrated just how uncomfortable a brother officer he must have been, and how cutting and insufferable his wit and his perception must have seemed to those less intellectually well-endowed than himself. His committee style, for instance, is well illustrated by his response, when attending the Army Reconstruction Committee in 1919, to the somewhat horsy question: 'How many hours a day can a tank run?' Fuller had replied: 'Thus far we have not exceeded twenty-four.' Indeed, the chapters in the *Memoirs* which cover his service in the War Office are among the most sardonic and amusing things he ever wrote. The last twenty-six pages form a final chapter called 'Synthetic-Iconoclasm', and this was a horse of a different colour and represented Fuller's 1936 politico-military 'credo'.

This final chapter begins with the admission that the author has been credited with the introduction of mechanization and with the stirring up of the Army. Mechanization, he argued, would have come anyway and his own role was merely that of an assistant; mechanization was an inevitable consequence of the operation of the law of military development and the constant tactical factor. Moreover it was obvious, as he had pointed out before, that the attack on the army's brains, proposed in 'Plan

1919' would soon switch to the nation's nerves, and that war was more likely to be eliminated by weapons than by words. Such influence as he had exerted had mostly had its effect abroad. At home he had been accused over and over again of exaggeration. As regards the stirring up of the Army he accepted this but pointed out that his military and political scepticism stemmed from his truth-loving nature as a child. It was this scepticism which led him to question old assumptions and beliefs and which had lately turned from the military to the political context. 'Synthetic-Iconoclasm', however, then took a more strident and polemic turn. He argued that he was seeking a new spirituality which would lead to the elimination of the moral causes of war—greed and fear. The masses were generally wrong, so he normally started his thinking from the opposite of the mass opinion. Democracy led to war. The Age of Plenty might eliminate the economic cause of war and lower birth rates might diminish the biological cause in Europe, but growing Asiatic population pressures might lead to new invasions in the face of which European unity would be essential. The First World War delivered Europe from the bondage of its old political system but a new system was now necessary and its development was being inhibited by the League powers' defence of the status quo. The present struggle was between 'outworn democracy' and 'emergent fascism'. Democracy was unsuited to industrial society but fascism was concerned with 'the creation of a higher freedom'. Moreover, great men, as Carlyle propounded, were instrumental in bringing about human accomplishments; in the war there were no such men but now they had arisen again—Lenin, Stalin, Pilsudski, Atatürk, Mussolini and Hitler. Men, and most of all great men, must conquer fear; in Carlyle's words: 'A man shall and must be valiant.' 'Truth,' Fuller wrote, 'is courage intellectualized,'[61] and although he used this aphorism to explain the emphasis on great men in his study of war he must surely have regarded it as his principal article of faith for he certainly displayed throughout his life a most valiant devotion to the truth as he saw it. Indeed he admitted on the last page of his *Memoirs* that he had often sinned against the ark of the British military covenant by attacking not only the system but those who controlled it or were controlled by it—in its way an act, be it said, as courageous and foolhardy as any open to an army officer.

In April Churchill wrote to him and acknowledged that the *Memoirs* contained some complimentary passages about the ways in which he had helped with the development of tanks [62] while the July number of the *Fascist Quarterly* [63] likened Fuller to 'Gulliver Among the War-House Lilliputians'. Others were also awakening to the dangers to Britain which were brewing up in central Europe. In March Sir Thomas Inskip had been appointed to the new post of Minister for the Co-ordination of Defence, while Liddell Hart, sensing the approaching crisis, asked Ironside, now GOC-in-C Eastern Command, why Fuller could not be reinstated. Ironside, in spite of his long friendship with Fuller, was not prepared to move because it would upset promotion prospects. [64] Fuller himself sounded the alarm in the *Sunday Dispatch* on May 10th. 'Europe's Next War', his headline ran, 'Will Be The Spring of a Tiger'. Hitler was a man of peace but if he attacked it would be all over in a few weeks, or hours. [65] Such sentiments well illustrated the ambivalence of Fuller's political position at the time, and of all patriotic British fascists.

September saw him visiting Hitler's second autumn manoeuvres, this time in Bad Nauheim in Hesse. His visits, which were sponsored by the German Government and not by the Wehrmacht, annoyed many of the German generals, one of whom even thought that Fuller was a spy sent to Germany by Lord Rothermere and believed that Hitler placed more reliance on Fuller than on the information provided by his ambassadors and military attachés. Dill, who was visiting Berlin at the time, was displeased to hear that Fuller was also in Germany. [66] Fuller wrote up the manoeuvres in the *Daily Mail* and followed this up with an article in the *Fascist Quarterly* on the 'Air Defence Problem', [67] again illustrating his political dilemma. He also published articles in American journals, for instance one on 'Totalitarian War' in *Army Ordnance*, [68] and an American edition of *Generalship* was also brought out at about the same time. [69] By the end of the year, however, his enormous literary energy resulted in the publication of yet another new book, based on his Abyssinian adventure, *The First of the League Wars*. The League, of course, was the League of Nations, and the wars were those which Fuller believed would result, as had the Italo-Abyssinian War, from the League's attempt to maintain the status quo in the face of those powerful, and fascist, nations who were disadvantaged by it. The book is almost schizophrenic in its attitude towards 'totalitarian' war, when compared with his earlier, and later, views on the destructiveness of war, particularly the slaughter of the civil population. In *The First of the League Wars* Fuller appeared to admire and recommend what we know he deeply abhorred. There is again an echo of Clausewitz's attitude to absolute war in this; indeed, Fuller believed that totalitarian war itself, of which the leading tactical idea is attack on the civil will, would in the second of the League Wars, between the democracies and the dictatorships, become absolute in the form of a death struggle between contending ideologies.[70]

It is important to emphasize that Fuller had arrived at this position by both a military and a political route. The military route began with mechanization, proceeded via the possibilities which air power raised of raining destruction—explosive, incendiary and chemical—on the civilian population and through terror and panic achieving victory. The only possible defence against such a psychological attack was psychological strength—the avoidance of fear and panic through national and totalitarian discipline. The political route began with distaste for mass opinion and continued with the drawing of a distinction between democratic individual freedom, enabling some to exploit others, and fascist state freedom, in which all were subordinated to the common good. It was these sorts of argument which led him to adopt as his goal the fascist Corporate State or, as he significantly chose to call it, the Threefold State, catering for the bodies, minds and souls of men. Threefold States, of course, were most capable of waging the totalitarian warfare which mechanization made inevitable, and most capable of withstanding it. In all this there was considerable rationality, although he made four enormous errors in his assumptions: first, he grossly overestimated, as did almost everyone at the time, the destructive and moral effects of non-nuclear strategic bombing; second, he assumed that gas would be used in future wars (mustard and tear gas were used in Abyssinia); third, he totally underestimated the ability of some democracies to unite themselves and withstand the onslaught of the dictators; fourth, he failed to take into account the fallible and evil nature of the leadership thrown up in Nazi Germany, or the bedrock common sense of the majority in the democracies. That Fuller's natural authoritarianism, his intolerance of those he chose to regard as fools, his career bitterness and his belief in military and political reform led him up the fascist path is clear. It is more difficult to understand how he reconciled his culture and intelligence with the struttings and pretensions of the Blackshirts or with their more extreme, irrational or unpleasant views. Of the latter many abound in *The First of the League Wars*. He quoted Treitschke with approval: 'War is holy.... It is the supreme remedy for the ills from which States suffer.'[71] He praised the creativity and human challenge of war. He claimed that Hitler and Ludendorff had rationalized Clausewitz by demonstrating that politics, when the causes of war remain virulent, must become subservient to war because war is, in Ludendorff's words, 'the supreme expression of the people's will to life'.[72] He based much of his thinking about the causes of war on the fallacious and extreme geopolitical premise that states function as biological organisms and must expand racially and struggle for a mate.[73] He likened the Italian soldiers, whom he laughed at in the privacy of his diary, to anchorites who 'fought like Crusaders'.[74] But most unforgivably of all he larded the book with anti-Semetic gibes: the Jews, we learn, exploited the moral degradation of Germany in 1923;[75] cinemas, which were largely controlled or influenced by Jews, purveyed stories of vice and crime; the Jews had established Bolshevism in Russia and would in this way come to dominate the world;[76] President Wilson was completely under the influence of Jews; the German Reich was opposed to international capitalism and that is why it was anti-Jewish.[77] The proliferation of these distortions and smears was no doubt the price Fuller thought he had to pay for the power and influence which the establishment of a fascist state would have given him, and the opportunity it would have provided for military and political reform. The price was paid in pieces of silver which cost Fuller less because he was undoubtedly able for a while to rationalize the arguments. Wars have been creative in their ultimate consequences; war and peace do represent a continuum; states do take on a kind of life of their own; European soldiers in the desert must look something like Crusaders; Jews can make Gentiles jealous, guilty or angry. But none of these facts justifies the cult of military might, the practice of violent expansionism, the extermination of a race. It says much for the climate of opinion in England at the time that when *The First of the*

League Wars was reviewed in the *Army Quarterly* the editor, separately, devoted as much space to recommending its military interest as to recognizing the author's fascist viewpoint. 'No student of warfare can afford to disregard, or to treat lightly, his opinions'.[78]

In the same issue of the *Army Quarterly* he had an article on 'Our Recruiting Problem and a Solution'.[79] The war clouds were apparent to many now; two of Fuller's solutions were the establishment of Boys' Training Battalions and the creation of long careers for adult soldiers with discharge options every three years. He also wanted better conditions of service. These proposals, which anticipated post-war developments, were embedded in fascist sentiment and reference to Hitler's labour conscription policy. In January he sent Field Marshal Sir Cyril Deverell, the new CIGS, a copy of his paper on CDLs. The CIGS, an infantryman who had been given the unenviable nickname of 'Butcher' Deverell when commanding 3 Division in 1917, and who was eventually to be eased out by Hore-Belisha, wrote to thank him and to indicate that he would welcome periodic visits from Fuller to discuss military matters.[80] Duff Cooper, the Secretary of State for War, also received a copy of the paper.[81] At the end of February the CIGS wrote again to tell him that there had been a CDL trial on Salisbury Plain.[82] He also indicated that he was interested in a visit which Fuller was about to make to Franco's Army because Britain had no official military attaché with Franco. He invited Fuller to call at the War Office to inspect the information already collected before setting off and asked him to be particularly on the lookout in Spain for material on tanks, anti-aircraft fire, the effects of bombing on attacking troops and air–ground co-operation.

The outbreak of the Spanish Civil War had, of course, presented Fuller with the opportunity to undertake some more military journalism, this time as a freelance. Unfortunately his visits to Spain are not as well documented as his Abyssinian escapade. He went first in March 1937 and saw Franco and the front line. He submitted a full report to the War Office in which he categorized what he had seen as a 'city war', not a trench or guerilla war. The Reds were strong in the towns, but the 'Pinks' had made the previous government possible. Franco did not use terror and so it would be a long war. Bombing had done little damage and the German AA guns were effective; there were no tank tactics. Franco would win because he wanted to establish a better peace and had discipline and humanity on his side. The War Office was impressed with the report which Intelligence felt was 'les partisan' than most they had received.[83]

Before going to Spain he had received from Faber and Faber a copy of *The Last of the Gentlemen's Wars*, an account of his experiences three and a half decades previously in South Africa, based on diaries he had kept at the time. On his return he was met by favourable reviews, including one by Liddell Hart in *The Times*.[84] This was not surprising; the book was quiet, measured recollection, full of youthful adventure and untouched by the strident and turgid clamour of his reaction to the political and military environment of the late thirties.

This was, however, a brief interlude, a foretaste of what was eventually to come in the summer evening of his life when he turned his pen increasingly to history. For the moment he had more immediate fish to fry and was adopted as the British Union candidate for Duff Cooper's parliamentary constituency of St George's, Westminster. It was of course a symbolic choice of opponent. In April the *English Review* brought out a Fuller article on 'The Air Defence of London and our Great Cities' which was copied immediately in a German magazine *Die Auslese*, and in the same month Lovat Dickson published his last major polemic *Towards Armageddon: The Defence Problem and Its Solution*. Fuller had been writing on this theme for nearly twenty years and much of the book is repetition and updating; much also is fascist propaganda or apologia. He called once more for radical change in the British political system; he denied that Hitler wanted war but warned that if war came Hitler would, as he had said, hurl himself upon his enemy 'like a flash of lightning in the night';[85] he prophesied, as he had done in his writings on the Abyssinian War, that in future wars between major European nations surprise would become so vital that 'the first blow may well be the last';[86] he reiterated his belief that infantry were outmoded on the battlefield,[87] except in an occupational or defensive role, although he contradicted this on another page with the categorical statement: 'I do not for one moment suggest that infantry, and the bulk of our men belong to that arm, have no place on the modern battlefield';[88] he repeated his suggestion for longer other-rank careers with three-year options[89] and for Boys' Training Battalions;[90] and, finally, he reproduced his theories about area warfare, the tank–anti-tank concept, air power and the limitations of battleships.

There were also, however, some considerable new developments in his thinking in *Towards Armageddon*, brought to fruition, no doubt, by the application of his *Foundations* system; that is, through the analysis of the probable conditions of future war. Inskip, in contrast appears to have said: 'I am not going to attempt to foresee what another war will be like'.[91] In spite, or perhaps even because of, his sympathy for the fascist states, he saw clearly that the development of the peace–war continuum, and the fascist adherence to military surprise, would in future necessitate a military posture of constant political, economic and military readiness for war—a posture which has since become endemic among the great powers. He recommended that other ranks should be given more responsibility and freedom, that transfer between arms should be made easier and resettlement provision bettered, and that in the population at large diet and cooking should be improved, fit breeding through birth control and sterilization encouraged, and physical and intellectual education improved.[92] Turning to the more obviously military requirements of future war he mounted a characteristically unconventional attack on the 'team spirit', 'that pernicious ideal of our public schools' which resulted in committees and conferences being substituted for individual leadership.[93] As the advent of air power meant that victory could now be achieved by attacking the civil will, war would become national rather than regimental.[94] The advent of wireless, both for the transmission of words and the control of robot machines, might eliminate the fighting man altogether, as he had prophesied in the early twenties, and produce 'a kind of metaphysical war'.[95] But air power could also provide the Empire with a deterrent force which would inhibit any aggressor from attacking us. 'It would almost seem,' he wrote with an apparently uncanny touch of prescience, based, however on analysis, 'that an all-wise Providence had allowed the secret of flight to be discovered, not in order to turn humanity mad but in order to prevent it from losing its wits.'[96] Liquid fuel rockets, he suggested, could be used as anti-aircraft weapons.[97]

It was, however, when he came to consider the consequences

of the bombing of the civilian population that his gifts of analysis and foresight forsook him. Study of air raids in the First World War had shown him that the material damage caused by HE bombs was not then very great and, in spite of increases in the load and size of bombs dropped, would not be catastrophic in a future war when HE and incendiaries, and not gas, would be dropped, as he now thought the former two more effective. The moral effect of such bombing would on the other hand be cataclysmic in an undisciplined society; it would result in complete industrial paralysis and civil panic (the civilian equivalent of the strategical paralysis of 'Plan 1919') which could only be avoided by the imposition of a new leadership.[98] In 1914–18, he claimed, our citizens did not have the necessary stoutness of disposition, nor, he continued, did they have it today as

> is proved by the inability of the London police to control the underworld of the East End of the capital. For instance, on October 4th, 1936, Sir Oswald Mosley was granted permission to march some 7,000 Fascists through the East End, and though 6,000 police were called out, that is approximately one to each marcher, the Commissioner of Police called the march off, because he considered that, were it held, he would be unable to maintain law and order. Though I am in no way concerned here with the political questions involved, it seems to me that if the largest forces of police ever assembled in the East End were unable to deal with a political demonstration, how much less likely is it that, in the event of an air attack on London, they will be able to deal with the frantic terror-striken mobs which will surge through the city. Replace 7,000 Fascists by 7,000 twenty-pound high explosive and incendiary bombs, that is the load of no more than thirty bombing machines, and what will the police do and what will be the mental state of the Government when they have failed to accomplish the impossible?[99]

Fuller was out of touch with political and social reality when he wrote that. His theories, his background and environment, his anxiety for the survival of his country, his very intellectuality, made him see only what his white-hot and sometimes narrow rationality allowed him to believe could and would happen, and at the same time clouded his perception of what fallible, irrational, uneducated, warm, sentimental, patriotic and, often, noble human beings would do in a national and international crisis in which they felt themselves to be the standard-bearers of right and justice against a rampant evil.

Such canards upon the Cockney working classes notwithstanding, *Towards Armageddon* was sympathetically reviewed in *The Times*[100] and *The Times Literary Supplement*.[101] Both reviewers treated Fuller now with great respect. The latter pointed out that the detached student and the fervent political partisan were curiously mingled in the book while the former commented that Fuller's writings were 'above all, a stimulus to others to think, and think things out, for themselves'. It must be noted before leaving *Towards Armageddon* that fervent political partisanship did not dim his detailed military judgments or even perhaps his longer-term political perceptions. Since mechanization had made the dual military functions of providing a 'gendarmerie' and a war army out of one force less possible, as he had pointed out in *The Army in My Time*, he now proposed that 40 of the existing 136 infantry battalions should be converted to the 'gendarmerie' role, 51 should be motorized and formed, with mechanized artillery and mechanized cavalry, into a striking force, and the remaining 45 become purely the responsibility of the Government of India. The infantry battalions in the mechanized striking force would be used with artillery in the anti-tank role.[102] As regards political perception Fuller saw in 1937 that the forthcoming war would be a conflict between communism and fascism. He regarded communism as the logical goal of democracy whereas fascism was the recoil against it. He was on much sounder ground when he foresaw a German defeat as leading to the spread of communism; in the event it also brought about the survival of many of the democracies and led, of course, to another Armageddon, a metaphysical war founded on nuclear deterrence. Fuller believed that in democracies the generals would once again have to struggle for power with the politicians as they did in the First World War, whereas, in the event again, a civilian was given the supreme direction of the war in Britain. Our true Armageddon, Fuller concluded, lay in avoiding internal decay from which only a new leadership could save us. *Towards Armageddon* was very much a curate's egg.

It was at this time that his friendship with Liddell Hart, which had grown less close since he had joined Mosley, more or less broke down. Liddell Hart was about to achieve his greatest influence as the mentor of Hore-Belisha, who succeeded Duff Cooper at the War Office in May 1937. Liddell Hart and Fuller still had broadly similar military views although Liddell Hart laid more emphasis on the combination of air and tank and the importance of night attacks, and disagreed with Fuller's dismissal of the offensive role of infantry in armoured forces and with his lack of belief in parachute operations. Liddell Hart believed that infantry should become 'tank marines' and should be used as parachutists to seize key points in the rear.[103] These differences well illustrate the contrast between Fuller's rigid intellectuality and Liddell Hart's more pragmatic and flexible approach. For Fuller, infantry, with or without parachutes, were useless in offensive battles involving tanks because they were unarmoured and slow and could not penetrate tanks; Liddell Hart could see that there might be conditions in which men would have to get out of machines to fight. The two men also looked with distaste upon the involvement of the British Army in another Continental war. Both undoubtedly were influenced by their memories of the First World War; Fuller also wanted Britain to act as a neutral referee in any future European conflict.[104] It was Fuller's openly acknowledged fascism which drove a wedge between them in spite of Liddell Hart's earlier praise of Mussolini's armed forces.[105] Fuller's last but one letter to Liddell Hart before the split was rather too much for the latter. 'Why I am attracted towards Fascism', he wrote, 'is not because I want people to be enslaved, but free. Authority without Freedom is despotism and Freedom without Authority is anarchy. I want neither, instead a balance between Authority and Freedom. . . . In Germany, in spite of many puerile restrictions, I find more intellectual freedom than in England and far less hysterical freedom.' Liddell Hart replied with a restrained and reasoned defence of the freedom to criticize—of which Fuller's own life demonstrated the value.[106] Fuller also quarrelled with his brother Walter on the same score,[107] and found that the Press were less willing to publish his articles than they had been before he became a fascist parliamentary candidate. This drove him to concentrate on writing books to augment his income, which was less profitable and more time-consuming than journalism. Throughout 1937 he put in about ten hours a day at his desk, much of it in preparing the two-volume *Decisive Battles* which was to be published in 1939 and 1940.[108]

In October he made a second visit to Spain and again saw the CIGS before he went. This time he was asked to look into the methods used to protect troops from low-flying attacks, AA defences, modern German or Italian equipments in use and relations between the Nationalists and the Italians. He spent ten days in Spain and travelled 1,600 miles by car through the Biscay provinces and along the Aragon front. On return he told the War Office that it was the Nationalists, not the Reds, who made low-flying attacks, that the Vickers AA gun was more effective than the German 88 mm, that he saw little modern equipment and that there was friction with the Italians. Hore-Belisha saw his report and thought it intensely interesting,[109] although this did not cause him to act on Liddell Hart's suggestion in December, made in spite of the coolness between them, that Fuller should be brought back and made Director of Research in the War Office.[110] The *Sunday Dispatch* took an article from him on this Spanish visit and *Action*, a fascist magazine, carried the somewhat arguable headline over a Fuller article: 'The Spanish War from Within. People are United Behind Franco'.[111] The American Journal *Army Ordnance* published an article by him at the end of the year on 'Propaganda and War: The new technique of mendacity as a psychological weapon'.[112] Perhaps, however, Fuller's most remarkable publication of the year was *The Secret Wisdom of the Qabalah* in which he displayed his knowledge of Judaism and his continuing interest in the occult. This short book had been foreshadowed in a passage in *First of the League Wars* in which he had claimed to discern an Oriental and Jewish influence in Bolshevism, an influence based on the leading conception of Judaism, the rule of law under the god of justice, Jehovah, for whom justice was 'the exaltation of his chosen people over all the other races of the earth'. The Judaic law also was twofold, the written and the oral, the latter the reverse of the former, Satanic as opposed to God-like. This was 'the key to the hidden wisdom in the Hebrew Qabalah'.[113]

In 1938 the pace of Hitler's drive for *Lebensraum* began to quicken. Early in the year he took Austria and then turned his eyes towards Czechoslovakia. At home the decision, made in 1937, to mechanize the whole of the cavalry by putting them in light tanks was being implemented, but the conversion of the infantry into a mobile, motorized force was slowed up by some back-tracking in the Estimates for 1939–40 in which funds were only provided for lorries sufficient to lift one brigade at a time out of the three in each division. These developments tended to institutionalize the concept that tanks had a twin role—fast, armed reconnaissance and slow, infantry support—and that light and medium tanks were therefore required. Rearmament was under way but its pace and the tactics on which it was based were unlikely to make the British Army initially a match for the more full-blooded concepts of armoured warfare which the Germans were developing largely on the basis of the writings of Fuller and Liddell Hart themselves. In France there had been a voice calling for mechanization, that of Charles de Gaulle in his book *The Army of the Future*, but his words had had little impact on the defensive-minded establishment. In the Soviet Union, a great deal of progress had been made, again influenced, to a limited extent, by Fuller and Liddell Hart, but the purge of 1937 had put back the clock; armoured formations smacked of élitism, of expertise rather than redness.

Early in 1938 Fuller had a personal rearmament success. On January 28th the War Office ordered Vickers to design and produce a special CDL tank turret to be ready for trials by June 1939. At the same time the War Office took over the CDL patents from the Mitzakis syndicate, which was to cause Fuller a lot of anguish after the war.[114] The next day *Action* came out with an article by Fuller with the title, 'On What should our Foreign Policy be Based?'[115] His answer was that we should give Germany her colonies back, avoid antagonizing the US, Italy, France, Spain and Germany and look to the development of our inter-Imperial machinery. The CDL tank, then, was not to be used against Hitler; in Fuller's mind it was against Stalin that rearmament ought to have been directed, or perhaps against all as insurance. Two months later, however, he wrote to Mosley and withdrew as British Union candidate for St George's, Westminster, pointing out that now Duff Cooper had gone from the War Office, and a vast rearmament scheme was in progress, his special knowledge of defence was no longer required.[116] Mosley wrote a friendly letter in reply and thanked Fuller for his work.[117] When Fuller announced his withdrawal some weeks later it is significant that he then gave as his reason the fact that a Jew, Leslie Hore-Belisha, had already carried out many of the reforms he was advocating.[118] There was an openness of mind about Fuller which few other fascists possessed; he was an intellectual fascist, just as much as he had been an intellectual soldier. In April he visited Spain for the third time, again with a shopping list of questions from the CIGS. In his subsequent report he emphasized the moral effect of air bombardment and called the light tank 'a wretched little machine'.[119] While in Spain he met Arnold Lunn, the ski-ing expert, who recalled later that Fuller had then told him that the Maginot Line would prove to be the tomb of France.[120] In May he castigated the Anglo-French defensive agreement and prophesied that it would lead to war[121] and in July he wrote about CDL to the then General Lord Gort, the new CIGS and future commander of the British Expeditionary Force in 1939–40.[122] Towards the end of the year he suggested in the *Daily Mail* that the TA should be called the Home Army.[123] The year 1938 closed without the publication of another Fuller book—only the third since 1922.

He began 1939, the year of Poland's defeat and the outbreak of the Second World War, with the publication of an article in the *Army Quarterly* praising Franco's 'pacification' tactics and claiming that the hidden cause of the Spanish Civil War was 'a clash between two financial systems'.[124] The German propaganda machine made a deliberate attempt to capitalize on Fuller's activities. His name appeared not infrequently in the German Press and in February the *Völkischer Beobachter* even carried his photograph.[125] German editions of *Memoirs* and *The First of the League Wars* were brought out.[126] The German Military Attaché in London, Von Scheppenburg, engineered a meeting in his home in Fitzjohns Avenue between Fuller and Guderian and the two had a long talk over a cup of tea. Guderian, of course, was to achieve fame with Rommel as the foremost of Germany's panzer generals—perhaps the world's greatest tank practitioner. Von Schweppenburg, however, came to believe that Fuller's fascism was a cloak which enabled him to act as Lord Rothermere's agent in Germany.[127] It obtained for him also the dubious accolade of an invitation, sent on Ribbentrop's behalf, to attend Hitler's fiftieth birthday parade in Berlin on April 20th,[128] which he accepted.

The Times noted his visit on the 19th, and just before he left London he received a telephone call from the Foreign Office telling him that they had warned Sir Ian Hamilton, who had also been invited, 'against going as it might prove dangerous'.[129] Fuller, who claimed that he had expected that the telephone call would be to ask him to note what kind of tanks were on parade, was not deterred. In Berlin he stayed in the Adlon Hotel where he picked up hints that Hitler meant to take Danzig and, if war came, would quickly overrun Poland, but would not attack on the Western Front or bomb French or English cities. An American he met in the hotel told him that Chamberlain's Polish guarantee was the greatest British mistake since the Stamp act.[130] The parade itself was a magnificent and ominous occasion and Fuller's presence caused a considerable stir in the Press. He and Lord Brocket, a brewing magnate and barrister, were Hitler's only British guests. *News Review* reported:

> Face to face with the Fuehrer, though separated from him by the sixty-yards-wide Avenue of Triumph, sat explosive old English warrior Major-General John Frederick Charles Fuller. Wearing a plain grey top-hat among the respondent [*sic*] uniforms of his fellow-guests, he looked somewhat like a cheeky mouse on a gaudy-hued patchwork quilt.... At present Major-General Fuller is distinguished by his Polish wife Sonia, his Poona moustache, and his cosmopolitan collection of decorations, including the DSO, Légion d'Honneur and Order of Leopold of Belgium.[131]

According to the *News Chronicle*:

> The other [guest] was Major-General J. F. C. Fuller, a soldier with strong Fascist sympathies. In yesterday's German broadcast news this 'honest and cool-headed English general' was the subject of warm Nazi encomiums. The radio item introducing Major-General Fuller to world attention was preceded by a grand fanfare of trumpets and another feature speeded his departure from the stage. The 'Last Post', I think, would have been a still more appropriate accompaniment.[132]

Fuller's own words help to paint the picture:

> On the morning of April 20 the great parade took place.
> For some three hours a completely mechanized and
> motorized army roared past the Führer along the
> Charlottenburger Strasse. Never before or since have I
> watched such a formidable mass of moving metal. That
> afternoon all foreign guests were lined up in the new
> Chancellery to meet Herr Hitler. He walked down the line,
> and when he came opposite to me he shook me by the hand
> and said: 'I hope you were pleased with your children?' To
> which I answered: 'Your Excellency, they have grown up so
> quickly that I no longer recognize them', which was true.[133]

Some days after his return to England Fuller wrote to *The
Times* to point out that he was not an anti-democrat but only
believed in democracy which put duty to nation before individual
right or 'pluto-mobocracy'.[134] A number of letters subsequently
appeared congratulating him on this stand, including one from a
woman in the new Czech Protectorate. He also wrote an account
of his visit for the *Westfälische Landeszeitung*, entitled 'Great
Nations', which gives the reader a very clear insight right into the
heart of his ideological–patriotic dilemma:

> My first visit to Germany was in 1903, since when, except
> for the War years, scarcely a year has passed by that I have
> not repeated it; therefore I may claim to some knowledge of
> the country and its people. In 1911 I was in Rostock during
> the Agadir crisis; in 1919 in Cologne shortly after its oc-
> cupation; in 1922 I witnessed the devastating effects of
> inflation; in 1929 I commanded a brigade at Wiesbaden; in
> March 1933 I was in Cologne during Herr Hitler's final
> elections, in January 1935 ski-ing on the Feldberg when the
> Saar plebiscite was held and in 1936 I was present at the
> manoeuvres in Hesse. So it came about when I was hon-
> oured by an invitation from your Führer to attend his
> birthday celebrations, in spite of political events, I gladly
> accepted it, because to me it was not merely the birthday of a
> great man, but also that of a great nation.
> Thus it came about that, on April 19, I arrived in Berlin

to feel what Thomas Carlyle the philosopher and historian must have felt nearly a hundred years ago when he penned the following words: 'For, as I take it, Universal History, the history of what man has accomplished in this world, is at bottom the History of the Great Men who have worked here . . . all things that we see standing accomplished in the world are properly the outer material result, the practical realization and embodiment of Thoughts that dwell in the Great Men sent into the world; the soul of the whole world's history, it may justly be considered, were the history of these.'

Surely this is true. I could feel it in the streets, in the buildings, in the crowds, in the rush of aeroplanes overhead and in the roaring of tanks below. Also I felt it in the fields as one day I travelled along the road to Potsdam: there the soil is poor and sandy; yet from it were sprouting forth emerald green crops. Great leadership and great followership can alone accomplish such things, and it is the first which right through history has ever and always created the second.

From 1932 to 1939 what a change, and all in seven full years. As an Englishman should this make me envious or fearful? No, because throughout life I have held that what is strong and not what is weak is best. Therefore, I believe in the strong man, strong physically, mentally and culturally. Also I believe that strong nations, like strong men, respect each other and that mutual respect is the foundation of peace.

Of the celebrations themselves, it would on my part be a waste of words to describe them, for this has already been done. But I would like to record here the kindly way in which I was received wherever I went, and the chivalrous way in which I was treated. Nothing more could have been done for me than was done. At the Hotel Adlon the Union Jack fluttered from a window, and at the Reichsportfeld I again saw it standing out in the fresh breeze. Frankly, it always fills me with a sense of pride to see my national flag flying peacefully in a foreign city.

Thus it will be seen that in spite of my friendship for Germany, and my respect for her great leader, I remain an

Englishman, with perhaps this difference when compared to some Englishmen, that constant travel has made me also, I hope, a good European. Though Europe embraces many countries, she herself is a civilization. Therefore let us be proud of what is common to us all. Should it come to war, let us fight chivalrously, for chivalry was born in Europe. Should peace remain unbroken, which is my fervent hope, let us honourably work together, not bending the knee to each other, but together marching forwards proudly, not only because we happen to be Germans or English, but above all because we and the French and Italians and other Western European peoples are the standard-bearers of a common culture and common civilization which for the good of the world must not perish from this earth. That is what I felt in Berlin, and this is what I feel in London.[135]

The weeks ticked by. In May he dined with Mosley[136] and *The New Pioneer* blazoned forth, to the converted, his views on conscription. He preferred what he called national service which would have been threefold: a sort of Hitler Youth adapted to British ideals, character and tradition, a Militia for air defence and air raid precautions (ARP) and, on the outbreak of war, the call-up of all men and women 'into array'.[137] In June he wrote the preface to the first volume of *Decisive Battles* which was published later in the year. Fuller admitted in the sixties that both volumes had been too hurriedly written,[138] and this may be so, but in one form or another he had been researching and writing the book, sometimes with the help of brother officers, since he had been on the staff at Camberley.[139]

Fuller had never believed in history for its own sake or in the necessity for dusty accuracy; he studied and wrote history, like so many military historians, for its lessons, for what it could teach us about the present and about how we ought to behave in the future; he believed, moreover, that since man, the material of history, and of military history, remained much the same, history ought to be regarded as a laboratory in which relevant experiments have been ceaselessly conducted.[140] He divided history into two main periods named after 'the men who dreamed the dreams out of which each period awoke', and 'the geographic quantity in which their dreams fructified', the Alexandrian or

Thalassic Period from 336 BC to AD 1453 and the Columbian or Oceanic Period from 1454 onwards. The latter period he divided into Columbian Proper (1492–1763) and the Napoleonic or Continental Period. War itself, at the highest level of generalization, was caused by the clash of myths, cultures or dreams.[141] Volume One deals with the Alexandrian and Columbian Proper Periods and covers eighteen battles in detail linked with short synopses filling in the historical interstices. His sources were largely secondary and his canvas immense but he succeeded in breathing life into a great many once violent human episodes and he was at his best with strategy and tactics. His historical sweep and grasp were, however, remarkable for one who was not a professional historian and who led so active and consuming a life. Unfortunately, harshly discordant notes crept in from time to time from his fascist philosophy. Thus: Alexander appears as a Leader-like figure, the bringer of Unity in Concord; 'the goal of a virile nation is the establishment of unattackable frontiers—the Alexandrian drive';[142] Caesar's guiding trinity in unity were 'Authority, Order and Discipline', and he 'set about limiting the Money Power which had been the ruin of the Republic';[143] with capitalistic Protestantism Old Testament culture replaced New, the Bible ousted the Cross and 'the economically minded nations became Judaized'.[144] The book delivered to the publisher, he got down at once to completing Volume Two, and it was with this that he was involved when Hitler finally struck at Poland on Fuller's sixty-first birthday. The 'ridiculous Poles' became the occasion of Armageddon, but the first campaign, thanks to the combination of planes and tanks, only lasted eighteen days.

The dilemma between ideology and patriotism which had been growing for long in Fuller's mind quite suddenly became acute. His politics were undoubtedly fascist, his sentiments, encouraged by Sonia, were pro-German, whereas his whole upbringing and profession made him a patriot. He was, also, an acquaintance and admirer of Winston Churchill, the deliverer in the wings. There was no comparable dilemma in his military outlook. At the outbreak of war his position on mechanized warfare remained much as it had been when he retired. Tanks were essential, and, for the land offensive, only tanks. Infantry ought to become tanks. Tactics would be area, not linear. Unarmoured infantry were unnecessary except as a 'gendarmerie' or for occupation, defence and attack in non-tank terrain. The purpose of bombers was to destroy the civil will and win the war, and this made planes not tanks the master weapon. The latter's primary function therefore was the defence of the former on the ground. In Hitler's Polish *Blitzkrieg* his views on both bombers and tanks were to be borne out, although the use the Germans made of planes in a ground support role was one which he had never stressed. How much his views on air power owed to the Italian General Guilio Douhet is in doubt. He knew about Douhet in the thirties, but the latter's book, *The Command of the Air*, was not translated into English until 1943.[145] Douhet's belief in bombing civilian targets in order to win wars was close to Fuller's view at this time. A Continental observer, Max Werner, writing at the end of 1938, had read both Douhet and Fuller and concluded that Fuller's theory was more realistic than Douhet's, but still one-sided; Fuller's conversion to the primacy of the plane was very interesting because he was himself 'the Douhet of the tank'.[146] The paradox in all this was that it was to a large extent his military theories, and his burning and frustrated crusade for military reform, which had led to the political dilemma. What began as a not untypical middle-class dislike of mass opinion and turned into a very untypical fascism, was dedicated to military reform, and to the defence of a country about to be pitted against those others which had adopted fascist forms of government. That Fuller was not torn apart by this paradox is a compliment to his intellectuality, mental flexibility and self-confidence. A more emotional and modest man might have gone under.

For a variety of reasons, the British establishment had either not listened hard enough to Fuller or had reacted violently against the iconoclasm of many of his proposals, and particularly, in the early days, against his attacks on the cavalry and infantry. Others had listened, however, as must now be apparent, at least to his military prescriptions. *Lectures on FSR III* was the standard work on mechanized warfare at the Czech Staff College,[147] and although the Czech officer, Major F. O. Miksche, did not mention Fuller in his *Blitzkrieg*, published in 1941, he used a lot of his ideas.[148] De Gaulle had listened too. When publicly asked to comment on *The Army of the Future* in 1943 he replied: 'But what about your best soldier, General Fuller? He was the prophet, we only followed him. . . . You will find prophesied in his books everything that the Germans did with tanks. I have often wondered why he is never used.'[149] Some Russians listened too, and Fuller's influence was apparent even in the twenties, in *The Preliminary Correct Line for the War Doctrine of Tanks*, although his arguments for an independent striking force tended to be suspect as anti-proletarian. By early 1937, however, the Russians had infantry support tanks and long-range tanks for deep penetration in independent formations, a compromise of course between Fuller and his opponents. Marshal Tukhachevski, who was familiar with some of Fuller's theories,[150] pioneered the development of tanks in the Red Army; he was careful to avoid being branded with acceptance of what he called the new 'Manoeuvre Theory', that tank speeds limited their use as infantry support, but he died in the purge of 1937, after which tanks became relegated to the role of infantry support until at least 1942. Fuller's insistence on small, technically developed armies was seen in the Soviet Union at the time in the same light as nuclear weapons were regarded in Mao's China in the fifties. On the one hand these developments offered the prospect of great power; on the other they represented a rejection of the value of the mass.[151] Nonetheless, three months before Hitler attacked Russia in 1941, Marshal Timoshenko made *Lectures on FSR III* a 'table book' or one that every officer had to have at his elbow, along with *On War* and *The Command of the Air*.[152] Even the Chinese listened, as Chiang Kai-Shek's military adviser testified,[153] and the Austrian General von Eimannesberger had read some of his books and knew enough about him to quote Fuller's opinion that 'except for the Church there is no organization which hangs on to tradition more than the army'.[154] But of course of all the listeners the most attentive were the Germans and the least the Americans. For the latter any attempt to produce independent armoured forces would have looked militaristic and extravagant; the American contribution was technical, the Christie tank. The German contribution was essentially strategic and tactical, the *Blitzkrieg*, and that this was largely based on the writings of Fuller and Liddell Hart is incontrovertible. It is important here to note that when one of these names is mentioned by writers apportioning the credit for the theories of mechanized warfare, the other is usually added; they formed, in foreign eyes, the British mechanized school and were not distinguished the one from the other.

onel Fuller asserts that the traditional soldier is doomed.' A drawing by George
Werveke in the *New York Times* Book Review and Magazine, 5 August 1923

The sort of advertisement for Fascism which Fuller encountered in Abyssinia in 19

Fuller with Italian troops in Abyssinia

Guderian, the architect and executor of success in 1940, told
Brigadier Daly, the military attaché in Berlin in 1939, that he had
studied Fuller's writings at length [155] and, after the war, wrote in
his memoirs: 'It was principally the books and articles of the
Englishmen, Fuller, Liddell Hart and Martel, that excited my
interest and gave me food for thought. These far-sighted soldiers
were even then trying to make of the tank something more than
just an infantry support weapon. ... I learned from them the
concentration of armour, as employed in the Battle of
Cambrai.' [156] A Czech officer stated in 1940 that the Germans
regarded *Lectures on FSR III* as their bible and that the entire
attack in France and Flanders was based on Fuller's teaching.[157]
Fuller himself never discovered whether or not a privately
printed edition of *Lectures on FSR III* was produced but there
was no openly published German version.[158] Knowledge of
Fuller's opinions must have come from his personal contact with
German officers and from reading his articles and the German
editions of *Generalship, Memoirs of an Unconventional Soldier*
and *The First of the League Wars.* Werner gave Eimannesberger
the credit for the idea of large tank armies used to carry out
decisive breakthrough operations and stated that German
strategy had taken over this concept. Eimannsberger, however,
took his ideas from Fuller as Werner's description of German
strategy clearly indicates: 'Close connection with the infantry
robs the tank of its advantage in speed and increases the risk of
destruction by hostile defensive forces. ... German strategy
refuses to adapt the speed of the tank to that of slow-moving
infantry.' [159] This is pure Fuller. Werner also praised the Hore-
Belisha reforms of March 1938 as a step in the direction of the
theories of Fuller and Liddell Hart. That was true but it is also
true that on September 3rd, 1939 Britain had only one lightly
equipped armoured division available for France, one in Egypt
and another still very much in the process of formation, whereas
the Germans had a force constructed very much along the lines of
the 1927 experiment and imbued with a doctrine of rapid, deep
penetration, supported by air power, flowing round obstacles and
dedicated to decisive actions. In effect Fuller and Liddell Hart,
through the public dissemination of their military theories,
helped the Germans to some enormous initial victories. Whether
they would have achieved them without this help, by drawing

their own conclusions from Cambrai and Amiens and the logic of technological progress, can never be determined. Unfortunately, war is no longer a sport on the playing of which books can be written for the mutual benefit of both sides and the development of a better game—unless the excellence produced in the armed forces of all potential combatants is such that war becomes ludicrous because it could result in no political gain. And this was the view of Fuller the philosopher if not that of Fuller the fascist. In 1939 the possibilities of political gain seemed real enough.

9. 'So also is Criticism the Life of War'[1]—1939–48

The fact that Fuller was allowed to lead a normal life throughout Britain's war against fascism, and permitted to comment publicly, pungently and to some extent unrepentantly on its aims and conduct, is a notable tribute to the sturdiness of the democratic plant which he so much distrusted and despised. His loyalty to Britain and the Empire was never in doubt, but his membership of the British Union, and his connections with German Nazis, and Spanish and Italian fascists, made him the target of much popular and governmental doubt. It was fortunate for Fuller that he was so well known, not only as a political figure but also as a fighting soldier and military thinker. Much of this was in the future, however; in 1939 and early 1940 even Mosley was allowed to continue his activities and to mount a campaign against the continuance of the war.

The war and its aftermath presented Fuller with the necessity to make numbers of radical intellectual adjustments and with the opportunity to assess the validity of his many theories against the reality of experience, at least experience as perceived by Fuller. Throughout these violent years the greatest adjustments became necessary in three separate but related areas. First, the global storm which grew from the invasion of Poland forced him to take in the sails of his rather intellectual fascism, and his pro-Germanism; the type of rig best designed to survive that storm and to accommodate the seas of Fuller's own, now contradictory, patriotism, was difficult to devise. The resultant strains and gyrations were evident in the support he gave to the cause of political detainees in wartime Britain, in his rapid and total change of view on the efficiency of the strategic bombing of the civil will, in his crusade against the policy of unconditional surrender and in his dirge for the peace which he began to claim

had been lost soon after the war was won. In the end the adjust-
ment became fully possible when events made it rational for him
to claim that he had been right all along because the destruction
of Germany inevitably led to the rise of the threat from the East
and from world communism. Churchill, who had been at least a
friendly acquaintance in the past, came to symbolize for Fuller all
the mistakes which Britain was making by his insistence on
policies of unconditional surrender and area bombing. Second,
the war saw Fuller's military theories put to the test and he no
doubt greatly enjoyed the vindication of many of those views on
mechanized warfare which had led to both fame and obloquy. In
some matters the Second World War led him to make relatively
minor changes to his military theories, or at least to those
theories he had developed prior to the mid-thirties when his
flirtation with totalitarian tactics and the all-out bombing of civil
targets had begun. On the whole, however, the concept of mobile
armoured formations effecting deep penetrations or fighting area
wars against each other materialized in France in 1940 and in
1944, and in the Western Desert and the USSR. The fact that the
war was not actually won by a bold and rapid armoured thrust,
but instead by the operation of attrition in various ways, and at
various levels, is explicable, at least in part, in terms of a failure to
devise, organize and use armoured forces as Fuller had recommended. The fact that armoured forces did not much engage in
driving around the land like fleets at sea was perhaps also due in
part to lack of imagination but also undoubtedly to problems of
terrain, supply and self-sufficiency which Fuller underestimated.
The nearest approaches to Gold Medal Essay warfare were the
various campaigns in North Africa. Poison gas was never used
and Fuller probably misappreciated its potential effectiveness.
Horsed cavalry did not survive the war but infantry did and live
on today. Fuller can be held to have been wrong, but as has been
suggested before, the argument is probably semantic in that what
we call infantry today are much more like armoured troops than
they are like traditional foot soldiers. Moreover, before Fuller's
death the technologists had given the foot soldier himself a very
good answer to the tank in the form of the anti-tank missile.
Third, at the end of the war Fuller had to assimilate the atom
bomb into his thinking. This he did with his usual remarkable
mental agility, as we shall see. At the same time as he was

subjected to all these pressures for change he continued to pursue numbers of his old interests, his fascination with the occult, his campaign for the use of CDLs and his journalistic career. His talents as a military journalist were much in demand and his income from this source became considerable.

By the outbreak of war the Fullers had left Cheyne Court and moved to Eaton Place. From there they moved again to Queens Gate Place and finally to Queen's Gate. From Eaton Place he went to dine with Mosley on September 26th.[2] The next evening, at 8.15 p.m. he saw Ironside, now CIGS, to discuss the possibility of his being brought back to the active list and made Deputy CIGS. Ironside had changed his mind about upsetting promotion prospects but the War Cabinet subsequently squashed any suggestion Fuller should be re-remployed because of his recent and highly publicized political activities.[3] Whether Ironside, or the War Cabinet, knew that he went to the CIGS straight, as it were, from Mosley, is not known. Three weeks later he sent the CIGS a paper on 'Our Strategical Problem and a Possible Solution'. In this he suggested that, as the consequence of a long war would be to replace National Socialism with National Communism, we should use CDLs to win a quick victory.[4] In his reply Ironside wrote: 'I wish I had you here with me but I am afraid that that is impossible. The politicians, without any war to keep them in order, have full sway.' He also told Fuller that he was experimenting with the de Thoren lamp and intended to fit it to aeroplanes.[5] At this time also Fuller kept up his Spanish contacts and dined several times with the Duke of Alba, the Spanish Ambassador.[6] In November *Truth* published an article by him, which was virtually an apologia for Hitler's concentration camps and contained the statement that he had never seen so many degenerates collected together as those forming the anti-social and Jewish groups in the camp he saw in Oranienburg.[7] This was the era of the 'phoney war'. At the beginning of 1940 Fuller toyed with the rationalization that the war was not against Hitlerism but against Hitler's attempt to create an autarchic empire[8] while in the March–April edition of the American *Army Ordnance* he prophesied that Russia could become the most autarchic country of all and so was the true enemy. It would have been better had we allowed him to advance and become embroiled with Russia.[9] In the spring of 1940 also the second volume of *Decisive Battles* was published.

There was more fascist sentiment in this than in the first and, perhaps more surprisingly, no mention whatsoever of the tank. Indeed Fuller's choice of battles from 1914 onwards was not a little odd. He began with the Marne and Tannenberg in 1914, which is understandable, and then continued with Sari Bair and Sulva Bay in 1915, Vittorio Veneto in 1918, Warsaw in 1920, Mai Chio in 1936 and Aragon in 1938, some of which are less than familiar today. Fascism emerges in numerous places. Thus Fuller believed that after 1815 financiers became the real world masters, led by Byron's 'Jew Rothschild';[10] Napoleon's gift was 'an idea of ethnographical groups of people governing the soil they are born on and the soil they work, live on and die on';[11] parliamentary systems were incapable of conducting wars;[12] in twenty years fascism had grown into a national religion, the three great tenets of which were discipline, authority and self-sacrifice;[13] the foundation of the Spanish Republic in 1931 led to the appearance of pornographic works on every Spanish bookstall 'as well as all the trappings of so-called intellectualism, which more often than not is a combination of highbrow flapdoodle and free fornication'.[14] These are strange words and judgments in a serious work on military history. Stranger still today are the words on the last page, page 1031: 'I, for one, agree with this prediction.' The prediction was that the Spanish Civil War was the beginning of a world war in which Absolutism and Democracy would fight it out. The strangeness lay in the fact that Fuller, just prior to British democracy's greatest military disaster and finest hour, favoured Absolutism not Democracy. The War Office received its copy on April 2nd. On the 9th Hitler took Denmark and invaded Norway and a short month later the German forces crossed the Dutch and Belgian frontiers at the beginning of an operation, using armoured forces much in accordance with the ideas of Fuller and Liddell Hart, which ended with Dunkirk and the collapse of France. On May 10th Churchill took Chamberlain's place as Prime Minister and on the 22nd, with the Germans on the Channel coast and an invasion of England seeming imminent, Defence Regulation 18B was amended in such a way as to make it possible for any member of the British Union to be interned. Mosley was arrested on the 23rd but his wife was allowed to remain at liberty until June 29th. In all, some 747 British Union members and sympathizers were detained by the end of June but neither Fuller nor Sonia was amongst them. Even today the Mosleys admit to a little puzzlement.[15] Fuller was, after all, an eminent fascist who had visited both Hitler and Mussolini and stood as a fascist parliamentary candidate. Rank did not save him since both Captain A. H. Ramsay, a Conservative MP, and Admiral Sir Barry Domvile were taken. Liddell Hart believed that Churchill himself probably saved Fuller from internment[16] and this seems very likely; it was after all inherently improbable that so distinguished a soldier would have given aid and comfort to the enemies of his country. He was, moreover, well known to the Prime Minister; acquaintanceship and even family connections did not save the Mosleys because the public wanted their arrest, but the public did not pursue Fuller in the same way. Fuller's own feelings at the time are not recorded. He had lunched with Mosley on April 20th[17] and he must have anticipated arrest but did nothing to avoid it. He actually had Diana Mosley openly to lunch in the interval between her husband's arrest and her own.[18] So far in fact was Fuller from arrest that the question of his re-employment was again raised.[19] No doubt those who supported his claims had omitted to read *Decisive Battles*; it is unlikely that Government could be so liberal today in a similar situation after our post-war experience of ideological warfare.

In June the final trials of the CDL apparatus took place and the War Office took over the whole project and ordered the initial construction of three hundred projector turrets and, a little later, the establishment of a CDL School.[20] In June also *Action* was suppressed and Fuller henceforth channelled most of his English journalism towards the popular Press and the less weighty periodicals. He wrote a lot. In June readers of the *Evening Standard* were told that we must never surrender the Channel line;[21] those taking the *Sunday Express* were advised that the Germans would try blockade before invasion;[22] while the clientèle of the *South Wales Echo* was treated to a humorously critical appraisal of Italian Blackshirt troops in which the 'Pirates of Penzance' simile was employed.[23] To balance this, however, Fuller advised readers of the *Leicester Mail* not to laugh at Italy's sturdy peasant soldiers.[24] Later in the year, after the Battle of Britain was on the way to being won, his published attitude became more pro-war. However, in early October he told readers of the *Daily Express* that bombing Berlin was like shooting your enemy through his foot whereas attacking the Ruhr would be going for his heart.[25] This was a significant shift in Fuller's thinking and its timing must be related to the ineffectiveness of the German Douhet-like air campaign against Britain. In October also he called for an attack in the Middle East;[26] in November he suggested that Britain needed a war dictator,[27] and in December he told the readers of the *Sunday Pictorial* that a victory was essential and should be sought against Italy first.[28] 1940 had been for Fuller a year of personal loss, since his mother, the highly cultured and intelligent Thelma de la Chevallerie, had died at the age of ninety-two. Also many of his own personal papers, including a semi-official diary of his years at the War Office between 1918 and 1922, were destroyed in a warehouse in the Blitz and the entire stock of the first edition of both volumes of *Decisive Battles* was burnt in Eyre & Spottiswoode's store in Paternoster Row. He later felt like thanking Hitler for this because it forced him to rewrite the book;[29] it also, of course, enabled him to omit much of the fascism.

At about this time the Fullers moved out of London and took a house in Camberley. From there he continued to write for the Press throughout 1941, recommending in January a small, highly mechanized army of the 'FSR III' variety[30] and calling for the release of the detainees.[31] In February he wrote an account of the campaign in Eritrea for the *Evening Standard*.[32] He was still remembered in the Army, which was not surprising since many of his contemporaries and immediate juniors were now in positions of authority and high command. Martel, for instance, was Commander of the Royal Armoured Corps and was another who tried unsuccessfully to bring him back, this time in February 1941, to plan future requirements for tank design. 'No one,' Martel wrote in 1945, 'would have done this vital work better than Major-General Fuller. What did it matter if some officers had not agreed with his views before the war? Better than being a peacemonger. . . . It was very unfortunate that more work was not done in this direction and the valuable services of General Fuller were never used.'[33] It was not, of course, Fuller's warlike views which were now a problem any more; in addition to the disadvantage of his recent political past, he was now well over sixty, and seven years on the retired list.

In April some of his articles for the *Sunday Pictorial* were censored in whole or part because of his strategic criticisms.[34] In May he had lunch at the Savoy with General Lee, the US Military Attaché in London. MI5 warned Lee of Fuller's political attitude before the lunch. Lee wrote in his diary:

> Fortunately, Fuller brought his wife along. She is a Pole and not very pretty and rather tiresome, with very strong ideas which are reflections of his. . . . Fuller is now a very little, old, wizened-up man, who is bitter and outspoken against the War Office, the British Government, and the way the war is being conducted. I size him up as having a very much better than usual brain, but an impatient disposition, so that he irritated his superiors and everyone else because they did not accept his views about warfare and tanks. If such revolutionary views are advanced in the wrong way, people resent them, regardless of their value. . . . He is an outspoken admirer of German effectiveness, but a lot of his ideas are all mixed up. He kept saying that the war need never have occurred, and his wife chimed in with the remark that none of the British people wanted it and had no enthusiasm for it.

After lunch MI5 rang Lee up and arranged to send someone round to 'debrief' on Fuller's conversation and attitude.[35] He may not have been arrested but he was obviously under surveillance. Moreover his private conversation appears to have changed less than his public attitude. In Lee's account Sonia revealed the pro-German and anti-British attitude with which Estelle Fuller credits her.[36]

In June he wrote an article for the *Sunday Pictorial* on the fall of Crete. The censor cut five hundred words but allowed Fuller to indulge in a little 'I told you so' about his earlier views on the aeroplane as a master weapon.[37] At dawn on the 22nd Hitler invaded the Soviet Union. On the 29th Fuller commented that Russia had given us our chance at last.[38] In July he likened the Russian plains to a tank ocean,[39] the context at last of naval warfare on land. August saw him in the *Evening Standard* telling the homeward commuter that mud was Stalin's ally and that the American Lieutenant-Colonel S. L. A. Marshall had written that 'Fuller' and not Heinz Guderian . . . Seeckt . . . or Ludendorff . . .

is the missing prophet of the new age of warfare. He harvested
the true kernels of strategy from his World War experience, and
he winnowed out the chaff.'[40] Certainly the Soviet Union was
providing a more rigorous testing ground for armoured forces
than Poland or France had done, and a testing ground in which
size, climate and manpower, coupled with the development of
effective anti-tank techniques, were to defeat an over-ambitious,
and perhaps unnecessarily dissipated, series of armoured thrusts.
In October Fuller dubbed the war an 'Engineer's war'; 'a war of
spanners and spades in intimate co-operation',[41] and at the end of
the year he was calling, most uncharacteristically, for the reinforce-
ment of Stalin's armies of the Lower Volga by an advance from
the Middle East to the Caucasus.[42] Military priorities appeared, at
least temporarily, to have overcome political imperatives in his
thinking. In some respects the Russo-German war became a test
of symmetrical mechanization, the initial superiority of German
tactics and organization being neutralized by long lines of communication, and as a consequence it reached a sort of stalemate,
as Fuller had prophesied it would, until Russian manpower and
Russian and Allied resources tipped the balance. Study of the war
therefore became a fascinating exercise for the author of *Lectures
on FSR III*.

   Pearl Harbor was the next substantial pabulum for Fuller's
military and political mind. America was in the war. 'Atlantic
Charter' was ranged against 'New Order'. Fuller wanted none of
this but saw the war from Britain's viewpoint as aimed at the
achievement of an era of political liberty and freedom from
poverty. The price of victory was the utilization to the limit of
one's resources for one's purpose. All this and much more was
contained in a series of four articles he wrote for the *Evening
Standard* in January 1942.[43] Frank Owen, the Editor, wrote in
reply to a correspondent the day after the fourth had appeared: 'I
have long thought that General Fuller should have a post in this
Government, and said so to the people in it. I do not agree with
the General's politics, but I have a very great respect for his
military strategy. It is a scandal that he is not given employment.
Of course, he should be War Minister.'[44] This squarely identified
the key to Fuller's gradual public rehabilitation and at the same
time increased the level of his proposed re-employment. He had
been militarily right all along, people began to say; let us listen

now. In March he again called for an Army to be sent to Russia,[45] suggested that MacArthur should fight in Australia[46] and recommended an invasion on the Channel coast.[47] In the midst of all this popular journalism *The Occult Review*, in its April number, carried an article by Fuller on 'Magic and War'. It is further evidence that his interest in the occult was a deep and continuing one and that it ran parallel to, and often supported, his military and political thinking. For Fuller the occult was the hidden, the inner meaning, and a great many of his theories had an occult dimension. But in this article there came a new and startling analogue: the general and the magician had a similar purpose, it seemed. 'Both magic and war,' he wrote, 'are coercive, propitiatory and dynamic. Their purpose is to influence events. ... When in his Manuals the soldier states that his object in war is to impose his will on his enemy, he enters the realm of magic; and when the magician sets out to impose his will on his victim he steps into the kingdom of war ... the wolf-man is no myth; in wartime he may be smelt in nearly every headline.'[48] In this way Fuller was able to reconcile his two major interests; he would not have felt that any explicit reconciliation was necessary. Later in the year he argued that propaganda was a form of magic and Dr Goebbels a magician.[49]

1942 also saw the publication of yet two more Fuller books. The first, *Machine Warfare: An enquiry into the influence of mechanics on the art of war* was slender and showed signs of being hurriedly put together. In the Preface, completed in the previous November, Fuller claimed that he had no politics and that all politicians were anathema to him. He then went on to suggest that all parliaments, houses of representatives, reichstags 'and such like talking-shops' should be closed down and that a sort of military government should be set up in Britain.[50] His personal position shone through another sentence: 'Today we are not only fighting for an ideal, which history alone can pronounce to be good or bad, but, what more immediately concerns us, for our existence.'[51] In other words, survival itself was a war aim Fuller could embrace. The book begins with much quotation from Lewis Mumford's *Technics and Civilization* in order to demonstrate that the mechanization of society had led to war, with armies filling the role of ideal industrial consumers, and that it had led also to the class war. Next, in Part One, Fuller demon-

strated his continuing misunderstanding of Clausewitz by accus-
ing the latter of producing doctrines aimed at turning the nation
into a military machine.[52] He praised Hitler's military originality[53] and accepted the validity of what he called the 'Stuka-Flak-
Panzer' tactics although he had not earlier, of course, placed a
high value on close air support.[54] Part Two, he admitted, contained no new ideas and most of it came from *Lectures on FSR
III*. The law of military development and the constant tactical
factor, from *The Dragon's Teeth* and *Memoirs*, reappear[56] and
were to lead eventually to a full-scale historical analysis of
weapon development and its interaction with social, political and
economic change. Also he now came out against bombing the
civil population, and called it mass murder, because it became an
ineffective exercise in terms of spreading terror once its novelty
had worn off. However he still quoted advice he had given in the
twenties that if done at all, it should be done when the enemy
situation had been rendered critical by other means.[57] For the
rest, however, it was very much a restatement, although so
accurate had Fuller's military vision been in the twenties and
thirties that much of it still seemed quite advanced even in 1942;
an example was his view that in armoured battles of the future
the object would not be to effect penetration but to close off an
enemy's salient, prevent him retiring and annihilate him, not by
pursuit but by boxing-up.[58] The Germans had just failed to do
this definitively in Russia; Falaise was to come. In Part Three he
trod on stranger ground. The war was a clash of philosophies—
Oceanic based on money against Continental based on labour, the
framework of *Decisive Battles*. The USA and Britain were
Oceanic and the USSR and Germany Continental. Here was his
difficulty once again. Britain and the USA were fighting Germany
in alliance with Russia. England was Hitler's one great obstacle,
he considered, and yet there is no criticism of Hitler anywhere in
the book. Instead Fuller praised the wisdom of French capitula-
tion,[59] referred to 'the British' rather than 'we'[60] and accused the
Government and the people of panicking in the face of threatened
invasion instead of welcoming it as an opportunity to defeat the
Germans.[61] In a less provocative vein he gave the reason for
Hitler's attack on Russia as a desire to clear his flank before
striking at British sea bases in the Eastern Mediterranean[62] and
accounted for the misfire of the initial attack on the grounds that

the Germans were not correctly organized to defeat a mechanized army such as Stalin possessed because the German armoured division did not have a proper anti-tank wing and had no tracked supply vehicles. Moreover the Russians did not surrender as the French had done.[63] The book ends with a chapter called 'Multiples of Victory'. These were lessons of war, and one of them read: 'In total war a nation can only be fully organized when all freedom is exorcised ... logically it follows that all who are incapable of fighting or working should be liquidated.'[64] It is almost unbelievable that the publication of such a book was allowed. The extraordinary mixture of cool and rational military analysis and tortured, shrill, only half-disguised political extremism cannot have aided the war effort. The 'panic' of 1940, particularly, is surely a figment of Fuller's imagination. The Government's coolness in 1942 is in any case well illustrated by the fact that *Machine Warfare* saw the light of day and that no action was taken against it.

At the end of May Fuller recommended the taking of Tunis and Bizerta.[65] In June a paragraph advocating the same action was censored from an article in the *Evening Standard* as was another prophesying a withdrawal to Tobruk.[66] At this time too he became involved with the Social Credit Party,[67] there was some more Press pressure for his re-employment,[68] and he began to correspond once again with Liddell Hart. In September he told the latter: 'The war as it is being run is just a vast Bedlam with WC as its glamour boy: a kind of mad hatter who one day appears as a cow puncher and the next as an Air Commodore—the man is an enormous mountebank.'[69] It was from this period that Fuller's hatred of Churchill grew into an obsession. That it was a new growth is obvious from what had gone before; its roots lay in reluctant gratitude, in intellectual disapproval of Churchill's political aims and military strategies and in emotional distaste for Churchill's style.

By this time the Fullers were living in the country again in half of a house called Chartlands at Limpsfield in the extreme north-eastern corner of Surrey, very close, ironically, to Churchill's home at Chartwell. There were five acres of grounds to cope with. It was from this retreat that Fuller saw the publication in both London and New York of his second 1942 book *The Decisive Battles of the United States*. Dedicated to Hoffman

Nickerson, this was an altogether less strident affair than *Decisive Battles*, partly at least because the author had less of a political axe to grind in an American context. The book was well researched and was based on primary as well as secondary sources. With it Fuller came of age as a military historian; the special pleading and the distortion of previous works were put aside and the system outlined in *Foundations* in 1926 was fairly applied. So little doctrinaire was the new book that instead of accounting for the Confederate defeat at Gettysburg mainly in terms of Pickett's foolhardy charge against a hail of steel (the bullet versus woollen jacket problem) he laid the chief blame on the character of General Lee himself. He mentioned the fire-power issue, of course, but only in one sentence of his own and by implication through the words of two Confederate writers, Fitzhugh Lee and A. L. Long.[70] The problem with a man who claims that weapons are 99 per cent of victory but that the other 1 per cent, which includes leadership, makes the whole possible, is that you cannot defeat him in an argument based on his own premise!

On Cambrai Day in November Fuller took the opportunity offered by Montgomery's victory at El Alamein to point out that it contained nothing tactically new compared with Cambrai, but he, of course, emphasized that it had far greater consequences.[71] On this the *Evening Standard*'s new Editor, Michael Foot, wrote and congratulated him.[72] After Christmas, Fuller wrote the first of three articles on strategic bombing for the same paper. He developed in some depth his thesis that the aeroplane was the master, but not necessarily the decisive, weapon; it would set the pace but not on its own conclude the issue; neither British nor Maltese civilian morale had been cracked from the air. Terror, if intermittent, would not win the war and to do so must be preceded by economic or military attack. Land and sea power must also therefore be developed, in conjunction with air power, and used against their like.[73] The second article, at the end of January, pointed out the contradictions as regards air resources between policies based on winning the war by bombing and by invasion,[74] while the title of a third, in February, 'Bomb Mind is The Somme Mind' speaks for itself.[75] In March he developed his views on El Alamein and likened Montgomery's tactic of penetration to those of Alexander at Arbela in 321 BC;

he also pointed out that it would all have gone much quicker if the British Army had had some mine-sweeping tanks, as they would have done had the battle been fought in 1919 rather than 1942.[76] He followed this up in April with a masterly criticism of the German and British use of armour, which appeared to rely on mass rather than velocity, and he called for the creation of special formations for each operation; he was particularly scornful of formations which, by mixing wheels and tracks, destroyed armoured mobility.[77]

In May he wrote two extremely barbed and funny articles for Michael Foot: 'Grenadiers on Castors'[78] and 'Cuirassiers on Wheels'.[79] The first began: 'Throughout history the soldier has lacked but one thing—he has steadfastly refused to think. And, as a rider, may I add, he has steadfastly opposed whoever has troubled to think for him.' He then provided some telling illustrations of this and made most effective fun of the Army's decision in 1900 that cyclists were infantry, 'grenadiers on castors'. Similarly tanks were classed as machine guns in 1916, and now there was a movement to regard them as close-support weapons for the infantry. Tanks, he claimed, should be regarded as tanks and should not be mixed with infantry (how old a cry was that). 'In fact, our so-called armoured divisions are no more than buns of infantry dough sprinkled with a pinch of steel currants.' In the second article he developed his long-held view that anti-tank developments ought not to lead to the relegation of the tank to a support role, but rather to the development of armoured and mobile anti-tank weapons and devices, to the 'cuirassier on wheels'. The day before the first of these articles was published Foot wrote to Fuller: 'The orange certainly was not dry! Your two articles are gems. They have made me laugh and weep. . . . I am looking forward to tomorrow. The War Office don't know what is going to hit them!'[80]

It was at this time that Fuller reopened his 1942 call for a second front on the Channel coast[81] and attacked the Allied policy of seeking the unconditional surrender of Germany and Italy since such a policy would be unlikely to lead to a stable peace.[82] For the same reason he also attempted to mount another attack on strategic bombing, not because of its ineffectiveness, but on the grounds that terror, although a powerful moral weapon, destroys the foundation upon which future peace must be built. This time his pen ran right away from his judgment with such statements as: 'the worst devastations of the Goths, Vandals, Huns, Seljuks and Mongols pale into insignificance when compared to the material and moral damage now wrought.'[83] However, the centre of Hamburg had just been virtually destroyed from the air, in which accomplishment the general public took some pride. It is understandable, therefore, that Foot, although in broad agreement with Fuller's views on unconditional surrender and strategic bombing, wrote and told him that he had not the nerve to publish the article.[84]

The major literary event of 1943 for Fuller was the publication, both in England and America, of *Armoured Warfare*. This was a reissue of *Lectures on FSR III*, but it is of considerable interest because Fuller added numerous footnotes which brought his 1932 theories, where necessary, up to date. A careful reading of the 1943 edition shows what a remarkably accurate vision of the future Fuller had committed to paper in 1932, a vision which had, of course, developed from the light he had seen near his 'Damascus' on the Western Front in 1918. In a new Preface[85] he claimed that by motor guerillas he had meant regular troops fighting in an irregular way, as the Germans had used their motorcyclists in France in 1940. He also admitted that as regards the tank he had overestimated the protective power of speed and underestimated the increases which would take place in the thickness of armour; although he stood by his earlier belief in the need for reconnaissance, artillery and combat tanks. In fact the British Army had only two major tank types in the Second World War—infantry and cruiser—but today, with its combat reconnaissance vehicles, self-propelled armoured guns and main battle tank, it has Fuller's three types at last. He concluded the preface by pointing out that the speed and range of the tank had not fundamentally changed since 1932 and that therefore there had been no fundamental changes in tactics.

The footnotes to the old text are imbued with Fuller's disarming intellectual honesty. There are admissions that the author had been wrong to prophesy that great battles would not take place soon after the outbreak of war,[86] and that his earlier prediction, that civil demoralization would replace military destruction as the chief war-winning factor, was an over-statement.[87] This latter is the strategic bombing issue. There is also an almost audible

chortle of delight in the reproduction of the sentence: 'The Royal
Engineers should, therefore, be divided into two bodies of men—
field engineers and mechanical engineers,' with the 1943 footnote:
'A corps of Electrical and Mechanical Engineers was created in
1942.'[88] However, the most interesting footnotes are those relat-
ing to the theory and practice of armoured warfare itself. When
Liddell Hart first read *Lectures on FSR III* he made some notes
on it which indicated general agreement, but he did take Fuller to
task in four main areas.[89] First, he considered that Fuller had not
recognized the value of combined air and tank attacks, and Fuller
himself admitted in *Armoured Warfare* that the advent of the
dive-bomber had increased the importance of ground–air co-
operation.[90] Second, he disagreed with Fuller's virtual dismissal
of the value of night attacks. In 1943 Fuller did not retract from
this viewpoint and one wonders if this was because the CDL trial,
under security wraps, inhibited him. Next Liddell Hart pointed
out that Fuller did not recognize the need to use infantry in
transported armoured-carriers to help tanks in overcoming
defended obstacles. This is the most serious criticism. It must be
remembered, of course, that in the 1920s and early 1930s the
British infantry were only in the process of motorization and are
not, even today, fully mechanized in the sense of being carried
onto the objective in armoured vehicles from which they can
fight. In *Armoured Warfare* Fuller clarified his epigram that the
combination of tanks and infantry was 'tantamount to yoking a
tractor to a draught horse' with the footnote: 'When I wrote this
I had in mind infantry as commonly understood—namely as
footsoldiers whose 'raison d'être' is to fight their like. Motorized
infantry equipped with anti-tank weapons are not infantry, they
are anti-tank mounted foot.'[91] The chief defence which can be
deployed of Fuller's 'all-tank' philosophy is that he regarded
armoured self-propelled guns as tanks, and that from 1930
onwards he saw the necessity for an anti-tank element in tank
forces. Nevertheless, even in 1943, he still appeared to under-
estimate the necessity for infantry to be used on foot in
mechanized battles. In *Lectures on FSR III* there had been only
one passing reference to 'infantry in armoured carriers' and there
was no elaboration of this in *Armoured Warfare*.[92] Liddell Hart's
last point was that Fuller dealt only with tactical and not
strategic penetration. This does not seem entirely fair as a

criticism and in any case the difference between tactical and strategic moves is hard to define. In *Armoured Warfare* Fuller pointed out in his footnotes that experience had proved that in open country mobile battles would replace infantry battles and that whole nations could be defeated through the demoralization occasioned by such mobility.[93] He also emphasized that the all-round protection he had claimed would be necessary in area warfare had been demonstrated in Russia as had the probability of decision through manoeuvre rather than fire, the necessity for supply convoys, the reintroduction of foraging and the need for cross-country supply transport. Such developments led to, and were the consequence of, strategic penetration. Of course Fuller's ultimate point, that static war would re-emerge once means had been found of slowing down tank penetration, was also borne out in Russia as he indicated in *Armoured Warfare*.[94] In conclusion it can be said that he used the occasion to demonstrate that this more than ten-year-old vision had been farsighted and only minimally distorted. That naval warfare on land did not fully come to pass was a consequence of lack of will and imagination and of what Clausewitz called friction and the fog of war. If Fuller made any serious miscalculations they were ones, not of the role of infantry, where the argument is largely semantic, but of logistics. Independent ground formations, tank and anti-tank, could no doubt have behaved like fleets before the advent of effective air, submarine and missile forces, and have done so in favourable climatic and topographic conditions, but for how long could they have been supplied with petrol, food and ammunition? It must also be said that the *Lectures on FSR III* vision was, to an extent, a self-fulfilling prophecy; some of those who planned and fought the Second World War had read and understood it, as we know.

On November 20th the Mosleys were let out of prison but this had little effect on war-torn Britain, or on Fuller. His other vision, the consequence of mystical, rather than armoured or political penetration, forced him into print again at the end of 1943. Uncharacteristically the *Evening Standard* carried an article on December 1st with the heading: 'Is War Inevitable? No, but the only way to prevent it is by a—Return to The Religious Way of Life'. And the religious way recommended was Hindu: 'to the mastership over the beast by spiritual awe . . . thus spake the Lord Shri Krishna . . . whenever spirituality decays and materialism is rampant, then O Arguna! I reincarnate myself. To protect the righteous, to destroy the wicked, and to establish the Kingdom of God, I am reborn from age to age.'[95]

The emphasis, however, of Fuller's journalism in the next few months was upon strategic bombing. In January 1944 he compared it with artillery bombardment in 1917, since both prevented subsequent exploitation through destruction of the ground, in one case, over which victory had to come, and the grounds, in the other, on which peace had to be built. Moreover the bomber which had replaced the gun would in turn be replaced by the rocket, when 'it will be possible to fire upon targets at any range—round the entire globe if need be ... possibly to the moon!' This, Fuller hoped, would lead to the elimination of war.[96] He followed this up with articles about the absurdity of war without rules,[97] the probable post-war revolutionary consequences of bombing[98] and the greater effectiveness of bombing industrial rather than population targets.[99] In the latter connection Fuller argued very cogently for the bombing of 'sources of the enemy's military and industrial energy', a proposal which post-war research has vindicated. In April he concluded that bombing was not shortening the war and quoted Clausewitz: 'Only great and general battles can produce great results'.[100]

One great and general battle was about to be launched. Before this event, however, Odhams published a glossy illustrated book called *Warfare Today* of which Fuller was a co-editor along with Admiral Sir Reginald Bacon and Air Marshal Sir Patrick Playfair. The first five chapters, obviously written by Fuller, provided an admirably simple and illustrated account of his theories on armoured warfare, while the chapter on Combined Operations ended with a reference to 'the greatest military campaign to be undertaken by the United Nations—namely, the invasions of the fortress of Europe'. The very first illustration in the book, 'Infantry Go in to the Final Assault' indicated that Fuller had by now accepted that 'mopping-up' in machine warfare was still a matter for infantry.

After D-Day most of Fuller's articles were published in the *Sunday Pictorial* or later, after the war, in the *Daily Mail*, *The People*, *Sunday Graphic*, *Daily Telegraph*, and various journals and periodicals both British and American. He had by this time become military analyst of the American *Newsweek* and his friendship, founded in the twenties, with Colonel Leo Codd of the Army Ordnance Association of the United States led to a series of articles in *Army Ordnance* in the period July 1944 to July 1945 which were later published in book form as *Armament and History*. He also contributed to numbers of somewhat obscure publications such as the *New English Weekly*, the *Peace News* and the *Leader*. It was in the *Sunday Pictorial*,[101] in July, that he attempted to explain Germany's failure. To win, he argued, Germany would have had to conquer Europe less Russia before America entered the war. This meant the reduction of England, but the naval problem involved in that operation was never seriously tackled by the German General Staff, who believed that the destruction of the BEF would drive Britain out of the war. The collapse of France was as much a surprise to the Germans as to anyone else, and the first German blunder lay in lack of preparation for an invasion. Blunder No. 2 was in not putting enough resources into the Mediterranean area to take Tunisia and Egypt in 1940. Blunder No. 3 was the decision to turn away from Moscow and head south in 1942, and the final blunder was the decision which followed, to take Stalingrad at all costs. He refused to call Hitler's decision to attack Russia in 1941 a blunder because he implied that it might have been necessary in case Stalin had decided to attack Hitler when he became involved in the Eastern Mediterranean. This sort of analysis led to the writing and publication of *The Second World War* in 1948.

By October 1944, it had become apparent that the naval-style land warfare which followed the Normandy breakout had exhausted itself. Why, Fuller asked, again in the *Sunday Pictorial*,[102] are we bogged on the Rhine? His answer was both military and political: we did not have enough ports for supply and we should have coupled the airborne attack on Arnhem with a seaborne invasion north of the Rhine in Friesland; but bogging was also a consequence of the policy of unconditional surrender, and the threat of war-crimes trials and dismemberment, which emanated from the politicians and built up the German will to resist to the last. 'Truth', he told Starr, when writing about his war-time journalism, 'actually terrifies people.'[103]

Terrified or not, the public appeared to want to read his articles, and a collection of them was published at the end of 1944 under the title *Watchwords*. His literary earnings in the financial

years 1943–4 and 1944–5 amounted to £2,413 and £2,557 respectively, not inconsiderable sums at that time.[104] One piece of
writing for which he got no fee but much protest was a letter to
the *Sunday Express* dated January 7th, 1945, in which he questioned the accepted views about German atrocities in Belgium in
1915. In February he pleaded again for an invasion north of the
Rhine.[105] Events then gathered pace. The Rhine was crossed in
March and the German armies crumbled; Vienna fell in April;
Eisenhower left Berlin to the Russians, who encircled it on the
25th, and joined hands with the Americans two days later on the
Elbe, where they had been halted for a fortnight; on the 28th
Mussolini and his mistress were assassinated; on the 29th the
German commander in Italy surrendered and on the 30th Hitler
shot himself; at midnight on May 8th the war in Europe officially
ended with Germany's unconditional surrender. In most of this,
tanks played a great part and yet all Fuller's political fears were
realized, since it has often been argued that, through adherence to
purely military criteria, and through lack of political foresight,
the West gained little from its victory apart from the destruction
of Hitler and Mussolini. Stalin, on the other hand, brought the
Soviet frontiers up to the Elbe and set the scene for the eclipse of
West European power and the rise of a bipolar world centred on
Washington and Moscow. There was, however, a final act to
come which, through its unbridled destructiveness, gave to
Washington and Moscow so absolute a power of annihilation that
this very power has maintained between them so far a balance of
mutual fear which has terrorized the world into the avoidance of
further global wars. This act was the explosion of atomic
weapons above the cities of Hiroshima and Nagasaki in August
1945 and the subsequent surrender of Japan. Fuller wrote in the
Daily Mail on August 8th: 'From August 5, 1945, onwards,
armies, navies, and air forces as we know them, have metaphor-
ically been sunk in the rubble and dust of Hiroshima,'[106] but a few
days later he added that the causes of war cannot be eliminated
'by pulverizing cities'.[107]

The advent of the atomic bomb gave Fuller the sort of intellectual jolt which most of us would not welcome in our prime; he
was almost sixty-seven years old when this ultimate perfection of
destructive machine warfare was achieved—perfection in the
sense in which Clausewitz uses the word *Vollkommenheit* in

defining absolute war. It meant that victory in conventional warfare on land, sea or air could no longer be the final arbiter of international conflict if any of the belligerents possessed nuclear weapons and the means and will to deliver them. It appeared to mean that tanks, warships and aeroplanes would become irrelevant, since it would obviously be possible to deliver nuclear explosives by rocket. It appeared to have knocked the bottom out of Fuller's life and work. In March he had delivered the seventh and final chapter of *Armament and History* to Leo Codd for publication in *Army Ordnance*.[108] These seven chapters traced the relations between military technology and historical development from the earliest times to 1945, and this analysis, which is fascinating and scholarly in itself, confirmed for Fuller his 1919 statement that weapons were 99 per cent of victory, his 1932 law of military development and constant tactical factor and his long-held view that quality of weapon-power was more important than quantity.[109] *Soviet News*, however, accused him of dreaming of a new war 'in the journal of American gun manufacturers'. It was proof, *Soviet News* claimed, that 'the roots of fascism and imperial aggression have not been finally extirpated'.[110] In fact what he had actually written was that weapons and their quality were of supreme importance in war, that 'civilization is environment, and armies must adapt themselves to its changing phases in order to remain fitted for war'[111] (the law) and that 'every improvement in weapon-power has aimed at lessening the danger on one side by increasing it on the other. Therefore every improvement in weapons has eventually been met by a counter-improvement which has rendered the improvement obsolete: the evolutionary pendulum of weapon-power, slowly or rapidly, swinging from the offensive to the protective and back again in harmony with the pace of civil progress; each swing in a measurable degree eliminating danger'[112] (the factor). No doubt such sentiments were good for the armaments industry but they were advanced against a background of great concern at the contemporary destructiveness of war and were expressed in almost precisely the same words as he had used in the thirties.

In August, therefore, Fuller had to set about the immediate reconsideration of his whole position. He took time off to write kindly in *The Tank*[113] about Elles on the occasion of his death and received a letter of thanks from his wife.[114] He added a footnote to the American edition of *Armament and History*, which was published before the end of the year, but he then sat down and re-read the manuscript and came to the conclusion that the bomb had not destroyed his arguments.[115] It certainly confirmed that weapons were of enormous importance; it in no way invalidated the law except that it tended to reverse it, making war the environment of civilization; it both confirmed and contradicted the quality argument since while on the one hand it 'deproletarianized' war, on the other it enormously increased the quantity of 'quality' explosives; finally it remained to be seen whether the factor would continue to operate.[116] He therefore decided to leave the first seven chapters alone and to add an eighth which was first published in *Army Ordnance* in January 1946.[117] Perhaps the most important sentences in this postscript are: 'the whole idea of maintaining peace through power to destroy is unadulterated madness'.[118] 'To found civilization on the destructive power of war is as idiotic as to found health on the destructive power of surgery.'[119] Such were Fuller's first pronouncements upon nuclear deterrence. They came in the shadow of a great and terrible war and were influenced by his very powerful feelings about the bombing of civil populations rather than by his earlier views on the possibility of eliminating war as a consequence of the growth of weapon-power and the resultant political absurdity of war. He lived to change his opinion. It is nevertheless greatly to his credit that he was able to conceive and comment at all upon a concept which did not materialize in most Western minds until the early fifties. There is space only to give a few more of Fuller's atomic views in 1945. He contended that the causes of war would remain; atomic power would not abolish war but wars fought with such weapons could not achieve any rational political ends. He foresaw with uncanny accuracy in most respects the ABM system:

> Instead of cities being walled in as happened in the Viking Age, we can picture whole countries girt about by radar sets, ceaselessly 'listening-in' for the first jazz note of the broadcast of annihilation. In the vicinity of these instruments will be hidden away two tactical organizations of atom-charged and -propelled rockets—the one offensive and the other defensive. The first will be ranged on every great foreign

city in the world, because before war is launched—to declare it would be sheer madness—no single nation will
know who among the rest is its true enemy. The second
organization will be directed by the radar sets, and as soon
as they signal a flight of offensive rockets speeding towards
them, the defensive rockets will automatically be released by
radar, to speed into the heavens and explode in whatever
cubic space in the stratosphere radar decides the enemy's
offensive rockets will enter at a calculated time. Then,
hundreds of miles above the surface of the earth, noiseless
battles will be fought between blast and counter-blast. Now
and again an invader will get through when up will go
London, Paris or New York in a 40,000 feet high mushroom
of smoke and dust, and as nobody will know what is happen-
ing above or beyond, or be certain who is fighting whom—
let alone what for—the war will go on in a kind of bellicose
perpetual motion until the last laboratory blows up. Then
should any life be left on earth, a conference will
undoubtedly be held to decide who was victor and who was
vanquished, the latter being forthwith liquidated by the
former as war 'criminals'.[120]

He also foresaw the possibilities of counter electronic warfare[121]
and accidental war[122] and recommended the construction of
atomic rocket-ships for the speedy occupation of enemy countries.[123] *Armament and History*, when published in London in
1946, contained as much food for thought as any of his books had
ever done in spite, or even perhaps because, some of it repeated
and reconfirmed a pre-war position. He summed up his views in
an article published in *Maclean's Magazine* in November when he
wrote: 'You can't win atomic war.'[124] Of course one must
remember that Fuller's definition of the object of war was based
on the inscription on the plinth of Sherman's statue in
Washington which reads: 'The legitimate object of war is a more
perfect peace.'[125] Victory and destruction were not enough—or
very often too much. As he wrote to Starr at the time, in his
more mystical style: 'Man was not made to destroy, he was made
to create but he has been endowed with both powers. . . . He is
not Shiva alone, or Vishnu alone or Brahma alone; but all three in
one. Every cosmos is born with a "Fiat Lux'—this is what the

Western World is waiting for today. Not a new religion or a new politics, but a spark of Divine Imagination which will detonate yet another cycle in world history.'[126]

On a more mundane plane, the war being over, Fuller set about writing its history and considering the temporal problems of peace, particularly the problem of the spread of Soviet power. He was still living in Limpsfield but had begun to look for another and smaller house as Chartlands was becoming too expensive to run.[127] Somewhat ironically a Swedish edition of *Armoured Warfare* was published at the end of the war and a second collection of his journalistic ventures called *Thunderbolts* was issued in 1946. His output of articles for the newspapers diminished sharply but he launched a major campaign aimed at gaining a greater financial recompense for the CDL syndicate than the £10,000 which it had been awarded in 1941. On April 30th he wrote to twenty-six senior officers including three field marshals and Lord Mountbatten.[128] Eight tank battalions had been fitted with CDLs in Britain and America but they were not used in the invasion because this was carried out in daylight. Six battalions were landed in Normandy in August 1944 but they were never used in a CDL role. Eventually twenty-eight tanks were re-equipped with CDL and used in a static role in the Rhine crossing and a few American CDLs were used later. One re-equipped battalion was sent to SEAC but arrived too late to fight in Burma.[129] Field Marshal Alanbrooke in his reply to Fuller's letter wrote that he encouraged their use but that they never seemed to take on.[130] Martel thought it was a great pity that they had not been used and rather put the blame on Hobart and Alanbrooke.[131] Lieutenant-General Sir Frederick Morgan, incidentally, told Fuller that he had derived immense benefit from his writings, which is an important tribute as Morgan had drawn up the original invasion plans.[132] Lord Mountbatten stated that he would have used CDLs for the capture of Malaya[133] and Lieutenant-General Sir Neil Ritchie agreed that they had proved of great value in the Rhine crossing.[134] It was partly as a consequence of these accolades that the syndicate was awarded £20,375, which included, however, the £10,000 paid in 1941, and costs against the Ministry of Supply in January 1949.[135]

After the war, also, his correspondence with Liddell Hart again began to assume voluminous proportions and the two quite frequently met, now, of course, like two elder statesmen of mechanized war who not infrequently indulged in the pleasures of mutual admiration. Liddell Hart told Fuller that Chiang Kai-Shek's military adviser had told him that he and his fellows had been brought up on his Fuller's writings 'as their bibles'.[136] Fuller speculated to Liddell Hart that navies and armies might share the fate of the bath-chair[137] and told him that he believed the Empire was in dissolution, but that he objected to a retreat before Russia—'as an Empire, let us die as slowly as we can'.[138] They also discussed CDLs and re-examined their own first meetings.[139] In *Army Ordnance*, in March 1947, Fuller asked the fundamental question about whether Britain and America had merely effected the replacement of Nazi tyranny with a more barbaric hegemony.[140] This article was no doubt a spin-off from his pre-occupation with writing the history of the Second World War. In September, in the *Daily Mail*, he called for the withdrawal of our 100,000 troops in Palestine and our 100,000 in Germany and suggested handing over the defence of West Germany to the Germans.[141] In 1948 he wrote for the *Sunday Pictorial*, *Cavalcade* and *Everybody's*. He argued for a rational move towards the Total State which we were approaching anyway,[142] told Liddell Hart that he still saw no use for riflemen and machine gunners with tanks except as occupation troops brought forward in armoured carriers,[143] attacked the trial of war criminals,[144] regretted it was not possible to resurrect German military power since Russia was the enemy, called for the use of Spain as a 'strategic area'[145] and pointed out in the middle of the Berlin blockade that the situation was the consequence of the policy of unconditional surrender. To Churchill he was particularly rude. In *Cavalcade* he wrote, for instance: 'Yet Mr Churchill, one of the two initiators of Unconditional Surrender, still goes about making his V-sign in the air. Little, I suspect, is he aware that in the Middle Ages it was the sign wherewith the sorcerers invoked the Devil!'[146] Such references to a more spiritual or mystical frame of reference occurred more frequently, of course, in his letters to Starr. In one he defined Brahma as imagination, Shiva as will and Vishnu as reason. When we rely on these separately we act intellectually, when we compound them, spiritually. This is what spiritually meant to Fuller—the combination of will, reason and imagination, another threefold order. Indeed, in 1947, he still founded much of his thinking on this order and believed that the chaotic state of the world stemmed from a disequilibrium in the order.[147]

In the summer of 1948 Eyre and Spottiswoode brought out *The Second World War*. This was undoubtedly one of the high peaks of Fuller's career as a criticizer of war. He made no claim that the book was free of error or that it was a full-dress history; it was, he stated, a strategical and tactical account and he claimed, somewhat modestly it must be said, that he had made no attempt to cover the political, economic and psychological aspects. The book was extremely well received in the British Press and the *Economist* went so far as to label it 'an outstanding book' in which the history was balanced and unemotional, and the criticism of the conduct of war dogmatic, but always interesting.[148] An American reviewer was less kind and accused Fuller of 'embittered hindsight' and clinging 'to the theory that wars are inevitable and that it is well to fight them cleanly and reasonably, like well-regulated prize fights'.[149] One detects here principally the American distaste for the realities of the international system, perhaps less evident today than it was in 1948. A great deal of what Fuller put into his history has already been referred to in this chapter, for the book is a structured presentation of views which he first expressed in his journalism. It would, therefore, be tedious to summarize its contents here. It is, however, a stimulating piece of work and, although his analysis was sometimes still distorted, it often had an academic elegance about it and an insight which has stood the test of time. There is room for a few examples. Britain's war aims, he claimed, were ideological, the destruction of the Nazi Evil; instead they should have been to re-establish the balance of power. The ideological aim led to the establishment of Russian hegemony over Europe.[150] Churchill 'subordinated the political point of view to the military, and, therefore, according to Clausewitz, acted, "contrary to common sense".'[151] Actually Fuller, himself, was still not sound on Clausewitz, even as late as 1948, and in one place he stated that Hitler believed in Clausewitz's doctrine of absolute war and in war as a political instrument, thus ignoring the fact that the whole point about Clausewitzian absolute war is that it had escaped political control and become a *Ding an sich*.[152] In places his continuing fascist sympathies peeped through, notably when he held that many of the peoples overrun by Hitler were in sympathy with his aims, if not his methods, and even more when he noted, as an excuse, that Major Quisling learnt to detest Communism when he served as Norwegian Military Attaché in Moscow.[153] He also laid the blame for the brutalization of the war in Russia solely at the feet of the Russian partisans operating behind the lines.[154] Such distortions were, however, rarer than in the past. His treatment of Japan's war aims and strategy was particularly good. Japan, he believed, could only have achieved a limited victory and her attack on Pearl Harbor prevented her from gaining that because it united America behind Roosevelt in the war.[155] On armoured warfare he was more pragmatic than before and used the analogy of medieval battles between armoured knights rather than naval warfare; the castle and the wagon laager had reappeared as the 'box'; mobile forces were needed in the defensive, as well as 'boxes', to break up the enemy attack and render it vulnerable to counter-attack—indeed once the momentum of attack was exhausted, and the enemy able to counter-attack, the attacker should retire and draw the enemy after him until he could counter-attack himself. Thus did Fuller come to an at least partial acceptance of Clausewitz's principle of the defensive—as-the-stronger-form-of-war, which Fuller later redefined as the defensive—offensive.[156] On 'strategic' bombing he reiterated his judgment that it had made the peace unprofitable, but he further concluded that it had lengthened the war by diverting resources from the production of landing craft and transport aircraft, which had resulted in shortages which distorted the Italian, and ruined the Arnhem, operations, and made an invasion in Friesland impossible. Until 1944 the targets had been wrongly selected, the civil will was not broken and only from the spring of 1944 was some real success gained, although the continuation of area bombing was counter-productive.[157] Unconditional surrender also prolonged the war and this, together with the Allied halt on the Elbe, handed over East Germany and much else to Stalin.[158] 'Unconditional surrender spelt political victory for the USSR. Therefore, occultly, the war was being fought to stimulate and expand Communism.'[159] The book contains no prophecies about deterrence; the atomic bomb had made Douhet possible; the ruined cities of Germany would stand for fifty or a hundred years 'as monuments to the barbarism of their conquerors' and 'will remain to beckon generation after generation of Germans to revenge'.[160]

German revenge is relatively unthinkable today for many complex reasons. Area bombing, of West Germany at least, has not endangered the peace and has had a hand in facilitating the German economic miracle. But Liddell Hart, in his 1970 *History of the Second World War*, in which he made no mention of Fuller's earlier work, agreed that until 1944 the strategic air offensive had fallen short of the claim made for it as an alternative to invasion and had failed to break the civil will; he also agreed that unconditional surrender prolonged the war and this 'proved of profit only to Stalin—by opening the way for Communist domination of central Europe'.[161] It is very important to note that in the last years of their lives, and in spite of many disagreements, the two men were broadly at one in their overall political and military judgments on the Second World War. It must be to Fuller's resounding credit that many of the unpopular and radical views he pioneered in the war and distilled in his history, overt or hidden fascist sympathies apart, have come to represent today the balance of informed Western judgment.

10. 'Grow Old along with Me! The Best is yet to be?'—1949–66

At seventy Fuller was still full of health and energy, and his mental powers were in no discernible way dimmed by age; he attributed this at least in part to the practice of yoga. As the years passed his opinions softened and he tended to seek the middle ground more often; that this was more the consequence of a broader, longer view than of any diminution in acuity is undoubtedly true, but it is also true that the pleasing, mellow hues of autumn are themselves portents of winter.

Good health was a major factor in Fuller's literary productivity in his seventies and eighties, when he published no fewer than six new or greatly revised books and many articles for journals and newspapers. After his medical misfortunes in South Africa and India his life had been remarkably free of illness. As he told Liddell Hart: 'One of the surest prescriptions for health is to avoid the doctors.'[1] He spent many hours in writing to Liddell Hart and his letters were sometimes reminiscent, often in answer to Liddell Hart's insistent questions. In the spring of 1949 they exchanged letters about the Tidworth affair of 1927 and Fuller's part in the definition of the principles of war.[2] Liddell Hart took the opportunity of reminding Fuller that it was he who had suggested him to Milne as his MA.[3] Later in the year Fuller told Liddell Hart that he regarded Churchill as 'the greatest mountebank since Nero . . . Nero, however, had the better of him in that he committed suicide when comparatively young; that, at least, is a decent act.'[4] This sort of venom echoes some of the near-adolescent barbs contained in his youthful letters home. Perhaps, in personal relationships and judgments, age was a factor. His published articles showed little trace of this. He prophesied a Red victory in China,[5] wrote a kindly review of Eisenhower's *Crusade in Europe*,[6] called for moral, as well as physical and economic opposition, to Russia[7] and recommended survival through emigration—the scattering of Britons along the air routes in the Dominions.[8] When the Russians exploded an atomic device he ridiculed the banning of atom weapons, envisaged that Stalin would use his new power psychologically, and demanded the US should share her nuclear knowledge with the UK.[9] Next year he greeted the impending advent of a fusion bomb with the headline: 'Three Cheers for the H-Bomb'.[10] For Fuller this was obviously a step towards deterrent thinking; the H-bomb had rendered war ridiculous, and so he was back to his pre-war thoughts about the elimination of war through absurdity.

In 1949 *The Second World War* had been published in the US; in 1950 it was also published in Buenos Aires. Back in Surrey the Fullers finally sold their half of Chartlands and its five acres, and moved a few miles south into 'The Manor', a hotel and country club at Duddleswell near Uckfield in Sussex. Part of the object was to give Sonia a rest among the somewhat barren and austere, if somewhat tamed, beauties of that small stretch of heathland called Ashdown Forest.[11] Here he got down to the revision of *Decisive Battles* which its own imperfections and the warehouse fire had made necessary. Military events, however, crowded in upon him. The Korean War burst like a star shell above a confused world and he was quick to tell the readers of the *Sunday Graphic* that Stalin's real aim was to divert attention from probes in Europe and get the US tangled up in the Far East.[12] The real danger spot, he argued in another paper, was Germany, and he called for the immediate raising of twenty armoured divisions by the US, Britain and France for the defence of Europe.[13] In August he told an interviewer from *US News and World Report* that the atom bomb was a deterrent and guarantee against the spread of the Korean War.[14] In September the *Washington Post* reported that he wanted the creation of 'fire brigades', ready to go anywhere globally.[15] In these ways he was once again articulating thought processes through which the West would have to go. In November the *Chicago Tribune* reported him as calling for the careful bombing of military objectives in Manchuria, and perhaps China;[16] here he entered for a while into the heart of a white-hot American controversy, as he was later to do over the whole question of containment versus liberation.

He continued to correspond regularly also with Starr, who was by this time established with his wife in the small and romantic port of Kyrenia on the north coast of a still peaceful Cyprus. His letters show his continuing interest in the occult and are yet more evidence that his Edwardian association with Crowley had made a deep and indelible impact upon him. However he told Starr that he had never kept a full account of his mystical experiences and had destroyed such notes as he had made in the Crowley era. He had discovered, he wrote, that,

> the whole problem is one of balance and that when the + and the − are reduced to zero, the wise (possibly foolish) man does not attempt to carry on the task beyond that point. . . . To penetrate beyond the zero . . . is of no practical use, for its discoveries are not communicatable [*sic*] to others. It probably leads to a super zero, but of this I have no experience. I have however taught myself, more especially as regards conflict (war), to see the essential parts of any problem instantaneously, which is the first step towards balancing them out.[17]

It was this ability to see problems whole which gave bite and mobility to his thinking, just as it was his sense of the practical, even in mysticism, which prevented him from allowing the incommunicable to overflow, except occasionally, and principally in *Foundations*, into his military and political writing.

Liddell Hart, meanwhile, was engaged in writing *The Tanks* and in November he sent Fuller a draft of his paragraph on the latter's retirement in 1933, asking if he was commemorated at all at Bovington. Fuller's reply is worthy of extended quotation:

> I appreciate your generosity in championing my ancient efforts far more than that my name should decorate a road or my portrait a mess. In Westerham there is a lane, unsuitable for all traffic other than flat feet, called 'Fuller's Lane', which quite possibly one day may be attributed to me as a horse-hater—incidentally nothing but a tank could go up it, which also seems to fit in. If a completely unnegotiable road can be found in the neighbourhood of Bovington, as a warning to posterity I should have no objection to see it christened after me—'Boney' preferred. But as to the hang-

Betreuungsstelle für ausländische Ehrengäste

20. April 1939

Der Inhaber dieses Ausweises

......Herr..General..F u l l e r...

ist

Ehrengast des Führers

vom 18. – 22. April 1939

Fuller's pass. 'General Fuller, an honoured guest of the Führer from 18–22 April 1939'

Fuller the Fascist. A drawing in the magazine *Action*, Issue No 59

Fuller in 1949

'Boney' and Sonia in old age

ing of my portrait—unless on a horse-halter—the question had better not be raised.[18]

Behind such flippancy lurked an understandable, but extreme personal bitterness, as became apparent later in the Rutgers incident. And today there is certainly a Fuller Lecture Theatre at Bovington.

In the New Year he wrote a slim pamphlet which Eyre and Spottiswoode published at one shilling. It was called 'How to Defeat Russia', and recommended a psychological offensive coupled with a strong military defensive posture, rather than mere containment. The psychological offensive should be aimed at undermining communist power within the Soviet Union and its satellites, and suppressing it elsewhere. The military posture should be based on a strong West Germany, the prospect of German reunification, the use of German and Spanish troops and the creation of 100 divisions, forty stationed in West Germany. It should concentrate on a stopping force of tank and anti-tank formations, a mobile armoured and motorized infantry force to break through the Russian front and paralyse his communications, together with a powerful supporting tactical air force. 'History shows again and again that a combination of Resistance and Mobility—of Shield and Sword—is the true answer to Mass.'[19] The interest of this pamphlet today lies in the fact that no psychological offensive ever really got under way, except perhaps inside America under McCarthy, while NATO has only been able to afford a part of Fuller's military prescription—the stopping force and tactical air force—partly of course, because the sword behind the shield very soon took on a nuclear or 'massive retaliation' look about it, and the shield shrank, at least temporarily, into a trip-wire. Fuller saw that nuclear weapons could not be used to defeat Russia; he does not even mention them in the pamphlet. Congratulations on the pamphlet came from an unusual source, from Guderian, with whom it appears he had corresponded before. Guderian included a complaint about the Labour Government's attitude over Heligoland and added: 'We feel the diminishing influence of the white man in the world but cannot recognize a growing understanding of our commun [*sic*] danger.'[20]

That spring the Fuller's set up house again, this time in a wing of West Poundgate Manor near Crowborough, a very short distance from the hotel in Duddleswell.[21] It cost them considerable effort and expense to carry out the necessary reconstruction but here Fuller was able to continue his work on *Decisive Battles* and write numbers of articles on the theme of defeating Russia. In the *Saturday Evening Post*, for instance, he put forward the view that the Kremlin most feared a new revolution within its own borders.[22] The Duke of Alba, whom Fuller had known as Spanish Ambassador in London, wrote and congratulated him on this[23] as did many emigrés in the United States. Between 1952 and 1954 his journalistic output and literary income dropped, and much of what he did write was published abroad, in America, Germany or Spain. The *Marine Corps Gazette* published an account of the CDL tank,[24] *Ordnance* took an article on the dangers to the defensive of unusual weapons which might make normal warfare seem useless,[25] and *Die Deutsche Soldatenzeitung*[26] and other German and Spanish military journals, carried Fuller articles. In *Armour* he propounded the view that in spite of everything, the essentials of tactics remained the same,[27] while in a journal, the *Ukrainian Independent* published in Munich, he espoused that self-evident cause with enthusiasm.[28] *The Tank* published an article by him on 'The Tank in Future Warfare' in which he stressed that armour and mobility would be vital in atomic warfare.[29]

Life in West Poundgate Manor was quiet. Fuller disliked the way in which Christmas upset his ordered existence; it was a time of disequilibrium. He also began to resent such small matters as having to pay duty on a parcel of wine sent to him from Cyprus by the Starrs.[30] He suffered from bronchial colds; Sonia often became over-tired, and in the summer of 1953 tripped over a telephone wire, the fall affecting her heart.[31] He read voraciously but spurned fiction which he found less satisfying than real life. The only fiction he ever enjoyed, and that was in his youth, was of the Zane Grey and Fenimore Cooper variety, because there was no humbug about it. Of the fifties he privately despaired. 'The aristocrats of this age,' he wrote, 'are the clowns and bitch-goddesses, in one word the entertainers—the undertakers of the soul.'[32] 'There is nothing fixed, nothing permanent, no central principle, no governing idea. It is all like a dance of inebriated skeletons.'[33]

Between 1954 and 1956 the revised three-volume version of

Decisive Battles was published in both London and New York. The British title was *The Decisive Battles of the Western World and Their Influence upon History*, while the American publisher, Funk and Wagnall, preferred *A Military History of the Western World*. This time Fuller carried his analysis up to the end of the Second World War. The reviews were very favourable on the whole and most were enthusiastic. As Jay Luvaas wrote in 1964 in his *The Education of An Army*—which contains an excellent chapter on Fuller—this was his 'magnum opus and marks his coming of age as a military historian'.[34] *The Times* reviewer wrote of the first volume: 'Scholars may on occasion raise their eyebrows when they read what concerns their own field, but very few, if any, of them could emulate this writer over the whole field.'[35] *The Times Educational Supplement* compared Fuller to Delbrück rather than Clausewitz;[36] the *Spectator* called him 'the most eminent living writer on war',[37] while the Princeton Professor of History, writing in the *New York Herald Tribune* stated that the book 'belongs on the shelf of every serious student of war'.[38] After the publication of all three volumes, *History Today* considered that the 'work will stand the test of time and will be consulted and quoted when the very name of Creasy has been forgotten',[39] and *The Times Literary Supplement*, while admitting that some would disagree with Fuller, called for the payment of homage 'to the imagination and vitality of this major work'.[40] Such unstinted praise must have gone some way towards soothing the wounds of the past, as must the publication in *Soldier*, the British Army magazine, of a kindly article on 'The Provocative General'.[41] The new *Decisive Battles of the Western World* was greatly expanded and much of the strident fascism of the earlier version was softened or removed. Byron's 'Jew Rothschild', the 'Judaization' of commercial nations and the whole chapter on the Spanish Civil War were gone. *Lebensraum* remained but was treated more rationally.[42] The Alexandrian drive for unattackable frontiers,[43] Caesar's belief in authority, order and discipline and his attack on Money Power[44] were retained, however, although democracy was substituted for parliamentary systems as being incapable of conducting wars.[45] In Volume III Fuller lavished a great deal of praise on Mussolini's reforms in the twenties[46] but concluded that Hitler was a Jekyll and Hyde.[47] His view of Hitler had become much more balanced and his judgment on his brutal treatment of the Jews and the occupied countries was almost unequivocal. The impression created on the reader is of a lapsed Catholic brought back to his religion by force of circumstance but still from time to time unable to prevent his past doubts and heresies from appearing through the chinks in his new orthodoxy—a Catholic determined, moreover, to point out that perhaps his error was only a response to error in the Church itself. What Fuller was unprepared to renounce was his belief that the Allies in 1939 should have gone into alliance with all Germans opposed to Hitler,[48] and that after the failure of Hitler's assault on the Soviet Union the chief requirement was to prevent Russian hegemony from replacing German in Europe. By 1945, he wrote, with the frontier of Russia on the Elbe, 'a thousand years of European history had been rolled back'.[49] The policy of unconditional surrender could only be explained by blind hatred in the hearts of Roosevelt and Churchill.[50] There was nothing new here, but at the very end of the book Fuller tackled the problem of deterrence again and pointed out that as nuclear weapons had made international warfare absurd, it would be replaced by cold war—psychological, economic, guerilla and civil cold war between the Soviet Union and the United States. The resolution of this conflict would come not from military action but from an answer to the question: Which of the two political, social, economic and cultural systems 'is the more fitted to solve the crucial problem set to mankind by the Industrial Revolution—the status of man, his government and way of life in a fully mechanized world?'[51]

In contrast to this measured pronouncement Fuller told Liddell Hart in March 1956 that he had never looked upon NATO 'other than as eyewash and, so far as I can see, our only possible hope is that Germany will produce another Hitler, and that next time we back him.'[52] His more private thoughts opened up greater chinks in the armour of his repentance than did his published work. In November he attacked the Suez War in an article in *The People*.[53] In 1956 also, and most surprisingly, a book was published in Moscow called Вторая Мировая Война; this was *The Second World War*.

Jay Luvaas, by now Professor of History at Allegheny College in Pennsylvania, had first written to Fuller in 1950 about the British military view of the American Civil War. He contacted him again early in 1957 to ask for a copy of the paper Fuller wrote on Chancellorville while at Camberley.[54] It was the beginning of a correspondence between them in which Fuller made some frank and illuminating comments on his life and work. In April William Sloane wrote another seminal letter to Fuller from America. Sloane had been at Funk and Wagnall when that firm contracted for *Decisive Battles of the Western World*, but had since moved as Director to Rutgers University Press in New Brunswick, New Jersey. He had heard that Fuller intended to follow up *Decisive Battles of the Western World* with a book on Alexander the Great. Indeed this had been occupying much of Fuller's time for the past year and had been a venture at the back of his mind since 1917, when he had read Colonel Dodge's two volumes on Alexander in his 'Great Captains' series.[55] At Camberley in the twenties he had lectured at length on Alexander.[56] Sloane suggested that Rutgers should bring out the American edition of *Alexander the Great*. In reply Fuller told him that his agents would be offering it to Funk and Wagnall but that if they did not want it he would remember Sloane's offer. He also told Sloane that he had not decided what to tackle next, and whatever it was would have to be fairly short because of his age, but that he would keep Rutgers in mind.[57] Before the receipt of this letter Helen Stewart, Sloane's assistant, had written to Eyre and Spottiswoode, who had replied advising Rutgers to approach Fuller's agents at once.[58] Sloane and Stewart developed a great enthusiasm and fondness for Fuller and were determined to capture his books for Rutgers University Press. As with Luvaas this began a correspondence in which Fuller threw very considerable light on his motives and the development of his opinions. That same month *Ordnance* included an article by Fuller on 'The Changing Face of War' in which he emphasized the importance of industrial power, science and technology, and concluded that victory on the 'inner front' was as important as on the battlefield.[59] In November General Wedemeyer invited him to visit the US and lecture at the National War College.[60] This offer he did not, at the age of seventy-nine, take up, but 1957 had clearly shown that he had become a well-known and greatly respected figure in many American military and academic circles, as he still is. In this respect his publicity for minority groups in the Soviet Union, well represented in America, was no doubt also important. At the end of the year, for instance, he had an article in *ABN*, the organ of the Anti-Bolshevik Bloc of Nations, headed 'The Kremlin is Living on a Volcano'.[61]

By 1958, the year in which a Polish edition of *The Second World War* was produced, he had become a little frail and a boast in a letter to Liddell Hart that he had not been near a doctor since 1905 had a note of defiance about it.[62] The strikes, petrol rationing and rising prices of 1957 had not been pleasant and he even considered emigrating like the Starrs to an island, but felt Majorca the best because it came under a dictatorship.[63] He appeared to be unafraid of death but in his eighties began to resent the limitations which age and infirmity increasingly imposed upon him. His letters to Liddell Hart sometimes betrayed the way in which minor anxieties were beginning to prey upon him; 'try and be on time as the club fills up rapidly at lunch time', he wrote rather querulously on one occasion.[64] On another, a few days later, however, he launched forth into a comment on Harold Macmillan's statement that 'military forces today are not designed to wage war; their purpose is to prevent it' which was as telling as ever, although still reluctantly deterrent. War had causes, he wrote, and only their elimination would ensure prevention; Russia should be attacked psychologically, but in physical war you cannot 'save men by increasing the destructive power of their weapons. As weapon-power goes up, more and more men creep into the military and industrial tail.'[65] In July he had to put off a planned visit to see the Liddell Harts because Sonia had fallen ill.[66] In November he sold West Poundgate Manor and negotiated for another and smaller house called Forest Gate in the same area. This he could not obtain immediately, and so Sonia and he moved into the Highlands Hotel, in Crowborough.[67] While this move was taking place, *Alexander the Great* was published.

Fuller's interest in Alexander, and later in Caesar, is not difficult to understand. Here were Great Men, whose activities had been both military and political, who did not—or at least no longer did—attract the opprobrium which clung to Hitler or Mussolini. Moreover their generalship could be analysed by using the method outlined so many years ago in *Foundations*. In *Alexander the Great* Fuller was most disarmingly open about his refusal to be bound slavishly to the product of detailed research. When a historian made an improbable statement about

Alexander, Fuller thought it safer to check against what was known of Alexander's character and activities rather than delve further into sources. 'At times, even unreliable historians hit the nail on the head.' As regards filling in tactical detail he used the method of 'inherent probabilities'.[68] The book is interesting as history, although Fuller used English translations of his sources, and for this reason *The Times* thought it a still more outstanding achievement than Volume III of *Decisive Battles of the Western World*;[69] it is however the lessons and contemporary asides and implications which are most striking. He used such phrases as 'pure Aryan stock', compared the Sogdiana campaign with the Boer War, commented on the arrogance of the mounted warrior and likened the Hellenic League to the League of Nations and the UN.[70] It is in the Epilogue, however, that he came closest to the present. Ignorance of history caused it to repeat itself, he argued, but valid lessons could only be drawn from periods in which prevailing conditions were similar to those of today. Conditions in the fifth and fourth centuries BC were similar to those of today in that there was then emotional and irrational democracy and a socialist welfare state. History could have taught statesmen that since the First World War had destroyed the political age which gave it birth, a new war policy and different military means would henceforth be required. Hitler should have exploited the inner front in Russia; he was defeated by his own stupidity. Churchill blundered in refusing to support the anti-Hitler movement in Germany. Unconditional surrender was a policy which stemmed from historical ignorance. Fuller was an unashamed historical utilitarian, but one who also deeply enjoyed the re-creation of the past.[71] In *Alexander the Great* he finally came to terms with the principles of war, defined them as guides rather than irrevocable principles, agreed that they could sometimes be discarded with impunity, but only after deep consideration, and reduced them to seven: maintenance of the aim, security, mobility, offensive, economy of force, concentration of force and surprise.[72] The baneful influence of the threefold order was at last expunged. He told Luvaas privately some years later that he had unwisely tried to universalize tactical principles in *Foundations* but that his best exposition of them was contained in *Alexander the Great*.[73] The book was well reviewed.[74] Fuller heard that his agent had placed the American contract with

Sloane and in a letter to the latter he wrote that he thought that, of all his works, *Alexander the Great* was 'the most likely to have permanent value', while in 1961 he still believed it was the best he had written.[75]

In 1959 he appears to have been relatively quiescent; he was writing his next book, *The Conduct of War*, and already thinking about following up *Alexander the Great* with *Caesar*. In January, however, he gave Liddell Hart's *The Tanks* a very favourable review in the *Spectator*.[76] In March he moved into Forest Gate and that same month heard from one of his two remaining close relatives, his younger brother Lionel, who had worked in India but now lived in Ireland.[77] His other brother, Walter was too deaf to practise his profession as a lawyer and lived with his wife in a converted coach-house and stable on Streatham Hill where he collected Polynesian artefacts.[78] In August Fuller had lunch with Liddell Hart who brought Luvaas with him,[79] while in September he attended Ironside's funeral.[80] The next month Sonia was ill with sciatica.[81] On October 18th he took her away for a week's rest to a hotel in Herstmonceux, near Eastbourne, but there himself fell victim to sciatica. Back home his right leg below the knee became numb, cold and painful. A specialist diagnosed disc trouble. Hotels were not good for Fuller, and doctors did not help.[82] From this time onwards his letters to Liddell Hart tended to catalogue the problems of the old—colds, Sonia's health, the lack of summer, the difficulties of running a house. Writing *The Conduct of War* took up a lot of his time in 1960, and in June Luvaas told him that he was proposing to write a book on British military thought since Napoleon, in which both Fuller and Liddell Hart would figure.[83] Sonia still got about and visited Tunbridge Wells once a week to go shopping.[84] In August he took her to visit the Liddell Harts in Medmenham and some time also that year gave Helen Stewart, of Rutgers University Press, lunch in the 'Senior', an occasion she has remembered with great vividness. In the autumn a drain overflowed and flooded the ground floor of Forest Gate, causing much anguish to the old couple, but not preventing Fuller from concluding a letter to Liddell Hart with a long analysis of Clausewitz's defensive—the-stronger-form-of-war theory.[85] In December he finished *The Conduct of War* and sent it off to Eyre and Spottiswoode. He was asked to modify his criticism of

Churchill and Roosevelt, which he agreed to do.[86]

At the end of January 1961, Sloane, who was going to publish *The Conduct of War* in America, wrote to Fuller and told him that he had got the impression that his intention was nothing less than the outmoding of Clausewitz. The reply he got was characteristic:

> As regards Clausewitz, my intention is not to outmode him, but—were there such a word—to in-mode him; to bring him into fashion and get people to read him instead of quoting him. The unfortunate thing about 'On War' is that nine-tenths of it are now obsolete, and the one-tenth, which is pure gold, gets lost in the rubble. ... In my opinion, Clausewitz's level is on that of Copernicus, Newton and Darwin. ... If my 'Conduct' is to follow suit it will not be because of what I have written, but because my study of Clausewitz has compelled me to write it. The difficulty of dealing with readers whose minds have been addled by propaganda is to step into their shoes, and one is apt to put things in ways which irritate rather than enlighten them. I frequently catch myself out doing this. ... I am not very good at sugaring pills.[87]

June saw him reading the proofs, which it took him a week to go through twice.[88] In July he wrote a long and slightly rambling letter to Liddell Hart about the necessity to base a philosophy of war on a philosophy of peace.[89] An advance copy of *The Conduct of War* was sent to Liddell Hart in October and the book itself was published on November 9th in England and on the 20th in the States. That year also a Spanish version of *Decisive Battles of the Western World* came out as well as a German *Alexander the Great*. Fuller believed that *The Conduct of War* would not be greatly admired in England 'because the English soldier is unteachable and the public not seriously interested in war', nor, perhaps, in America, but that it would sell on the Continent where it was later published in French, Spanish and German.[90] He regarded it, however, as important because it gave his 'mature views on war'.[91] What these views were must now be explained.

The Conduct of War does not contain anything startlingly new but in it are distilled most of the theories and values which Fuller spent a lifetime in developing. Perhaps 'distilled' is the wrong word, suggesting as it does the concentration of a fiery spirit; better words might be 'refined' or 'aged', matured in cask and bottle until the dross becomes a sediment which is discarded before one drinks; the beverage itself improves and mellows, and the quiet and cool of the cellar, far from the vineyard's sun and rain, turns raw fermented grape juice into a great wine. Gone from *The Conduct of War* are the convoluted rationalities of *Foundations*, the embittered outbursts of the *Memoirs* or *The Army in My Time* and the strident, nauseous fascist battle-cries, of *The First of the League Wars* or *Towards Armageddon*. Liddell Hart told him that it was 'a masterly work. . . . It is a wonderful feat to have achieved such a "tour de force" at eighty-three. It whets one's appetite for what you produce at ninety!'[92]

The book is an examination of the impact of social, economic, political and technological change upon the conduct of war since 1789, and Fuller's 'mature views on war' were related to that framework. The problem of war aims was examined in depth, and Fuller repeated his quotation from the plinth of Sherman's statue and argued that Clausewitz never understood that the true aim of war was peace and not victory.[93] This led him to a final condemnation of Churchill's adoption of the policy of unconditional surrender and a final reiteration of his view that this had led to prolongation of the war against both Germany and Japan, and to an enormous expansion of Russian influence in Europe and the Far East. He also placed on record once again his condemnation of Churchill's espousal of the policy of bombing of civil populations.[94] The causes of the reversion to barbarism in war since 1789, which Fuller exemplified graphically and statistically, included the fall of aristocracy, the rise of democracy, the industrial and technological revolutions, the emergence of socialism, the growth of populations, the popular Press and materialism, and the decay of religion.[95] The restricted warfare of the eighteenth century was only possible in an aristocratic civilization.[96] With the emergence of the theory of the 'general will' mass emotion began to exacerbate wars which, with conscription, became affairs of peoples as well as armies. Democracies brought war, not peace, because their 'in-group' love, or solidarity, depended on the development of hatred of the 'out-group'.[97] Thus unlimited war was reborn, and when communism was added to democracy as a driving force unlimited war became essentially ideological and unending, even if cloaked under the guise of 'peaceful co-existence'.[98] The industrial and technological revolutions led to the rise of communism, but also to enormous changes in military technology. These technological developments happened too quickly for soldiers and politicians to keep up with and the ultimate consequence was the stalemate and slaughter of the First World War.[99] The atom bomb was 'the ultimate military expression of the Industrial Revolution' and it 'eliminated physical warfare as a profitable instrument of policy'.[100]

On fascism Fuller was very circumspect, although he clung to the view that what really mattered in the Second World War was 'not whether Hitler was more evil than Stalin, or Stalin more so than Hitler, but which of their aims was the more dangerous to the democratic way of life'.[101] Perhaps this view would now be rather more widely accepted than in the past. To what extent Fuller himself believed in any sort of democracy is a point to which he did address himself in a later correspondence with Luvaas. It is doubtful, however, if anyone even today would agree that the Ascot Concentration Camp, where 18B detainees were collected in 1940, was worse than Dachau, yet Fuller gave space and approval to such a claim in the book.[102] He saw clearly, of course, that one of Hitler's greatest mistakes was to treat the Ukrainians as *Untermenschen* but he also implied that Hitler could have done little else if he wanted to establish a German *Lebensraum* in Eastern Europe.[103] There was no mention this time of the partisans as a cause of the brutality.

On mechanized warfare *The Conduct of War* contains Fuller's last substantial message. He admitted that tanks had only begun the breakage of the 1918 deadlock and that, although they had had the potential to complete it, this was achieved by economic means;[104] he retained his belief in gas and put down its non-usage to 'popular emotionalism';[105] he questioned the validity of the Douhet theory in any non-nuclear context;[106] he recognized that his theory of strategic paralysis could only be based on an offensive policy which Britain did not have in the inter-war period;[107] he saw that technological developments made it necessary in 1940 for Guderian to attack the front prior to the headquarters, to use the Liddell Hart strategy of indirect approach.[108]

He admitted, as we have seen, that nuclear weapons had rendered physical warfare unprofitable between members of the two great camps because strategic and tactical nuclear weapons would henceforth act as deterrents at both levels.[109] Pacifists could not see that they should welcome such weapons.[110] The result was that we had to live in a state of cold war, of permanent emergency, in which there was no real distinction between peace and war. The problem of China was a complicating factor and one which might lead to our advantage—or disadvantage in the end.[111]

Cyril Falls reviewed *The Conduct of War* on the day of its publication. 'Age,' he wrote, 'has not dimmed the power of this veteran. On the other hand, he has become slightly less pugnacious and prejudiced, without losing drive; and this is a benefit, because, while it does not weaken his forcefulness it makes him less inclined to be unreasonable, if not at times maddening.'[112] *The Conduct of War* was well received, made *Ordnance* Book of the Month in America, has been twice reprinted in this country and fifteen years after its publication is studied in some depth in numbers of universities. Perhaps the military and political worlds had at last caught up with the octogenarian soldier-scholar so that his views, no longer those of a visionary, ahead, or out of touch, with his time, were more or less acceptable. *The Conduct of War* bends few frontiers but it is compulsive reading because, from a highly informed and original standpoint, it presents, in just over three hundred readable pages, a coherent view, over nearly two centuries, of the relations of war and policy against the environment of change. Clausewitz is certainly 'in-moded' because Fuller was a neo-Clausewitzian whether he accepted the fact or not. He teased Clausewitz for his recommendation that states should attempt to fight absolute war, and attacked him for his defensive—the-stronger-form-of-war theory and for his belief that the aim of war was the overthrow of the enemy. The teasing was justified. Clausewitz's absolute war was a theoretical model drawn from the philosophies current in his day; his recommendation that states should attempt to make wars absolute came in the unrevised Book VIII of *On War*;[113] it did not sit well with his argument in the completed Chapter 1 of Book 1 that wars could in reality never be absolute and should always be fought for a political end. The attack on Clausewitz's belief that the defensive was the stronger form of war was arguable, but on this point it is unfair to take Clausewitz out of the conditions of his day. Fuller's main attack, that Clausewitz never grasped that the true aim of war was peace not victory, does not succeed. Clausewitz's whole system was based on the fact that war was a political instrument; the aims of any war must therefore be those given to it by its makers—the rulers or politicians. Only if the military object overruled the political, and war became absolute, did victory become the superior and only aim. Fuller was berating the wrong man; it was numbers of Allied political leaders, not Clausewitz, who placed victory above peace, and that 'complete non-Clausewitzian soldier', General Eisenhower; the description is Fuller's.[114]

Liddell Hart devoted a considerable amount of time and effort to reading and commenting on *The Conduct of War*. He told Fuller that he thought it was his best book but, because it would probably go into a second edition, he sent Fuller numerous comments and criticisms for his consideration. On this occasion Fuller did not explode with wrath as he had done over Lord God Almighty's criticisms of his *Grant* in 1929. The two exchanged a series of letters about such matters as Douhet's influence in England, the state of British armoured preparedness in 1940, de Gaulle's claims as a theorist of armoured warfare, and the nature and credibility of deterrence. Fuller held that nuclear weapons had proved their value in deterring the outbreak of a war which could only lead to mutual destruction; Liddell Hart believed that no proof of such an effort was possible and that the Russians did not appear to be aiming at domination through the use of military means and feared, moreover, to allow their troops to see the greater prosperity of the West. This fear of contact had just been exemplified in the construction of the Berlin Wall. It was in this exchange of letters that Fuller admitted that he had been obliged to give up lecturing because he had become subject to fits of coughing. 'At 94 my father choked to death, and his father did the same.'[115] Sonia, also, had a number of bad falls at this time.[116]

Fuller's brother, Walter, died in 1962, and this meant that, apart from the bachelor Lionel in Eire, he had no close blood relations left. He was old, increasingly infirm, as was Sonia, and finding the burden of looking after a house tiresome and exhausting. It was at this juncture that he received a letter from Sloane in New Brunswick which was to have considerable consequences.

Sloane merely asked him where he intended to have his archives kept after his death, so that Sloane could send his collection of Fuller's letters there.[117] Fuller replied in a long letter, full of invaluable information for his biographer, that he hardly had any archives worth keeping because his peripatetic military life had prevented their serious collection, while most of his papers had been destroyed in the blitz. This led him on to reminisce about his activities in the thirties and also to some self-revelation. 'I am by nature a shy man,' he wrote, 'a defect I think. I am no prophet, no expert and perhaps too imaginative to be a good historian. . . . I am a student of war and a military critic. "Prophet!" always amuses me.'[118] It appeared that Fuller might even destroy his papers, for he began to wonder if anyone was interested in them. He spent many hours turning the problem over in his mind while writing *Caesar* and this must have led him to make the depressed comment to Liddell Hart in August that his Army service had been 'thirty years of unprofitable labour'.[119] Then, towards the end of the year he decided to turn Sloane's offer on its head and, instead of telling him where to send his collection of letters, wrote and made a strange suggestion.

> Such heirs as I have [he told the American publisher] are distant ones, and in any case are not interested in my work, nor do I know of any institution in this country which is. I have a complete collection of the books I have written, some forty in all, and of nearly all my articles in some eight volumes, three still unbound. So far I have not found the time to go through letters and papers, but will do so as soon as *Caesar* is off my hands. What I suggest is, that I have a clause inserted in my will leaving all these things to you to do with as you see fit. . . . Since our acquaintance, which unfortunately has been through correspondence only, may I say that you are the only man who has taken a real interest in me, and nothing would give me greater pleasure than to know that my life's work eventually rested in your hands.[120]

In the first draft of this letter he had written 'taken a real interest in my work' but crossed out the last two words and substituted 'me'.[121] In making this decision he misjudged the changed climate of opinion; public recognition and modest honour were just around the corner, and numbers of British universities would have been extremely anxious to house his papers; the proposition that no man had taken a real interest in him was untenable and would have hurt both Liddell Hart and Meredith Starr deeply. The wounds inflicted by general scorn and neglect take long to heal.

Sloane 'found the letter extremely touching and more than a little sad'. He must have been very surprised but he immediately secured the agreement of the Rutgers University President and its Librarian to the papers being housed in the University Library [122] and wrote to tell Fuller this. [123] He also told Fuller that he found it hard to believe that he had 'not attracted the interest and attention of a great many people in a great many places'. So he had, but because of a continuing feeling of rejection a large proportion of his books and papers eventually found their unlikely way to a small New Jersey university town of frame houses and campus buses, not far from New York.

At the end of the year the Fullers spent a holiday in Bavaria; [124] in spite of their age the urge to travel never left them. In January 1963 they were snowed up in Forest Gate [125] but in the spring he was particularly busy writing letters to Liddell Hart, about John Wheldon (who subsequently wrote a book on mechanized armies in which both Fuller and Liddell Hart appear prominently)[126] and about what foreign editions of his works had been published. [127] Then in June he was told by Brigadier John Stephenson of the RUSI that he and Liddell Hart were to receive the Chesney Gold Medal. It was Fuller's second gold medal, and this time it was to be a genuine accolade from the military community and not a contentious prize almost surreptitiously awarded to a military bolshevik by a very small group. This medal, the highest honour in the gift of the RUSI, is awarded to authors of eminent work or works, 'calculated to advance military science or knowledge in the Empire'. The list of previous recipients includes Mahan, Corbett and Churchill. It was particularly appropriate that Fuller and Liddell Hart should both receive it and at the same ceremony.

Before this event could take place Fuller took time off from writing *Caesar* to read the draft of the chapter on himself which Luvaas had sent him from Meadeville in Pennsylvania. The chapter was to form part of the book about which Luvaas had written to Fuller eighteen months before. Fuller liked what he read and this was understandable because, for perhaps the first time, a balanced but sympathetic account of his life's work was to be presented to the public. He sent Luvaas some comments, the most important of which were concerned with a wish to have the emphasis on *Foundations* decreased and on *The Conduct of War* increased, with an attempt to explain his fascism and with an explanation of his attitude to Churchill, whom he regarded as an outstanding national leader but 'an emotional and capricious strategist'.[128] In a later letter he told Luvaas that he 'was never a fascist in the German sense' because National Socialism stemmed from tribalism whereas Mussolini's fascism was medieval in concept. His own political views had been formulated, he implied, merely from a desire to bring about the mechanization of the British Army.[129] That this explanation had a basis in fact there is no doubt; that Fuller had been a fascist there is also no doubt; whether his route to fascism was Italian or German is perhaps important, but difficult to determine. Certainly it was the Corporate State he admired but, as we have seen, he gave Hitler public support late into 1939.

His visit to Whitehall to receive the Chesney Gold Medal was also preceded by the departure of the Fullers from Forest Gate. Running the house had become too burdensome. They spent many days in looking for a flat in Tunbridge Wells; Sonia liked gardening although she felt too frail for it, but Fuller himself was prepared to settle for a 'piazza' and one geranium in a pot. Sonia had retained her delicate beauty and Fuller remained dapper and distinguished; the pair must have looked entirely appropriate amidst the fading gentility of the royal spa although Fuller's quiet but precise and penetrating voice shattered the equanimity of more than one public place. Alison Starr, for example, remembers that once in the 'Old Barn', a well-known Tunbridge Wells restaurant, he announced that Edith Summerskill had said that boxing should be forbidden because it damaged the boxers' brains. 'I don't agree with her,' he then pronounced. 'I don't believe they have any.' He also made no secret of his views about Churchill.[130]

A suitable flat was difficult to find, so in September 1963 the Fullers moved into the Royal Mount Ephraim Hotel in Tunbridge Wells where they were to remain for over a year. One is, I suppose, fortunate to be able to afford to live in a hotel in Tunbridge Wells when over eighty and in declining health. There is, however, in the psychic atmosphere of such places, an intimation of fear publicly suppressed, and decay temporarily arrested, which the Fullers found distasteful. Fuller feared senility greatly and the Royal Mount Ephraim Hotel was bad for him. The irony was that it was the same hotel in which he and Sonia had stayed when he had become GSO 3 Second Army in December 1914. He told Liddell Hart that in the First World War the hotel drawing room, by this time a sort of palm court, had been on the first floor but that this had subsequently been divided into three bedrooms,

> each virtually two rooms—half bedroom and half palm court. The reason we came here was that we were able to book the largest of the three. Except for this advantage over the other hotels, and that the cooking is passable, the rest is archaic. There is no getting over it, our main obstacle is that we are too old to run a house, possibly also a flat. Our plan, however, is to try out a flat, and should we find it too much for us, to sell up and end our days in a hotel, although we loathe the idea.[131]

It had been decided that the Chesney Gold Medals would be presented in the RUSI lecture theatre on October 31st. Fuller asked the Liddell Harts and the Stephensons to dine after the ceremony, and Liddell Hart in reply asked Fuller what he intended to say. Fuller, who knew by this time that the then Lieutenant-General Sir John Hackett, the DCIGS, was going to speak, told Liddell Hart that, if DCIGS mentioned it, he would deny being a prophet 'because it was obvious that the tank could cancel out the bullet. . . . As thinking was penal servitude to the soldier of forty odd years ago, emulating the ostrich he buried his head in the manure heap until Disaster . . . wrenched out his tail feathers'.[132]

In the event General Hackett did not actually call Fuller a prophet. The setting was august; the Duke of Gloucester, President of the RUSI, sat on the dais behind the long, heavy, wooden desk. The Chairman, Air Chief Marshal Sir Claude Pelly, referred to Fuller and Liddell Hart as 'two distinguished gentlemen'. General Hackett emphasized the irony that 'the enemies of Britain in war should have brought Britain nearly to her knees through the use of tactical techniques evolved in Britain but largely ignored there'. He called Fuller 'the gadfly of Socrates, pricking people to awareness of false complacency, not always a popular pursuit in armies. . . . Not everyone would agree with his political conclusions nor accept his interpretations of history. In so provocative a writer, this would be impossible. But no one would deny the vigour of the first nor the penetration of the second.' It was a very laudatory speech. Fuller and Liddell Hart, he concluded, were alike in many ways, unlike in many more, but with two outstanding things in common: 'Each is possessed by a powerful and enquiring mind and by a passion for truth.'

In reply Fuller stuck close to his intentions. He expressed his pleasure in the honour of having his name 'coupled with that of my old friend, Basil Liddell Hart'. He told General Hackett that he did not know whether he deserved the bouquet he had been given, 'but it gave me great pleasure to receive it and I think back some forty odd years when bouquets which were not bouquets were usually thrown at me. . . . I was not a prophet. I have never thought of being a prophet. I think I have got too much common-sense to be a prophet. I was a missionary and I had only one little thing really to do. It was a little propaganda on the slogan, "Half an inch of steel will keep out half an ounce of lead". . . . It was really very simple but its implications were enormous.' Liddell Hart, on the other hand, complained of losing his 'clean sheet' as regards awards but said that to share the award with his 'old friend and comrade "Boney" Fuller' was a pleasurable compensation. 'The extent, to which we have worked in unison,' he said, his tall figure dwarfing the now sitting Fuller, 'over a span of more than forty years is far more remarkable than any differences of view. Our association in the crusade for military progress has been one of my happiest experiences.' As missionaries and crusaders both medallists were blessed with remarkable longevity. For Fuller, at least, October 31st, 1963, and the medal which the Duke handed to him, represented, as he said, some very pleasurable recognition.[133]

Soon after this event the Fullers found a first-floor flat but the kitchen proved difficult to improve and the deal fell through. The strain imposed by flat-hunting so soon after packing up Forest Gate told on him and a cough, aggravated by a bad cold, led to what he called a 'heart collapse' at the beginning of December. He recovered from this but began to find the mornings trying.[134] Fortunately he was able to finish *Caesar* in January and to spend the early months of 1964 less energetically than usual. However even in the summer he still felt unwell and complained of lack of energy, shortage of breath and coughing paroxysms. Sonia was becoming increasingly immobile. In July they found a flat in Nevill Park, on the outskirts of Tunbridge Wells, and in August began looking for domestic help, without which they felt they could not contemplate a move out of the Royal Mount Ephraim Hotel. The flat was on the ground floor of a Victorian house and comprised five large rooms.[135] He made plans to send Sonia off to stay with friends in Germany to cushion the problems of the move, but before this could take place she fell seriously ill, went into a nursing home and everything had to be delayed.[136]

A German edition of *The Conduct of War* came out in the summer and was well reviewed. It was also at this time that the first reactions to his last book began to come in. Sloane read the typescript in New Brunswick and was excited. He found Fuller's surgical analysis as striking as ever but expressed a hope that he would write another book, perhaps on Augustus, in spite of his declaration at the end of the preface that *Caesar* would be his last.[137] In reply Fuller reaffirmed his decision not to start another book; he cited his declining health and deteriorating memory as reasons, together with the enormous literature on Augustus which he would have had to absorb and the need he felt to sort out such papers as he intended to leave to Rutgers.[138] Sloane was not deterred by this and set out to interest his Council in the Augustus venture. When doing so he paid Fuller a tribute which would have touched and amused him had he heard it.

> General Fuller has a nineteenth-century mind. He is intel-lectually quite unafraid, romantic, specifically virile and masculine, never asexually impersonal. It is the mind of a commander and while the General is a good deal of a scholar, he is a personal scholar; the details of much of what he says are open to argument and criticism very often from men of infinitely less stature than his own. . . . General Fuller has been playing all his life for mortal stakes and his books . . . reflect that.[139]

On October 10th Sonia was discharged from the nursing home and on the 30th the move to the flat took place. In a letter to Sloane telling him of this Fuller admitted that he saw a great similarity between Hitler and Caesar and the ages in which they lived but had not said as much in the book because he would have then been branded a Nazi.[140] Once intalled in the flat he began sorting out his books, for he realized that if flat-living was not a success he would have to part with them. Possessions had become an increasing encumbrance.[141]

Throughout the year he had been exchanging letters regularly with Liddell Hart but in the autumn he paid a visit, without Sonia, to States House at Medmenham where the Liddell Harts had made their home. He saw the house at its best set against the richly decorated autumnal trees. Liddell Hart had converted the stables into a garage for his Rolls-Royce and a library for his enormous collection of letters, papers and books. Fuller was at once reminded of his hut in the Headquarters at Bermicourt in 1917 and christened the States House library the 'Brain Barn' as the hut had been called nearly fifty years before.[142] Meanwhile Estelle Fuller, Walter's widow, visited America and discovered that Fuller's fame there ensured her the most lavish welcome and hospitality.[143]

An inscribed copy of Luvaas's book arrived at Nevill Park in March 1965. The chapter on Fuller ended with the words:

> Fuller's tone has mellowed considerably over the years. At eighty-five [he was eighty-six by the time he read it] he retains much of his vitality and the strength of his convictions and no one can deny his mind is still as sharp as his pen. . . . In music discord produces tension, provokes attention, sustains interest, and demands resolution—all effects that Fuller tried to achieve through his writings. But it is no longer Fuller's function to blow Reveille, which of necessity is impatient, authoritative, and usually displeasing.[144]

This was valid, although *Caesar* was to shatter not a few illusions and prove that the Fullers of this world do not take kindly to the secluded paddock. In May the Starrs, concerned at the problems which beset the Fullers in their attempts to run a large flat, offered to come and look after them. Fuller declined the offer for the time being.[145] In fact at one time the Fullers and the Starrs did seriously consider this proposition but the two women were apprehensive that the men would spend each entire day in over-stimulating conversation. In June the Liddell Harts visited the Tunbridge Wells flat and were given detailed instructions to park the Rolls-Royce in the road as there was insufficient space to turn it in the drive. Lunch was taken in a restaurant and the journey thence accomplished in a taxi because Fuller was concerned that it would be difficult to park the Rolls-Royce in the centre of Tunbridge Wells. Kathleen Liddell Hart admired a chair in the flat and was promptly, in somewhat Arabic fashion, promised that she should have it after it had been repaired. It duly arrived at States House and is there today.[146]

Caesar was published in London on July 1st, and in the autumn in America. This was forty-five years after the publica-tion of his first full-length book, *Tanks in the Great War*. Most of *Caesar* was about Caesar. It was a masterly re-statement and analysis of a very important piece of history, written with wit and economy. Fuller concluded that Caesar had been too much of a general to a be a creative statesman. His basic problems were the corruption brought about by the pursuit of wealth, the power of the money-lender and the dilemma of being unable to give up control of the army to the Senate and the people—the only way to a lasting peace—without destroying himself. As a statesman he had grave deficiencies but as a demagogue and a fighting general he was a genius. However he was not so good at other sorts and levels of generalship; he failed to put right defects in the Roman Army's logistic system and in its order of battle, notably its lack of trained cavalry and light infantry, which latter deficiency prevented it from making an adequate response when faced with guerilla warfare; he failed also to be consistently sound as a strategist. His greatest genius lay in his complete and well-placed self-confidence as a tactician; but it fell to Augustus, his succes-sor, to solve the political problems of the Roman world by establishing a disguised form of one-man rule safeguarded by the creation of a professional standing army and a Praetorian Guard, rather than a militia or conscript force. The possibilities of military 'coups' were diminished by producing, for the most able officers, a combined military and civil career.[147]

Fuller believed that *Caesar* was his best written book.[148] The reviews were enthusiastic. The *Wall Street Journal*, for instance, called the book a 'new, satisfying study in biography, power politics and military tactics ... by Major-General J. F. C. Fuller who has been called a modern Clausewitz. Some consider him superior'. *The Times Literary Supplement* praised his clarity and expertise and commented that there were few historians 'who would not be vastly improved by a rigorous military apprenticeship'. The *Supplement* thought his campaign narratives 'pure professional delight'.[149]

In July that year he was at his best. He told Sloane that there was a big difference between a study of war based on concepts and one based on percepts. The former approach led to a sort of military metaphysics and to the situation in which the American government could accept the concept that communism in Vietnam could be defeated by bombing. Fuller's own thinking, he claimed, in happy forgetfulness of *Foundations*, was largely based on percepts and the percepts of the Second World War showed that ideas could not 'be dislodged by bombs'.[150] Sonia and he then conceived the idea of giving up the Nevill Park flat and going to live in Malta.[151] Sloane wrote and suggested that he might care to consider writing a book 'out of your own knowledge and experience' which would not pose the necessity for a great deal of research. He went on: 'I believe that it would be a valuable enterprise coming from you. I have never before recommended any such undertaking to an established writer, especially academic ones who quite often fail to produce anything of the least interest unless they are crowded into it by an oftentimes inordinate amount of meticulous research. But in your case, it might be a good idea.'[152] Fuller's reply to this rather patronizing offer has not survived. Before receiving Sloane's suggestion, however, he wrote another letter to him in which he elaborated on his earlier comment on the Vietnam bombing and compared such a method of attacking guerillas in a jungle to Braddock's disastrous campaign against the Red Indians in 1755. He also told Sloane that he had sorted out most of his papers and had now decided to annotate and link them with a series of notes. Sonia unfortunately was unwell again and so they had decided to give up the flat at the end of September and, a little later, to go to Malta for the winter. This, he implied, might interfere with the production of the notes.[153] Sloane replied at once, offering to help Fuller with clerical expenses or even to pay transport costs so that he could take his papers with him to Malta.[154] Sloane was very anxious to get the papers; it is, therefore, not a little odd that when he eventually did, he never actually read them.[155]

The decision having been made to winter in Malta, Fuller set about selling some of his books for which he would have no more room. Francis Edwards, the London bookseller, took his military books, while Keith Hogg, another bookseller, sold his occult collection. Fuller helped to produce a catalogue for this latter sale. Here were listed the poetry, erotica, plays, novels, translations and pamphlets he had collected, the other side of Fuller's genius, his extremely unconventional spirituality, his search for the hidden meaning of life and death, his life-long and absorbing interest. It was the alternative destination to which his rationality led him, alternative that is to mechanized warfare or the authoritarian state, and yet in so many ways linked to them, as best exemplified by the threefold order and the wartime article on 'Magic and War'. The whole collection was bought by the University of Texas; *The Soul of Osiris, Rosa Mundi, Korix Om Pax, Bagh-l-Mualtar, The Scented Garden of Abdullah the Satirist, Thumbs Up! A Pentagram—a Pantacle to Win the War, A Handbook of Geomancy*—these, the 'Bibliotheca Crowleyana', have been found, like his papers, an improbably inappropriate resting place.[156]

It was in this last summer, however, that Fuller's sight began to go. Cataract was diagnosed and arrangements were made for him to enter hospital. On September 30th they gave up the Nevill Park flat and on October 4th Fuller had an operation during which the lens of his right eye was removed. He was allowed to leave hospital on the 17th and he and Sonia then moved into a small furnished flat, still in Tunbridge Wells, in Regina Court, Molyneux Park Road. This they took for three months. On the 20th he wrote to Liddell Hart, who had gone to California as a visiting professor, and told him that he would have to wait a month for glasses to be fitted and meanwhile saw and wrote in a fog.[157] Two days later he wrote to Sloane, in a shaky hand, with the same message.[158] He was not only half-blind but also felt a sick man. When the spectacles arrived, those intended for reading were no good and had to be remade. In order to read he was forced to use the distant spectacles with a magnifying glass which made both reading and writing tedious. He also had bronchitis and then, on December 10th, he experienced a 'heart collapse' similar to the one two years before. He was taken to the Clarence Nursing Home in Tunbridge Wells and forced to remain there until the end of the year.[159]

Men and women who achieve great age often have to suffer attendant indignities in their later years; Fuller was obviously not immune. With failing sight, and short of breath, his books disposed of, his papers sorted out, and his only alternative to a hospital bed a small and undistinguished flat in a town for the elderly and infirm, he contemplated, in enforced and unusual idleness, the pageant of his life. Self-evaluation was a process he had carried out many times before, but now he must have wanted to draw the threads together, both for the notes he never wrote on his papers and because it seems he had a premonition that the end was near. There were to be no more books or articles and very few letters. It is therefore also time for his biographer to stand back and, before the final curtain descends, to ask, and attempt to answer, some questions about this man and his life and work, as the man himself asks questions of the same sort and gives answers at the nature of which one can only guess.

Fuller was so many things that it is difficult to evaluate his life and work. His most notable characteristic, his finest quality, was the excellence and energy of his brain, while his principal and life-long activity was writing. He wrote forty-five books and many hundreds of articles and papers; he was not only a prolific writer but in most of his works a lively, pungent, amusing and controversial one, whose style, though sometimes didactic in the extreme, could rise to heights of telling brevity, devastating invective, and side-splitting aphorism or anecdote. It is probable that very few of his non-historical books will be reprinted because they deal with problems which have been resolved, or technologies which have been overtaken. It is, however, as a man of intellect, who was also a superb craftsman of words, that he ought most to be remembered. Few other serious thinkers and writers have published so much, or written so stimulatingly, as Fuller did. But with these fundamental attributes accepted one must begin by dealing separately with the major directions of his thought and activity. As a career soldier he was only modestly successful. He was never given the opportunity, in peace or war, to hold high military office or to command large formations. He saw his share of action, but it was as a staff officer, both in France in 1917–18, and in the War Office subsequently, that he principally distinguished himself. As a trainer of officers he was fertile of ideas, immensely forward-looking and stimulating to the able and intelligent, but for the lazy, the less than intelligent, the disbelievers, he operated at a level they could not, or did not want to, reach. His military service by no means represented 'thirty unprofitable years'; in France in 1917–18, and during his fight for the Tank Corps after the war, he had great influence; throughout the remainder of his service career he acted as a catalyst, as a 'stirrer-up' of indolent and comfortable thinking, as a bleak and strident military conscience and as a herald of 'the budding technical civilization'. In this latter respect he compared himself, characteristically, 'with the Spanish-fly (*cantharides*) in former ages used as an aphrodisiac to overcome impotence'.[160] His ultimate and relative lack of success as a soldier was in part due to the cause of mechanization, which he espoused too strongly and too early from the point of view of his career interests; but it was also due to central factors of his personality, his extreme intellectual competence, his superlative rationality, his barbed and irrepressible wit, his somewhat clinical human relations, his rejection of compromise even when his future was at stake. When he was finally retired from the Army he realized at last that change from within would more easily have come through compromise and conversion than abuse and opposition.[161] Outside his long-standing friendships with those he respected, he was an uncomfortable and all too aggressively cerebral member of the military organization—regarded by many senior officers as 'too clever by half'.[162] In peacetime such men have problems. In 1930 it would not have been difficult to regard him as an arrogant, self-opinionated, disloyal, bad-tempered crank, with an impossible wife, no political sense and some pretty strange affiliations and activities. His over-reaction during the 'Tidworth Affair' in 1927 was unforgivable in the eyes of the military establishment and this was his greatest career crime.

He was much more than a career soldier, of course, and apart from the limitations it imposed on his influence on the British Army in the thirties, the fact that he did not rise above the rank of major-general is of little ultimate significance. As a military

theorist he must rank with the world's greatest. His attempt to
bring about technological, tactical and strategic innovation was
of the greatest military significance in and after the First World
War, and was a major factor in the development of 'blitzkrieg'
and its post-Second World War adaptations. His immediate
influence on the British Army in the late twenties and thirties was
not great, but the impact of his thinking and experience on
Liddell Hart and others was to bring about great changes in the
late thirties and in the Second World War itself. The differences
between his views on mechanized warfare and those of Liddell
Hart were not great. Fuller had the more rigorous rationality
while Liddell Hart was a great deal better with people and understood that politics was the art of the possible. Fuller dealt in
absolutes, Liddell Hart in relativities. That is why Fuller can be
accused of promoting the all-tank 'fallacy' whereas Liddell Hart
always recognized the need for other arms. But both could claim
to have been right; there are still separate arms in most major
armies but they nearly all travel, and generally fight, in vehicles
which look very like tanks. Fuller's influence on other armies,
particularly the German, was far greater in the thirties than his
influence on the British, and the ways in which he continued to
adapt his military theories to increasingly rapid technological and
political change from 1939 onwards was quite remarkable. His
vision of armoured tank fleets was never to be fully realized but
had it not been for recent nuclear and electronic developments it
well might have been. All his military visions were rational; like
Clausewitz's absolute war they represented the logical development of the essence of things and like absolute war they were
unlikely to come to pass in their perfect state because of what
Clausewitz called 'friction' or reality. But Fuller was realist
enough to see that in the end symmetry of military development
would lead to stalemate again and, of course, to deterrence. We
need the Fullers of this world, who are few in number, to show us
where things might go. It was unfortunate, nevertheless, that he
showed our enemies the same straight path.

The distinction between military theory and military
philosophy is a fine one. Military theory, as commonly understood, is more concerned with action, and with ways of acting,
than is philosophy, which asks questions, sets up models and
attempts to determine general principles and laws. The determin-

ation of general laws and principles takes philosophy towards a science of war, but also leads in another direction, that of principles of action to be used in the art of war; back in other words, to theory. Fuller must be regarded as a philosopher and scientist of war, as well as a theoretician. His preoccupation with principles of war spans the fields of theory, philosophy and science, and his principles have had great influence on armies and their trainers. The principles, however, as guides to action, were conflicting, and as explanations, less than complete. In his later years his views softened and the principles became little more than guides. His attempt to create a science of war was brave, but unsuccessful, and for a while diminished his reputation as a thinker. His numerical metaphysic, the threefold order, was unprovable and unhelpful, and owed a lot to his mystical interests, while his later and temporary advocacy of totalitarian tactics and total war was a regrettable aberration. His attempts to better Clausewitz on the relations of war and policy were not particularly enlightening, but his 'in-moding' of Clausewitz was very relevant to contemporary strategic thinking; his views on war aims and unconditional surrender were startlingly original at the time. He did not have the rigorous academic training required of a philosopher, particularly of one who derived his basic position from academic philosophy, but his rationality brought him to positions the rectitude and insight of which many philosophers would have admired in themselves. The problem was that sometimes this rationality, coupled with his mysticism, led him into very strange countries of the mind and into positions which were pragmatically absurd.

He was also a politician and must be judged as such. He came to politics through military and bureaucratic frustration, and in choosing his party he made one of the gravest errors of his life, although his previous views on democracy led him naturally to a political grouping not then so obviously tainted with racial murder and aggression as it later became. In spite of all his post-war denials he was a committed fascist in the thirties and as guilty as any of them in disseminating anti-Semitic and other racial propaganda, although always maintaining his patriotism. To the end of his life he distrusted mass democracy and believed that much of the violence and irrationality of the nineteenth and twentieth centuries were a consequence of its growth. It was his fascist sympathies which precluded any possibility of his military re-employment in the Second World War.

As a journalist he had a long career. For twenty years or more after his retirement he worked almost full time in this field, except when he was writing books. His journalism, unlike some of his other writing, was direct and popular stuff—popular, that is, in being directed at the ordinary reader. For one who despised the people's judgment he spent a great deal of his time writing for them. He was an excellent mass journalist, ready with a wealth of home-spun images, biting ironies and startling conclusions. Some of his wartime articles were journalistic classics. As a historian, and in a quite different way, he made a unique contribution. His system of writing military history, of drawing lessons from it for the future, either as prescriptions, or predictions, first exposed in *Foundations*, was used again and again with great effect. He was never an academic, impartial seeker after the truth, and he used his imagination extensively, but the total insight he achieved by this method more than compensated, in his later, less strident works, for his faults of scholarship. Some of his deductions, notably the law of military evolution and the constant tactical factor, are important contributions to historical understanding.

He denied, it must be remembered, being a prophet, and in the sense of being magically endowed with knowledge of the future we must accept his denial, although we must at the same time recognize that he was an outstanding scholar of the occult, highly regarded by others with claims to judgment and eminence in that area, as well as being, as some of his friends have claimed, a man of great spirituality and meditative ability. However he certainly gave voice to many prophecies which subsequently came true. He prophesied, among other things, Indian partition, the end of white global supremacy, the use of military rockets, the Chinese problem, the conflict which would arise between the use of infantry as gendarmerie and as mechanized soldiers, the weakness of air power in anti-guerilla warfare, the limitation of war through the development of weapons, the development of 'metaphysical' war as a consequence, and the spread of communism across Europe from the East. Others, no doubt, had similar visions, though perhaps no other man had so many. Fuller's prophecies were derived from a process of reasoning about the future on the basis of the past and the present. He was, above all else, a man of reason, whose rationality could sometimes lead him into positions which either appeared irrational, or which were irrational because they failed to take account of man's heart as well as his head. The heart also has its reasons.

It is permissible to wonder if, as he lay in that Tunbridge Wells nursing home, he ever questioned decisions he had taken in the past. Did he ever wish he had resisted the temptation to associate himself with Crowley? Did he ever doubt the wisdom of his attacks on Camberley orthodoxy, or of his Gold Medal Essay? Did he ever wonder if his lectures at the Staff College had been worthwhile, as he came in late years to see that *Foundations* had been something of a mistake?[163] Did he ever feel that it would have been more sensible to have made the test of the Tidworth job and to have gone to Bombay? Did he ever regret his long association with Mosley or his vociferous criticism of Churchill? Perhaps there were some few decisions he regretted. He was not, however, the sort of man to worry about his past. There was also about his life an inevitability, a chain of consequence in some ways reminiscent of the action–reaction phenomena of his own constant tactical factor. His early characteristics—his intellectuality, cleverness, intolerance, pro-Germanism, belief in authority and fascination for the occult—led through his experiences in Ireland, South Africa and India, to his preoccupation before 1914 with morale and training, with the principles of war, with magic and mysticism and with the tactics of penetration. Some of these things, via Southampton and Tunbridge Wells, led to the beginnings of his historical research and writing, and to his ability to develop the tactics and strategy of tanks. This, in turn, together with his growing awareness of the political dangers from communism, led to his exhaustive study of warfare and to his models of asymmetrical and symmetrical mechanized warfare, and to the ultimate elimination of warfare through the development of weapons. His personal characteristics were at least in part the explanation of the failure of his crusade for mechanized warfare and the failure of that crusade, and of his own military career, led him to fascism, which in turn prevented his employment in the Second World War. Denied military or political office, he turned to journalism and, increasingly at the end of his life, to history, to comment on and explanation of the past—but never entirely to the exclusion of predictions or recommendations for the future.

In no sense is this interpretation offered as justification for a belief in predestination! It is, however, remarkable how little Fuller deviated from a path that could have been mapped out for him by some extra-terrestrial being able to foresee what problems, conditions and phenomena would surround him at every point in his life. Even the maturity and wisdom of his later books are not after all surprising.

He was fond of drawing lessons from history. What lessons would he have drawn from his own life had he written his autobiography in the mid-sixties rather than the mid-thirties? We cannot know. Lessons which could be drawn, but perhaps would not have been by Fuller himself, certainly ought to include the facts that it is almost impossible to bring about violent change from within a conservative human institution, that Englishmen distrust obvious cleverness, that the conditions of struggle dictate, as Fuller knew full well on the physical battlefield, the tactics one ought to use, that if one allows the end to justify the means then one will only achieve that end if the means one selects are compatible with it, and this virtually involves saying that the end cannot justify the means. Today there is growing acceptance, for instance, of his position on strategic bombing, but not of his espousal of fascism. But perhaps the greatest lesson of all to be learnt is that men are governed by the situations in which they find themselves. Given, however, the right man and the right situation, great actions, mental or physical, may result. Hence Cambrai, Amiens, 'Plan 1919' and the Gold Medal Essay; hence also *Lectures on FSR III*, *The Second World War*, *Decisive Battles of the Western World*, *Alexander the Great*, *The Conduct of War* and *Caesar*. We have freedom, essentially, to play the balls we are bowled.

While still in the nursing home he received a letter from Sloane asking him if he would 'have any use for a slightly obsolete five-sided building requiring only an intercom for modernization'. Sloane offered to rent it to him cheaply.[164] This was an offer to which he never replied. At the beginning of January he went back to the flat in Regina Court but because he felt so feeble gave up the idea of wintering in Malta. Sonia and he then decided to go to Falmouth at the end of the month and spend the remainder of the winter there. Accordingly they booked a room in the Royal Duchy Hotel and Fuller wrote to Liddell Hart in

California to tell him about it. He also wrote to congratulate Liddell Hart on his knighthood and to tell him that he thought it thirty years overdue. 'You must be getting somewhat weary of teaching the Yanks the perils of war', he continued, mentally active to the last.

> What a mess they seem to have made in Vietnam. In one of your talks you might rub in Clausewitz's little-heeded maxim, that no war should be begun without first replying to the question 'What is to be gained by it' and that the first step should not be taken without considering what may be the last one. Your budding Lees and Grants will find them in my *Conduct of War*. It would appear that a similar folly has been committed over Rhodesia. Instead of declaring economic war ... it would have been more profitable ... had Wilson and Co. ... offered to buy out at a fair price all white Rhodesians who could or would not tolerate being ruled by negroes.[165]

This lively letter was the last he wrote to Liddell Hart. The friendship between these two, spanning nearly half a century, is in some ways the most remarkable and important aspect of each of their lives. Fuller was at first the senior partner and always perhaps intellectually superior, if intellect is regarded as sheer cerebral ability; Liddell Hart was much more the man of affairs, better with people, allowing practical and human considerations to mellow and inform his judgment.

On January 28th the Fullers left for Cornwall and the Royal Duchy Hotel. They intended to visit Lieutenant-General Sir Francis Tuker, who lived nearby, but Fuller developed pneumonia. British seaside hotels are not always the best of places in winter for octogenarian convalescents. He was taken to Tehidy Hospital and there, on February 10th, 1966 he died. Sonia was not with him in the hospital at the end and this caused her great pain.[166] The two of them had been very close throughout their long marriage and had lived inside a privacy which was and is difficult to pierce.

The obituaries were balanced and flattering on the whole. *The Times* considered that his greatest contribution was to armoured . warfare in the First World War but that his influence might have been greater had he been less testy and capricious. However, it had been *The Times* conceded, considerable, especially in Germany.[167] *The Tank*, the journal of the Royal Tank Regiment, successor to the RTC, gave him the final military accolade, and a British one at that. 'Boney Fuller,' the obituary reads, 'was an intellectual giant.' The reviewer went on to praise his practical and literary abilities and the debt owed to him by the men who manned the tanks in the First World War. But the debt of the RTR was even greater. 'We owe our existence very largely to his efforts, his conception of armoured warfare has been the basis of current practice, while his independence of thought, his distaste for convention sanctified by history and his eager grasp of new ideas have characterized successive generations of Tank soldiers.' After reference to his bitter, sardonic tongue the writer concluded that Boney had 'earned an undying name in the RTR who will always remember him and his work with gratitude'.[168]

There was a memorial service at the end of April in St Margaret's, Westminster. The Liddell Harts took Sonia but the turn-out on the whole was rather poor.

So passed a man with real claims to be regarded as a significant world figure. He was a man of very great vitality, intelligence, application and integrity. He made mistakes but was greater than many of those who did not, and who rose higher in their lifetime. He was, above all things, a thinking man and even his aberrations were intellectual. He carried the process of rationality too far to be a career success. He was not the equal of Clausewitz, whose insights were more original and comprehensive, as regards war and policy at least. Fuller's was a flawed genius, and one who could have been more systematically educated. He was as important, in different ways, as Liddell Hart, and can be regarded as the latter's original mentor and life-long associate, and this was a process of two-way traffic and benefit. His contribution to military theory and history will have a lasting relevance principally because he was above all else a brilliant and critical student of war, who was able to bring to that study the inside knowledge and understanding of a professional soldier, who was also a scholar. His influence abroad was very considerable, in Germany before the war, and in America after it; his influence at home has increased as the memory of his 'military bolshevism' grows less painful. He was a considerable figure of the twentieth century and a very intellectual general. Let us hope that the age of men of such breadth of interest and achievement is not past. It will be a poorer world if we have to rely upon narrow and highly trained specialists for our future development. Let us also hope that some few of such men will continue to find at least part of their life satisfaction in service of one sort or another to their countries or to some wider community. Boney was a warrior in many important battles of both mind and body—and he fought well and hard and long. That is probably epitaph enough for a soldier.

Sources

Unpublished

1. The main unpublished sources used in the preparation and writing of this biography were:

(a) *Fuller's correspondence with his parents and others.* Now held in the Fuller Collection in the Liddell Hart Centre for Military Archives at King's College, London. Referred to in the source notes as 'King's'.

(b) *Fuller's correspondence with Liddell Hart.* Retained during his lifetime by Sir Basil Liddell Hart and now part of the Liddell Hart Centre for Military Archives but held for the time being in States House, Medmenham, Buckinghamshire. Referred to in the source notes as 'States House'.

(c) *Liddell Hart's papers.* Referred to in the source notes as 'States House'.

(d) *Fuller's personal papers.* Now held in the Fuller Collection in the Liddell Hart Centre for Military Archives at King's College, London, or in the Fuller Papers in Rutgers University Library, New Brunswick, New Jersey, USA. The latter source is referred to in the source notes as 'Rutgers'.

(e) *Fuller's correspondence with Meredith Starr.* Now in the possession of Gordon Grey Esq., Clayton, Douro Road, Cheltenham. Referred to in the source notes as 'Starr'.

(f) *Fuller's correspondence with William Sloane of Rutgers University Press.* Now in Rutgers University Press. Referred to in the source notes as 'RUP'.

(g) *Fuller's correspondence with Professor Jay Luvaas of Allegheny College, Meadville, USA.* In Professor Luvaas's possession and referred to in the source notes as 'Luvaas'.

(h) *Files held in the Public Record Office.* Referred to in the source notes as 'PRO'.

(i) Records in the Staff College, Camberley.

Oral

2. Conversations and discussions with numerous people but principally, as regards information about Fuller himself, with Sir Basil and Lady Liddell Hart, Mrs Estelle Fuller, Mrs Alison Starr and Sir Oswald and Lady Mosley. These are referred to in the source notes as BLH, 12.12.69, Estelle Fuller, 24.8.71, Alison Starr, 15.11.75, Mosley, 18.3.75.

Published books

3. The principal published sources were Fuller's own published works which are listed on pages 301–3, together with numerous references to Fuller and his life and work in other contemporary and later published work. Full details are given in the source notes.

4. The only substantial studies so far published of Fuller's work are contained in Luvaas's *Education of an Army* and Higham's *The Military Intellectuals in Britain, 1918–1939*.

Published (journals, magazines and newspapers)

5. The *RUSI Journal*, the *Army Quarterly* and the *Cavalry Journal* were invaluable.

6. In addition Fuller published many articles in other journals and magazines and in many British, American and other newspapers. His books and activities were also widely reviewed from time to time in the press. Full details are given in the source notes.

Source Notes

NOTE: *The letters F and LH in the notes identify the writer of the letter under reference as either Fuller or Liddell Hart.*

Chapter One

1. *Memoirs*, p. 1; information provided by Mrs Estelle Fuller, widow of Fuller's brother Walter; King's, IV/3/2
2. King's, IV/3/2
3. *Memoirs*, p. 2
4. Ibid., pp. 2–3
5. King's, IV/1/1
6. Ibid., IV/1
7. *Memoirs*, p. 2
8. Ibid., p. 3
9. King's, IV/1/13
10. Ibid., IV/1/15
11. *Memoirs*, p. 3
12. Ibid., p. 3
13. Ibid., p. 4
14. Ibid., p. 4
15. King's, IV/2/1
16. Ibid., IV/2/2
17. Ibid., IV/3/2
18. Ibid., IV/3/2
19. Ibid., IV/3/3
20. Ibid., IV/3/4
21. *Generalship*, p. 73
22. *Memoirs*, pp. 5–6
23. Ibid., p.5

24. King's, IV/2/4–5
25. Ibid., IV/2/6
26. Ibid., IV/2/7
27. *Memoirs*, p. 26
28. Ibid., p. 7
29. King's, IV/3/10
30. Ibid., IV/4/1
31. Ibid., IV/3/18
32. Ibid., IV/3/8
33. *Memoirs*, pp. 7–8
34. King's, IV/3/19
35. Ibid., IV/3/21; *Memoirs*, p. 8
36. King's, IV/3/21
37. *Memoirs*, p. 8
38. The remainder of the narrative of Fuller's part in the South African War is mainly based on pp. 8–16 of his *Memoirs* and on his *The Last of the Gentlemen's Wars*. These sources are not henceforward acknowledged in detail unless direct quotation is made
39. *Memoirs*, p. 8
40. King's, IV/3/24
41. *The Last of the Gentlemen's Wars*, p. 29
42. King's, IV/3/26
43. Ibid., IV/3/27
44. Ibid., IV/3/28
45. Ibid., IV/3/36
46. Ibid., IV/3/47. At this time known, for British officers joining local regiments, as the Indian Staff Corps and so referred to by Fuller
47. *The Last of the Gentlemen's Wars*, p. 94
48. King's, IV/3/59
49. Ibid., IV/3/60
50. Ibid., IV/3/64
51. Ibid., IV/3/70
52. Ibid., IV/3/81
53. Ibid., IV/3/78
54. *The Last of the Gentlemen's Wars*, p. 150
55. Ibid., p. 149
56. Ibid., p. 180
57. Ibid., p. 252
58. Ibid., p. 252
59. King's, IV/3/93
60. Ibid., IV/3/105
61. *The Last of the Gentlemen's Wars*, p. 263
62. Ibid., p. 265
63. Rutgers, draft of letter from F. to Adjutant 1 OXLI dated 19.7.02
64. King's, IV/3/110
65. *The Last of the Gentlemen's Wars*, p. 244
66. Ibid., pp. 171–2
67. *Memoirs*, p. 16
68. Ibid., pp. 17–18
69. King's, IV/12/1–2

70. Ibid., IV/3/137–8
71. *India in Revolt*, pp.91–3
72. King's, IV/3/139b
73. Ibid., IV/12/4; Rutgers, medical report dated 17.2.06
74. King's, IV/12/6
75. Estelle Fuller believed that he met her before he went to India but Fuller gives the date as 1906 in *Memoirs*, p. 18. Estelle Fuller, 24.8.71, and letter to the author dated 6.5.76
76. King's, IV/11/27; Sir Basil Liddell Hart believed that Sonia's father had been the Kaiser's doctor but I have been unable to find other evidence of this. BLH, 12.12.69
77. Estelle Fuller, 24.8.71
78. Estelle Fuller believed that he had to leave his regiment because of his marriage. None of the family would see them until 1914. Estelle Fuller, 24.8.71, and letter to the author dated 6.5.76

Chapter Two

1. King's, IV/12/8–9
2. Ibid., IV/3/18
3. Ibid., IV/3/24
4. Alison Starr, 15.11.75
5. *Memoirs*, p. 459
6. Ibid., p. 460
7. King's, IV/3/139c
8. *Memoirs*, p. 20
9. 'Hints on Training Territorial Infantry'
10. King's, IV/2/7
11. Ibid., IV/12/35; States House LH, 21.12.27
12. King's, IV/12
13. *Memoirs*, p. 21
14. King's, IV/3/140b
15. States House
16. States House, 'Training Soldiers for War', p. viii
17. *The Conduct of War*, p. 124
18. *The Army Review*, July 1913
19. Ibid., July 1914
20. States House
21. *RUSI Journal*, vol. LVII, pp. 1187–1214. The RUSI is now called the Royal United Services Institute for Defence Studies
22. Henderson, G. F. R., *The Science of War*, pp. 347, 361 and 413, Longmans (London, 1906)
23. *The Army Review*, January 1914
24. *RUSI Journal*, vol. LVIII, pp. 63–84
25. Ibid., p.63 note
26. Ibid., p. 64
27. Ibid., p. 81
28. Ibid., p. 84
29. Henderson, op. cit., pp. 372–6 and 411
30. Ibid., pp. 372 and 376

31. *RUSI Journal*, vol. LIX, pp. 378–89
32. Henderson, op. cit., p. 74
33. *Field Service Regulations*, Part 1, Operations, p. 112, HMSO (1909)
34. Bloch, I. S., *The War of the Future in its Technical, Economic and Political Relations*, Grant Richards (London, 1897)
35. Henderson, op. cit., p. 419
36. *Memoirs*, p. 27
37. Ibid., p. 25
38. *Foundations*, p. 13
39. *Field Service Regulations*, op. cit., p. 11
40. King's, IV/3/141
41. *RUSI Journal*, vol. LXI, pp.779–90
42. *Memoirs*, p. 50
43. King's, IV/3/152
44. Ibid., IV/3/153
45. Ibid., IV/3/155
46. *RUSI Journal*, vol. LXI, pp. 1–40
47. King's, IV/3/148–50
48. Ibid., IV/3/176
49. Ibid., IV/3/190
50. *Memoirs*, pp. 62–9
51. King's, IV/3/196
52. *Memoirs*, p. 79
53. Foot, S., *Three Lives*, p. 159, Heinemann (London, 1934)
54. *Memoirs*, pp. 78–9

Chapter Three

1. For the British tank see Swinton, E. D., *Eyewitness*, pp. 32 and 81, Hodder and Stoughton (London, 1932); for the French tank see Ogorkiewicz, R. M., *Armoured Forces*, pp. 169–70, Arms and Armour Press (London, 1970)
2. Swinton, op. cit., p. 79
3. Ibid., pp. 31–2
4. See Ogorkiewicz, op. cit., p. 141
5. *Tanks in the Great War*, pp. 19–20
6. Swinton, op. cit., p. 129
7. Ibid., pp. 129–31
8. Ibid., p. 131
9. Ibid., pp. 131–4
10. Stern, Sir A. G., *Tanks 1914–18: The Log-Book of a Pioneer*, pp. 58 and 87–8, Hodder and Stoughton (London, 1919)
11. Swinton, op. cit., pp. 144–6
12. Ibid., pp. 183–4
13. Ibid., pp. 197–8 and *Memoirs*, pp. 169
14. Swinton, op. cit., p. 203
15. Ibid., p. 209
16. Ibid., p. 210
17. Ibid., p. 211
18. *Tanks in the Great War*, p. 52
19. Foot, *Three Lives*, p. 170

20. Swinton, op. cit., p. 243
21. Martel, G. Le Q., *Our Armoured Forces*, p. 38, Faber & Faber (London, 1945)
22. Ibid., pp. 396–402
23. Ibid., p. 38
24. See Ogorkiewicz, op. cit., p. 57
25. *Tanks in the Great War*, p. 55
26. Ibid., p. 57
27. Ibid., p. 59
28. Liddell Hart, B. H., *The Tanks*, vol. 1, p. 122, Cassell (London, 1959)
29. Ibid., pp. 120–1
30. *Tanks in the Great War*, Preface, P. XIX
31. King's, IV/3/214
32. *Memoirs*, p. 96
33. *Tanks in the Great War*, p. 73
34. *Memoirs*, p. 97
35. Stern, op. cit., p. 131
36. Martel, *Our Armoured Forces*, p. 38
37. *Memoirs*, p. 107
38. Ibid., pp. 122–30
39. Ibid., p. 130
40. *Memoirs*, p. 200
41. Ibid., p. 207
42. Ibid., p. 237
43. Ibid., p. 241
44. Ibid., p. 262
45. Stern, op. cit., p. 215
46. States House, F, 22.9.22; *The Conduct of War*, pp. 242–3; *Memoirs*, pp. 321–2
47. States House, F, 22.9.22
48. Ibid., F, 19.1.64
49. Ibid., F, 19.5.63
50. Ibid., F, 19.2.64
51. Orgill, D., *The Tank*, p. 90, Heinemann (London, 1970)
52. PRO WO 106/314; *Memoirs*, p. 320
53. *Memoirs*, pp. 320–1
54. Ibid., p. 340
55. Foot, op. cit., pp. 215–18
56. Ibid., pp. 345–9
57. Martel, *Our Armoured Forces*, p. 401
58. *Memoirs*, p. 336
59. All quotations from 'Plan 1919' are taken from *Memoirs*, ch. XIII
60. *Memoirs*, p. 331
61. King's, IV/3/232
62. *Memoirs*, p. 338; Rutgers, letter from Harington to Foch, 20.7.18
63. Ibid., p. 340; PRO WO 106/315; Rutgers, letter from Foch to Wilson, 6.8.18
64. *Memoirs*, p. 317
65. Foot, op. cit., pp. 219–20
66. Stern, op. cit., p. 247
67. *Memoirs*, p. 321
68. BLH, 12.12.69

69. Crow, D. (Ed.), *AFVs of World War 1*, p. 90, Profile Publications (London, 1970)
70. PRO WO 32/5933
71. Martel, G. Le Q., *In the Wake of the Tank*, p. 71, Sifton Praed (London, 1935)
72. States House, LH to Col. R. J. Icks, 26.8.49
73. *Official History of the Great War: Military Operations in France and Belgium 1918*, vol. IV, HMSO (London, 1947)
74. Liddell Hart, op. cit., p. 185

Chapter Four

1. Estelle Fuller, 24.8.71
2. *Memoirs*, p. 343
3. *The Naval Review*, vol. X, no. 1, pp. 129–30, February 1920
4. *Memoirs*, p. 355
5. Foot, *Three Lives*, pp. 228–9
6. *Memoirs*, p. 391
7. Rutgers
8. Liddell Hart, *The Tanks*, vol. I, pp. 225–6
9. Wheldon, J., *Machine Age Armies*, p. 39, Abelard-Schuman (London, 1968); Rutgers; *Memoirs*, pp. 406–7
10. *Army Quarterly*, vol. 3, p. 301
11. *RUSI Journal*, vol. LXI, p. 291
12. *Reformation*, p. 187
13. *Weekly Tank Notes*, nos. 1–42 in PRO WO 106/377
14. *RUSI Journal*, vol. LXV, pp. 281–98
15. Ibid., p. 281
16. Ibid., p. 281
17. Ibid., pp. 291–3
18. Ibid., p. 294
19. Ibid., p. 296
20. *Daily Mail*, 18.2.20
21. *Observer*, 24.4.20
22. *Daily News*, 12.3.20
23. *Daily Herald*, 24.2.20
24. *RUSI Journal*, vol. LXV, p. 441
25. *Tanks in the Great War*, p. 319
26. Ibid., p. 319
27. *RUSI Journal*, vol. LXV, pp. XVII–XIX; the other judge was Lt.-Gen. Sir Herbert Miles
28. Ibid., pp. 239–74
29. *Memoirs*, p. 392
30. *RUSI Journal*, vol. LXV, p. 250
31. Ibid., p. 254
32. Rutgers, Box 1
33. *Memoirs*, p. 393
34. Rutgers, Box 1
35. *Cavalry Journal*, vol. X, pp. 109–32, 307–22, 510–30, 1920
36. Ibid., p. 109

37. Ibid., p. 110
38. Ibid., p. 528
39. Ibid., p. 529
40. Ibid., pp. 323–30
41. Ibid., pp. 331–3
42. Ibid., pp. 531–41
43. Ibid., pp. 557–8
44. *The Naval Review*, vol. X, no. 1, pp. 73–104, February 1922
45. Liddell Hart, B. H., *Memoirs*, vol. 1, p. 46, Cassell (London, 1965)
46. BLH, 12.12.69
47. Liddell Hart, *Memoirs*, vol. 1, p. 46; States House, F, 7.6.20 and 10.6.20
48. States House, LH, 11.3.28
49. Ibid., F, 26.4.48
50. Ibid., LH, 5.5.48
51. Ibid., LH, 16.1.22
52. Ibid., F, 19.1.22
53. Ibid., F, 8.2.22
54. Liddell Hart, *Memoirs*, vol. 1, p. 63
55. States House, F, 11.12.22
56. Ibid., F, 15.9.22
57. Ibid., F, 27.3.23
58. Ibid., F, 27.3.23; Starr, 18.9.22, 20.9.22, 18.11.22
59. Ibid., F, 25.8.22
60. *Reformation*, p. ix
61. Ibid., p. xi
62. Ibid., p. xiv
63. Ibid., p. ix
64. Ibid., p. 9
65. Ibid., p. 16
66. Ibid., p. 29
67. Ibid., p. 136
68. Ibid., p. 176
69. Ibid., p. 283
70. *Foundations*, p. 14

Chapter Five

1. Betjeman, J., *Collected Poems*, p. 10, Murray (London, 1958)
2. Ibid., p. 98
3. *Memoirs*, p. 416
4. See Williams, P., 'The Decline of Academic Strategy', *RUSI Journal*, December 1972, p. 35
5. This was generally true, as regards deterrence between states, until the 1950s
6. Wheldon, *Machine Age Armies*, p. 42
7. Starr, 14.10.23
8. *RUSI Journal*, vol. LXV, p. 74
9. Ibid., p. 164
10. Custance, Admiral Sir Reginald, *A Study of War*, Constable (London, 1924)
11. *Decisive Battles*, vol. 2, p. 890

12. Hamilton, Sir Ian, *The Soul and Body of An Army*, p. 184, Arnold (1921)
13. Ibid., p. 185
14. Ibid., p. 279
15. Ibid., pp. 279–81
16. Ibid., p. 20
17. Ibid., p. 185
18. *RUSI Journal*, vol. LXV, pp. 155–63
19. *RUSI Journal*, vol. LXV, p. 466
20. *RUSI Journal*, vol. LXVIII, pp. 556–8; *Army Quarterly*, vol. 6, pp. 173–6; *Sunday Times*, 25.2.23; *Sunday Times*, 4.3.23; *The Outlook*, 24.3.23; *John O'London's Weekly*, 17.2.23; *Observer*, 4.3.23; *Tank Corps Journal*, April 1923; *Spectator*, 28.4.23; *New Statesman*, 19.5.23; *New York Times Book Review and Magazine*, 5.8.23
21. *Memoirs*, p. 417
22. Junior Division Files, 1923, The Army Staff College when all information about Fuller's lectures at the Staff College also comes
23. Conversation with Maj.-Gen. G. S. Hatton, 7.5.71
24. Estelle Fuller, 1.9.76
25. Reproduced in *On Future Warfare*
26. *Sir John Moore's System of Training*, pp. 222–3
27. *British Light Infantry in the Eighteenth Century*, pp. 242–3
28. *Memoirs*, p. 420; Rutgers, Box 1
29. Rutgers, Scrapbook 1
30. Rutgers, Box 1
31. *RUSI Journal*, vol. LXX, p. 73
32. Ibid., p. 73
33. States House, F, 13.11.24
34. *The Occult Review*, April 1923
35. *Yoga*, p. vii
36. Starr, 8.8.25
37. *Army Quarterly*, vol. 1, pp. 90–111, October 1920
38. Ibid., p. 91
39. Clausewitz, *On War*, vol. 1, p. 10, Trubner (London, 1873)
40. States House, F, 13.6.43
41. *Army Quarterly*, vol. 1, p. 111
42. See *Memoirs*, pp. 388–9; *Foundations*, p. 14; States House, F, 11.4.49; Rutgers, Box 1
43. *Foundations*, p. 18
44. States House, F, 27.3.23
45. Ibid., F, 7.12.25
46. *Foundations*, p. 227
47. Ibid., p. 195
48. Liddell Hart, *Memoirs*, vol. 1, p. 102
49. *Foundations*, p. 48
50. States House, F, 22.5.24
51. *Foundations*, p. 51
52. Luvaas, J., *The Education of An Army: British military thought, 1815–1940*, p. 349, Cassell (London, 1965)
53. *Foundations*, p. 51
54. Ibid., p. 68

55. Ibid., p. 77
56. Clausewitz, op. cit., vol. 2, p. 78
57. Spelt 'moral' by Fuller
58. *Foundations*, p. 174
59. Ibid., p. 204
60. Ibid., p. 324
61. Ibid., p. 335
62. Clauzewitz, op. cit., vol. 1, p. 62
63. *Foundations*, p. 201
64. States House, passim, 1923–5
65. Liddell Hart, *Memoirs*, vol 1, p. 99
66. *Memoirs*, p. 421
67. Ibid., p. 421
68. States House, F, 28.9.25
69. *Memoirs*, p. 422
70. Rutgers, Box 1
71. *Owl Pie*, Christmas 1925

Chapter Six

1. The chief general sources for this chapter are the *Memoirs* of Fuller and Liddell Hart, and Rutgers
2. *Memoirs*, p. 434
3. States House, F, 7.12.25
4. *Army Quarterly*, vol. 12, pp. 354–6; *Observer*, 28.2.26; *The Times*, 18.3.26; *Saturday Review*, 29.9.26; *Manchester Guardian*, 7.4.26
5. *Army Quarterly*, vol. 12, pp. 300–14
6. Ibid., pp. 165–9; Fuller's note on his copy now in Rutgers
7. States House, F, 7.4.26
8. Ibid., LH, 7.4.26
9. Ibid., Headlam, 12.2.26
10. *Army Quarterly*, vol. 12, pp. 354–61
11. Ibid., pp. 232–3
12. States House, F, 9.7.26
13. *Memoirs*, p. 429; PRO WO 32/2820–2821
14. PRO WO 32/2820
15. Ibid.
16. Ibid.
17. Ibid.
18. Ibid., WO 32/2822
19. Liddell Hart, *The Tanks*, vol. I, p. 244
20. States House, F, 3.9.26
21. *Memoirs*, p. 430
22. Ibid., p. 430
23. PRO WO 32/3533
24. *Memoirs*, p. 431
25. Ibid.
26. *India in Revolt*, pp. 196–203
27. *Memoirs*, p. 433
28. *On Future Warfare*, pp. 262–82

29. *On Future Warfare*, pp. 38–82
30. Ibid., pp. 350–90
31. States House, F, Nov. 26
32. PRO WO 32/2820
33. See Liddell Hart, *Memoirs*, vol. I, p. 109 amd *The Tanks*, vol. I, p. 242
34. The basis of the story is contained in Fuller's, *Memoirs*, p. 431–41; Liddell Hart's, *Memoirs*, vol. I, pp. 112–18; Liddell Hart's, *The Tanks*, vol. I, pp. 244–6; and Rutgers, Boxes 1 and 2
35. States House, F, 7.1.27
36. Rutgers, Box 2, Paget, 6.2.27
37. *Memoirs*, p. 436
38. Rutgers, Box 2, Fuller's paper
39. *Memoirs*, p. 437
40. Rutgers, Box 2, Burnett Stuart, 18.2.27
41. *Memoirs*, p. 438
42. Ibid., p. 439
43. Liddell Hart, *Memoirs*, vol. I, p. 114
44. *Memoirs*, p. 439; Rutgers, Box 2, Campbell, 7.3.27
45. Rutgers, Box 2, Burnett Stuart, 8.3.27
46. *Memoirs*, p. 439
47. Rutgers, Box 2, Campbell, 18.3.27
48. Estelle Fuller, 24.8.71
49. Liddell Hart, *Memoirs*, vol. I, p. 115
50. Rutgers, Box 2, Fuller's draft letter to MS.
51. *Memoirs*, p. 440
52. Liddell Hart, *Memoirs*, vol. I, p. 117; States House, F, 28.4.27
53. PRO WO 32/2828
54. Starr, 23.5.27

Chapter Seven

1. States House, F, 1.2.49
2. Germains, V. W., *The 'Mechanization' of War*, Sifton Praed (London, 1927)
3. Ibid., p. x
4. Ibid., p. xi
5. Ibid., p. xii
6. Ibid., pp. xii–xiii
7. Ibid., pp. 6–7
8. Ibid., pp. 10–11
9. *Foundations*, p. 29
10. Germains, op. cit., p. 55
11. Ibid., pp. 103–4
12. Ibid., p.177
13. Ibid., p. 185–6
14. Charrington Lt.-Col. H. V. S., *Where Cavalry Stands Today*, Hugh Rees (London, 1927)
15. Ibid., p. 48
16. *Memoirs*, pp. 443–4
17. Starr, 30.10.28

18. 'The Changing Conditions of War', *The Nineteenth Century and After*, CI, pp. 685–93
19. 'The Reign of the Bullet', *The Fighting Forces*, October 1927
20. 'The Problems of Air Warfare', *The Journal of the Royal Artillery*, October 1927
21. *On Future Warfare*, pp. 334–49
22. *The Nineteenth Century and After*, CIII, pp. 88–96
23. Ibid., CIV, pp. 650–8
24. *La Guerra Futura* (Toledo, 1929)
25. States House, F, 12.3.28 (to J. L. Garvin)
26. Ibid., F, 21.12.27
27. Ibid., F, 12.3.28 (to J. L. Garvin)
28. Ibid., LH, 11.3.28
29. Ibid., Mrs Fuller, 13.3.28
30. Ibid., F, 14.3.28
31. Ibid., F, 3.4.28
32. Rutgers, Box 2, notes by Fuller 1928–9
33. Ibid., Ironside, 1928–9
34. Ibid., Churchill, 27.3.28 and invitation for 21.6.28
35. Ibid., Milne, 6.7.28 and India Office, 11.7.28
36. *Army Quarterly*, vols. 19 and 22; States House, F, 13.12.28
37. *Mechanized and Armoured Formations*, War Office (London, 1929)
38. States House, F, 7.9.29
39. States House, F, 12.7.29
40. *Grant*, p. ix
41. States House, F, 4.11.29
42. Ibid., F, 25.11.29
43. *Daily Telegraph*, 24.12.29
44. Starr, 31.1.30
45. *The Army, Navy and Air Force Gazette*, 24.10.29
46. Ibid., 3.4.30
47. States House, F, 6.11.29
48. Rutgers, Box 2, War Office letter, 2.10.30; States House, F, 14.12.30
49. Ibid., MS letter, 5.2.31
50. Ibid., F, 9.1.33
51. Ibid., Ironside, 16.12.30
52. *Memoirs*, p. 448
53. Rutgers, Box 2, F, 11.2.31
54. Ibid., Army Council letter, 28.2.31
55. Ibid., draft, 28.2.31
56. Ibid., Ironside, 22.5.31
57. Estelle Fuller, 24.8.71, confirmed by a letter to the author dated 6.5.76
58. *Operaciones entre Fuerzas Mecanizados* (Toledo, 1933)
59. *Operace Mechanisovanych Vojsk* (Prague, 1935)
60. States House, LH, 5.10.49
61. *Army Quarterly*, vol. XLIV, no. 2, p. 216
62. *Lectures on FSR II*, p. 14
63. Ibid., p. 16
64. States House, F, 26.4.48
65. *Lectures on FSR II*, pp. 59, 76, 77–8

66. Ibid., p. 123
67. Ibid., p. 126
68. *Lectures on FSR III*, p. 12
69. *Lectures on FSR II*, pp. 77–8
70. *Lectures on FSR III*, p. 3
71. Ibid., p. 5
72. Ibid., p. 6
73. Ibid., pp. 6–7
74. Ibid., p. 9
75. Ibid., p. 11
76. Ibid., p. 14
77. Ibid., pp. 15–16
78. Ibid., p. 16
79. Ibid., p. 17
80. Ibid., p. 20–2
81. Ibid., p. 23
82. Ibid., p. 39
83. Ibid., p. 89
84. Ibid., pp. 106–7
85. Ibid., p. 113
86. Ibid., p. 115.
87. Ibid., p. 152
88. *Memoirs*, pp. 466–8
89. *India in Revolt*, p. 217
90. Ibid., p. 10
91. Ibid., p. 95
92. Ibid., p. 190
93. Ibid., p. 257
94. Ibid., p. 115
95. Ibid., p. 268
96. Ibid., p. 240
97. Ibid., p. 174
98. States House, F, 13.12.31
99. *The Dragon's Teeth*, p. VI
100. Ibid., p. 7
101. Ibid., p. 83
102. Ibid., p. 117
103. Ibid., p. 119
104. Ibid., p. 11
105. Ibid., p. 42
106. Ibid., p. 48
107. Ibid., p. 115
108. Ibid., p. 205
109. Ibid., pp.212–16
110. Ibid., pp.222–3
111. Ibid., p. 229
112. *War and Western Civilization*, p. 8
113. Ibid., p. 26
114. Ibid., p. 48
115. Ibid., p. 159

116. Ibid., pp. 254–5
117. Ibid., p. 267
118. Ibid., p. 268
119. States House, F, 15.7.31 and 18.8.31
120. Liddell Hart, *Memoirs*, vol. 1, pp. 196–8
121. *Memoirs*, p. 455; States House, LH, 5.10.49
122. Rutgers, Box 2, letters dated 30.7.29 and 8.8.29
123. Ibid., War Office, 9.12.32
124. Ibid., F, 15.12.32
125. Ibid., War Office, 13.1.33
126. Ibid., F, 9.1.33
127. *Army Quarterly*, vol. 25, pp. 227–36
128. Ibid., vol. 26, pp. 316–25
129. *Everyman*, 28.4.32
130. Ibid., 19.5.32
131. Ibid., 9.6.32
132. *Daily Mail*, 4.12.33; *Daily Mirror*, 12.12.33
133. Rutgers, Box 2, F, 15.6.33
134. States House, de Watteville, 26.4.33
135. Ibid., LH, 1.5.33
136. Liddell Hart, *Memoirs*, vol. 1, p. 231
137. Detailed evidence is to be found in notes and letters in States House particularly of talks with Ironside (11.5.36) and Montgomery-Massingberd (20.4.27, 27.4.26, 25.8.26, 23.7.26, 11.1.27)
138. Liddell Hart, *Memoirs*, vol. 1, p. 172

Chapter Eight

1. Fuller's own copy of his *Memoirs*, now in King's College, London, Library, contains a note in his own handwriting of a projected work: 'The Memoirs of an Unconventional Journalist'
2. Starr, 1934
3. *Sunday Dispatch*, 15.3.34
4. *Daily Mirror*, 19.3.34
5. *Manchester Evening Chronicle*, 18.4.34
6. *Evening Standard*, 27.6.34
7. *Daily Mail*, 9.8.34
8. *Evening Standard*, 23.8.34
9. Ibid., 8.8.34
10. Ibid., 21.9.34
11. See Skidelsky, R., *Oswald Mosley*, pp. 365–78, Holt, Rinehart and Winston (New York, 1975)
12. Mosley, 18.3.75
13. Starr, 27.9.31; 15.6.33; 3.8.33; 27.2.34
14. Mosley, 18.3.75
15. Rutgers, Box 2, Mosley, 20.8.34
16. Mosley, 18.3.75
17. Luvaas, F, 28.7.63
18. *The Second World War*, pp. 413–15; Rutgers, Box 2, Mitzakis, 15.8.33; PRO WO 32/10389

19. King's, 1934. Paper by Fuller
20. *Empire Unity and Defence*, pp. 7–9
21. Ibid., p. 20
22. Ibid., p. 186
23. Ibid., pp. 187–282
24. Ibid., p. 62
25. Ibid., p. 88
26. Ibid., pp. 89–90
27. Ibid., pp. 289–94
28. Ibid., p. 210
29. Ibid., p. 289
30. Ibid., p. 62
31. Ibid., pp. 286–7
32. *Blackshirt*, 9.11.34
33. Rutgers, Box 3, F, 18.4.62 and Box 4, African Diary
34. *Fascist Quarterly*, vol. 1, no. 1
35. *Weltpost*, 8.8.35
36. King's, IV/4/28
37. States House, F, 9.1.35
38. See Luvaas, J., *The Education of An Army*, p. 365, Cassell (London, 1965)
39. States House, F, 28.2.35.
40. Ibid., Swinton, 16.3.35.
41. *National Review*, May 1935.
42. *The Army in My Time*, pp. 6–7
43. Ibid., p. 19
44. Ibid., pp. 172–3
45. Ibid., p. 173
46. Ibid., p. 190
47. Ibid., pp. 195–209.
48. *Daily Mirror*, 20.3.35
49. *Fascist Quarterly*, vol. 1, no. 2
50. Rutgers, Elles, 17.4.35; 28.4.35; 30.4.35
51. Rutgers, F, 18.4.62; *Daily Mail*, 5, 6, 7.9.35
52. Luvaas, F, 1.9.63
53. Mosley, O., *My Life*, pp. 369–70, Nelson (London, 1968)
54. *Blackshirt*, 23.8.35
55. The details of the Abyssinian expedition are taken from Rutgers, Box 4, African Diary and *The First of the League Wars*.
56. *Natal Advertiser*, 9.1.36
57. *Daily Mail*, 4.12.35
58. Liddell Hart, *Memoirs*, vol. 1, pp. 301–6
59. *Army Quarterly*, vol. 31, pp. 237–46
60. Starr, 14.8.34
61. *Memoirs*, p. 477
62. Rutgers, Box 2, Churchill, 7.4.36
63. *Fascist Quarterly*, vol. II, no. 3, pp. 436–40
64. Liddell Hart, *Memoirs*, vol. 1, p. 231
65. *Sunday Dispatch*, 10.5.36
66. Letter from General Freiherr Geyr von Schweppenburg dated 30.3.70 to the author

67. *Fascist Quarterly*, vol. II, no. 4
68. *Army Ordnance*, vol. XVII, no. 99
69. *Generalship, its Diseases and Their Cure* (Harrisburg, Pa., 1936)
70. *The First of the League Wars*, p. 165
71. Ibid., p. 105
72. Ibid., p. 167
73. Ibid., pp. 229–37
74. Ibid., p. 63
75. Ibid., p. 120
76. Ibid., pp. 132 and 138
77. Ibid., p. 183
78. *Army Quarterly*, vol. 33, pp. 202–3, 371–3
79. Ibid., pp. 222–33
80. Rutgers, Box 2, Deverell, 26.1.37
81. Ibid
82. Ibid., Deverell, 27.2.37
83. PRO WO 106/1578
84. *The Times*, 5.3.37
85. *Towards Armageddon*, p. 55
86. Ibid., p. 51
87. Ibid., p. 141
88. Ibid., p. 105
89. Ibid., p. 97
90. Ibid., p. 100
91. Ibid., p. 33
92. Ibid., chs. VI and VII
93. Ibid., p. 127
94. Ibid., pp. 129–31
95. Ibid., p. 132
96. Ibid., p. 149
97. Ibid., p. 187
98. Ibid., ch. X
99. Ibid., pp. 170–1
100. *The Times*, 4.5.37
101. *The Times Literary Supplement*, 15.5.37
102. *Towards Armageddon*, pp. 220–4
103. States House, LH, 26.8.49
104. *Towards Armageddon*, p. 17
105. See Liddell Hart, *The British Way in Warfare*, 1932
106. States House, F, 5.5.37 and LH, 6.5.37
107. Estelle Fuller, 24.8.71
108. Rutgers, Box 2, F to Mosley, March 1938
109. PRO WO 106/1579
110. Liddell Hart, *Memoirs*, vol. II, p. 68
111. *Sunday Dispatch*, 24.10.37; *Action*, 6.11.37
112. *Army Ordnance*, Nov/Dec. 1937
113. *The First of the League Wars*, pp. 130–2
114. *The Second World War*, p. 413; King's, 11/4; Rutgers, Box 2, F to Lt.-Gen. Forbes-Adam, June 1939; PRO WO 32/10389
115. *Action*, 29.1.38

116. Rutgers, Box 2, F to Mosley, March 1938
117. Rutgers, Box 2, Mosley, 10.3.38
118. *News Review*, 17.6.38
119. PRO WO 106/1585
120. *Machine Warfare*, p. 62
121. *Pioneer*, 12.5.38
122. Rutgers, Gort, 28.7.38
123. *Daily Mail*, 11.10.38
124. *Army Quarterly*, vol. 37, pp. 312–21
125. *Völkisher Beobachter*, 9.2.39
126. *Erinnerungen Eines Freimütigen Soldaten* (Stuttgart, 1939), and *Der Erste der Völkerbundskriege* (Stuttgart, 1939)
127. Letter to the author from General von Schweppenburg, 30.6.70; 'Kampftruppen', Jan/Feb 70
128. Rutgers, Ribbentrop, 5.4.39
129. *Machine Warfare*, p. 13
130. Ibid., p. 13
131. *News Review*, 27.4.39
132. *News Chronicle*, 25.4.39
133. *Machine Warfare*, p. 14
134. *The Times*, 27.4.39
135. *Westfälische Landeszeitung*, 30.4.39
136. King's, IV/4/34
137. *The New Pioneer*, May 1939
138. Rutgers, Box 3, F to Sloane, 18.4.62
139. Rutgers, Box 2
140. *Decisive Battles*, vol. 1, p. IX
141. Ibid., pp. X–XI
142. Ibid., p. 35
143. Ibid., pp.81–2
144. Ibid., p. 356
145. States House, F, 3.11.61
146. Werner, M., *The Military Strength of the Powers*, pp. 27–8, Gollancz (London, 1939)
147. King's, IV/7/5
148. Miksche, F. O., *Blitzkrieg*, Faber (London, 1941)
149. States House, F, 3.11.61
150. *The Conduct of War*, pp. 246–7
151. For an account of Russian armoured developments see Milsom, J., *Russian Tanks 1900–1970*, Arms and Armour (London, 1970)
152. King's, IV/7/8a
153. States House, LH, 24.9.46
154. Eimannsberger, L. R. von., *Der Kampfwagenkrieg*, p. 82, Lehmanns (Munich/Berlin, 1938)
155. *Army Quarterly*, vol. XLIV, no. 2, p. 216
156. Guderian, H., *Panzer Leader*, p. 20, Michael Joseph (London, 1970)
157. King's, IV/7/5
158. Luvaas, 28.7.63 and 1.9.63
159. Werner, op. cit., p. 149

Chapter Nine

1. *Machine Warfare*, p. 17
2. King's, IV/4/34
3. King's, IV/4/34; Liddell Hart, *Memoirs*, vol. 1, p. 231
4. Rutgers, Box 2, F, 16.10.39
5. Ibid., Ironside, 27.10.39
6. King's, IV/4/34–5
7. *Truth*, 24.11.39
8. *The Weekly Review*, 4.1.40
9. *Army Ordnance*, vol. XX, no. 119, Mar–Apr. 1940
10. *Decisive Battles*, Vol. 2, pp. 658–9
11. Ibid., p. 661
12. Ibid., p. 888
13. Ibid., p. 927
14. Ibid., p. 1005
15. Mosley, 18.3.75
16. BLH, 12.12.69
17. King's, IV/4/35
18. Mosley, 18.3.75
19. States House, LH, 15.8.42
20. *The Second World War*, pp. 413–14
21. *Evening Standard*, 1.6.40
22. *Sunday Express*, 2.6.40
23. *South Wales Echo*, 10.6.40
24. *Leicester Mail*, 8.6.40
25. *Daily Express*, 2.10.40
26. *Sunday Pictorial*, 27.10.40
27. Ibid., 17.11.40
28. Ibid., 1.12.40
29. Rutgers, F, 18.4.62
30. *Sunday Pictorial*, 7.1.41
31. *Truth*, 10.1.41
32. *Evening Standard*, 8.2.41
33. Martel, *Our Armoured Forces*, p. 103
34. Rutgers, Box 6; *Sunday Pictorial*, 13.4.41 and 27.4.41
35. Leutze, J., 'The London Observer', *The Journal of General Raymond E. Lee 1940–41*, pp. 282–3, Hutchinson (London, 1972)
36. Estelle Fuller, 24.8.71, confirmed by letter to the author dated 6.5.76
37. Rutgers, Box 6; *Sunday Pictorial*, 9.6.41
38. *Sunday Pictorial*, 29.6.41
39. *Evening Standard*, 19.7.41
40. Ibid., 2.8.41
41. Ibid., 25.10.41
42. *Sunday Pictorial*, 16.11.41
43. *Evening Standard*, 5, 6, 7, 8.1.42
44. Ibid., 9.1.42
45. *Sunday Pictorial*, 15.3.42
46. *Evening Standard*, 21.3.42
47. *Sunday Pictorial*, 22.3.42 and 19.4.42

48. *The Occult Review*, April 1942
49. Copied in *Watchwords*, pp. 12–15
50. *Machine Warfare*, p. 9
51. Ibid., p. 17
52. Ibid., p. 28
53. Ibid., p. 49
54. Ibid., pp. 59–60
55. Ibid., p. 15
56. Ibid., pp. 73–4
57. Ibid., p. 83
58. Ibid., pp. 103–4
59. Ibid., p. 143
60. Ibid., p. 144
61. Ibid., pp. 146–7
62. Ibid., pp. 164–5
63. Ibid., p. 172
64. Ibid., p. 177
65. *Sunday Pictorial*, 31.5.42
66. Rutgers, Scrapbook 7; *Evening Standard*, 15.6.42
67. Rutgers, Scrapbook 7
68. *Catholic Herald*, 10.7.42
69. States House, F, 6.9.42
70. *The Decisive Battles of the United States*, pp. 169–71
71. *Evening Standard*, 20.11.42
72. Rutgers, Scrapbook 7, Foot, 19.11.42
73. *Evening Standard*, 28.12.42
74. Ibid., 25.1.43
75. Ibid., 8.2.43
76. Ibid., 11.3.43
77. Ibid., 6.4.43
78. Ibid., 6.5.43
79. Ibid., 24.5.43
80. Rutgers, Scrapbook 7, Foot, 5.5.43
81. *Sunday Pictorial*, 30.5.43
82. *Evening Standard*, 15.8.43
83. *Watchwords*, p. 100
84. Rutgers, Scrapbook 7, Foot, 31.8.43
85. *Armoured Warfare*, pp. 5–6
86. Ibid., p. 85
87. Ibid., p. 13
88. Ibid., p. 27
89. States House, Notes on Fuller's *Lectures on FSR III* by Liddell Hart.
90. *Armoured Warfare*, p. 29
91. Ibid., p. 19
92. Ibid., p. 116
93. Ibid., p. 43
94. Ibid., p. 109
95. *Evening Standard*, 1.12.43
96. Ibid., 4.1.44
97. Ibid., 4.2.44

98. Ibid., 18.2.44
99. *Thunderbolts*, pp. 40–2
100. Ibid., pp. 55–6
101. *Sunday Pictorial*, 9.5.44
102. Ibid., 27.10.44
103. Starr, 1.8.45
104. King's. Fuller's Accounts
105. *Newsweek*, 26.2.45
106. *Daily Mail*, 8.8.45
107. *Sunday Pictorial*, 12.8.45
108. *Armament and History*, p. v
109. Ibid., chs. I and V.
110. *Soviet News*, 27.11.45
111. *Armament and History*, p. 32
112. Ibid., p. 33
113. *The Tank,* vol. 27, no. 317, September, 1945
114. Rutgers, Box 8
115. *Armament and History*, p. V
116. Ibid., pp. 188–90
117. *Army Ordnance*, Jan.–Feb. 1946, pp. 34–9
118. *Armament and History*, p. 193
119. Ibid., pp. 195–6
120. Ibid., pp. 194–5
121. Ibid., p. 206
122. Ibid., p. 195
123. Ibid., p. 207
124. *Maclean's Magazine*, 1.11.45
125. Referred to by Fuller in numbers of books e.g. *The Conduct of War*, p. 111
126. Starr, 8.3.46
127. Ibid., 20.5.47
128. King's, II/1
129. *The Second World War*, Appendix, pp. 413–15; PRO WO 32/10389
130. King's, II/5
131. Ibid., II/45
132. Ibid., II/50
133. Ibid., II/56
134. Ibid., II/74
135. Rutgers, Box 5
136. States House, LH, 24.9.46
137. Ibid., F, 30.6.46
138. Ibid., F, 12.8.46
139. Ibid., LH, 5.5.48 and 5.6.48; F, 26.4.48
140. *Army Ordnance*, Mar.–Apr. 1947
141. *Daily Mail*, 2.9.47
142. *Cavalcade*, 20.3.48
143. States House, F, 26.4.48
144. *Ordnance*, May–June 1948
145. *Sunday Pictorial*, 25.4.48
146. *Cavalcade*, 31.8.48
147. Starr, 18.7.47 and 3.11.47

148. *Economist*, 24.8.48
149. States House, Review by Richard E. Danielson.
150. *The Second World War*, pp. 26–7
151. Ibid., p. 400
152. Ibid., p. 40–1
153. Ibid., p. 59
154. Ibid., p. 122
155. Ibid., pp. 129–33
156. Ibid., pp. 164, 173–4, 257; *The Conduct of War*, pp. 71–3
157. *The Second World War*, pp. 89, 220–31, 313–17, 343–5
158. Ibid., chs. IX and XI
159. Ibid., p. 391
160. Ibid., pp. 407–8
161. Liddell Hart, *History of the Second World War*, pp. 712–13, Cassell (London, 1970)

Chapter Ten

1. States House, F, 19.8.49
2. Ibid., letters Mar.–Apr. 1949
3. Ibid., LH, 2.5.49
4. Ibid., F, 7.9.49
5. *Cavalcade*, 22.1.49
6. *Truth*, 4. 2.49
7. *Everybody's*, 23.4.49
8. *The People*, 2.4.49
9. *Sunday Pictorial*, 25.9.49
10. *The People*, 9.4.50
11. States House, F, 3.4.50
12. *Sunday Graphic*, 2.7.50
13. *Daily Telegraph*, 20.7.50; *Sunday Pictorial*, 9.5.50
14. *US News & World Report*, 25.8.50
15. *Washington Post*, 9.9.50
16. *Chicago Tribune*, 18.11.50
17. Starr, 9.2.50
18. Liddell Hart, *The Tanks*, vol. 1, pp. 302–3; States House, F, 20.11.50
19. *How to Defeat Russia*, p. 16
20. King's, IV/7/14a
21. States House, F, 16.3.51
22. *Saturday Evening Post*, 27.10.51
23. Rutgers, Scrapbook 8, Alba, 16.1.52
24. *The Marine Corps Gazette*, Apr. 1952
25. *Ordnance*, May–June 1952
26. *Die Deutsche Soldatenzeitung*, 1952
27. *Armour*, Mar.–Apr. 1953
28. *Ukrainian Independent*, 1953
29. *The Tank*, Apr. 1954
30. Starr, 9.2.50
31. Ibid., 22.10.53
32. Ibid., 28.11.53

33. Ibid., 3.2.53
34. Luvaas, J., *The Education of An Army: British military thought, 1815–1940*, p. 370, Cassell (London, 1965)
35. *The Times*, 19.6.54
36. *The Times Educational Supplement*, 11.6.54
37. *Spectator*, 2.7.54
38. *New York Herald Tribune*, 2.1.55
39. *History Today*, Aug. 1956
40. *The Times Literary Supplement*, 20.7.56
41. *Soldier*, Sep. 1956
42. *Decisive Battles of the Western World*, vol. 1, p. 2
43. Ibid., p. 122
44. Ibid., p. 200
45. *Decisive Battles of the Western World*, vol. 3, p. 261
46. Ibid., pp. 322–4
47. Ibid., p. 367
48. Ibid., pp. 378–9
49. Ibid., p. 589
50. Ibid., p. 631
51. Ibid., pp. 634–6
52. States House, F, 8.3.56
53. *The People*, 4.11.56
54. Luvaas, L, 8.1.57
55. *Alexander the Great*, p. 5
56. Junior Division Files, 1923, The Army Staff College, Camberley
57. RUP, F, 14.4.57
58. Ibid., Eyre and Spottiswoode, 12.4.57
59. *Ordnance*, Mar.–Apr. 1957
60. Rutgers, Box 3
61. *ABN*, Nov.–Dec. 1957
62. States House, F, 3.9.58
63. Starr, 31.3.57
64. States House, F, 11.1.58
65. Ibid., F, 19.1.58
66. Ibid., F, 20.7.58
67. Ibid., F, 15.11.58; RUP, F, 14.12.58
68. *Alexander the Great*, pp. 6–7
69. *The Times*, 1.1.59
70. *Alexander the Great*, pp. 116, 122, 149, 265
71. Ibid., pp. 306–14
72. Ibid., p. 292
73. Luvaas, 28.8.63
74. *The Times Literary Supplement*, 14.11.58; *The Times*, 1.1.59
75. RUP, F, 4.12.58 and 23.1.61
76. *Spectator*, 30.1.59
77. Rutgers, Box 3, Lionel Fuller, 12.3.58
78. Estelle Fuller, 24.8.71
79. Luvaas, L., 10.6.60
80. Rutgers, Box 3
81. States House, F, 27.10.59

82. Starr, 17.11.59
83. Luvaas, L, 10.6.60
84. Starr, 25.7.60
85. States House, F, 4.11.60
86. King's, IV/6/7 and IV/6/11
87. Ibid., IV/6/6
88. RUP, F, 30.6.61
89. States House, F, 5.7.61
90. Luvaas, F, 28.7.63
91. Ibid., F, 28.7.63
92. States House, LH, 30.10.61
93. *The Conduct of War*, pp. 76 and 111
94. Ibid., ch. XIII, passim
95. Ibid., p. 11
96. Ibid., p.25
97. Ibid., pp. 26–38
98. Ibid., ch. XI, passim
99. Ibid., chs. V, VIII and IX, passim
100. Ibid., p. 303
101. Ibid., p. 249
102. Ibid., p. 261
103. Ibid., pp. 263–4
104. Ibid., pp. 176–7, 317
105. Ibid., p. 239
106. Ibid., pp. 240–2, 281
107. Ibid., p. 244
108. Ibid., pp. 255–6
109. Ibid., pp. 316–17
110. Ibid., p. 317, note 1
111. Ibid., pp. 317–33
112. *Listener*, 9.11.61
113. Clausewitz, *On War*, vol 3, p. 45
114. *The Conduct of War*, p. 296
115. States House, LH, 30.10.61, 10.11.61, 6.12.61; F, 3.11.61, 21.11.61, 9.12.61
116. Starr, 18.9.61
117. Rutgers, Box 3, Sloane, 22.3.62
118. Ibid., F, 18.4.62
119. States House, F, 14.8.62
120. RUP, F, 12.12.62
121. King's, IV/6/25
122. Rutgers, Box 3, Sloane to Cameron, 19.12.62; RUP, Cameron to Sloane, 27.12.62
123. RUP, Sloane, 2.1.63
124. Rutgers, Box 3
125. Starr, 4.2.63
126. Wheldon, J., *Machine Age Armies*, Abelard-Schuman (London, 1968)
127. States House, F, 19.5.63, 24.5.63, 31.5.63
128. Luvaas, 28.7.63
129. Ibid., 1.9.63
130. Alison Starr, 14.11.75

131. States House, F, 29.1.64
132. Ibid., F, 24.10.63
133. *RUSI Journal*, vol. CIX, pp. 68–72
134. States House, F, 16.12.63
135. Starr, 5.12.64
136. States House, F, 29.1.64, 23.7.64, 27.8.64, 14.9.64, 17.9.64
137. RUP, Sloane, 24.7.64; *Caesar*, p. 14
138. RUP, F, 2.8.64
139. Rutgers, Box 3, Sloane to Cameron, 17.9.64
140. RUP, F, 9.11.64
141. Starr, 5.12.64
142. States House, F, 28.11.64
143. Estelle Fuller, 24.8.71
144. Luvaas, op. cit., p. 375
145. Starr, 18.5.65
146. States House, F, 24.6.65
147. *Caesar*, pp. 308–27
148. States House, F, 23.6.65
149. *Wall Street Journal*, 30.12.65; *The Times Literary Supplement*, 3.3.66
150. RUP, 5.7.65
151. States House, F, 29.7.65
152. RUP, Sloane, 29.7.65
153. Ibid., F, 3.8.65
154. Ibid., Sloane, 9.8.65
155. Letter from Sloane to the author dated 2.2.70
156. Rutgers, Boxes 3 and 5
157. States House, F, 20.10.65
158. RUP, F, 22.10.65
159. States House, F, 16.1.66
160. Luvaas, F, July 1962
161. Starr, 1934
162. See *Kampftruppen*, Jan.–Feb. 1970, article by General von Schweppenburg
163. Luvaas, July 1962
164. King's, IV/6/48
165. States House, F, 16.1.66
166. States House, Mrs Fuller, 1966
167. *The Times*, 11.1.66
168. *The Tank*, Vol. 48, no. 563, pp. 182–4

Books published by Major-General Fuller

Dates given before titles show years of first publication in the United Kingdom. Shortened form of title in square brackets is that used in the source notes. Many of Fuller's books were also published in translation in France, Spain, Germany, the Soviet Union, Poland, Sweden and the Argentine.

1. 1907 *The Star in the West—A Critical Essay upon the Works of Aleister Crowley*, The Walter Scott Publishing Co., Ltd, London/New York (reprinted 1974 Gordon Press, New York)
2. 1913 *Hints on Training Territorial Infantry*, Gale and Polden, London
3. 1914 *Training Soldiers for War*, Hugh Rees, London
4. 1920 *Tanks in the Great War*, Murray, London: Dutton, New York
5. 1923 *The Reformation of War [Reformation]*, Hutchinson, London: Dutton, New York
6. 1925 *Sir John Moore's System of Training*, Hutchinson, London
7. 1925 *British Light Infantry in the Eighteenth Century (An Introduction to 'Sir John Moore's System of Training')*, Hutchinson, London
8. 1925 *Yoga: A Study of the Mystical Philosophy of the Brahmins and Buddhists*, W. Rider, London: McKay, Pa (?1925)
9. 1926 *The Foundations of the Science of War [Foundations]*, Hutchinson, London
10. 1926 *Imperial Defence, 1588–1914*, Sifton Praed, London
11. 1926 *Atlantis—America and the Future*, Kegan Paul, London
12. 1926 *Pegasus—Problems of Transportation*, Kegan Paul, London: Dutton, New York
13. 1928 *On Future Warfare*, Sifton Praed, London
14. 1929 *The Generalship of Ulysses S. Grant [Grant]*, Murray, London: Dodd Mead, New York (2nd ed. 1958, Indiana U.P., Bloomington, Indiana)
15. 1931 *India in Revolt*, Eyre and Spottiswoode, London
16. 1931 *Lectures on F.S.R. II*, Sifton Praed, London
17. 1932 *Lectures on F.S.R. III (Operations Between Mechanized Forces) [Lectures on F.S.R. III]*, Sifton Praed, London
18. 1932 *The Dragon's Teeth: A Study of War and Peace [The Dragon's Teeth]*, Constable, London

19. 1932   *War and Western Civilization, 1832–1932: A Study of War as a Political Instrument and the Expression of Mass Democracy* [*War and Western Civilization*], Duckworth, London; 1969 Books for Libraries Press, Freeport, New York

20. 1933   *Grant and Lee: A Study in Personality and Generalship* [*Grant and Lee*], Eyre and Spottiswoode, London; Scribner's, New York; 1957 Indiana U.P., Bloomington, Indiana

21. 1933   *Generalship: Its Diseases and their Cure: A Study of the Personal Factor in Command* [*Generalship*], Faber and Faber, London; 1936 Military Service Publishing Co., Harrisburg, Pa

22. 1934   *Empire Unity and Defence*, Arrowsmith, Bristol

23. 1935   *The Army in my Time*, Rich and Cowan, London

24. 1936   *The First of the League Wars: Its Lessons and Omens* [*The First of the League Wars*], Eyre and Spottiswoode, London

25. 1936   *Memoirs of an Unconventional Soldier*, Ivor Nicholson and Watson, London

26. 1937   *Towards Armageddon: The Defence Problem and its Solution* [*Towards Armageddon*], Lovat Dickson, London

27. 1937   *The Last of the Gentlemen's Wars: A Subaltern's Journal of the War in South Africa 1899–1902* [*The Last of the Gentlemen's Wars*], Faber and Faber, London

28. 1937   *The Secret Wisdom of the Qabalah*, Rider, London

29. 1939   *Decisive Battles: Their Influence Upon History and Civilization, Vol. I—From Alexander the Great to Frederick the Great* [*Decisive Battles*, Vol. I], Eyre and Spottiswoode, London; 1940 Scribner's, New York

30. 1940   *Decisive Battles: Their Influence Upon History and Civilization, Vol. II—From Napoleon the First to General Franco* [*Decisive Battles*, Vol. II], Eyre and Spottiswoode, London; Scribner's, New York

31. 1942   *Machine Warfare: An Enquiry into the Influence of Mechanics on the Art of War* [*Machine Warfare*], Hutchinson, London; 1943 *The Infantry Journal*, Washington, D.C.

32. 1942   *The Decisive Battles of the United States*, Hutchinson, London; Harper, New York (reprinted 1953 Beechhurst Press, New York)

33. 1943   *Armoured Warfare: An Annotated Edition of Fifteen Lectures on Operations between Mechanized Forces* [*Armoured Warfare*], Eyre and Spottiswoode, London; Military Service Publishing Co., Harrisburg, Pa

34. 1944 *Warfare Today: How Modern Battles are Planned and Fought on Land, at Sea and in the Air* (with Admiral Sir R. Bacon and Air Marshal Sir P. Playfair), Odhams, London
35. 1944 *Watchwords*, Skeffington, London/New York
36. 1946 *Thunderbolts*, Skeffington, London/New York
37. 1946 *Armament and History: A Study of the Influence of Armaments on History from the Dawn of Classical Warfare to the Second World War* [*Armament and History*], Eyre and Spottiswoode, London; 1945 Scribner's, New York
38. 1948 *The Second World War, 1939–45: A Strategical and Tactical History* [*The Second World War*], Eyre and Spottiswoode, London; 1949 Duell, Sloan and Pearce, New York (reprinted 1968 Meredith Press, New York)
39. 1951 *How to Defeat Russia*, Eyre and Spottiswoode, London
40–42.   *The Decisive Battles of the Western World and their Influence upon History*
     1954 *Vol. 1—From the Earliest Times to the Battle of Lepanto*
     1955 *Vol. 2—From the Defeat of the Spanish Armada to the Battle of Waterloo*
     1956 *Vol. 3—From the American Civil War to the End of the Second World War*
           [*Decisive Battles of the Western World*, Vols 1, 2 and 3], Eyre and Spottiswoode, London (abridged and republished in a new edition edited by John Terraine 1970, 1972 and 1975 Granada Publishing Ltd (Paladin), St Albans); 1954–6 *A Military History of the Western World*, Funk and Wagnalls, New York (reprinted 1967 Minerva Press, New York)
43. 1958 *The Generalship of Alexander the Great* [*Alexander the Great*], Eyre and Spottiswoode, London. 1960 Rutgers U.P., New Brunswick, N.J. (reprinted 1968 Minerva Press, New York)
44. 1961 *The Conduct of War, 1789–1961: A Study of the Impact of the French, Industrial and Russian Revolutions on War and its Conduct* [*The Conduct of War*], Eyre and Spottiswoode, London, reprinted 1962 and 1972 and first University Paperback edition by Eyre Methuen; Rutgers U.P., New Brunswick, N.J. (reprinted 1968 Minerva Press, New York)
45. 1965 *Julius Caesar: Man, Soldier and Tyrant* [*Caesar*], Eyre and Spottiswoode, London; Rutgers U.P., New Brunswick, N.J. (reprinted 1969 Minerva Press, New York)

Glossary of Abbreviations

Modern military organizations tend to appear to outsiders to be alphabetic jungles. The following glossary of abbreviations may help.

AG	Adjutant General
ARP	Air Raid Precautions (Second World War)
ATGW	Anti-tank Guided Weapon
BEF	British Expeditionary Force
BGS	Brigadier General Staff
CDL	Canal Defence Lights (Code name for a light projector for night armoured warfare)
CID	Committee for Imperial Defence
CIGS	Chief of the Imperial General Staff (now CGS)
C-in-C	Commander-in-Chief
DCIGS	Deputy Chief of the Imperial General Staff
DDSD (Tanks)	Deputy Director of Staff Duties (Tanks)
DMO and I	Director of Military Operations and Intelligence
DSD	Director of Staff Duties
FSR	Field Service Regulations
GHQ	General Headquarters
GOC	General Officer Commanding
GS	General Staff
GSO 1, 2 or 3	First, Second or Third Grade General Staff Officer (Lieutenant-Colonel, Major, Captain)
HE	High Explosive
HQ	Headquarters
MA	Military Assistant
MGO	Master General of Ordnance
QMG	Quarter Master General
RA	Royal Artillery
RAC	Royal Armoured Corps
RE	Royal Engineers
RTC	Royal Tank Corps
RTR	Royal Tank Regiment
RUSI	Royal United Service Institute (now Royal United Institute for Defence Studies
SD7	Staff Duties 7 (a War Office branch dealing with Tanks in Fuller's day)
SD4	Staff Duties 4 (a War Office branch dealing with Training in Fuller's day)

Index

Fuller's writings are indexed under the entry for Fuller himself